DAVID BUSCH'S
CANON® EOS® REBEL® T7i/800D

GUIDE TO DIGITAL SLR PHOTOGRAPHY

David D. Busch

David Busch's Canon® EOS® Rebel® T7i/800D
Guide to Digital SLR Photography
David D. Busch

Project Manager: Jenny Davidson
Series Technical Editor: Michael D. Sullivan
Layout: Bill Hartman
Cover Design: Mike Tanamachi
Indexer: Valerie Haynes Perry
Proofreader: Mike Beady

ISBN: 978-1-68198-286-1
1st Edition (1st printing, September 2017)

All images © David D. Busch unless otherwise noted

Rocky Nook, Inc.
1010 B Street, Suite 350
San Rafael, CA 94901
USA
www.rockynook.com

Distributed in the U.S. by Ingram Publisher Services
Distributed in the UK and Europe by Publishers Group UK

Library of Congress Control Number: 2017934688

This book is printed on acid-free paper.
Printed in Korea

For Cathy

Acknowledgments

Thanks to everyone at Rocky Nook, including Scott Cowlin, managing director and publisher, for the freedom to let me explore the amazing capabilities of the Canon EOS Rebel T7i/800D in depth. I couldn't do it without my veteran production team, including project manager, Jenny Davidson, and series technical editor, Mike Sullivan. Also thanks to Bill Hartman, layout; Valerie Hayes Perry, indexing; Mike Beady, proofreading; Mike Tanamachi, cover design; and my agent, Carole Jelen, who has the amazing ability to keep both publishers and authors happy.

About the Author

With more than two million books in print, **David D. Busch** is the world's #1 bestselling camera guide author, and the originator of popular series like *David Busch's Pro Secrets, David Busch's Compact Field Guides,* and *David Busch's Quick Snap Guides.* He has written dozens of hugely successful books for Canon and other digital SLR models, including the all-time #1 bestsellers for several different cameras, additional user guides for other camera models, as well as many popular books devoted to dSLRs, including *Mastering Digital SLR Photography, Fourth Edition* and *Digital SLR Pro Secrets.* As a roving photojournalist for more than 20 years, he illustrated his books, magazine articles, and newspaper reports with award-winning images. He's operated his own commercial studio, suffocated in formal dress while shooting weddings, and shot sports for a daily newspaper and an upstate New York college. His photos and articles have appeared in *Rangefinder, Professional Photographer,* the late, lamented *Popular Photography,* and hundreds of other publications. He's also reviewed dozens of digital cameras for CNet and other CBS publications.

When About.com named its top five books on Beginning Digital Photography, debuting at the #1 and #2 slots were Busch's *Digital Photography All-In-One Desk Reference for Dummies* and *Mastering Digital Photography.* He has had as many as 18 books listed in the Top 100 of Amazon.com's Digital Photography Bestseller list—simultaneously! Busch's 200-plus other books published since 1983 include bestsellers like *Digital SLR Cameras and Photography for Dummies.*

Busch is a member of the Cleveland Photographic Society (www.clevelandphoto.org), which has operated continuously since 1887. Visit his website at http://www.canonguides.com.

Contents

Preface   xiv

Introduction   xv

Chapter 1
Thinking Outside of the Box   1

First Things First 2
Initial Setup 7
    Battery Included 7
    Final Steps 10

Chapter 2
Quick Start   13

Navigating the Rebel T7i 13
    Guided Shooting Mode 14
    Guided Menus 15
    Using the Physical Controls 16
    Mastering the Touch Screen 17
Enabling Conventional Menus and Modes. 19
    Accessing Display Level Settings. 19
Initial Settings 20
    Setting Date and Time 20
    Formatting a Memory Card 23
Selecting a Shooting Mode 24
    Basic Zone Modes 25
    Special Scene Modes. 26
    Creative Filters. 27
    Creative Zone Modes. 27
Choosing a Metering Mode 28
Choosing a Focus Mode. 29
Selecting an AF Area Selection Mode 30

Other Settings 31
   Adjusting White Balance and ISO 31
   Using the Self-Timer 32
   Using the Built-in Flash 32
Taking a Picture 34
Reviewing the Images You've Taken 34
   Cruising Through Index Views 36
Transferring Photos to Your Computer 36
Shooting Tips 37

Chapter 3
Your Rebel Roadmap   45

Front View 46
The Canon EOS Rebel T7i's Business End .49
   Jumping Around 54
Going Topside 55
Underneath Your Rebel T7i 57
Lens Components 57
Shooting and Playback Information 59
While You're Shooting 60
   Image Playback Displays 65

Chapter 4
Nailing the Right Exposure   69

Getting a Handle on Exposure 70
How the Rebel T7i Calculates Exposure 75
   Correctly Exposed 76
   Overexposed 76
   Underexposed 76
Choosing a Metering Method 78
Choosing an Exposure Method 81
   Basic Zone Exposure Methods 82
   Aperture-Priority 82
   Shutter-Priority 85
   Program Mode 86
   Manual Exposure 87
Adjusting Exposure with ISO Settings 89
   Dealing with Visual Noise 90
Making EV Changes 91
   Fast EV Changes 91
   Slower EV Changes 92

Bracketing 93
Working with HDR 95
   HDR Backlight Control 95
Bracketing and Merge to HDR 98
Fixing Exposures with Histograms 101
   Tonal Range 102
   Histograms and Contrast 104
   Understanding Histograms 105
Basic Zone Modes 108
   Making Changes in Basic Zone Modes 110

Chapter 5
Mastering the Mysteries of Autofocus   115

How Focus Works 115
   Contrast Detection 116
   Phase Detection 117
   Dual Pixel CMOS AF 120
   Cross-Type Focus Point 121
Focus Modes 125
   Adding Circles of Confusion 125
Your Autofocus Mode Options 127
   One-Shot AF 128
   AI Servo AF 128
   AI Focus AF 128
   Manual Focus 129
Selecting an AF Area Selection Mode 129
AF with Color Tracking 131
   Other Important AF Parameters 132
Back-Button Focus 132
   Activating Back-Button Focus 133

Chapter 6
Movies and Live View   135

Working with Live View 135
   Live View Essentials 136
   Enabling Live View 137
   Activating Live View 139
   Quick Control 143
Focusing in Live View 144
   Selecting an AF Method 144
   Focus Operation 148
   Servo AF 148

Using the Touch Shutter 149
Shooting Movies 150
    Resolution and Frame Rates. 152
    Movie Settings 154
    Capturing Video/Sound 160
Special Movie Modes 161
    Video Snapshots. 161
    Shooting HDR Movies. 165
    Shooting Movies with Creative Filters 165
    Time-Lapse Movies 167
    Playback and Editing 170
Tips for Shooting Better Movies. 172
    Lens Craft 172
    Keeping Things Stable and on the Level 174
    Shooting Script. 174
    Storyboards 175
    Storytelling in Video. 176
    Composition 176
    Lighting for Video 179
    Audio. 182

Chapter 7
Advanced Shooting   185

Continuous Shooting 185
More Exposure Options. 187
A Tiny Slice of Time. 188
    Working with Short Exposures. 189
Long Exposures 192
    Three Ways to Take Long Exposures 193
    Working with Long Exposures 194
Delayed Exposures. 198
    Self-Timer. 198
Using Wi-Fi/NFC and Bluetooth 199
    General Wi-Fi Guidelines 200
    Connecting to Your Camera. 200
Using Your Connection 206
    Transferring Images Between Cameras. 207
    Communicating with your Smart Device 208
    Save Images to Connect Station 210
    Remote Control with EOS Utility. 210
    Printing from a Wi-Fi Printer 211
    Uploading to a Web Service 211

Chapter 8
Customizing with the Shooting and Playback Menus   213

Anatomy of the Rebel T7i's Menus 214
Shooting Menu Options. 216
  Image Quality 217
  Image Review. 221
  Release Shutter without Card. 221
  Lens Aberration Correction 221
  Electronic Manual Focus 226
  Exposure Compensation/Automatic Exposure Bracketing 226
  Flash Control 228
  Red-Eye Reduction. 231
  ISO Speed. 231
  ISO Auto 232
  Auto Lighting Optimizer 232
  Metering Mode 234
  Color Space 235
  Picture Style 238
  White Balance 247
  Custom White Balance. 247
  White Balance Shift and Bracketing 248
  Long Exposure Noise Reduction 250
  High ISO Speed Noise Reduction. 252
  Dust Delete Data 253
  Anti-Flicker Shooting. 254
  Aspect Ratio. 255
  Live View Shooting 256
Playback Menu Options. 256
  Protect Images 256
  Rotate Images 258
  Erase Images 259
  Print Order. 259
  Photobook Set-up. 261
  Creative Filters. 261
  Cropping 264
  Resize. 265
  Rating 266
  Slide Show 266
  Set Image Search Conditions 268
  Image Jump with Main Dial. 269
  AF Point Display 270
  Histogram Display 271
  Ctrl over HDMI. 271

Chapter 9
Customizing with the Set-up Menu, Display Level Menu, and My Menu   273

Set-up Menu Options 273
    Select Folder 274
    File Numbering 276
    Auto Rotate 277
    Format Card 278
    Wireless Communication Settings 278
    Eye-Fi Settings 279
    Auto Power Off 279
    LCD Brightness 280
    LCD Off/On Button 280
    Date/Time/Zone 281
    Language 282
    Viewfinder Display 282
    GPS Device Settings 283
    Video System 284
    Touch Control 284
    Beep 285
    Battery Info 285
    Sensor Cleaning 285
    Custom Functions 286
    Clear Settings 296
    Copyright Information 300
    Manual/Software URL 301
    Certification Logo Display 301
    Firmware Version 301
Display Level 302
My Menu 302

Chapter 10
Working with Lenses   305

But Don't Forget the Crop Factor 306
Your First Lens 307
    Buy Now, Expand Later 309
What Lenses Can You Use? 312
    EF vs. EF-S 314
Ingredients of Canon's Alphanumeric Soup 315

Your Second (and Third...) Lens 318
    What Lenses Can Do for You. 319
    Zoom or Prime?. 322
Categories of Lenses. 324
Using Wide-Angle and Wide-Zoom Lenses. 324
    Avoiding Potential Wide-Angle Problems 327
Using Telephoto and Tele-Zoom Lenses 329
    Avoiding Telephoto Lens Problems. 330
    Telephotos and Bokeh 332
Add-ons and Special Features. 333
    Lens Hoods 333
    Telephoto Extenders. 333
    Macro Focusing 334
    Image Stabilization. 334

Chapter 11
Working with Light   **337**

Continuous Illumination versus Electronic Flash 338
Continuous Lighting Basics 343
    Living with Color Temperature 343
    Daylight. 344
    Incandescent/Tungsten Light 345
    Fluorescent Light/Other Light Sources 345
    Adjusting White Balance 347
Electronic Flash Basics 347
    Fire When Ready! 348
    How Electronic Flash Works 349
    Determining Exposure 354
Getting Started with the Built-in Flash 355
    Basic Zone Flash 355
    Creative Zone Flash. 355
    Flash Range 356
    Red-Eye Reduction and Autofocus Assist. .357
    Using FE Lock and Flash Exposure Compensation. 358
More on Flash Control Settings 359
    Flash Firing 360
    E-TTL II Metering 361
    Flash Sync Speed in AV mode. 361
    Built-in Flash Settings. 363
    Using Flash Mode 365
    External Flash Function Settings 367
    External Flash Custom Function Settings 372
    Clear External Flash Custom Function Setting 372

Using External Electronic Flash 372
  Speedlite 600EX-RT/600EX II-RT 374
  Speedlite 580EX II 376
  Speedlite 430EX III-RT 377
  Speedlite 320EX. 378
  Speedlite 270EX II 378
  Close-Up Lites 379

Chapter 12
Working with Wireless Flash   381

Wireless Evolution 381
Elements of Wireless Flash 383
  Flash Combinations 383
  Controlling Flash Units 384
  Why Use Wireless Flash? 385
  Key Wireless Concepts 386
  Which Flashes Can Be Operated Wirelessly? 387
Getting Started. 389
  Easy Wireless Flash Shooting 390
  Custom Wireless Flash Shooting. 391
Setting Up an External Master Flash or Controller. 394
  Using a Speedlite or Transmitter as the Master in Optical Mode 394
  Using the ST-E2 Transmitter as Master. 395
  Using the Speedlite 600EX-RT/600EX II-RT as Radio Master. 396
  Using the Speedlite 430EX III-RT as Radio Master 397
  Using the ST-E3-RT as Radio Master 397
  Setting Up a Slave Flash 398
More Wireless Options and Capabilities 399
  Internal/External Flash Ratio Setting 399
  Wireless Flash Only 403
  Using Wireless and Built-in Flash 405
Working with Groups 405
  Ratio Control. 407
  Choosing a Channel 407
Flash Release Function 408

Chapter 13
Troubleshooting and Prevention   411

Updating Your Firmware 412
  Official Firmware. 412
  Upgrading Your Firmware 413
Protecting Your LCD 416
Troubleshooting Memory Cards 417
  All Your Eggs in One Basket?. 417
  What Can Go Wrong? 418
  What Can You Do? 419
Cleaning Your Sensor. 421
  Dust the FAQs, Ma'am 422
  Identifying and Dealing with Dust 423
  Avoiding Dust 424
  Sensor Cleaning 426

Index   431

Preface

You don't want good pictures from your new Canon EOS Rebel T7i/800D—you demand *outstanding* photos. After all, this camera is one of the most advanced entry/mid-level cameras that Canon has ever introduced. It boasts 24 megapixels of resolution, built-in Wi-Fi, blazing-fast automatic focus, cool features like the real-time live view preview system, full high-definition movie shooting, a touch screen that allows you to make many settings with a tap of the LCD, and an amazing wireless flash capability. Although this camera has an innovative optional "Guide" mode, the available built-in help isn't comprehensive. In addition, the camera's manual doesn't offer much information on photography or digital photography.

What you need is a guide that explains the purpose and function of the T7i's basic controls, how you should use them, and *why*. Ideally, there should be information about file formats, resolution, exposure, and other special autofocus modes available, but you'd prefer to read about those topics only after you've had the chance to go out and take a few hundred great pictures with your new camera. Why isn't there a book that summarizes the most important information in its first two or three chapters, with lots of illustrations showing what your results will look like when you use this setting or that?

Now there is such a book. If you want a quick introduction to the T7i's focus controls, wireless flash synchronization options, how to choose lenses, or which exposure modes are best, this book is for you. If you can't decide on what basic settings to use with your camera because you can't figure out how changing ISO or white balance or focus defaults will affect your pictures, you need this guide.

Introduction

Once you've confirmed that you made a wise purchase decision, the question comes up, *how do I use this thing?* All those cool features can be mind-numbing to learn, if all you have as a guide is the manual furnished with the camera. Help is on the way. I sincerely believe that this book is your best bet for learning how to use your new camera, and for learning how to use it well.

I've tried to make *David Busch's Canon EOS Rebel T7i/800D Guide to Digital SLR Photography* different from the other T7i learn-up options. The roadmap sections use larger, color pictures to show you where all the buttons and dials are, and the explanations of what they do are longer and more comprehensive. I've tried to avoid overly general advice, including the two-page checklists on how to take a "sports picture" or a "portrait picture" or a "travel picture." Instead, you'll find tips and techniques for using all the features of your Canon EOS Rebel T7i to take *any kind of picture* you want. If you want to know where you should stand to take a picture of a quarterback dropping back to unleash a pass, there are plenty of books that will tell you that. This one concentrates on teaching you how to select the best autofocus mode, shutter speed, f/stop, or flash capability to take, say, a great sports picture under any conditions.

David Busch's Canon EOS Rebel T7i/800D Guide to Digital SLR Photography is aimed at both Canon and dSLR veterans as well as newcomers to digital photography and digital SLRs. Both groups can be overwhelmed by the options the T7i offers, while underwhelmed by the explanations they receive in their user's manual. The manuals are great if you already know what you don't know, and you can find an answer somewhere in a booklet arranged by menu listings and written by a camera vendor employee who last threw together instructions on how to operate a camcorder.

Who Am I?

After spending years as the world's most successful unknown author, I've become slightly less obscure in the past few years, thanks to a horde of camera guidebooks and other photographically oriented tomes. You may have seen my photography articles in leading photographic magazines but, first, and foremost, I'm a photojournalist and made my living in the field until I began devoting most of my time to writing books.

Although I love writing, I'm happiest when I'm out taking pictures, which is why I invariably spend several days each week photographing landscapes, people, close-up subjects, and other things. I spend a month or two each year traveling to events, such as Native American "powwows," Civil War re-enactments, county fairs, ballet, and sports (baseball, basketball, football, and soccer are favorites). I spent a full two weeks in Salamanca, Spain. I went there to shoot photographs of the people, landscapes, and monuments that I've grown to love, with about five hours a day set aside for study at a *colegio* located in an ancient monastery in the old part of the city, just steps from the cathedral. I can offer you my personal advice on how to take photos under a variety of conditions because I've had to meet those challenges myself on an ongoing basis.

Like all my digital photography books, this one was written by someone with an incurable photography bug. My first Canon SLR was a now-obscure model called the Pellix back in the 1960s, and I've used a variety of newer models since then. I've worked as a sports photographer for an Ohio newspaper and for an upstate New York college. I've operated my own commercial studio and photo lab, cranking out product shots on demand and then printing a few hundred glossy 8 × 10s on a tight deadline for a press kit. I've served as a photo-posing instructor for a modeling agency. People have actually paid me to shoot their weddings and immortalize them with portraits. I even prepared press kits and articles on photography as a PR consultant for a large Rochester, NY, company, which shall remain nameless. My trials and travails with imaging and computer technology have made their way into print in book form an alarming number of times.

Like you, I love photography for its own merits, and I view technology as just another tool to help me get the images I see in my mind's eye. But, also like you, I had to master this technology before I could apply it to my work. This book is the result of what I've learned, and I hope it will help you master your T7i digital SLR, too.

In closing, I'd like to ask a special favor: let me know what you think of this book. If you have any recommendations about how I can make it better, visit my website at www.canonguides.com, click on the E-Mail Me tab, and send your comments, suggestions on topics that should be explained in more detail, or, especially, any typos. (The latter will be compiled on the Errata page you'll also find on my website.) I really value your ideas, and appreciate it when you take the time to tell me what you think! Some of the content of the book you hold in your hands came from suggestions I received from readers like yourself. If you found this book especially useful, tell others about it. Visit http://www.amazon.com/dp/1681982862 and leave a positive review. Your feedback is what spurs me to make each one of these books better than the last. Thanks!

Guide to the Guide

Here's a quick guide to what you'll find in this book.

The first three chapters explain all the essentials you need to hit the ground running:

- **Chapter 1, "Thinking Outside of the Box."** This is a "Meet Your T7i" introduction, where you'll find information about what came in the box with your camera and, more importantly, what *didn't* come with the camera that you seriously should consider adding to your arsenal. I'll also cover some things you might not have known about charging the T7i's battery, choosing a memory card, setting the time and date, and a few other pre-flight tasks. This is basic stuff, and if you're a Canon veteran, you can skim over it quickly. A lot of this first chapter is intended for newbies, and even if you personally don't find it essential, you'll probably agree that there was some point during your photographic development (so to speak) that you would have wished this information was spelled out for you. There's no extra charge!

- **Chapter 2, "Quick Start."** Here, you'll find a Quick Start aimed at those who may not be old hands with Canon cameras having this level of sophistication. The T7i has some interesting new features, including one of the most advanced autofocus systems ever seen in a mid-level camera body (and which deserves an entire chapter of its own later in this book). But even with all the goodies to play with and learning curve still to climb, you'll find that Chapter 2 will get you shooting quickly with a minimum of fuss.

- **Chapter 3, "Your Rebel Roadmap."** This is a Streetsmart Roadmap to the Canon EOS Rebel T7i/800D. Confused by the tiny little diagrams and multiple cross-references for each and every control that send you scurrying around looking for information you know is buried somewhere in the small and inadequate manual stuffed in the box? This chapter uses multiple, large full-color pictures that show every dial, knob, and button, and explain the basics of using each in clear, easy-to-understand language. I'll give you the basics up front, and, even if I have to send you deeper into the book for a full discussion of a complex topic, you'll have what you need to use a control right away.

Even if you've learned the fundamentals and controls of the Canon EOS T7i, there is lots of room to learn more. The next four chapters will help you master the features of your camera.

- **Chapter 4, "Nailing the Right Exposure."** This chapter explores all your options for fine-tuning exposure with the Canon T7i. You'll learn when to use—and not use—each of the camera's metering modes, how to work with histograms, and the rationale for choosing the built-in HDR feature—or whether to capture high dynamic range images "manually." I'm also going to explode the myth of the 18-percent gray card.

- **Chapter 5, "Mastering the Mysteries of Autofocus."** As autofocus features like the T7i's new "hybrid" AF system are added, this useful capability often becomes more confusing, even for veteran photographers. I'm going to show you exactly how autofocus works so you can better understand the strengths and limitations of each mode. You'll discover how to select the mode that will give you tack-sharp focus time after time.

- **Chapter 6, "Movies and Live View."** This is your introduction to shooting in Live View mode and capturing movies, with complete descriptions of the T7i's shooting features, along with tips for better video.

- **Chapter 7, "Advanced Shooting."** Here you'll find discussions of some more advanced techniques, including how to make people "invisible" with long exposures, and getting the most from the T7i's continuous shooting capabilities. I'll also show you how to use the camera's built-in Wi-Fi features.

The next two chapters are devoted to helping you dig deeper into the customization capabilities of your EOS T7i, so you can exploit all those cool features that your previous camera might have lacked.

- **Chapter 8, "Customizing with the Shooting and Playback Menus."** In this chapter, you'll learn some easy stuff, along with some very important capabilities, like using the camera's lens aberration correction facility to banish vignetted corners and color fringes. I explain Picture Styles, recap the most important Live View/Movie options originally discussed in Chapter 6, and show you how to apply creative filters and assemble your own photo books.

- **Chapter 9, "Customizing with the Set-up Menu, Display Level Menu, and My Menu."** A broad array of set-up options are found here. You'll learn how to format memory cards, adjust LCD brightness and screen colors, and enter time zones and dates. You'll even discover how to set up your own command listings with the My Menus option.

The next four chapters are devoted to helping you dig deeper into the capabilities of your Canon EOS Rebel T7i. Here's what you can expect:

- **Chapter 10, "Working with Lenses."** Working with lenses is the goal of this chapter, where I'll show you how to select the best lenses for the kinds of photography you want to do, with my recommendations for starter lenses as well as more advanced optics for specialized applications.

- **Chapter 11, "Working with Light."** This chapter is devoted to the magic of light—your fundamental tool in creating any photograph. There are entire books devoted to working with electronic flash, but I hope to get you started with plenty of coverage of the EOS T7i's capabilities. I'll show you how to master your camera's built-in flash—and avoid that "built-in flash" look—and offer an introduction to the use of external flash units.

- **Chapter 12, "Working with Wireless Flash."** This chapter goes a little more deeply into the use of flash, and covers working with the T7i's wireless flash capabilities.

- **Chapter 13, "Troubleshooting and Prevention."** Even the best cameras need firmware updating from time to time, protection from sensor dust, and other housekeeping chores. I'll show you the basics in this handy chapter.

1

Thinking Outside of the Box

Whether you subscribe to the "my camera is just a tool" theory, or belong to the "an exquisite camera adds new capabilities to my shooting arsenal" camp, picking up a new Canon EOS Rebel T7i/800D is a special experience. Those who simply wield tools will find this camera as comforting as an old friend, a solid piece of fine machinery ready and able to do their bidding as part of the creative process.

Other photographers see the low-light capabilities (up to the equivalent of ISO 52100), the 6 frames-per-second continuous shooting, commendable ruggedness, and 24-megapixel resolution of the T7i, and gain a sense of empowerment. *Here* is a camera with fewer limitations and more capabilities for exercising renewed creative vision. In either case, using less mawkish terms, the T7i is one of the coolest cameras Canon has ever offered. Whether you're upgrading from another brand, from another Canon model (like one of the "lesser" Rebel models), or your T7i is your first digital camera and/or single-lens reflex, welcome to the club.

But, now that you've unwrapped and recharged the beast, mounted a lens, and fueled it with a memory card, what do you *do* with it? That's where this chapter—and the chapters that follow—should come in handy. Like many of you, I am a Canon user of long standing. And, like other members of our club, I had to learn at least some aspects of my newest EOS camera for the very first time at some point. Regardless of your experience level, you bought this book because you wanted to get the most from a very powerful tool, and I'm here to help.

So, I'm going to provide a basic pre-flight checklist that you need to complete before you really spread your wings and take off. You won't find a lot of detail in these first two chapters. Indeed, I'm going to tell you just what you absolutely *must* understand, accompanied by some interesting tidbits that will help you become acclimated to your T7i. I'll go into more depth and even repeat some of what I explain here in later chapters, so you don't have to memorize everything you see. Just relax, follow a few easy steps, and then go out and begin taking your best shots—ever.

Even if you're a long-time Canon shooter, I hope you won't be tempted to skip this chapter or the next one. I realize that you probably didn't purchase this book the same day you bought your camera and that, even if you did, the urge to go out and take a few hundred—or thousand—photos with your new camera is enticing. As valuable as a book like this one is, nobody can suppress their excitement long enough to read the instructions before initiating play with a new toy.

You don't need to fret about wading through a manual to find out what you must know to take those first few tentative snaps. I'm going to help you hit the ground running with this chapter, which will help you set up your camera and begin shooting in minutes. Because I realize that some of you may already have experience with Canon cameras similar to the T7i, each of the major sections in this chapter will begin with a brief description of what is covered in that section, so you can easily jump ahead to the next if you are in a hurry to get started.

> **Note**
>
> Throughout this book, you'll find short highlighted tips labeled **My Recommendation** or **My Preference**, intended to help you sort through the available options for a feature, control, or menu entry. I'll provide my recommendations, suitable for most people in most situations, or my personal preferences, which work for me, and might work for you, too. I don't provide these recommendations for every single feature, and you should consider your own needs before adopting any of them.

First Things First

This section helps get you oriented with all the things that come in the box with your Canon EOS Rebel T7i/800D, including what they do. I'll also describe some optional equipment you might want to have. If you want to get started immediately, skim through this section and jump ahead to "Initial Setup" later in the chapter.

The Canon EOS Rebel T7i/800D comes in an impressive box that contains the basic stuff you need to get started. The most important components are the camera and lens (if you purchased your T7i with a lens), battery, battery charger, and, if you're the nervous type, the neck strap. Also in the package is a compact small-format version of the Canon user manual. (Page 4 of that manual tells you to visit www.canon.com/icpd to download PDF versions of the camera, Wi-Fi, lens, and software instruction manuals.)

The first thing to do is carefully unpack the camera and double-check the contents with the checklist on one end of the box, helpfully designated with a CONTENTS heading. The box should include a Digital Camera EOS Rebel T7i/800D, Wide Strap EW-400D neck strap, Battery Charger LC-E17 or LC-E17E, a rubber eyecap, and Battery Pack LP-E17. You'll also find a lens, if the camera was purchased in a kit. You also got an instruction manual and warranty information. The contents I've listed will vary slightly depending on when and where you bought the camera.

While this level of setup detail may seem as superfluous as the instructions on a bottle of shampoo, checking the contents *first* is always a good idea. No matter who sells a camera, it's common to open boxes, use a camera for a demonstration, and then repack the box without replacing all the pieces and parts afterward. Someone might have helpfully checked out your camera on your behalf—and then mispacked the box. It's better to know *now* that something is missing so you can seek redress immediately, rather than discover two months from now that the video cable you thought you'd never use (but now *must* have) was never in the box.

At a minimum, the box should have the following:

- **Canon EOS Rebel T7i/800D digital camera.** This is hard to miss. The camera is the main reason you laid out the big bucks, and it is tucked away inside a nifty Bubble Wrap envelope you should save for protection in case the camera needs to be sent in for repair.

- **Rubber eyecup Ef.** This slide-on soft-rubber eyecup should be attached to the viewfinder when you receive the camera. It helps you squeeze your eye tightly against the window, excluding extraneous light, and also protects your eyeglasses (if you wear them) from scratching.

- **Body cap RF-3.** The twist-off body cap keeps dust from entering the camera when no lens is mounted. Even with automatic sensor cleaning built into the T7i, you'll want to keep the amount of dust to a minimum. The body cap belongs in your camera bag if you contemplate the need to travel with the lens removed.

- **Lens (if purchased).** The Rebel T7i may come in a kit with the Canon Zoom Lens EF-S 18-135mm f/3.5-5.6 IS STM lens or the EF-S 18-55mm f/3.5-56 IS STM lens. You may purchase it with another lens. I purchased my T7i as a camera body only, because I already own both of the two "kit" lenses. The lens will come with a lens cap on the front, and a rear lens cap aft.

- **Battery pack LP-E17 (with cover).** The power source for your Rebel T7i is packaged separately. You'll need to charge this 7.2V, 1120mAh (milliampere hour) battery before using it. It should be charged as soon as possible and inserted in the camera. Save the protective cover. If you transport a battery outside the camera, it's a good idea to re-attach the cover to prevent the electrical contacts from shorting out.

- **Battery charger LC-E17 or LC-E17E.** One of these two battery chargers will be included.

- **Wide strap EW-400D.** Canon provides you with a suitable neck strap, emblazoned with Canon advertising. While I am justifiably proud of owning a fine Canon camera, I prefer a low-key, more versatile and secure strap from UPstrap (www.upstrap.com). If you carry your camera over one shoulder, as many do, I particularly recommend the UPstrap shown in Figure 1.1. That patented non-slip pad offers reassuring traction and eliminates the contortions we sometimes go through to keep the camera from slipping off. I know several photographers who refuse to use anything else. If you do purchase an UPstrap, be sure you mention to photographer-inventor Al Stegmeyer that I sent you hence. You won't get a discount, but Al will get yet another confirmation of how much I like his neck straps.

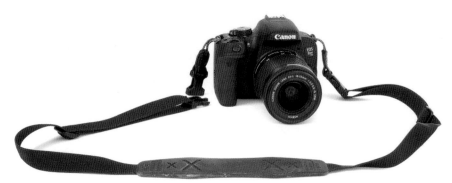

Figure 1.1
Third-party neck straps, like this UPstrap model, are often preferable to the Canon-supplied strap.

- **Printed instruction manuals.** These include a basic instruction manual for camera and Wi-Fi/NFC functions. For more detailed information, you'll need to view the PDF manuals available for download from the Canon website Support page for your country. In Chapter 9 I'll explain how to use the Manual/Software URL entry in the Set-up 4 menu to retrieve the manuals using a QR code the camera will display on the LCD monitor. Even if you have this book, you'll probably want to check the printed user's guide and PDF manuals that Canon provides, if only to check the actual nomenclature for some obscure accessory, or to double-check an error code.

- **Warranty and registration card.** Don't lose these! You can register your Canon T7i by mail, although you don't really need to to keep your warranty in force, but you may need the information in this paperwork (plus the purchase receipt/invoice from your retailer) should you require Canon service support.

Don't bother rooting around in the box for anything beyond what I've listed previously. There are a few things Canon classifies as optional accessories, even though you (and I) might consider some of them essential. Here's a list of what you *don't* get in the box, but might want to think about as an impending purchase. I'll list them roughly in the order of importance:

- **Secure Digital card.** First-time digital camera buyers are sometimes shocked that their new tool doesn't come with a memory card. Why should it? The manufacturer doesn't have the slightest idea of how much storage you require, or whether you want a slow/inexpensive card or one that's faster/more expensive, so why should they pack one in the box and charge you for it? For a 24-megapixel camera, you really need one that's a minimum of 8GB in size, although 16GB cards and larger are more common these days.

  Perhaps you want to use tiny 8GB cards—and lots of them. I've met many paranoid wedding photographers who like to work with a horde of smaller cards (and then watch over them *very* protectively), on the theory that they are reducing their chances of losing a significant chunk of the event or reception at one time (of course, that's why you hire a second shooter as backup). Others, especially sports photographers, instead prefer a 16GB or 32GB card with room to spare. If you are shooting fast action at high frame rates, or transfer lots of photos to your computer with a speedy card reader, you might opt for the speediest possible memory card. Buy one (or two, or three) of your own and have your flash memory ready when you unpack your T7i.

My recommendation: I've recently standardized on 64GB and 128GB Lexar cards with up to 150 MB/second transfer rates. I like having that much capacity because I always shoot RAW, and frequently RAW+JPEG with my camera.

■ **Interface cable.** Canon no longer includes an interface cable to connect your T7i to your computer. You can use such a cable to transfer photos from the camera to your computer, although I don't recommend that mode, because direct transfer uses a lot of battery power. You can also use the cable to upload and download settings between the camera and your computer (highly recommended), and to operate your camera remotely using the EOS Utility downloaded from the Canon website. The cable can also be used to link the camera to PictBridge-compatible printers.

My recommendation: This cable is a standard USB 2.0 Mini B cable—one that works with many other digital cameras—Canon and otherwise—so you might already own one. They are available from Amazon and other retailers for $5 or less. There is no need to purchase the more costly Canon IFC-400PCU (4.3 feet), IFC-200/IFC-500 (6.2 and 15.4 feet, respectively).

■ **EOS Digital Solution Disc CD.** The disc contains useful software, including Digital Photo Pro Professional, EOS Utility, Lens Registration Tool, Web Service Registration Tool, Sample Music, and the Picture Style Editor. It's no longer supplied with the camera.

My recommendation: Canon still offers what it calls *EOS Digital Solution Disk Software* as a download. However, despite the name, you're retrieving only the software (not a disc) in a self-installing format. You may have to supply your camera's serial number for access. The Canon support site for your country will also allow you to download and install the individual programs found on the "disc."

■ **Extra LP-E17 battery.** Even though you might get 820 shots from a single battery, it's easy to exceed that figure in a few hours of shooting sports at 6 fps. Batteries can unexpectedly fail, too, or simply lose their charge from sitting around unused for a week or two.

My recommendation: Buy an extra (I own four, in total), keep it charged, and free your mind from worry.

■ **Add-on Speedlite.** One of the best uses for your Canon T7i's built-in electronic flash is as a remote trigger for an off-camera Speedlite such as the 600EX-RT, or the more affordable 430EX III-RT strobe, which was designed especially for cameras in this class. Your built-in flash can function as the main illumination for your photo, or softened and used to fill in shadows. If you do much flash photography at all, consider an add-on Speedlite as an important accessory.

My recommendation: At around $169, the Canon Speedlite 270EX II is an affordable flash with an excellent combination of power, compact size, and features. For a bit more, the 430EX III-RT has more power and additional capabilities. I'll offer more information on choosing and using electronic flash in Chapters 11 and 12.

- **AC Adapter Kit ACK-E18.** This includes the AC Adapter AC-E6 and DC Coupler DR-E18, which are used together to power the T7i independently of the batteries. There are several typical situations where this capability can come in handy: when you're cleaning the sensor manually and want to totally eliminate the possibility that a lack of juice will cause the fragile shutter and mirror to spring to life during the process; when indoors shooting tabletop photos, portraits, class pictures, and so forth for hours on end; when using your T7i for remote shooting as well as time-lapse photography; for extensive review of images on your television; or for file transfer to your computer. These all use prodigious amounts of power, which can be provided by this AC adapter. (Beware of power outages and blackouts when cleaning your sensor, however!)

  My recommendation: Unless you regularly do time-lapse or interval photography for long periods of time using an external intervalometer, you can probably skip this expensive accessory.

- **Angle Finder C right-angle viewer.** This handy accessory fastens in place of the standard rubber eyecup and provides a 90-degree view for framing and composing your image at right angles to the original viewfinder, useful for low-level (or high-level) shooting. (Or, maybe, shooting around corners!)

- **Magnifier MG-Ef.** Provides a 1.2X magnification factor of the entire viewing area, which enlarges the center of the image, making it easier to check focus. You might have to move your eye around a little to see all the indicators outside the image frame, but this magnifier is still suitable for everyday use.

  My recommendation: This is not the best accessory for those who wear glasses while shooting. I tend to flip my glasses up on my forehead, and have adjusted the diopter setting for my vision, so this magnifying eyepiece works fine for me.

- **Remote switch RS-60E3.** You can plug this two-foot long accessory electronic release cable into the socket hidden behind a rubber cover on the side of the camera, and then fire off shots without the need to touch the camera itself. In a pinch, you can use the T7i's self-timer to minimize vibration when triggering the camera. But when you want to take a photo at the exact moment you desire (and not when the self-timer happens to trip), or need to eliminate all possibility of human-induced camera shake, you need this release cord.

  My recommendation: These sometimes get lost in a camera bag or are accidentally removed. I bought an extra RS-60E3 cable and keep it in a small box in the trunk of my car, along with an extra memory card.

- **Remote Controller RC-6.** The Rebel has infrared sensors that can receive signals from this optional remote control. It works best when pointed at the sensor, but, unlike the plug-in remote, you can be positioned farther away than two feet.

  My recommendation: Because the IR remote is easily overpowered by bright lights, I use it as my secondary remote control. However, they are also cheap and small, so I've bought a couple to keep handy in several camera bags

Initial Setup

This section helps you become familiar with the important controls most used to make adjustments. You'll also find information on charging the battery, mounting a lens, and making diopter vision adjustments.

The initial setup of your Canon EOS Rebel T7i/800D is fast and easy. Basically, you just need to charge the battery, attach a lens, and insert a memory card. I'll address each of these steps separately, but if you already feel you can manage these setup tasks without further instructions, feel free to skip this section entirely. You should at least skim its contents, however, because I'm going to list a few options that you might not be aware of.

Battery Included

Your Canon EOS Rebel T7i/800D is a sophisticated hunk of machinery and electronics, but it needs a charged battery to function, so rejuvenating the LP-E17 lithium-ion battery pack furnished with the camera should be your first step. A fully charged power source should be good for approximately 820 shots if you're not using the built-in flash, and around 600 shots if using flash 50 percent of the time. These figures are based on standard tests defined by the Camera & Imaging Products Association (CIPA) document DC-002, and don't involve live view shooting.

My experience is that the CIPA figures are often a little optimistic, so it's probably a good idea to have a spare battery on hand. I always recommend purchasing Canon-brand batteries (for less than $75) over less-expensive third-party packs. My reasoning is that it doesn't make sense to save $20 on a component for an advanced camera, especially since batteries (from Canon as well as other sources) have been known to fail in potentially harmful ways. Canon, at least, will stand behind its products, issue a recall if necessary, and supply a replacement if a Canon-brand battery is truly defective. A third-party battery supplier that sells under a half-dozen or more different product labels and brands may not even have an easy way to get the word out that a recall has been issued.

In addition, sellers of third-party batteries may note that their batteries are not *fully decoded* and may require use of their battery charger instead of the Canon LC-E17 or LC-E17E chargers. Translated into plain English, those batteries don't contain the computer chip that conveys to the camera and charger exactly how much power they contain. So, when used in the T7i, your battery status indicator may be inaccurate, and there is some danger that the Canon-brand chargers may overcharge your batteries, with unpleasant results. (Exploding hoverboards and Samsung Galaxy Note 7 tablets demonstrate the danger of mishandled Li-Ion batteries.) If your pictures are important to you, always have at least one spare battery available, and make sure it is an authentic Canon product. If you decide to try out a third-party battery, if it is not decoded you will get messages like those shown in Figure 1.2.

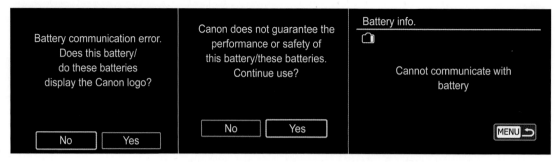

Figure 1.2 Your T7i will let you know if your third-party battery is not fully decoded.

All rechargeable batteries undergo some degree of self-discharge just sitting idle in the camera or in the original packaging. Lithium-ion power packs of this type typically lose a small amount of their charge every day, even when the camera isn't turned on. Li-ion cells lose their power through a chemical reaction that continues when the camera is switched off. So, it's very likely that the battery purchased with your camera is at least partially pooped out, so you'll want to revive it before going out for some serious shooting.

There are many situations in which you'll be glad you have that spare battery:

- **Remote locales.** If you like to backpack and will often be far from a source of electricity, rechargeable cells won't be convenient. They tend to lose some charge over time, even if not used, and will quickly become depleted as you use them. You'll have no way to recharge the cells, lacking a solar-powered charger that might not be a top priority for your backpacking kit.

- **Unexpected needs.** Perhaps you planned to shoot landscapes one weekend, and then are given free front-row tickets to a Major League Baseball game. Instead of a few dozen pictures of trees and lakes, you find yourself shooting hundreds of images of Edward Encarnación and company, which may be beyond the capacity of the single battery you own. If you have a spare battery, you're in good shape.

- **Unexpected failures.** I've charged up batteries and then discovered that they didn't work when called upon, usually because the rechargeable cells had passed their useful life, the charger didn't work, or because of human error. (I *thought*, I'd charged them!) That's one reason why I always carry three times as many batteries as I think I will need.

- **Long shooting session.** Perhaps your niece is getting married, and you want to photograph the ceremony, receiving line, and reception. Several extra batteries will see you through the longest shooting session.

Power Options

Several battery chargers are available for the Canon EOS Rebel T7i/800D. Purchasing an additional charging device offers more than some additional features: You gain a spare that can keep your camera running until you can replace your primary power rejuvenator.

Here's a list of your power options:

- **LC-E17.** This is the standard charger for the T7i and charges a single battery (see Figure 1.3). It may be the most convenient for some, because of its compact size and built-in wall plug prongs that connect directly into your power strip or wall socket and require no cord. This charger, as well as the LC-E17E (described next), has a switching power module that is fully compatible with 100V to 240V 50/60 Hz AC power, so you can use it outside the US with no problems. When I travel to Europe, for example, I take my charger and an adapter to convert the plug shape for the European sockets. No voltage converter is needed.

- **LC-E17E.** This alternate version requires a cord. That can be advantageous in certain situations. For example, if your power outlet is behind a desk or in some other semi-inaccessible location, the cord can be plugged in and routed so the charger sits on your desk or another more convenient spot. The cord itself is a standard one that works with many different chargers and devices (including the power supply for my laptop), so I purchased several of them and leave them plugged into the wall in various locations. I can connect my T7i's charger, my laptop computer's charger, and several other electronic components to one of these cords without needing to crawl around behind the furniture. The cord itself draws no "phantom" power when it's not plugged in to a charger.

- **AC Adapter Kit ACK-E18.** As mentioned earlier, this device consists of the AC Adapter AC-6 and DC Coupler DR-E18, and allows you to operate your Rebel T7i directly from AC power, with no battery required. Studio photographers need this capability because they often snap off hundreds of pictures for hours on end and want constant, reliable power. The camera is probably plugged into a flash sync cord (or radio device), and the studio flash are plugged into power packs or AC power, so the extra tether to this adapter is no big deal in that environment. You also might want to use the AC adapter when viewing images on a TV connected to your T7i, or when shooting remote or time-lapse photos.

- **Battery Grips.** Although Canon offered the BG-E18 battery grip for the previous model Rebel T6i, as I write this there is no equivalent grip from Canon for the T7i (or stablemate 77D), even though these models all use the same LP-E17 batteries. There may be some issue with the BG-E18 grip, or with the cameras themselves that make the grip incompatible.

  However, a suitable grip may be added after this book is published, and it is almost certain that third-party vendors like Meike or Vello will make one available. Previous models held two batteries (another reason to own a spare, or two). It can also be equipped with six AA cells with a battery holder accessory. You can potentially increase your shooting capacity, while adding an additional shutter release, Main Dial, AE Lock/FE Lock, and AF point selection controls for vertically oriented shooting. If a grip for this camera is offered, you'll find it on Amazon and other online retailers, and, perhaps, at your local camera store. It's probably a good idea to monitor online forums to see if early adopters of third-party grips discover any issues.

Charging the Battery

When the battery is inserted into the LC-E17 charger properly (it's impossible to insert it incorrectly), a Charge light begins glowing orange-red. When the battery completes the charge, the Full Charge lamp glows green, approximately two hours later. When the battery is charged, remove it from the charger, flip the lever on the bottom of the camera, and slide the battery in. (See Figure 1.4.) To remove the battery, you must press a lever, which prevents the pack from slipping out when the door is opened.

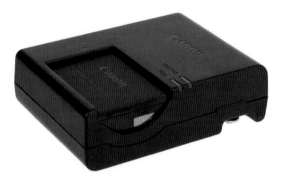

Figure 1.3 A flashing status light (not shown) indicates that the battery is being charged.

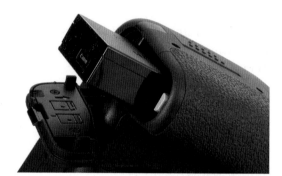

Figure 1.4 Insert the battery in the camera; it only fits one way. Press the button to release the battery when you want to remove it.

Final Steps

Your Canon EOS Rebel T7i is almost ready to fire up and shoot. You'll need to select and mount a lens, adjust the viewfinder for your vision, and insert a memory card. Each of these steps is easy, and if you've used any Canon EOS camera in the past, you already know exactly what to do. I'm going to provide a little extra detail for those of you who are new to the Canon or digital SLR worlds.

Mounting the Lens

As you'll see, my recommended lens mounting procedure emphasizes protecting your equipment from accidental damage, and minimizing the intrusion of dust. If your T7i has no lens attached, select the lens you want to use and loosen (but do not remove) the rear lens cap. I generally place the lens I am planning to mount vertically in a slot in my camera bag, where it's protected from mishaps, but ready to pick up quickly. By loosening the rear lens cap, you'll be able to lift it off the back of the lens at the last instant, so the rear element of the lens is covered until then.

After that, remove the body cap by rotating the cap toward the shutter release button. You should always mount the body cap when there is no lens on the camera, because it helps keep dust out of the interior of the camera, where it can settle on the mirror, focusing screen, the interior mirror box, and potentially find its way past the shutter onto the sensor. (While the T7i's sensor cleaning mechanism works fine, the less dust it has to contend with, the better.) The body cap also protects the vulnerable mirror from damage caused by intruding objects (including your fingers, if you're not cautious).

Once the body cap has been removed, remove the rear lens cap from the lens, set it aside, and then mount the lens on the camera by matching the alignment indicator on the lens barrel (red for EF lenses and white for EF-S lenses) with the red or white dot on the camera's lens mount (see Figure 1.5). Rotate the lens away from the shutter release until it seats securely. (You can find out more about the difference between EF and EF-S lenses in Chapter 10.) Set the focus mode switch on the lens to AF (autofocus). If the lens hood is bayoneted on the lens in the reversed position (which makes the lens/hood combination more compact for transport), twist it off and remount with the edge facing outward (see Figure 1.6). A lens hood protects the front of the lens from accidental bumps, stray fingerprints, and reduces flare caused by extraneous light arriving at the front element of the lens from outside the picture area.

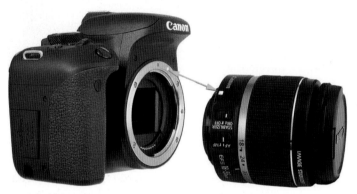

Figure 1.5 Match the white dot on EF-S lenses with the white dot on the camera mount to properly align the lens with the bayonet mount. For EF lenses, use the red dots.

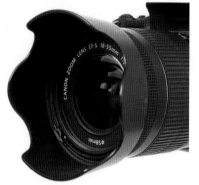

Figure 1.6 A lens hood protects the lens from extraneous light and accidental bumps.

Adjusting Diopter Correction

Those of us with less than perfect eyesight can often benefit from a little optical correction in the viewfinder. Your contact lenses or glasses may provide all the correction you need, but if you are a glasses wearer and want to use the EOS Rebel T7i/800D without your glasses, you can take advantage of the camera's built-in diopter adjustment, which can be varied from –3 to +1 correction. Press the shutter release halfway to illuminate the indicators in the viewfinder, then rotate the dioptric adjustment knob next to the viewfinder (see Figure 1.7) while looking through the viewfinder until the indicators appear sharp.

If the available correction is insufficient, Canon offers 10 different Dioptric Adjustment Lens Series E correction lenses for the viewfinder window. If more than one person uses your T7i, and each requires a different diopter setting, you can save a little time by noting the number of clicks and direction (clockwise to increase the diopter power; counterclockwise to decrease the diopter value) required to change from one user to the other. There are 18 detents in all.

Dioptric adjustment knob

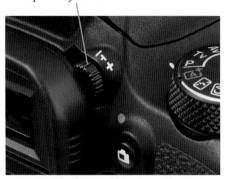

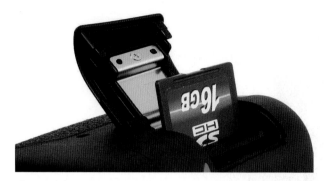

Figure 1.7 Viewfinder diopter correction from −3 to +1 can be dialed in.

Figure 1.8 Insert the memory in the slot with the label facing the back of the camera.

Inserting a Secure Digital Memory Card

You can't take photos without a memory card inserted in your EOS Rebel T7i/800D (although there is a Release Shutter without Card entry in Shooting 1 menu that enables/disables shutter release functions when a memory card is absent—learn about that in Chapter 8). So, your final step will be to insert a memory card. Slide the door on the right side of the body toward the back of the camera to release the cover, and then open it. (You should only remove the memory card when the camera is switched off, but the T7i will remind you if the door is opened while the camera is still writing photos to the memory card.)

Insert the memory card with the label facing the back of the camera, as shown in Figure 1.8, oriented so the edge with the connectors goes into the slot first. Close the door, and your pre-flight checklist is done! (I'm going to assume you remember to remove the lens cap when you're ready to take a picture!) When you want to remove the memory card later, push it inward to make the memory card pop out.

That's all you need to do to prep your camera for operation. In the next chapter, I'll give you a Quick Start that shows how to power up the camera, enter the date and time, and format a memory card. Then, we'll move on to mastering the T7i's touch screen, and the basics of capturing a photo or movie using the easiest settings.

2

Quick Start

Now it's time to fire up your EOS T7i and take some photos. The easy part is turning on the power—that On/Off switch on the right shoulder, labeled with On, Off, and a movie camera icon. Avoid rotating the switch past the On setting to Movie—unless you intend to shoot movies! Simply turn on the camera, and, if you mounted a lens and inserted a fresh battery and memory card—as I prompted you in the last chapter—you're ready to begin. You could just rotate the Mode Dial (located to the left of the On/Off switch) to the P (Program mode) or green A+ (Scene Intelligent Auto mode) labels and begin taking pictures immediately.

However, you'll enjoy your introduction to the camera more if you first learn from this chapter some basic functions, such as how to use the touch screen, take care of some initial housekeeping (like setting the time and date or formatting a card), select a shooting mode, metering mode, focus mode, and, if need be, elevate the built-in flash.

Navigating the Rebel T7i

Canon has introduced an optional "guided" system for the screens displayed when shooting, navigating menus, and choosing shooting modes. It is enabled by default, so the first thing we need to do is explain the displays you'll see while you are shooting or making adjustments using the menus. You'll find complete instructions for using every menu option the T7i offers in Chapters 8 and 9, but a quick introduction to the guided options are in order now.

Guided Shooting Mode

When you first turn on the T7i with Guided modes enabled, a screen like the one at top in Figure 2.1 appears. In the top-left corner of the screen, the current shooting/exposure mode is displayed. In the example figure, Tv (for Time Value) is shown, indicating that the camera is set for Shutter Priority. The current shutter speed is shown above a scale displaying all the available shutter speeds from 30 seconds to 1/4000th second, along with icons flanking the scale indicating that slower shutter speeds allow action to blur (or "flow"), while faster shutter speeds can stop or "freeze" movement. Don't panic at this point if you're a new photo enthusiast; I'll explain all these modes in Chapter 4.

At the bottom of the screen are labels showing various adjustments that you *can* make (but don't need to fuss with quite yet), changing the brightness/darkness of your images; switching from taking a single picture to continuous or self-timer shooting; and making two focusing adjustments. You'll learn how to use those shortly.

When you rotate that Mode Dial I mentioned earlier, a screen like the one at bottom in Figure 2.1 pops up. It tells you a little about the mode. Tap the touch screen at the down-pointing arrow to read more about the mode. To dismiss the screen and begin shooting, tap the OK icon on the LCD touch screen or press the SET button located on the back of the camera (Figure 2.3 accompanying an upcoming discussion shows you exactly where it is). Once you've become more familiar with your camera, you will not need to use the guided modes, and I'll show you how to turn them off later in this chapter.

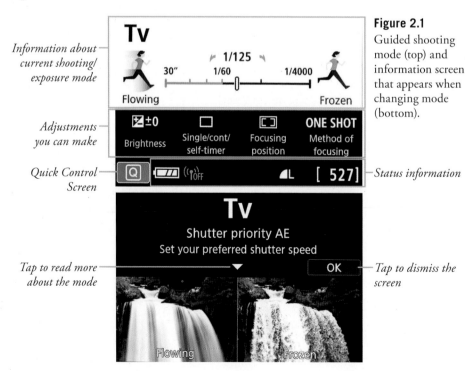

Figure 2.1
Guided shooting mode (top) and information screen that appears when changing mode (bottom).

Information about current shooting/exposure mode

Adjustments you can make

Quick Control Screen

Status information

Tap to read more about the mode

Tap to dismiss the screen

Guided Menus

Some of the Quick Start suggestions that follow ask you to navigate through some simple menu adjustments. Canon gives you a guided mode for the menus, too. When you press the MENU button (located in the upper-left corner of the back of the camera), the default guided menu pops up, shown at top left in Figure 2.2. It has four "tabs" labeled Shooting Settings, Playback Settings, Function Settings (also known as Set Up adjustments), and Display Level Settings (which enables/ disables the guide modes).

You can use the left/right buttons on the back of the camera (shown in Figure 2.3 in the next section) to move from one tab to another, or tap the tab's icon on the touch screen. Once you've selected one of the tabs, you can press the SET button (also seen in Figure 2.3) or tap OK to view the underlying menus (Figure 2.2, center right). These menus are very similar to the non-guided menus (as shown in Figure 2.2, lower left), but include pop-up "tool tip" displays explaining what the selected menu does. As with guided shooting modes, you probably won't need the hand-holding the guided menus offer after you've used your T7i for a short time.

Now that you have been introduced to the guided screens, you can jump right into putting your Rebel T7i to work. I'm going to show you how to use the basic camera controls, work with the touch screen, and select some basic settings next.

Figure 2.2
Top-level guided menu (top left); guided menu (center right); conventional menu (lower left).

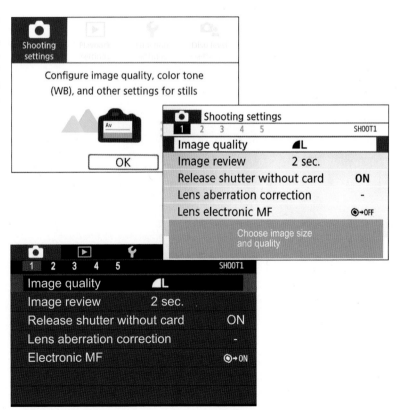

Using the Physical Controls

Before I introduce you to the touch screen on the back of the camera, it's a good idea to become familiar with the most important of the physical controls first:

- **Access menus.** You can produce the T7i's main menus by pressing the MENU button, located at the far-left corner of the back of the camera (and shown at left in Figure 2.3).
- **Navigate among menus.** Use the directional buttons (seen at center in Figure 2.3) to move within the menu system. Note that each of these buttons has a secondary function, such as setting white balance, that I'll explain in Chapter 3.

Note
With some previous versions of the Rebel series, these directional buttons were often referred to as "cross keys." While the T7i retains the same layout, for simplicity's sake, I will refer to the directional controls as *directional buttons* and/or *up/down/left/right buttons* in this book.

- **Main Dial.** This dial (shown at right in Figure 2.3) can often be used to move highlighting left and right, say, to scroll among the main menu heading tabs.
- **Quick Control button.** The Quick Control button (Q button) (shown in the center image in Figure 2.3) produces a Quick Control menu (described later), which offers fast access to many adjustments.

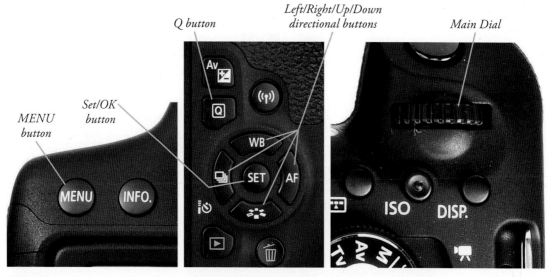

Figure 2.3 Your basic controls include the MENU button (left), directional buttons, SET/OK button, and Q button (center), and Main Dial (right).

Mastering the Touch Screen

When a main menu, adjustment screen, or the Quick Control menu is displayed, you will often elect to use the touch screen to make your changes. Optionally, you can resort to the physical controls that provide the equivalent functions, including the available buttons and navigational buttons. However, I think that once you become familiar with the speed with which the touch screen allows you to make these adjustments, you'll be reluctant to go back to the "old" way of doing things.

The T7i's touch screen is *capacitive* rather than *resistive*, making it more like the current generation of smartphones than earlier computer touch-sensitive screens. The difference is that your camera's LCD responds to the electrical changes that result from *contact* rather than the force of *pressure* on the screen itself. That means that the screen is able to interpret your touches and taps in more complex ways. It "knows" when you're using two fingers instead of one, and can react to multi-touch actions and gestures, such as swiping (to scroll in any direction), and pinching/spreading of fingers to zoom in and out. Since you probably have been using a smartphone for a while, these actions have become ingrained enough to be considered intuitive. Virtually every main and secondary function or menu operation can be accessed from the touch screen. However, if you want to continue using the buttons and dials, the T7i retains that method of operation.

YOUR CHOICE

Throughout this book, I may not explicitly say "tap the screen" or "use the button" for every single operation. I'm assuming that once you master the touch screen using the information in this section, you'll make your own choice and use whichever method you prefer. Unless I specifically say to use the touch screen or physical controls, assume I mean you can use either one.

Here's what you need to know to get started:

- **Tap to select.** Tap (touch the LCD screen briefly) to select an item, including a menu heading or icon. Any item you can tap will have a frame or box around it. Figure 2.4 shows the taps needed to select a menu tab and specific entry within that menu. (The Guided menu is used as an example.)
- **Drag/swipe to select.** Many functions can be selected by touching the screen and then sliding your finger to the right or left until the item you want is highlighted. For example, instead of tapping, you can slide horizontally along the main menu's tabs to choose any Shooting, Playback, Custom, or My Menu tab, and slide vertically to choose an individual menu entry.
- **Drag/swipe to adjust scales.** Screens that contain a sliding scale (say, to make an image brighter or darker) can be adjusted by dragging. Figure 2.5 shows how you can drag along the LCD Brightness scale to select a value or, alternatively, tap the small sun (darker) or large sun (brighter) icons to either side of the scale. (Note that you can also press the left/right directional buttons if you prefer.)

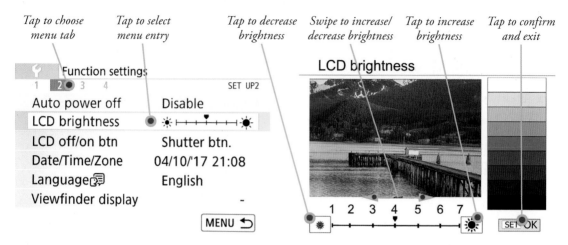

Tap to choose menu tab   *Tap to select menu entry*   *Tap to decrease brightness*   *Swipe to increase/decrease brightness*   *Tap to increase brightness*   *Tap to confirm and exit*

Figure 2.4 Tap menu tabs or entries to select them.

Figure 2.5 Tap or swipe to adjust sliding scales.

■ **Drag/swipe to scroll among images.** In Playback mode, as you review your images you can drag your finger left and right to advance from one image to another, much as you might do with a smartphone or tablet computer. This is probably the coolest use for the touch screen. Figure 2.6 shows you can use either one finger to scroll or two fingers to jump among playback images.

■ **Pinch to reduce/enlarge.** During playback, you can use two fingers to "pinch" the screen to zoom out from single-frame display to multiple thumbnails, and spread those two fingers apart to zoom in again to a single frame and magnified image—also very cool and intuitive. (See Figure 2.7.)

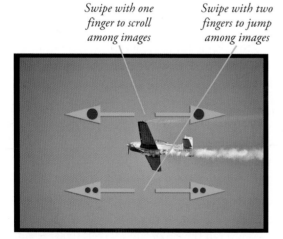

Swipe with one finger to scroll among images   *Swipe with two fingers to jump among images*

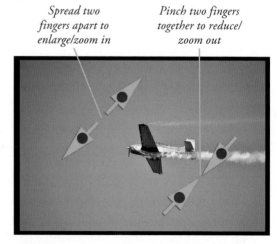

Spread two fingers apart to enlarge/zoom in   *Pinch two fingers together to reduce/zoom out*

Figure 2.6 Swipe left or right with one finger to scroll among images; swipe with two fingers to jump.

Figure 2.7 Spread two fingers apart to enlarge/zoom in, or pinch two fingers together to zoom out/view thumbnails.

■ **Enable/Disable touch features.** As I'll explain in Chapter 9, you can enable or disable touch operation in the Set-up 3 (Function Settings 3) menu under the Touch Control entry, and turn the click sound the touch feature makes on or off using the Beep setting in the Set-up 3 (Function Settings 3) menu.

■ **Avoid "protective" sheets, moisture, sharp implements.** The LCD uses capacitive technology to sense your touch, rather than pressure sensitivity. LCD protectors or moisture can interfere with the touch functions, and styluses or sharp objects (such as pens) won't produce the desired results. I have, in fact, used "skins" on my T7i's LCD with good results (even though the screen is quite rugged and really doesn't need protection from scratches), but there is no guarantee that all such protectors will work for you.

As I noted, the choice of whether to use the traditional buttons or touch screen is up to you. I've found that with some screens, the controls are too close together to be easily manipulated with my wide fingers. The touch screen can be especially dangerous when working with some functions, such as card formatting. In screens where the icons are large and few in number, such as the screen used to adjust LCD brightness, touch control works just fine. Easiest of all is touch operation during Playback. It's a no-brainer to swipe your finger from side to side to scroll among images and pinch/spread to zoom out and in.

Enabling Conventional Menus and Modes

As I noted earlier, the Guided menus and modes can be quite useful if you are new to digital photography, or to Canon digital cameras in particular. However, veteran users (and you'll join their ranks before you finish this book), especially those who have previously used Rebels, find the Guided modes add needless extra steps and provide information they already have mastered (for example, using fast shutter speeds to freeze action).

So, I'm going to show you how to enable the conventional menus and modes you are probably already familiar with, as a time-saver for those who don't need extra hand-holding. Those of you who *are* new to photography can skip this section and come back to it when you're ready to ditch the Canon user interface's helpful, but temporary, training wheel guides. For most of the rest of this book, the figures will show the conventional menus and screens, which are functionally almost identical to the "guided" screens, but use a different color scheme.

Accessing Display Level Settings

The display type options reside in a new menu tab, called Display Level Settings. Follow these steps to change how menus and other screens appear:

1. **Access menus.** Turn the camera on and press the MENU button, shown earlier in Figure 2.3. Use the touch screen or directional buttons to select Disp Level Settings (highlighted in green in Figure 2.8, left). Press the SET/OK button or tap OK to reveal the settings screen, shown at right in the figure.

2. **Choose category to change.** Four options appear, shown at right in Figure 2.8. Unless they have been changed, all will be set to Guided/Enabled mode:

- **Shooting Screen.** Change from Guided or Standard by tapping the Shooting Screen selection, or pressing SET, highlighting your choice, and pressing SET/OK again. Choosing Guided enables the LCD monitor shooting screen discussed earlier, and shown in the thumbnail image at top left in Figure 2.9. Selecting Standard produces a more detailed screen like the one shown at top right in the figure. (I'll explain how to use the Standard screens in Chapter 3.)

- **Menu Display.** As above, toggle between Guided or Standard modes by tapping the Menu Display selection, or pressing SET/OK, highlighting your option, and pressing SET/OK again. I already showed you the Guided menu screen, shown at lower left in Figure 2.9. The Standard menu displays look like the thumbnail at lower right in the figure. I'll use the standard menus for most of the rest of the book, and explore all their options in greater detail in Chapters 8 and 9.

- **Shooting Mode Guide.** Choose Enable or Disable as described above. I showed you a typical Shooting Mode Guide at right in Figure 2.1. When enabled, a different guide for each shooting mode appears as you rotate the Mode Dial. Press the down button to scroll to any additional information. Tap OK, press SET or the Q button, or depress the shutter halfway to return to the shooting screen.

- **Feature Guide.** When enabled, pop-up tool tips appear with information about a particular setting or feature. You can see a typical tip at center right in Figure 2.2, earlier. Note that shooting tips will appear, even if Shooting Screen has been set to Standard and Feature Guide set to disabled, if you are using Basic Zone modes—the automatic, effects, and scene modes (such as Close-up). I'll explain Basic Zone modes in more detail later in this chapter. In addition, even if the tips have been disabled, you can also summon them when shooting pictures by pressing the Trash button (located at the bottom-right corner of the back of the camera).

3. **Switch back (optional).** If you disable the Guided modes, you can always turn any or all four back on by using the steps just outlined.

Initial Settings

This section will give you a quick start to making the most important settings you'll need while taking photos with your T7i.

Setting Date and Time

When you rotate the On/Off switch on top of the camera (located on the right shoulder of the T7i) to the On position, automatic sensor cleaning takes place (unless you specifically disable this action) as the camera comes to life. The camera will remain on or in a standby mode until you manually turn it off. After 30 seconds of idling, the T7i goes into the standby mode to save battery power.

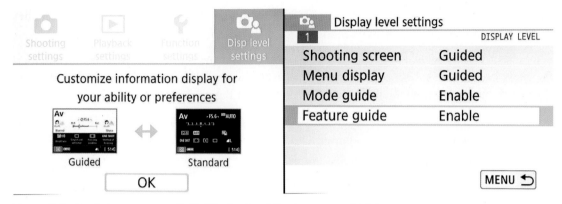

Figure 2.8 Guided menu screen (left); Display Level Settings screen (right).

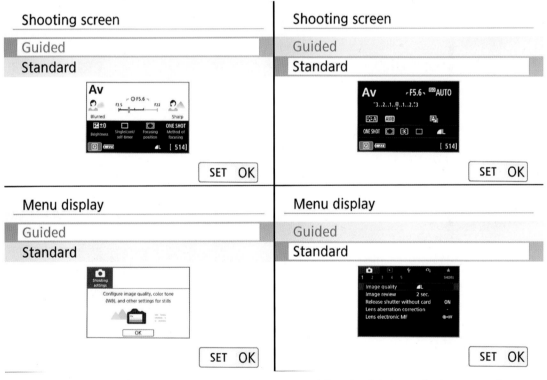

Figure 2.9 Shooting Screen Guided and Standard settings (top left and right); Menu display options (bottom left and right).

Just tap the shutter release button to bring it back to life. The automatic sensor cleaning operation does not occur when exiting standby mode.

The first time you use the Rebel T7i, it may ask you to enter the time and date. (This information may have been set by someone checking out your camera on your behalf prior to sale.) Just follow these steps, using the directional buttons shown earlier in Figure 2.3:

1. Press the MENU button, located in the upper-left corner of the back of the T7i.

2. Rotate the Main Dial (near the shutter release button on top of the camera) until the Function Settings menu is highlighted (Guided mode). Tap the tab on the touch screen or press SET. If using Standard menus, you can skip those steps and move directly to the Set-up 2 menu. In both cases, it's marked by a wrench icon, as shown earlier in Figure 2.4.

3. Use the up/down buttons to move the highlighting down to the Date/Time/Zone entry, and press the SET button in the center of the keypad located to the right of the LCD monitor.

4. When the screen shown in Figure 2.10 appears, use the directional buttons to scroll down to the date/time entry. When the gold box highlights the month, day, year, hour, minute, or second format (using a 24-hour clock) you want to adjust, press OK/SET to activate that value. A pair of up/down-pointing triangles appears above the value.

5. Press the up/down keys to adjust the value up or down. Press OK/SET to confirm the value you've entered.

6. Continue to enable/disable Daylight Savings Time (indicated by a box with a sun inside) and Time Zone (a list of the major city that represents each time Zone, such as New York, Chicago, Denver, and Los Angeles). If the currently selected time zone is not correct for your location, use the up/down buttons to highlight the appropriate city and press the SET/OK button.

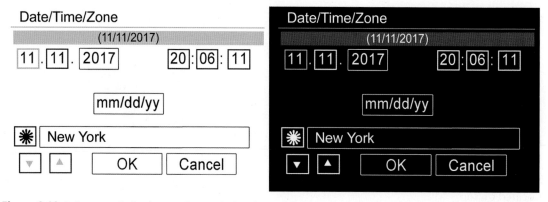

Figure 2.10 Like most dialog boxes, the Guided and Standard screens to adjust the date, time, format, and time zone are identical in layout.

7. When finished, navigate to select either OK (if you're satisfied with your changes) or Cancel (if you'd like to return to the menu screen without making any changes). Press SET/OK to confirm your choice.

8. When finished setting the date and time, press MENU to exit.

Your Canon EOS Rebel T7i is ready to go.

Formatting a Memory Card

There are three ways to create a blank memory card for your T7i, and two of them are at least partially wrong. Here are your options, both correct and incorrect:

■ **Transfer (move) files to your computer.** When you transfer (rather than copy) all the image files to your computer from the memory card (either using a direct cable transfer or with a card reader, as described later in this chapter), the old image files are erased from the card, leaving the card blank. Theoretically. This method does *not* remove files that you've labeled as Protected (choosing the Protect Images function in the Playback menu) nor does it identify and lock out parts of your memory card that have become corrupted or unusable since the last time you formatted the card. Therefore, I recommend always formatting the card, rather than simply moving the image files, each time you want to make a blank card. The only exception is when you *want* to leave the protected/unerased images on the card for a while longer, say, to share with friends, family, and colleagues.

■ **(Don't) Format in your computer.** With the memory card inserted in a card reader or card slot in your computer, you can use Windows or Mac OS to reformat the memory card. Don't! The operating system won't necessarily arrange the structure of the card the way the T7i likes to see it (in computer terms, an incorrect *file system* may be installed). The only way to ensure that the card has been properly formatted for your camera is to perform the format in the camera itself. The only exception to this rule is when you have a seriously corrupted memory card that your camera refuses to format. Sometimes it is possible to revive such a corrupted card by allowing the operating system to reformat it first, then trying again in the camera.

■ **Set-up/Function menu format.** The recommended way to format a memory card uses the T7i's menu system, as described next.

Easy Formatting

If you've set your camera's time and date, you've learned enough about navigating the menus to format a memory card. Just turn on the camera, press the MENU button, rotate the Main Dial (located on top of the camera, just behind the shutter release button), choose the Set-up 1/Function Settings menu, use the up/down directional buttons to navigate to the Format entry, and press SET/OK to access the Format screen. Press the left/right directional buttons again to select OK and press SET/OK one final time to begin the format process.

You can also use the Trash button (located in the lower-right corner of the back of the camera) or Trash icon on the touch screen to mark the Low-level format box on the Format screen. This tells the T7i to perform an additional, more thorough, formatting of the card after the initial format is finished. The low-level format serves to remove data from all writable portions of your memory card while locking out "bad" sectors, and can be used to restore a memory card that is slowing down as it "trips" over those bad sectors. This extra step takes a bit longer than a standard reformat, and need not be used every time you format your card.

Selecting a Shooting Mode

The following sections show you how to choose Scene, semi-automatic, or automatic shooting (exposure) modes; select a metering mode (which tells the camera what portions of the frame to evaluate for exposure); and set the basic autofocus functions. If you understand how to do these things, you can skip ahead to "Other Settings."

You can choose a shooting method from the Mode Dial located on the top right of the Canon EOS Rebel T7i. (See Figure 2.11.) There are eight Basic Zone shooting modes positions on the dial, plus seven more Special Scene modes that can be selected when the Mode Dial is set to the SCN position. With these 15 modes, the camera makes virtually all the decisions for you (except when to press the shutter).

The camera also offers four Creative Zone modes: Manual, Aperture-priority (Av), Shutter-priority (Tv), and Program Auto (P), which allow you to provide input over the exposure and settings the camera uses. You'll find a complete discussion of both Basic and Creative Zone modes in Chapter 4.

Turn your camera on by flipping the power switch to On. Next, you need to select which shooting mode to use. If you're very new to digital photography, you might want to set the camera to Scene Intelligent Auto (the green A+ icon on the Mode Dial) or P (Program mode) and start snapping

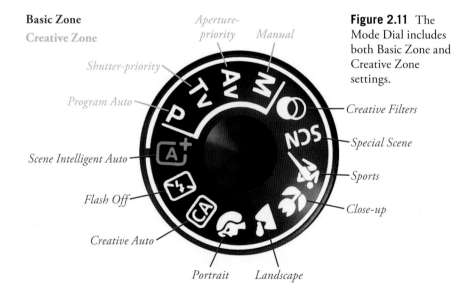

Figure 2.11 The Mode Dial includes both Basic Zone and Creative Zone settings.

away. Either mode will make all the appropriate settings for you for many shooting situations. If you have a specific type of picture you want to shoot, you can try out one of the other Basic Zone modes indicated on the Mode Dial with appropriate icons, as shown in Figure 2.11.

As you select a mode, a screen like the one at left in Figure 2.12 appears if you've enabled Guided modes. As always, the down arrow on the screen means you can tap/press down to view additional information about the selection. Choose OK/SET to dismiss the screen and begin shooting. When using Standard modes, this screen does not appear and you can skip the extra step and begin shooting immediately. Choosing a specific Special Scene mode (the SCN position on the dial) will be described shortly.

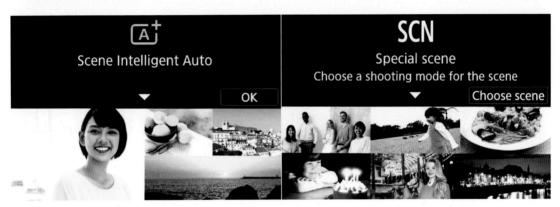

Figure 2.12 Guide mode information screen (left). Special Scene selection in Guided mode (right).

Basic Zone Modes

Here is a list of the nine Basic Zone modes available from the Mode Dial. I'll provide additional information about Special Scene and Creative Filter modes shortly.

- **Scene Intelligent Auto/Full Auto.** In this mode, marked with a green A+ icon, the EOS T7i makes all the exposure decisions for you, and will pop up the flash if necessary under low-light conditions.

- **Flash Off.** This mode is like Scene Intelligent Auto with the flash disabled. You'll want to use it in museums and other locations where flash is forbidden or inappropriate. It otherwise operates exactly like the Auto setting but disables the pop-up internal flash unit.

- **Creative Auto.** This Creative Auto mode is basically the same as the Full Auto option, but, unlike the other Basic Zone modes, allows you to change the brightness and other parameters of the image. The T7i still makes most of the decisions for you, but you can make some simple adjustments using the Creative Auto setting screen that appears when you press the Quick Control button (located on the back of the camera to the right of the LCD monitor). You can find instructions for using this mode and the other shooting modes in Chapter 4.

- **Portrait.** Use this mode when you're taking a portrait of a subject standing relatively close to the camera and want to de-emphasize the background, maximize sharpness, and produce flattering skin tones.

- **Landscape.** Select this mode when you want extra sharpness and rich colors of distant scenes.

- **Close-up.** This mode is helpful when you are shooting close-up pictures of a subject from about one foot away or less.

- **Sports.** Use this mode to freeze fast-moving subjects.

- **SCN.** Choose from seven Special Scene modes, described next.

- **Creative Filters.** You can apply 10 different filters to your images, as you shoot. (Sorry, no dog noses available.)

Special Scene Modes

With the dial in the SCN position, you can select any of seven additional Special Scene modes. When the screen shown at right in Figure 2.12 appears (in Guided mode), you can tap Choose Scene or press SET to continue to a screen with your seven options listed in a vertical column. Use the up/down arrows to highlight the scene mode you want to work with, and choose OK/SET. In non-Guided mode, press the Q button to highlight Choose Scene, then tap/press SET to open the screen with the same vertical column of selections. I'll show you how to make the small set of adjustments allowed when working with Special Scene modes in Chapter 4.

- **Group photo.** Provides settings that help ensure everyone in a group shot is in acceptably sharp focus.

- **Kids.** Produces pleasant skin tones, with bright colors and a fast-enough shutter speed to allow sharp pictures of rampaging children.

- **Food.** Gives you bright and vivid colors, to make your food look more appetizing than it probably was in real life. Shooting pictures of your food has become almost mandatory when dining out, thanks to Instagram.

- **Candlelight.** Preserves the warm, pleasant colors found in subjects illuminated by candlelight. The built-in flash is disabled, but if you have an external Speedlite connected and powered up, it will fire anyway and spoil your picture. Turn it off!

- **Night Portrait.** Choose this mode when you want to illuminate a subject in the foreground with flash, but still allow the background to be exposed properly by the available light. Be prepared to use a tripod or an image-stabilized (IS) lens to reduce the effects of camera shake. (You'll find more about IS and camera shake in Chapter 10.)

- **Handheld Night Scene.** The T7i takes four continuous shots and combines them to produce a well-exposed image with reduced camera shake.

- **HDR Backlight Control.** The T7i takes three continuous shots at different exposures and combines them to produce a single image with improved detail in the highlights and shadows.

Creative Filters

One useful feature of the T7i is the ability to apply Creative Filters to images *as you actually take the picture,* and, when shooting in live view, preview their effect before you take the photo. You can also add these filters to a new copy of the image during image review. (I'll show you how to do that in Chapter 8.) When the Mode Dial is in the Creative Filter position, you can choose which filter to apply with the same steps as selecting a Special Scene mode, as described above. The seven effects are shown in the list that follows. I'll provide examples of some of them in Chapter 8.

- **Grainy B/W.** Creates a grainy monochrome image. You can adjust contrast among Low, Normal, and Strong settings.
- **Soft Focus.** Blur your image using Low, Normal, and Strong options.
- **Fish-Eye Effect.** Creates a distorted, curved image.
- **Water Painting Effect.** Gives you soft colors like a watercolor painting, and allows you to adjust color density.
- **Toy Camera Effect.** Darkens the corners of an image, much as a toy camera does, and adds a warm or cool tone (or none), as you wish.
- **Miniature Effect.** This is a clever effect, and it's hampered by a misleading name and the fact that its properties are hard to visualize (which is not a great attribute for a visual effect). This tool doesn't create a "miniature" picture, as you might expect. What it does is mimic tilt/shift lens effects that angle the lens off the axis of the sensor plane to drastically change the plane of focus, producing the sort of look you get when viewing some photographs of a diorama, or miniature scene.
- **HDR Art Standard/Vivid/Bold/Embossed.** These are four separate options that provide special effects with excellent rendition of both highlights and shadows. The T7i takes three separate shots continuously and combines them to produce the special look.

Creative Zone Modes

If you have more photographic experience, you might want to opt for one of the Creative Zone modes. These, too, are described in more detail in Chapter 4. These modes let you apply a little more creativity to your camera's settings. These modes are indicated on the Mode Dial by letters M, Av, Tv, and P.

- **M (Manual).** Select when you want full control over the shutter speed and lens opening, either for creative effects or because you are using a studio flash or other flash unit not compatible with the T7i's automatic flash metering.
- **Av (Aperture-priority).** Choose when you want to use a particular lens opening, especially to control sharpness or how much of your image is in focus. The T7i will select the appropriate shutter speed for you. Av stands for *aperture value.*

- **Tv (Shutter-priority).** This mode (Tv stands for *time value*) is useful when you want to use a particular shutter speed to stop action or produce creative blur effects. The T7i will select the appropriate f/stop for you.

- **P (Program).** This mode allows the T7i to select the basic exposure settings, but you can still override the camera's choices to fine-tune your image.

You can change some settings when the shooting settings display is shown on the screen (press the INFO. button to the left of the viewfinder window if you want to make the display visible). Press the Quick Control button and then tap the touch screen or use the directional buttons to navigate to the setting you'd like to adjust. (See Figure 2.13.) The available adjustments change, depending on what Basic Zone or Creative Zone exposure mode you're using.

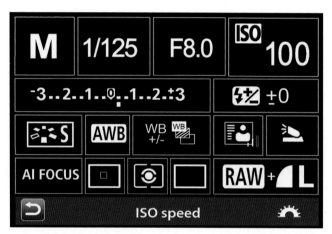

Figure 2.13
Some settings can be made quickly when the shooting settings display is visible.

Choosing a Metering Mode

You might want to select a particular metering mode for your first shots, although the default Evaluative metering (which is set automatically when you choose a Basic Zone mode) is probably the best choice as you get to know your camera. Guided mode won't let you change metering mode and some other parameters directly; it requires a trip to the menu, so for the rest of this chapter I'm going to assume you are using Standard mode with the conventional controls.

To change metering modes when using a Creative Zone mode, you'll need to use the Q button to access the Quick Control screen, as described earlier, or the T7i's menu system (navigated using the directional buttons or the touch screen, as described at the beginning of this chapter). To use the (slower) menus, press the MENU button and navigate to the Shooting 3 menu (a camera icon). Tap or press the down directional button to highlight Metering Mode and select SET. A screen pops up on the LCD offering four choices. Highlight the choice you want. Then select SET to confirm your choice. The options are shown in Figure 2.14. (The Quick Control screen is almost identical, with a different color scheme.)

The metering modes are as follows:

- **Evaluative metering.** The standard metering mode; the T7i attempts to intelligently classify your image and choose the best exposure based on readings from 63 different zones in the frame (measured using a whopping 7,560-pixel sensor that detects both RGB and infrared reflected light, with emphasis on the autofocus points).

- **Partial metering.** Exposure is based on a central spot, roughly six percent of the image area in the center of the frame.

- **Spot metering.** Exposure is calculated from a smaller central spot, about 3.5 percent of the image area.

- **Center-weighted averaging metering.** The T7i meters the entire scene, but gives the most emphasis to the central area of the frame.

You'll find a detailed description of each of these modes in Chapter 4.

Choosing a Focus Mode

You can easily switch between automatic and manual focus by moving the AF/MF switch on the lens mounted on your camera. However, if you're using a Creative Zone shooting mode, you'll still need to choose an appropriate focus mode. (You can read more on selecting focus parameters in Chapter 5.) If you're using a Basic Zone mode, the focus method is set for you automatically.

To set the focus mode, you must first have set the lens to the AF position (instead of the manual focus MF position). Then press the AF button (it's the right directional button) on the back of the camera to produce the selection screen shown in Figure 2.15. Choose the focus mode you want and select SET to confirm your focus mode.

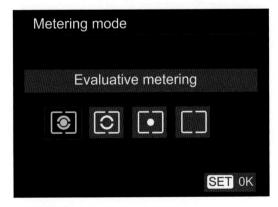

Figure 2.14 Metering modes (left to right): Evaluative, Partial, Spot, Center-weighted.

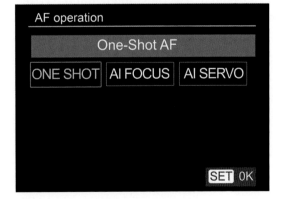

Figure 2.15 Set AF mode.

The three choices available in Creative Zone modes are as follows:

- **One-Shot.** This mode, sometimes called *single autofocus*, locks in a focus point when the shutter button is pressed down halfway, and the focus confirmation light glows in the viewfinder. The focus will remain locked until you release the button or take the picture. If the camera is unable to achieve sharp focus, the focus confirmation light will blink. This mode is best when your subject is relatively motionless. Portrait, Night Portrait, and Landscape Basic Zone modes use this focus method exclusively.

- **AI Servo.** This mode, sometimes called *continuous autofocus*, sets focus when you partially depress the shutter button, but continues to monitor the frame and refocuses if the camera or subject is moved. This is a useful mode for photographing sports and moving subjects. The Sports Basic Zone mode uses this focus method exclusively.

- **AI Focus.** In this mode, the T7i switches between One-Shot and AI Servo as appropriate. That is, it locks in a focus point when you partially depress the shutter button (One-Shot mode), but switches automatically to AI Servo if the subject begins to move. This mode is handy when photographing a subject, such as a child at quiet play, that might move unexpectedly. The Flash Off Basic Zone mode uses this focus method.

Selecting an AF Area Selection Mode

The Canon EOS Rebel T7i uses 45 different focus points to calculate correct focus. In any of the Basic Zone shooting modes, the focus point is selected automatically by the camera. In the Creative Zone modes, you can allow the camera to select the focus point automatically, or you can specify which focus point should be used. There are four AF Area Selection modes, which I'll explain in detail in Chapter 5. They are as follows:

- **Manual Selection: Single-point AF.** You can choose one AF point for focus.
- **Manual Select: Zone AF.** Select any of nine different focus zones, each with multiple focus points.
- **Manual Select: Large Zone AF.** Three focus zones are available at the left, right, and center areas of the middle of the frame.
- **Automatic Selection AF.** The camera will choose the focus point for you. This mode is always used in Basic Zone exposure modes.

To get up and running with this Quick Start, you should set the T7i to Automatic Selection AF mode. If you want to choose an individual point or zone yourself, skip ahead to Chapter 5 after you've finished reading this chapter. For now, just follow these steps:

1. Make sure the lens AF/MF switch is set to AF, and you are using a Creative Zone mode.
2. Tap the shutter release to activate the focus system.

3. Press the AF Area Selection Mode button. It's located on the top of the T7i, on the right side, and shown highlighted at left in Figure 2.16.

4. As you press the button, the camera will cycle among the four available focus area modes. Continue pressing, if necessary, until the Automatic Selection AF icon is highlighted, as seen at right in Figure 2.16.

Figure 2.16
Press the AF Area Selection Mode button (left) to choose focus area (right).

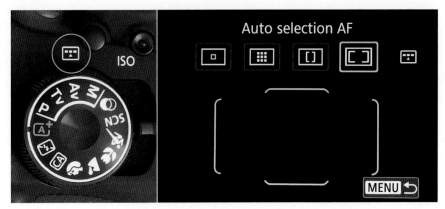

Other Settings

There are a few other options, such as ISO, using the self-timer, or working with flash. Use these right away if you're feeling ambitious, but don't feel ashamed if you postpone using these features until you've racked up a little more experience with your EOS T7i.

Adjusting White Balance and ISO

If you like, you can custom-tailor your white balance (color balance) and ISO sensitivity settings. To start out, it's best to set white balance (WB) to Auto, and ISO to ISO 100 or ISO 200 for daylight photos, and ISO 400 for pictures in dimmer light. You can adjust either one now by pressing the WB button (the up directional button) (for white balance) or the ISO button (just south of the Main Dial) and then navigating with the touch screen or directional buttons until the setting you want appears on the LCD.

If you've been playing with your camera's settings, or your T7i has been used by someone else, you can restore the factory defaults by selecting Clear Settings from the Set-up 4 menu. Just press the MENU button (located at the upper-left corner of the back of the camera), and highlight the yellow wrench icon with four dots, then select Clear Settings. A screen will pop up asking whether you'd like to Clear All Camera Settings, or Clear All Custom Func. (C.Fn). Choose the one you'd like to reset, and choose SET.

Using the Self-Timer

If you want to set a short delay before your picture is taken, you can use the self-timer. Press the drive/left directional button and then press the right directional button to select from the Self-timer: 10 sec/Remote control (which also can be used with the optional RC-6 infrared remote control), Self-timer: 2 sec, or Self-timer: Continuous, which allows you to press the up/down directional buttons to specify the number of shots to be taken (from 2 to 10) once the timer runs its course (see Figure 2.17). Select SET to confirm your choice, and a self-timer icon will appear on the shooting settings display on the back of the Rebel T7i. Press the shutter release to lock focus and start the timer. The self-timer lamp will blink and the beeper will sound (unless you've silenced it in the menus) until the final two seconds, when the lamp remains on and the beeper beeps more rapidly.

Canon recommends slipping off the eyepiece cup and replacing it with the viewfinder cap, to keep extraneous light from reaching the exposure meter through the viewfinder "back door." I usually just shade the viewfinder window with my hand (if I'm using the self-timer to reduce camera shake for a long exposure) or drape a jacket or sweater over the back of the camera (if I'm scurrying to get into the picture myself).

Using the Built-in Flash

Working with the EOS T7i's built-in flash as well as external flash units like the Canon 430EX II deserves a chapter of its own, and I'm providing it (see Chapter 11). But the built-in flash is easy enough to work with that you can begin using it right away, either to provide the main lighting of a scene or as supplementary illumination to fill in the shadows. The T7i will automatically balance the amount of light emitted from the flash so that it illuminates the shadows nicely, without overwhelming the highlights and producing a glaring "flash" look.

The T7i's flash has a power rating of 12/39.4 (meters/feet) at ISO 100, using the GN (guide number) system that dates back to the film era and before electronic flash units had any sort of automatic features. In plain terms, the flash's rating means that the unit is powerful enough to allow proper illumination of a subject that's 10 feet away at f/4 at the *lowest* ISO (sensitivity) setting of your camera. Boost the ISO (or use a wider f/stop) and you can shoot subjects that are located at a great distance. For example, at ISO 800, the T7i's flash is good enough for a subject at 20 feet using f/5.6 or, alternatively, you can expose that scene at the original 10 feet distance at f/11. Ordinarily, the T7i takes care of all these calculations for you. If you need a bigger blast of light, you can add one of the Canon external flash units, described in Chapter 11.

The flash will pop up automatically when using any of the Basic Zone modes except for Landscape, Sports, or No Flash modes. In Creative Zone modes, just press the flash button (marked with a lightning bolt as shown in Figure 2.18).

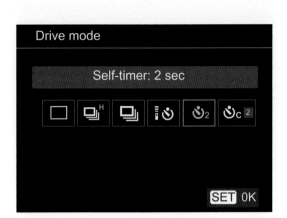

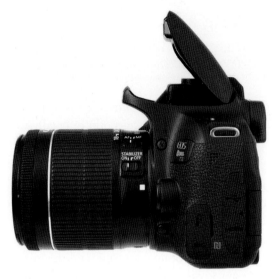

Figure 2.17 The drive modes include (left to right) Single shooting, High-Speed Continuous, Continuous, Self-timer: 10 sec/Remote control, Self-timer: 2 sec, and Self-timer: Continuous (which takes multiple shots when the self-timer's delay has elapsed).

Figure 2.18 The pop-up electronic flash can be used as the main light source, or for supplemental illumination.

When using these modes, the flash functions in the following way:

■ **P (Program mode).** The T7i selects a shutter speed from 1/60th to 1/200th second and the appropriate aperture automatically.

■ **Tv (Shutter-priority mode).** You choose a shutter speed from 30 seconds to 1/200th second, and the T7i chooses the lens opening for you while adjusting the flash output to provide the correct exposure.

■ **Av (Aperture-priority mode).** You select the aperture you want to use, and the camera will select a shutter speed from 30 seconds to 1/200th second, and adjust the flash output to provide the correct exposure. In low light levels, the T7i may select a very slow shutter speed to allow the flash and background illumination to balance out, so you should use a tripod.

■ **M (Manual mode).** You choose both shutter speed (up to 1/200th second) and aperture, and the camera will adjust the flash output to produce a good exposure based on the aperture you've selected.

You can read about flash exposure compensation, red-eye reduction options, and other built-in flash features in Chapter 11.

Taking a Picture

The final sections of the chapter guide you through taking your first pictures, reviewing them on the LCD, and transferring your shots to your computer.

Press the shutter release button halfway to lock in focus at the selected autofocus point. (Remember that you can select a focus point manually when using Creative Zone modes, whereas the camera always chooses the focus point in Basic Zone modes.) When the shutter button is in the half-depressed position, the exposure, calculated using the shooting mode you've selected, is also locked.

Press the button the rest of the way down to take a picture. At that instant, the mirror flips up out of the light path to the optical viewfinder (assuming you're not using Live View mode, discussed in Chapter 6), the shutter opens, the electronic flash (if enabled) fires, and your T7i's sensor absorbs a burst of light to capture an exposure. In fractions of a moment, the shutter closes, the mirror flips back down restoring your view, and the image you've taken is escorted off the CMOS sensor chip very quickly into an in-camera store of memory called a buffer, and the EOS T7i is ready to take another photo. The buffer continues dumping your image onto the Secure Digital card as you keep snapping pictures without pause (at least until the buffer fills and you must wait for it to get ahead of your continuous shooting, or your memory card fills completely).

Reviewing the Images You've Taken

The Canon EOS Rebel T7i has a broad range of playback and image review options, including the ability to jump ahead 10 or 100 images at a time. I'll cover them in more detail in Chapter 3. For now, you'll want to learn just the basics. Here is all you really need to know now, as shown in Figure 2.19, with the touch screen options shown earlier in Figures 2.4 and 2.5.

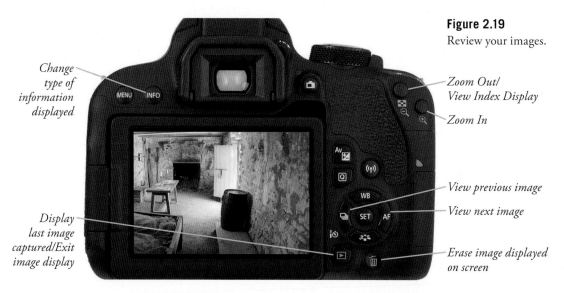

Figure 2.19
Review your images.

Change type of information displayed

Zoom Out/ View Index Display

Zoom In

View previous image

View next image

Display last image captured/Exit image display

Erase image displayed on screen

Here are your options.

■ **Display last image captured/Exit image display.** Press the Playback button (marked with a blue right-pointing triangle on the right side of the back of the camera) to display the most recent image on the LCD in full-screen Single Image mode. If you last viewed your images using the thumbnail mode (described later in this list), the Index display appears instead.

■ **View previous/next image.** Use the left and right directional buttons or swipe the touch screen left or right to view the next or previous image. Use a two-finger swipe to jump quickly among the images.

■ **Change type of information displayed.** Press the INFO. button repeatedly to cycle among overlays of basic image information, detailed shooting information, or no information at all.

■ **Zoom in on an image.** When an image is displayed full-screen on your LCD, magnify the image by spreading two fingers apart on the touch screen, or reduce the image to thumbnails by pinching two fingers together on the touch screen. You can also press the Zoom In button repeatedly to zoom in. The Zoom In button is located in the upper-right corner of the back of the camera, marked with a blue magnifying glass with a plus sign in it. The Zoom Out button, located to the left of the Zoom In button, zooms back out. Press the Playback button to exit the magnified display.

■ **Scroll around in a magnified image.** Use the left/right/up/down directional buttons or swipe the touch screen to scroll around within a magnified image. If you're using the touch screen, tap the "Return" arrow icon to go back to a single-image display.

■ **Zoom Out/View index display.** You can also rapidly move among a large number of images using the Index display mode described in the section that follows this list. The Zoom Out button in full-frame view switches from single-image display to display of 4, 9, 36, or 100 reduced-size thumbnails. To change from a larger number of thumbnails to a smaller number (from nine to four to single image, for example), press the Zoom In button until the display you want appears. You can also tap the highlighted image on the touch screen to view a full-screen rendition of that thumbnail.

■ **Jump forward or back.** You can set the jump increment in the Playback 2 menu. (I'll explain all the jump options in Chapter 3.) Once a jump increment has been selected, you can leap forward or back that number of pictures by rotating the Main Dial or by swiping the touch screen from left to right with *two* fingers. If using the Main Dial, turn it counterclockwise to review images from most recent to oldest, or clockwise to start with the first image on the memory card and cycle forward to the newest, using the jump size you've selected.

Cruising Through Index Views

You can navigate quickly among thumbnails representing a series of images using the T7i's Index mode. Here are your options.

- **Display thumbnails.** Press the Playback button to display an image on the color LCD. If you last viewed your images using Index mode, an Index array of four or nine reduced-size images appears automatically (see Figure 2.20). If an image pops up full-screen in single-image mode, press the Zoom Out button to view 4, 9, 36, or 100 thumbnails on a single screen; pressing the Zoom In button reverses the view to 100, 36, 9, 4, and full-screen display to see fewer/larger thumbnails.

- **Navigate within a screen of index images.** In Index mode, use the up/down/left/right directional buttons or the touch screen to move the orange highlight box around within the current Index display screen. Swipe the scroll bar at the right of the touch screen to scroll down or up.

- **View more Index pages.** To view additional Index pages, rotate the Main Dial. The display will leap ahead or back by the Jump increment you've set in the Playback 2 menu (as described in Chapter 8), 10 or 100 images, by index page, by date, or by folder.

- **Check image.** When an image you want to examine more closely is highlighted, press the Zoom In button or tap the thumbnail on the touch screen until the single-image version appears full-screen on your LCD.

Transferring Photos to Your Computer

The final step in your picture-taking session will be to transfer the photos you've taken to your computer for printing, further review, or image editing. Your T7i allows you to print directly to PictBridge-compatible printers and to create print orders right in the camera, plus you can select which images to transfer to your computer.

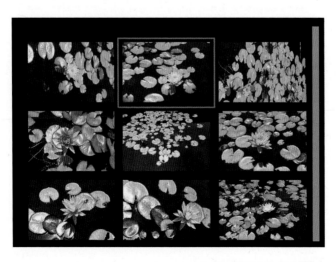

Figure 2.20
Review thumbnails of 4, 9, 36, or 100 images using Index review.

For now, you'll probably want to transfer your images either by using a cable transfer from the camera to the computer or by removing the memory card from the T7i and transferring the images with a card reader. The latter option is usually the best, because it's typically much faster and doesn't deplete the battery of your camera. However, you can use a cable transfer when you have the cable and a computer, but no card reader (perhaps you're using the computer of a friend or colleague, or at an Internet café).

To transfer images from the camera to a Mac or PC computer using an optional USB cable:

1. Turn off the camera.

2. Pry back the rubber cover that protects the Rebel T7i's USB port (located closest to the LCD monitor), and plug the USB cable into the USB port. (See Figure 2.21.)

3. Connect the other end of the USB cable to a USB port on your computer.

4. Turn the camera on. Your installed software usually detects the camera and offers to transfer the pictures, or the camera appears on your desktop as a mass storage device, enabling you to drag and drop the files to your computer.

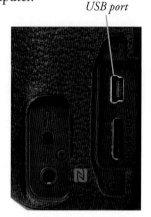

USB port

To transfer images from a memory card to the computer using a card reader:

1. Turn off the camera.

2. Slide open the memory card door, and press on the card, which causes it to pop up so it can be removed from the slot.

3. Insert the memory card into your memory card reader. Your installed software detects the files on the card and offers to transfer them. The card can also appear as a mass storage device on your desktop, which you can open, and then drag and drop the files to your computer.

Figure 2.21 Images can be transferred to your computer using a USB cable.

Shooting Tips

Here you'll find tips on settings to use for different kinds of shooting, beginning with recommended settings for some Playback, Shooting, and Custom Function menu options. You can set up your camera to shoot the main type of scenes you work with, then use the charts that follow to make changes for other kinds of images. Most will set up their T7i for my All Purpose settings, and adjust from there. Note that not all menu choices for the Shooting and Set-up menus have recommendations here. You'll find my personal preferences in Chapters 8 and 9.

Table 2.1 Default, All Purpose, Sports—Outdoors, Sports—Indoors

	Default	All Purpose	Sports–Outdoors	Sports–Indoors
Exposure mode	Your choice	P	Tv	Tv
Autofocus mode	One-Shot	AI Focus	AI Servo	AI Servo
AF-point selection	Automatic	Automatic	Automatic	Automatic
Drive mode	Single Shooting	Single Shooting	Continuous Shooting	Continuous Shooting
Shooting menus				
Image quality	Large/Fine	Large/Fine	Large/Fine	Large/Fine
Image review	2 sec.	2 sec.	Off	Off
Lens aberration correction	Peripheral Illumination: Enable	Peripheral Illumination: Enable	Peripheral Illumination: Enable	Peripheral Illumination: Enable
	Chromatic Aberration: Enable	Chromatic Aberration: Enable	Chromatic Aberration: Enable	Chromatic Aberration: Enable
	Distortion: Disable	Distortion: Disable	Distortion: Disable	Distortion: Disable
	Diffraction correction: Enable	Diffraction correction: Enable	Diffraction correction: Disable	Diffraction correction: Disable
Auto Lighting Optimizer	Standard	Standard	Disable	Disable
Metering mode	Evaluative	Evaluative	Evaluative	Evaluative
Color Space	sRGB	sRGB	sRGB	sRGB
Picture Style	Standard	Standard	Standard	Standard
ISO Auto	Auto	Max: 1600	Max: 3200	Max: 3200
Long exp. noise reduction	Off	Off	Off	Off
High ISO speed noise reduction	Standard	Standard	Standard	High
Anti-flicker shoot.	Disable	Disable	Disable	Enable
Set-up menus				
Auto power off	30 sec.	30 sec.	Disable	Disable
LCD brightness	4	4	5	4
Beep	Enable	Enable	Enable	Enable

Table 2.1 Default, All Purpose, Sports—Outdoors, Sports—Indoors (continued)

	Default	All Purpose	Sports–Outdoors	Sports–Indoors
Custom Functions				
C.Fn-1: Exposure level increments	0: 1/3 stop	0: 1/3 stop	0: 1/3 stop	0: 1/3 stop
C.Fn-2: ISO expansion	0: Off	0: Off	0: Off	1: On
C. Fn-3: Exposure comp. auto cancel	0: Enable	0: Enable	0: Enable	0: Enable
C.Fn-4: Highlight tone priority	0: Disable	1: Enable	0: Disable	0: Disable
C.Fn-5: AF-assist beam firing	0: Enable	0: Enable	1: Disable	1: Disable
C.Fn-6: AF-area selection method	0: AF-area selection button	0: AF-area selection button	1: Main Dial	1: Main Dial
C.Fn-7: Auto AF pt sel: Color tracking	0: One-Shot AF Only	0: One-Shot AF Only	1: Disable	1: Disable
C.Fn-8: AF point display during focus	0: Selected (Constant)	0: Selected (Constant)	2: Selected (pre-AF, Focused)	2: Selected (pre-AF, Focused)
C.Fn-9: VF display illumination	0: Auto	0: Auto	1: Enable	1: Enable
C.Fn-10: Mirror lockup	0: Disable	0: Disable	0: Disable	0: Disable
C.Fn-11 Warnings in Viewfinder	All enabled	All enabled	All enabled	All enabled
C.Fn-12: Shutter/ AE lock button	0: AF/AE lock	0: AF/AE lock	3: AE/AF, no AE lock	3: AE/AF, no AE lock
C.Fn-13: Assign SET button	0: Normal (disabled)	0: Normal (disabled)	0: Normal (disabled)	0: Normal (disabled)
C.Fn-14: LCD display when power ON	0: Display on	1: Previous display status	1: Previous display status	1: Previous display status
C.Fn-15 Retract lens on power off	0: Enable	0: Enable	0: Enable	0: Enable

Table 2.2 Stage Performance, Long Exposure, HDR, Portrait

	Stage Performances	Long Exposure	HDR	Portrait
Exposure mode	Tv	Manual	Tv	Tv
Autofocus mode	One-Shot	Manual	One-Shot	One-Shot
AF Point selection	Automatic	Automatic	Automatic	Automatic
Drive mode	Single Shooting	Single Shooting	Continuous Shooting	Continuous Shooting
Shooting menus				
Image quality	Large/Fine	RAW+Large/Fine	RAW	RAW+Large/Fine
Image review	Off	Off	Off	2 sec.
Lens aberration correction	Peripheral Illumination: Enable Chromatic Aberration: Enable Distortion: Disable Diffraction correction: Enable	Peripheral Illumination: Enable Chromatic Aberration: Enable Distortion: Disable Diffraction correction: Enable	Peripheral Illumination: Enable Chromatic Aberration: Enable Distortion: Disable Diffraction correction: Disable	Peripheral Illumination: Enable Chromatic Aberration: Enable Distortion: Disable Diffraction correction: Disable
Auto Lighting Optimizer	Standard	Standard	Disable	Disable
Metering mode	Spot	Center-weighted	Evaluative	Center-weighted
Color Space	Adobe RGB	Adobe RGB	Adobe RGB	Adobe RGB
Picture Style	User Def— Standard, Reduce contrast, add sharpening	Neutral	Standard	Standard
ISO Auto	Max: 3200	Max: 3200	Auto	Auto
Long exp. noise reduction	Off	On	Off	Off
High ISO speed noise reduction	High	High	Standard	Low
Anti-flicker shoot.	Disable	Disable	Disable	Disable

Table 2.2 Stage Performance, Long Exposure, HDR, Portrait (continued)

	Stage Performances	Long Exposure	HDR	Portrait
Set-up menus				
Auto power off	30 sec.	Off	Off	Off
LCD brightness	Dimmer	Dimmer	Medium	Medium
Beep	Disable	Enable	Enable	Enable
Custom Functions				
C.Fn-1: Exposure level increments	0: 1/3 stop	0: 1/3 stop	0: 1/3 stop	0: 1/3 stop
C.Fn-2: ISO expansion	1: On	1: On	0: Off	0: Off
C.Fn-3 Exposure comp. auto cancel	0: Enable	0: Enable	0: Enable	0: Enable
C.Fn-4 Highlight tone priority	1: Enable	1: Enable	0: Disable	1: Enable
C.Fn-5 AF-assist beam firing	1: Disable	1: Disable	1: Disable	1: Disable
C.Fn-6 AF-area selection method	0: AF-area selection button	0: AF-area selection button	1: Main Dial	1: Main Dial
C.Fn-7 Auto AF pt sel: Color tracking	0: One-Shot AF Only	0: One-Shot AF Only	1: Disable	0: One-Shot AF Only
C.Fn-8 AF point display during focus	0: Selected (Constant)	0: Selected (Constant)	0: Selected (Constant)	0: Selected (Constant)
C.Fn-9 VF display illumination	1: Enable	0: Auto	1: Enable	1: Enable
C.Fn-10: Mirror lockup	0: Disable	0: Disable	0: Disable	0: Disable
C.Fn-11: Warnings in Viewfinder	All enabled	All enabled	All enabled	All enabled
C.Fn-12: Shutter/ AE lock button	0: AF/AE lock	0: AF/AE lock	0: AF/AE lock	0: AF/AE lock

Table 2.2 Stage Performance, Long Exposure, HDR, Portrait (continued)

	Stage Performances	Long Exposure	HDR	Portrait
Custom Functions (continued)				
C.Fn-13: Shutter/ AE lock button	0: AF/AE lock	0: AF/AE lock	0: AF/AE lock	0: AF/AE lock
C.Fn-14: Assign SET button	3: LCD Monitor On/Off	0: Normal (disabled)	0: Normal (disabled)	0: Normal (disabled)
C.Fn-14: LCD display when power ON	1: Previous display status	1: Previous display status	1: Previous display status	1: Previous display status
C.Fn-15: Retract lens on power off	0: Enable	0: Enable	0: Enable	0: Enable

Table 2.3 Studio Flash, Landscape, Macro, Travel, E-Mail

	Studio Flash	Landscape	Macro	Travel	E-Mail
Exposure mode	Manual	Av	Tv	Tv	P
Autofocus mode	One-Shot	One-Shot	Manual	One-Shot	One-Shot
AF point selection	Automatic	Automatic	Automatic	Automatic	Automatic
Drive mode	Single Shooting	Single Shooting	Single Shooting	Single Shooting	Single Shooting
Shooting Menus					
Image quality	RAW+ Large/Fine	RAW+ Large/Fine	RAW+ Large/Fine	Large/Fine	Small 3
Beep	Enable	Enable	Enable	Disable	Enable
Image Review	2 sec.	2 sec.	Off	Off	2 sec.

Table 2.3 Studio Flash, Landscape, Macro, Travel, E-Mail (continued)

	Studio Flash	Landscape	Macro	Travel	E-Mail
Shooting Menus (continued)					
Lens aberration correction	Peripheral Illumination: Enable	Peripheral Illumination: Enable	Peripheral Illumination: Enable	Peripheral Illumination: Enable	Peripheral Illumination: Enable
	Chromatic Aberration: Enable	Chromatic Aberration: Enable	Chromatic Aberration: Enable	Chromatic Aberration: Enable	Chromatic Aberration: Enable
	Distortion: Disable	Distortion: Disable	Distortion: Disable	Distortion: Disable	Distortion: Disable
	Diffraction correction: Enable	Diffraction correction: Enable	Diffraction correction: Disable	Diffraction correction: Disable	Diffraction correction: Enable
Auto Lighting Optimizer	Standard	Standard	Standard	Standard	Standard
Metering mode	Manual	Evaluative	Spot	Evaluative	Evaluative
Color Space	Adobe RGB	Adobe RGB	Adobe RGB	sRGB	sRGB
Picture Style	Standard	Auto	Standard	Auto	Auto
ISO Auto	Auto	Max: 800	Auto	Auto	Auto
Long exp. noise reduction	Off	Off	Off	Off	Off
High ISO speed noise reduction	Low	Low	Standard	Standard	Low
Anti-flicker shoot.	Disable	Disable	Disable	Enable	Disable
Set-up menus					
Auto power off	Off	Off	Off	30 sec.	30 sec.
LCD brightness	Medium	Medium	Medium	Medium	Medium
Beep	Enable	Enable	Enable	Enable	Enable

Table 2.3 Studio Flash, Landscape, Macro, Travel, E-Mail (continued)

	Studio Flash	Landscape	Macro	Travel	E-Mail
Custom Functions					
C.Fn-1: Exposure level increments	0: 1/3 stop	0: 1/3 stop	0: 1/3 stop	0: 1/3 stop	0: 1/3 stop
C.Fn-2: ISO expansion	0: Off	0: Off	0: Off	0: Off	0: Off
C.Fn-3: Exposure comp. auto cancel	0: Enable	0: Enable	0: Enable	0: Enable	0: Enable
C.Fn-4: Highlight tone priority	1: Enable	1: Enable	0: Disable	1: Enable	1: Enable
C.Fn-5: AF-assist beam firing	1: Disable	1: Disable	0: Enable	0: Enable	0: Enable
C.Fn-6: AF-area selection method	0: AF-area Selection Button	0: AF-area Selection Button	1: Main Dial	1: Main Dial	1: Main Dial
C.Fn-7: Auto AF pt sel: Color tracking	0: One-Shot AF Only	0: One-Shot AF Only	1: Disable	0: One-Shot AF Only	0: One-Shot AF Only
C.Fn-8: AF-point display during focus	0: Selected (Constant)	0: Selected (Constant)	0: Selected (Constant)	0: Selected (Constant)	0: Selected (Constant)
C.Fn-9: VF display illumination	0: Auto	0: Auto	1: Enable	1: Enable	1: Enable
C.Fn-10: Mirror lockup	0: Disable	0: Disable	0: Disable	0: Disable	0: Enable
C.Fn-11: Warnings in viewfinder	All enabled	All enabled	All enabled	All enabled	All enabled
C.Fn-12: Shutter/ AE lock button	0: AF/AE lock	0: AF/AE lock	0: AF/AE lock	0: AF/AE lock	0: AF/AE lock
C.Fn-13: Assign SET button	0: Normal (disabled)	0: Normal (disabled)	0: Normal (disabled)	0: Normal (disabled)	0: Normal (disabled)
C.Fn-14: LCD display when power ON	0: Display on	1: Previous display status	1: Previous display status	1: Previous display status	1: Previous display status
C.Fn-15: Retract lens on power off	0: Enable	0: Enable	0: Enable	0: Enable	0: Enable

3

Your Rebel Roadmap

One thing that surprises new owners of the T7i is that the camera has a total of 496 buttons, dials, switches, latches, and knobs bristling from its surface. Okay, I lied. The real number is closer to two dozen controls and adjustments, just among the physical components and not counting the virtual controls on the touch screen. That's still a lot of components to master, especially when you consider that many of these controls serve double-duty to give you access to multiple functions.

Traditionally, there have been two ways of providing a roadmap to guide you through this maze of features. One approach uses two or three tiny 2 × 3–inch black-and-white line drawings or photos impaled with dozens of callouts labeled with cross-references to the actual pages in the book that tell you what these components do. You'll find this tactic used in the manual Canon provides with the Rebel T7i, and most of the other third-party guidebooks as well. Deciphering one of these miniature camera layouts is a lot like being presented with a world globe when what you really want to know is how to find the capital of Belgium.

I originated a more useful approach in my field guides, providing you, instead of a satellite view, a street-level map that includes close-up, full-color photos of the camera from several angles (see Figure 3.1), with a smaller number of labels clearly pointing to each individual feature. And, I don't force you to flip back and forth among dozens of pages to find out what a particular component does. Each photo is accompanied by a brief description that summarizes the control, so you can begin using it right away. Only when a feature deserves a lengthy explanation do I direct you to a more detailed write-up later in the book.

So, if you're wondering what the depth-of-field preview button does, I'll tell you up front, rather than have you flip to another page. This book is not a scavenger hunt. But after I explain how to use the ISO button to change the sensitivity of the T7i, I *will* provide a cross-reference to a longer explanation later in the book that clarifies noise reduction, ISO, and its effects on exposure. I think this kind of organization works best for a camera as sophisticated as the Rebel T7i.

By the time you finish this chapter, you'll have a basic understanding of every control and what it does. I'm not going to delve into menu functions here—you'll find a discussion of your Set-up, Shooting, Playback, and Display Level menu options in Chapters 8 and 9. Everything here is devoted to the button pusher and dial twirler in you.

Front View

When we picture a given camera, we always imagine the front view. That's the view that your subjects see as you snap away, and the aspect that's shown in product publicity and on the box. The frontal angle is, for all intents and purposes, the "face" of a camera like the Rebel T7i. But, not surprisingly, most of the "business" of operating the camera happens *behind* it, where the photographer resides. The front of the T7i has very few controls and features to worry about. Five of them are readily visible in Figure 3.1:

- **Shutter button.** Angled on top of the hand grip is the shutter button. Press this button down halfway to lock exposure and focus (in One-Shot mode and AI Focus with nonmoving subjects). The T7i assumes that when you tap or depress the shutter release, you are ready to take a picture, so the release can be tapped to activate the exposure meter or to exit from most menus.

- **Main Dial.** This dial is used to change shooting settings. When settings are available in pairs (such as shutter speed/aperture), this dial will be used to make one type of setting, such as shutter speed. The other setting, say, the aperture, is made using an alternate control, such as spinning the Main Dial while holding down an additional button like the exposure compensation button (which resides conveniently under the thumb on the back of the camera).

- **Card slot cover.** Slide this memory card access door toward the back of the camera to gain access to the Secure Digital card.

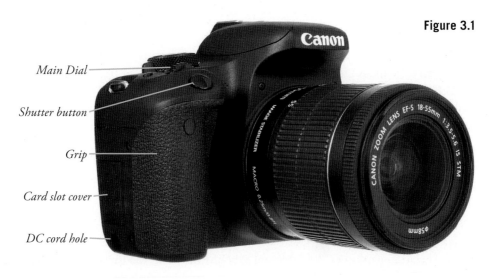

Figure 3.1

Main Dial

Shutter button

Grip

Card slot cover

DC cord hole

■ **Grip.** This provides a comfortable handhold, and also contains the T7i's battery.

■ **DC cord hole.** This small, flexible door opens to allow the cable from the optional DC coupler DR-E18 (which slides into the battery compartment to replace the battery) to connect to the AC Adapter AC-E6N.

When viewed from the front with the lens removed, you can see more components, as shown in Figure 3.2:

■ **Red-eye reduction/Self-timer lamp.** This LED provides a blip of light shortly before a flash exposure to cause the subjects' pupils to close down, reducing the effect of red-eye reflections off their retinas. When using the self-timer, this lamp also flashes to mark the countdown until the photo is taken.

■ **Remote control sensor.** The sensor behind this window receives signals from the optional Canon RC-6 infrared remote control. The RC-6 release gives the choice of triggering the camera immediately, or with the two-second delay. Note that the sensor is on the hand grip and thus would be blocked if you happened to be holding the T7i when trying to take a picture. In practice, of course, the camera will be mounted on a tripod or supported in some other way when using the remote control. The remote control generally must be used in front of the camera for the sensor to detect its signal.

■ **Lens mount.** This sturdy bayonet mount component mates with the matching bayonet mount on the lens to secure it to the camera body.

■ **EF lens mount index.** Match the round red bump on the lens with this mark to align EF-series lenses for mounting.

■ **EF-S lens mount index.** Match the raised white square on the lens with this mark to align EF-S-series lenses for mounting.

Figure 3.2

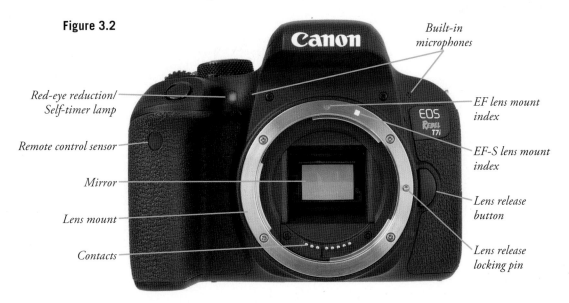

- **Lens release button/locking pin.** Press this button to retract the lens release locking pin so the lens can be rotated toward the shutter release and removed.
- **Contacts.** These eight electrical contacts convey information about aperture, focus, focal length, and distance between the lens and camera.
- **Mirror.** This partially silvered reflective component directs most of the light that passes through the lens upward toward the focus screen, exposure metering system, and viewfinder eyepiece. Some illumination is directed downward to the 45-point autofocus system in the floor of the mirror chamber.
- **Built-in microphones.** The stereo microphones record sound when shooting movie clips.

You'll find more controls on the other side of the T7i, shown in Figure 3.3.

- **Flash button.** This button releases the built-in flash in Creative Zone modes so it can flip up (see Figure 3.4) and start the charging process. If you decide you do not want to use the flash, you can turn it off by pressing the flash head back down.
- **Depth-of-field preview button.** This button, adjacent to the lens mount, stops down the lens to the aperture that will be used to take the picture, so you can see in the viewfinder how much of the image is in focus. The view grows dimmer as the aperture is reduced.
- **Lens switches.** Canon autofocus lenses have a switch to allow changing between automatic focus and manual focus, and, in the case of IS lenses, another switch to turn image stabilization on and off.
- **Strap mount.** This is one of two neck strap mounts (the other is on the other side of the camera).
- **Terminal covers.** These flip-away panels protect the connector ports underneath.
- **Speaker.** Sounds emanating from your T7i are emitted from this monaural speaker.

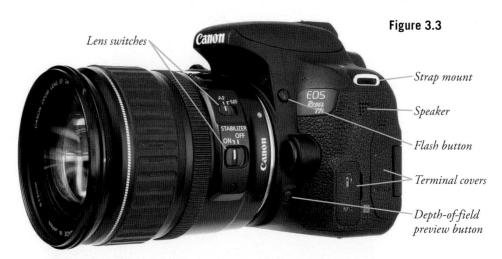

Figure 3.3

Lens switches

Strap mount

Speaker

Flash button

Terminal covers

Depth-of-field preview button

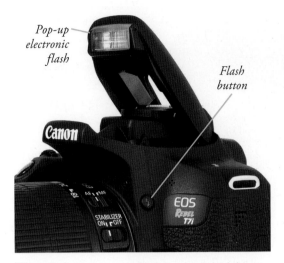

Pop-up electronic flash

Flash button

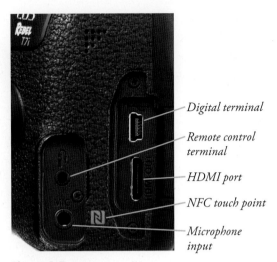

Digital terminal

Remote control terminal

HDMI port

NFC touch point

Microphone input

Figure 3.4 Pressing the Flash button (which has an arrow/lightning bolt symbol) pops up the built-in flash unit and starts the charging process.

Figure 3.5 Four ports allow connecting the T7i to external devices.

The four connectors and NFC touch point are shown in Figure 3.5 and described below.

- **Microphone input.** Plug a stereo microphone into this jack.
- **Remote control terminal.** You can plug various Canon remote release switches, timers, and wireless controllers into this connector.
- **Digital terminal.** Plug in an optional USB cable with your Rebel T7i and connect the other end to a USB port in your computer to transfer photos.
- **HDMI port.** Use a Type C HDMI cable (not included in the box with your camera) to direct the video and audio output of the T7i to a high-definition television (HDTV) or HD monitor.

The Canon EOS Rebel T7i's Business End

The back panel of the Rebel T7i (see Figure 3.6) bristles with nearly a dozen different controls, buttons, and knobs. That might seem like a lot of controls to learn, but you'll find, as I noted earlier, that it's a lot easier to press a dedicated button and spin a dial than to jump to a menu every time you want to change a setting.

You can see the controls clustered on the top back edge of the T7i in the figure. The key buttons and components and their functions are as follows:

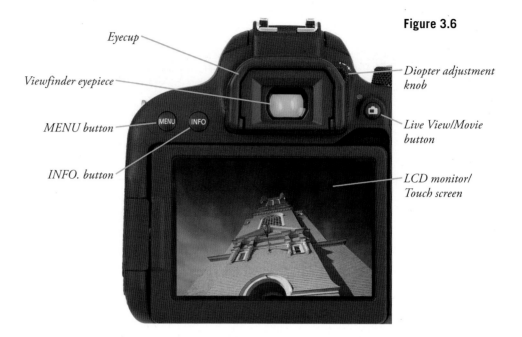

Figure 3.6

- **MENU button.** This button summons/exits the menu displayed on the rear LCD of the T7i. When you're working with submenus, this button also serves to exit a submenu and return to the main menu.

- **INFO. button.** When pressed repeatedly, this button changes the amount of picture information displayed in Shooting and Playback modes. In Playback mode, pressing the INFO. button cycles among basic display of the image; a detailed display with a thumbnail of the image, shooting parameters, and a brightness histogram; and a display with less detail but with separate histograms for brightness, red, green, and blue channels. (I'll show you what these look like later in the chapter.) When setting Picture Styles, the INFO. button is used to select a highlighted Picture Style for modification. In Live View mode, the INFO. button adjusts the amount of information overlaid on the live image that appears on the LCD screen.

- **Viewfinder eyepiece.** You can frame your composition by peering into the viewfinder. It's surrounded by a soft rubber frame that seals out extraneous light when pressing your eye tightly up to the viewfinder, and it also protects your eyeglass lenses (if worn) from scratching.

- **Diopter adjustment knob.** Use of this knob to adjust the viewfinder sharpness was explained in Chapter 1.

- **Live View/Movie button.** Press this button, marked with a red dot above it, to activate/deactivate live view. To shoot movies, turn the power switch on top of the camera to the Movie position, and then press this button to start/stop video/audio recording.

- **LCD monitor/Touch screen.** This is the three-inch display that shows your live view preview image review after the picture is taken, shooting settings display before the photo is snapped,

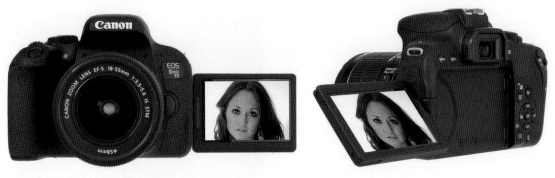

Figure 3.7

and all the menus used by the Rebel T7i. A significant feature is the swiveling LCD, which can be folded with the display screen facing inward to protect it or reversed into the normal position, flipped out, swiveled, or even turned around to allow you to view yourself while shooting self-portraits. As described in Chapter 2, the touch screen can be used instead of physical controls when reviewing images and making settings changes. (See Figure 3.7.)

The most-used controls reside on the right side of the Rebel T7i (see Figure 3.8). There are 12 buttons in all, many of which do double-duty to perform several functions. I've divided them into two groups; here's the first set of controls, found in the upper half of the panel:

■ **Reduce/Index/AE lock/FE lock button.** This button, which has a * label above it, has several functions, which differ depending on the AF point and metering mode. You can find more about these variations, available in Creative Zone modes only, in Chapter 4.

Shooting mode: The button locks the exposure or flash exposure that the camera sets when you partially depress the shutter button. In Evaluative exposure mode, exposure is locked at the AF point that achieved focus. In Partial, Spot, or Center-weighted modes, exposure is locked at the AF center point. The exposure lock indication (*) appears in the viewfinder and on the shooting settings display. If you want to recalculate exposure with the shutter button still partially depressed, press the * button again. The exposure will be unlocked when you release the shutter button or take the picture. To retain the exposure lock for subsequent photos, keep the * button pressed while shooting.

When using flash, pressing the * button fires an extra pre-flash that allows the unit to calculate and lock exposure prior to taking the picture. The characters "FEL" will appear momentarily in the viewfinder, and the exposure lock indication and a flash indicator appear. (See the description of the viewfinder display later in this chapter.)

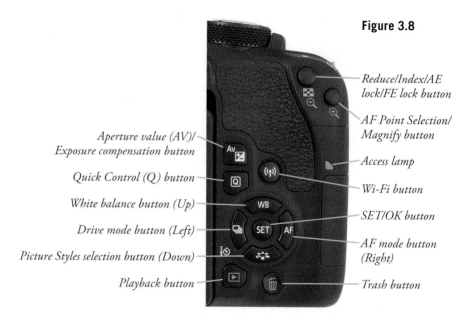

Figure 3.8

Reduce/Index/AE
lock/FE lock button

AF Point Selection/
Magnify button

Aperture value (AV)/
Exposure compensation button

Access lamp

Quick Control (Q) button

Wi-Fi button

White balance button (Up)

SET/OK button

Drive mode button (Left)

AF mode button
(Right)

Picture Styles selection button (Down)

Playback button

Trash button

Playback mode: Press this button to switch from single-image display to nine-image thumbnail index. (See Figure 3.9.) Move highlighting among the thumbnails with the touch screen, buttons, or Main Dial. To view a highlighted image, press the Zoom In button.

In Playback mode, when an image is zoomed in, press this button to zoom out, or use the touch screen.

- **AF Point Selection/Magnify button.** In Shooting mode, this button activates autofocus point selection. (See Chapter 4 for information on setting autofocus/exposure point selection when using Creative Zone exposure modes.) In Playback mode, if you're viewing a single image, this button zooms in on the image that's displayed. If thumbnail indexes are shown, pressing this button switches from 4 to 9 to 36 to 100.

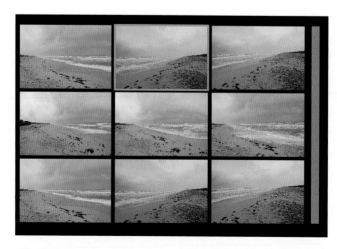

Figure 3.9
The Thumbnail/
Index/Zoom Out
button changes the
playback display
from single image to
four or nine
thumbnails.

■ **Aperture value (AV)/Exposure compensation button.** When using Manual exposure mode with the T7i, hold down this button and rotate the Main Dial to specify a lens aperture; rotate the Main Dial alone to choose the shutter speed. In other Creative Zone exposure modes—Aperture-priority (Av), Shutter-priority (Tv), or Program (P)—hold down this button and rotate the Main Dial to the right to add exposure compensation (EV) to an image (making it brighter), or rotate to the left to subtract EV and make the image darker.

■ **Wi-Fi button.** This button immediately produces the Wi-Fi Communication Settings menu screen. It's important to have a dedicated button to access the Wi-Fi menus because wireless communication uses a lot of juice, so you'll probably want to enable it just before you intend to use it, and disable it at all other times. Personally, I think it would be smarter to have this button simply turn Wi-Fi on and off, to avoid a trip to Menuland. When making most other Wi-Fi adjustments, it's almost as easy access the features with the MENU button. But we'll take what Canon offers us. I'll show you how to work with the T7i's Wi-Fi and Bluetooth capabilities in Chapter 9.

Some of the controls in the lower half of the panel perform dual functions, one for navigation and one for making various settings. I'll describe both.

■ **Directional buttons.** This array of four directional keys provides those who aren't using the touch screen an alternate method for movement to navigate menus, and is used to cycle among various options (usually with the left/right buttons) and to choose amounts (with the up/down buttons). The four buttons (which Canon calls *cross keys* on the T7i, but which for simplicity I will simply call *directional buttons*) also have secondary functions to adjust white balance, auto-focus mode, Picture Styles, and drive mode (I'll describe these separately).

■ **SET/OK button.** Located in the center of the button cluster, this button is used to confirm a selection or activate a feature, similarly to the SET icon on the touch screen.

■ **Playback button.** Displays the last picture taken. Thereafter, you can move back and forth among the available images by pressing the left/right buttons to advance or reverse one image at a time, or the Main Dial, to jump forward or back using the jump method you've selected. (See the section below for more on jumping.) To quit playback, press this button again. The T7i also exits Playback mode automatically when you press the shutter button (so you'll never be prevented from taking a picture on the spur of the moment because you happened to be viewing an image).

■ **Trash button.** Press to erase the image shown on the LCD during Playback mode. A menu will pop up displaying Cancel and Erase choices. Use the left/right buttons to select one of these actions, then press the SET button to activate your choice.

■ **Access lamp.** When lit or blinking, this lamp indicates that the memory card is being accessed.

■ **Quick Control (Q) button.** Press this button to produce the Quick Control screen, which gives you access to many feature adjustments when in Shooting mode. When you're reviewing images in Playback, a different Quick Control screen pops up that allows you to protect or rate images, change jump method, resize, or perform other functions.

The directional buttons also each have a secondary function:

- **White balance (Up).** The up button also serves to access the white balance function. Press this WB button when using one of the Creative Zone modes (M, Av, Tv, or P) to produce the White Balance screen. Then, use the touch screen or left/right buttons to select a white balance, and choose SET to confirm.

- **AF mode (Right).** Press the right button when using a Creative Zone mode to produce a screen that allows choosing the autofocus mode from among One-Shot, AI Focus, and AI Servo. Use the touch screen or press the button repeatedly until the focus mode you want is selected. Then select SET to confirm your focus mode.

- **Drive mode (Left).** Press the left button to produce a screen that allows choosing a drive mode, in both Creative Zone and Basic Zone modes. Then use the touch screen or press the right button to select Single Shooting (one shot at a time); High Speed Continuous (up to 6 shots per second); Low Speed Continuous (up to 3 shots per second); Self-Timer: 10 sec/Remote Control; Self-Timer: 2 seconds; and Self-timer: Continuous, which allows you to specify the number of shots to be taken (from 2 to 10) with the up/down keys. Choose SET to confirm your choice.

- **Picture Styles selection button (Down).** When in Shooting mode using a Creative Zone exposure setting, press the down button to pop up the Picture Styles menu on the LCD, so you can select a given style, or gain access to user-defined styles. To modify a Picture Style, you'll need to use the Shooting 3 menu, as described in Chapter 8.

Jumping Around

When a photo you've taken is displayed on the color LCD, you can move forward or backward one image at a time or "jump" ahead or back in different increments by rotating the Main Dial. As you jump, an overlay appears on the screen briefly showing the size of the leap you're making. (See Figure 3.10.)

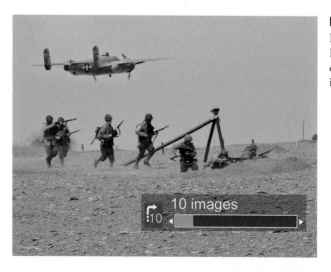

Figure 3.10
Rotate the Main Dial to jump ahead or back during image playback.

As I'll describe in Chapter 8, you can specify the exact increment using the Image Jump with Dial entry in the Playback 2 menu. Your options are as follows:

- **1 image.** Rotating the Main Dial one click or swiping jumps forward or back one image.

- **10 images.** Rotating the Main Dial one click or swiping jumps forward or back ten images.

- **Specified number of images.** Rotating the Main Dial one click or swiping jumps forward or back by a number you specify in the menu entry. The default value is 30, but you can specify jumps of any value from 1 to 100.

- **Display by Date.** Rotating the Main Dial one click or swiping jumps forward or back to the first image taken on the next or previous calendar date.

- **Display by Folder.** Rotating the Main Dial one click or swiping jumps to the next folder on your memory card.

- **Display Movies only.** Tells the T7i to jump only among movie images when using a card that contains both video clips and still images. This option is useful when you prefer to view only one kind of file.

- **Display Stills only.** Specifies jumping only between still images when using a card that has both video clips and still images.

- **Display protected images only.** This is a great new capability. You can mark images using the T7i's Protect feature, and thereafter jump between them (and only them) with the Main Dial. You'll need to work with the Playback 1 menu's Protect Images entry, and designate individual images, images in a folder, or a range of images. I'll explain the Protect feature in more detail in Chapter 8.

- **Display by Image Rating.** As explained in Chapter 8, you can rate a particular movie or still photo by applying from one to five stars, using the Rating menu entry in the Playback 2 menu. This Jump choice allows you to select a rating rank, and then jump among photos with that rating applied.

Going Topside

The top surface of the Canon EOS Rebel T7i has a few frequently accessed controls of its own. The key controls, shown in Figure 3.11, are as follows:

- **Mode Dial.** Rotate this dial to switch among Basic Zone and Creative Zone modes. Unlike the dial installed on some earlier Rebels you may have owned, this Mode Dial rotates a complete 360 degrees. You'll find the various modes and options described in more detail in Chapter 4.

- **Focal plane mark.** Precision macro and scientific photography sometimes requires knowing exactly where the focal plane of the sensor is. The symbol on the top side of the camera, to the left of the viewfinder, marks that plane.

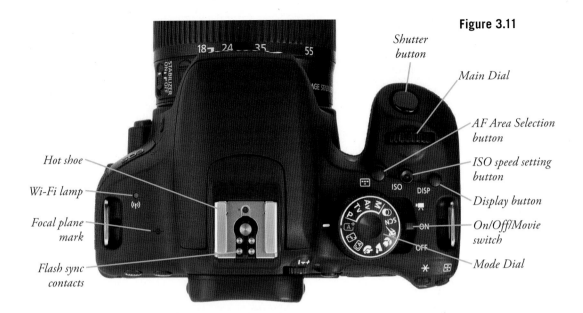

Shutter button

Figure 3.11

Main Dial

AF Area Selection button

ISO speed setting button

Display button

On/Off/Movie switch

Mode Dial

Hot shoe

Wi-Fi lamp

Focal plane mark

Flash sync contacts

- **Flash sync contacts.** Slide an electronic flash into this mount when you need a more powerful Speedlite. A dedicated flash unit, like those from Canon, can use the multiple contact points shown to communicate exposure, zoom setting, white balance information, and other data between the flash and the camera. There's more on using electronic flash in Chapter 11.

- **ISO speed setting button.** Press this button and use the touch screen or buttons to navigate until the setting you want appears on the LCD. Choose SET to confirm your choice. You'll find more about ISO options in Chapter 4, and flash EV settings in Chapter 11.

- **Main Dial.** This dial is used to make many shooting settings. When settings come in pairs (such as shutter speed/aperture in Manual shooting mode), the Main Dial is used for one (for example, shutter speed), while some other control, such as the Av button (when shooting in Manual exposure mode) is used for the other (aperture).

- **Shutter button.** Partially depress this button to lock in exposure and focus. Press all the way to take the picture. Tapping the shutter release when the camera has turned off the autoexposure and autofocus mechanisms reactivates both. When a review image is displayed on the back-panel color LCD monitor, tapping this button removes the image from the display and reactivates the autoexposure and autofocus mechanisms.

- **On/Off/Movie switch.** Flip forward one click to turn the Rebel T7i on in still photography mode, and one additional click to activate Movie mode. Flip back to the off position again to power down.

- **Display button.** Press this button to turn the LCD monitor on or off. You can change the on/off behavior in the LCD Off/On Button entry in the Set-up 2 menu, as I'll explain in Chapter 9. You can have the LCD display remain on all the time, turn off when the shutter release is held down, or use the DISP button as a switch to toggle the display on or off.

- **AF Area Selection button.** Pressing this button repeatedly cycles among the four AF area point modes, including three manual selection modes (Single-Point AF, Zone AF, Large Zone AF) and fully Automatic Selection AF.
- **Wi-Fi lamp.** Glows blue when Wi-Fi is active.
- **Hot shoe.** An external electronic flash, microphone, or other accessory can be attached to this mount.

Underneath Your Rebel T7i

There's not a lot going on with the bottom panel of your Rebel T7i. You'll find a tripod socket, which secures the camera to a tripod or other accessory, and the battery door and latch. Figure 3.12 shows the underside view of the camera.

Figure 3.12

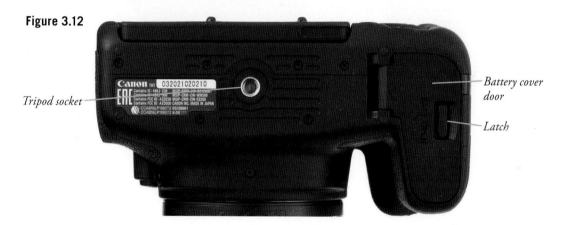

Tripod socket

Battery cover door

Latch

Lens Components

The typical lens, like the ones shown in Figures 3.13 and 3.14, has seven or eight common features. Not every component appears on every lens. The lens on the left, for example, lacks the distance scale and distance indicator that the lens on the right has. Lenses that lack image stabilization will not have a stabilization switch.

- **Filter thread.** Lenses have a thread on the front for attaching filters and other add-ons. Some also use this thread for attaching a lens hood (you screw on the filter first, and then attach the hood to the screw thread on the front of the filter).
- **Lens hood.** The lens hood shields the front element of the lens from extraneous light arriving from outside the image area, and serves as protection.
- **Lens hood bayonet.** This is used to mount the lens hood for lenses that don't use screw-mount hoods (the majority).

Figure 3.13

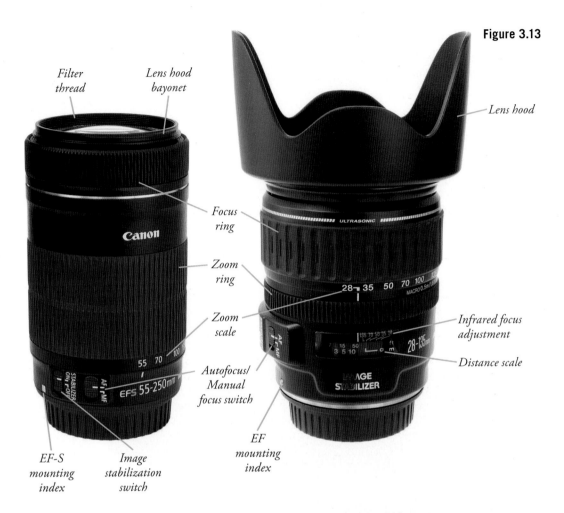

Filter thread

Lens hood bayonet

Lens hood

Focus ring

Zoom ring

Zoom scale

Autofocus/ Manual focus switch

Infrared focus adjustment

Distance scale

EF-S mounting index

Image stabilization switch

EF mounting index

Figure 3.14

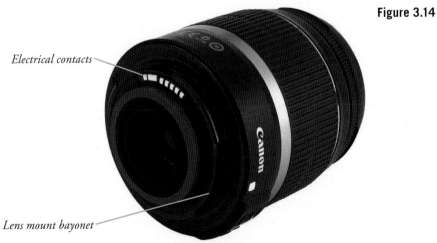

Electrical contacts

Lens mount bayonet

- **Zoom ring.** Turn this ring to change the zoom setting.

- **Zoom scale.** These markings on the lens show the current focal length selected.

- **Focus ring.** This is the ring you turn when you manually focus the lens.

- **Distance scale.** This is a readout that rotates in unison with the lens's focus mechanism to show the distance at which the lens has been focused. It's a useful indicator for double-checking autofocus, roughly evaluating depth-of-field, and for setting manual focus guesstimates.

- **Infrared focus adjustment.** IR illumination doesn't focus at the exact same plane as visible light, so if you're shooting infrared photos, move the focus ring to line up to the appropriate focal length opposite the distance determined by normal focusing.

- **Autofocus/Manual focus switch.** Allows you to change from automatic focus to manual focus.

- **Image stabilization switch.** Lenses with IS include a separate switch for adjusting the stabilization feature.

- **EF-S/EF mounting index.** EF-S lenses have a raised white square, while EF lenses have a raised red bump; line up these indexes with the matching white and red indicators on the camera lens mount to attach the lens.

- **Electrical contacts.** On the back of the lens (see Figure 3.14) are electrical contacts that the camera uses to communicate focus, aperture setting, and other information.

- **Lens mount bayonet.** This mount is used to attach the lens to a matching bayonet on the camera body.

Shooting and Playback Information

Your Rebel T7i provides a wealth of information both when you are taking pictures and when you are examining and evaluating the images you just captured. The *shooting* information can be seen by looking through the viewfinder, or checking out the electronic displays on the back-panel color LCD monitor. This data helps you make decisions on the settings to use as you take photographs. You can view the shooting modes, autofocus settings, and exposure controls, and then adjust any of them as necessary.

The *playback* information provides feedback after the fact, allowing you to examine the images you took and review the settings so you can make decisions about what adjustments need to be made when you resume shooting. Playback data is shown exclusively on the back-panel LCD monitor, using a series of screens that can show you an amazing amount of information about virtually every setting you've made, plus additional data, such as GPS location (if you've used the optional Canon GP-E1 accessory). Mastering this wealth of information can be the key to fine-tuning your photography as you explore your creative options.

The next sections will introduce you to the various information displays at your disposal, and show you how to use them effectively.

While You're Shooting

Canon knows you don't want your shooting to be bogged down with bewildering information displays, so your Rebel gives you the most essential information in the most efficient way possible. Your key shooting display will be the optical viewfinder, which gives you a through-the-lens view of your subject, accompanied by some relevant data. Alternatively, if you're shooting in Live View or Movie modes, the LCD monitor's display of what the sensor sees is overlaid with the most important data. In either view, not *all* the information is shown at one time.

Through the Viewfinder

When framing your subject through the optical viewfinder, you'll find some information overlaid on the focus screen, and an additional array of data presented along the bottom of the viewfinder image (see Figure 3.15). The key items of interest are described next. I'll explain many of these readouts in more detail later in this book, with those pertaining to exposure in Chapter 4, and those relating to flash in Chapter 11. Note that not all of the information shown in the figure appears in the viewfinder simultaneously. Your T7i may display different combinations of AF area brackets and AF points, for example, and the array of information along the bottom will change when appropriate as well. These readouts include:

- **Spot metering circle.** Shows the circle that delineates the metered area when Spot metering is activated.

- **Autofocus points.** Shows the 45 points used by the T7i to focus. The camera can select the appropriate focus point for you, or you can manually select one or all of the points, as first described in Chapter 1. The number and appearance of the points differ depending on the AF method you've selected, as explained in Chapter 4, which explores the mystery of autofocus in more detail.

- **Area AF frame.** The outer frame shows the area that encompasses the 45 points, while the inner frames appear when needed to show the left, right, top, bottom, and central AF zones when you're using Zone AF or Large Zone AF.

- **Grid.** Displays the lines of the type of grid you chose. You can select from two different grid layouts or turn grid display off in the Viewfinder Display entry of the Shooting 2 menu, as explained in Chapter 8.

- **Aspect Ratio frames (not shown).** Heavy bars appear in the viewfinder to indicate the aspect ratio, or *proportions*, of your frame when you select something other than the default 3:2 aspect ratio. It wasn't possible to show all three available frames in the figure, but I'll provide illustrations in Chapter 9, where I discuss how you can select 3:2, 4:3, 16:9, or 1:1 proportions using the Aspect Ratio entry in the Shooting 3 menu.

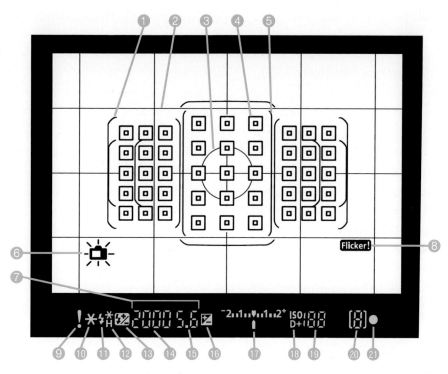

Figure 3.15

1. *Area AF frame*
2. *Grid*
3. *Spot metering circle*
4. *AF point*
5. *Large Zone AF frame*
6. *Electronic level*
7. *Bulb exposure/FE lock/Busy/ Built-in flash recharging/No card warning/Card error/Card full warning/Error code/ AF point readouts*

8. *Flicker detection*
9. *Warning icon*
10. *Autoexposure lock/Auto Exposure Bracketing in-progress*
11. *Flash-ready indicator*
12. *Flash status indicator/ High-speed sync*
13. *Flash exposure compensation/ FE lock/Flash exposure bracketing in-progress*
14. *Shutter speed*

15. *Aperture*
16. *Exposure compensation*
17. *Exposure level indicator/ AEB range/Red-eye reduction lamp on*
18. *Highlight Tone Priority*
19. *ISO speed*
20. *Maximum burst available*
21. *Focus indicator*

- **Electronic level.** This indicator, when activated using the Viewfinder Display entry of the Set-up 2 menu, shows when the camera is tilted, by means of an icon that changes to show the amount of tilt as you rotate the camera to make the camera level in either the horizontal or vertical orientations. (See Figure 3.16.)

- **Flicker detection.** This warning is displayed when the camera detects flickering caused by several types of blinking light sources. You can disable this warning in the Viewfinder Display entry of the Set-up 2 menu, detailed in Chapter 9.

- **Autoexposure lock/Auto Exposure Bracketing In-Progress.** Shows that exposure has been locked. This icon also appears when an automatic exposure bracketing sequence is in process.

- **Flash-ready indicator.** This icon appears when the flash is fully charged. It also shows when the flash exposure lock has been applied for an inappropriate exposure value.

- **Flash status indicator.** Appears along with the flash-ready indicator. The H is shown when high-speed (focal plane) flash sync is being used. The * appears when flash exposure lock or a flash exposure bracketing sequence is underway.

- **Flash exposure compensation.** Appears when flash EV changes have been made.

- **Shutter speed/aperture/AF point readouts.** Most of the time, these readouts show the current shutter speed and aperture. This pair can also warn you of memory card conditions (full, error, or missing), ISO speed, flash exposure lock, AF point selection and a buSY indicator when the camera is busy doing other things (including flash recycling).

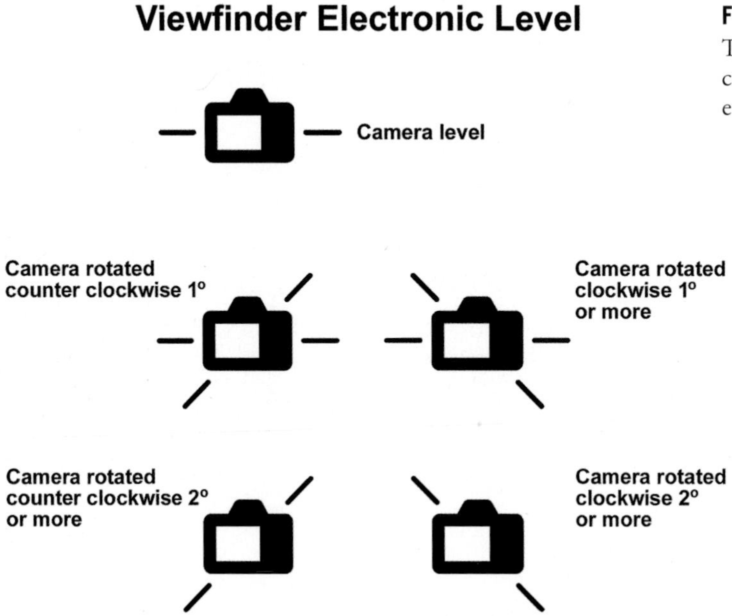

Viewfinder Electronic Level

Figure 3.16
The viewfinder icon changes as the camera is rotated.

Camera level

Camera rotated counter clockwise 1°

Camera rotated clockwise 1° or more

Camera rotated counter clockwise 2° or more

Camera rotated clockwise 2° or more

■ **Exposure level indicator.** This scale shows the current exposure level, with the bottom indicator centered when the exposure is correct as metered. The indicator may also move to the left or right to indicate under- or overexposure (respectively). The scale is also used to show the amount of EV and flash EV adjustments and the number of stops covered by the current automatic exposure bracketing range, and is used as a red-eye reduction lamp indicator.

■ **Exposure compensation.** Appears when EV changes have been made.

■ **ISO speed.** This useful indicator shows the current ISO setting value. Those who have accidentally taken dozens of shots under bright sunlight at ISO 1600 because they forgot to change the setting back after some indoor shooting will treasure this addition.

■ **Maximum burst available.** Changes to a number to indicate the number of frames that can be taken in continuous mode using the current settings.

■ **Focus indicator.** This glowing dot flashes, and then glows steadily when the subject covered by the active autofocus zone is in sharp focus.

■ **Highlight tone priority.** Shows status of this feature, which allows the T7i to adjust the rendition of the lighter tones in an image to provide full detail, possibly at the expense of shadow detail.

■ **Warning icon.** Appears under several different conditions: Monochrome Picture Style is selected, White Balance is corrected, and Multi-Shot Noise Reduction is active. I'll show you how to enable and disable each of these icons in Chapter 9.

On the LCD Monitor

As you are shooting using the optical viewfinder, the back-panel color LCD monitor can display different screens: shooting information and an electronic level, plus display off. You can cycle among the screen options by pressing the INFO. button. In Live View and Movie modes, the LCD monitor, of course, shows the sensor view with overlays that provide shooting information. I'll show you the Live View/Movie screens in Chapter 6. The non–live view/movie screens are these:

■ **Shooting function settings.** In Creative Zone modes—Manual (M), Shutter-priority (Tv), Aperture-priority (Av), and Program (P)—the LCD monitor screen will display the Quick Control screen, as shown in Figure 3.17. Not all of the information shown in the figure will be visible at one time. The display includes all the basic shooting information shown in the viewfinder, plus the additional data shown in the figure. When you press the Quick Control (Q) button, you can adjust many of these settings, as described in Chapter 2, by navigating around the screen, pressing SET, and using the directional buttons, dials, or other controls to modify them. (See Figure 3.18.)

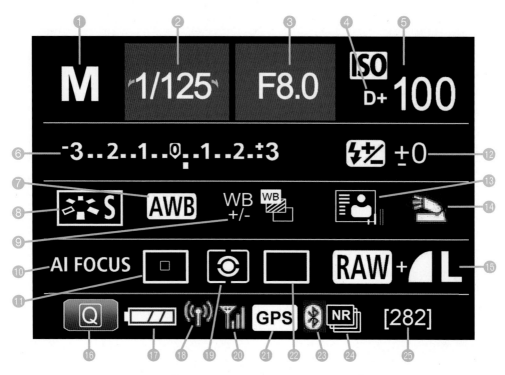

Figure 3.17 Shooting functions/Quick Control display.

1 Exposure mode

2 Shutter speed

3 Lens aperture

4 Highlight Tone Priority

5 ISO setting

6 Exposure level/Exposure compensation amount/Automatic exposure bracketing range

7 White balance

8 Picture control

9 White balance bracketing

10 Autofocus mode

11 AF area selection mode

12 Flash exposure compensation

13 Auto Lighting Optimizer

14 Built-in flash settings

15 Image quality

16 Access quick control screen

17 Battery level

18 Wi-Fi function

19 Metering mode

20 Eye-Fi transmission status/Wi-Fi signal strength

21 GPS

22 Drive mode

23 Bluetooth function

24 Multi-Shot Noise Reduction

25 Shots remaining/Shots remaining during WB bracketing/Self-timer countdown/Bulb exposure time

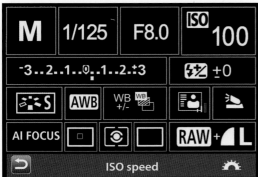
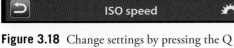

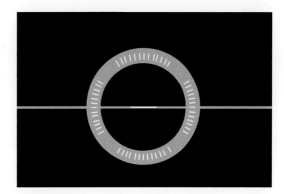

Figure 3.18 Change settings by pressing the Q button to access this screen.

Figure 3.19 Electronic level.

- **Electronic level.** The LCD monitor can display a virtual horizon with the same functionality as the one shown in the viewfinder, but with a larger, more easily viewed display, shown in Figure 3.19. The colored bar is red when the camera is tilted, and changes to green when the T7i is level. The markings on the scale surrounding the level line represent 5-degree increments. When you rotate from a horizontal to vertical shooting position, the virtual horizon display readjusts its orientation to match. An electronic level is also available during live view and movie shooting, as described in Chapter 6.

- **Screen off.** The T7i has an additional non-screen mode, in which the LCD monitor is turned off completely, which you can accomplish by pressing the DISP. button on top of the T7i, located to the immediate right of the ISO button. This mode is useful at concerts and other venues where you don't want you—or those around you—to be distracted by the LCD.

Image Playback Displays

When the T7i shows you a picture for review, you can select from among a variety of different information screens. To switch among them, press the INFO. button while the image is on the screen. The available displays include:

- **No information.** This screen gives you a clean, uncluttered view of the image you took, without any intrusive data overlays at all, as shown in Figure 3.20.

- **Basic information display.** This version still provides you with a full-screen look at your image, but provides some basic exposure and picture information at the top and bottom of the screen. (See Figure 3.21.)

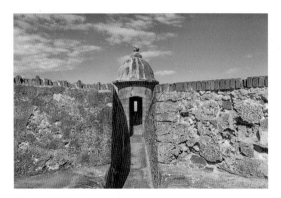

Figure 3.20 No Information screen.

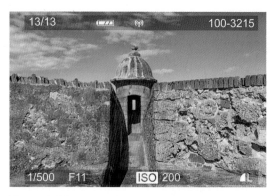

Figure 3.21 Basic information display.

- **Shooting information display.** This screen has two variations. Both show a reduced-size thumbnail of your image in the upper-left corner, and either an RGB *or* Brightness histogram immediately to the right of that. The thumbnails have additional information, such as battery status, picture and file number, date, and time located in the top row. The two versions are shown in Figure 3.22. You can select which type of histogram is the default using the Histogram Disp. entry in the Playback 3 menu, as described in Chapter 8.

At the bottom of the shooting information display, you'll find a scrolling panel of data. When the shooting information screen is visible, you can press the up and down directional buttons to scroll through the available "bonus" panels. They include:

- **Shooting data.** Includes exposure mode, shutter speed, f/stop, ISO, white balance, Picture Control, and metering mode (seen at the bottom of the two versions in Figure 3.22).

- **Lens/alternate histogram.** Shows information about the lens used to capture the image. The second, non-default type of histogram is shown in this panel. (See Figure 3.23, left.)

- **White balance information.** The white balance setting used to capture this image is shown, along with a graph that represents any color correction settings you've made. (See Figure 3.23, right.)

- **Picture Control settings.** Shows the Picture Control used for the image, and settings in effect. I'll show you how to create and manage Picture Controls in Chapter 8. (See Figure 3.24, left.)

- **Color space/Noise reduction information.** Here you can view the color space setting and both long exposure noise reduction and high ISO speed noise reduction settings. (See Figure 3.24, right.)

- **Lens aberration correction data.** Shows which lens correction settings were used for the picture, as explained in Chapter 9. (See Figure 3.25, left.)

- **GPS data.** If you used a GPS device when taking the picture, the GPS information embedded in your image file is displayed. Otherwise, you will not see this screen. (See Figure 3.25, right.)

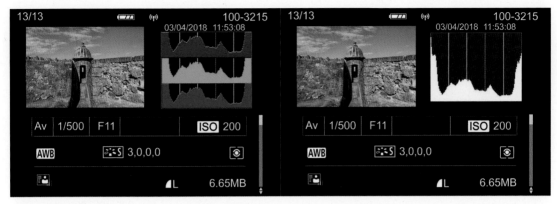

Figure 3.22 RGB histogram (left), brightness/luminance histogram (right).

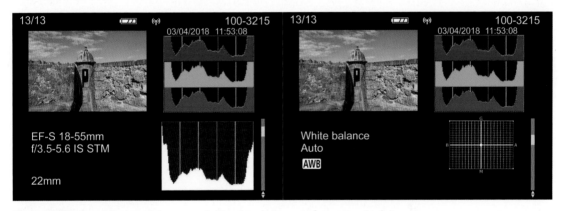

Figure 3.23 Lens/alternate histogram (left), white balance information (right).

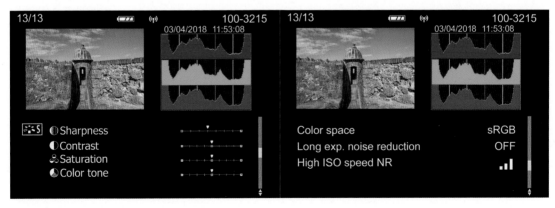

Figure 3.24 Picture Control settings (left), color space/noise reduction (right).

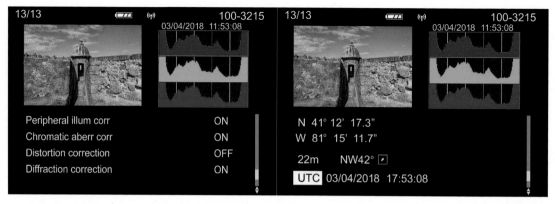

Figure 3.25 Lens aberration correction data (left), GPS data (right).

Nailing the Right Exposure

As you learn to use your T7i creatively, you're going to find that the right settings—as determined by the camera's exposure meter and intelligence—need to be *adjusted* to account for your creative decisions or to fine-tune the image for special situations.

For example, when you shoot with the main light source behind the subject, you end up with *backlighting*, which results in an overexposed background and/or an underexposed subject. The Rebel T7i recognizes backlit situations nicely, and can properly base exposure on the main subject, producing a decent photo. Features like Highlight Tone Priority and the Auto Lighting Optimizer can fine-tune exposure to preserve detail in the highlights and shadows.

But what if you *want* to underexpose the subject, to produce a silhouette effect? Or, perhaps, you might want to flip up the T7i's built-in flash unit to fill in the shadows on your subject. The more you know about how to use your T7i, the more you'll run into situations where you want to creatively tweak the exposure to provide a different look than you'd get with a straight shot.

This chapter shows you the fundamentals of exposure, so you'll be better equipped to override the Rebel T7i's default settings when you want to, or need to. After all, correct exposure is one of the foundations of good photography, along with accurate focus and sharpness, appropriate color balance, freedom from unwanted noise and excessive contrast, as well as pleasing composition.

The Rebel T7i gives you a great deal of control over all of these, although composition is entirely up to you. You must still frame the photograph to create an interesting arrangement of subject matter, but all the other parameters are basic functions of the camera. You can let your T7i set them for you automatically, you can fine-tune how the camera applies its automatic settings, or you can make them yourself, manually. The amount of control you have over exposure, sensitivity (ISO settings), color balance, focus, and image parameters like sharpness and contrast make the T7i a versatile tool for creating images.

In the next few pages, I'm going to give you a grounding in one of those foundations, and explain the basics of exposure, either as an introduction or as a refresher course, depending on your current level of expertise. When you finish this chapter, you'll understand most of what you need to know to take well-exposed photographs creatively in a broad range of situations.

Getting a Handle on Exposure

This section explains the fundamental concepts that go into creating an exposure. If you already know about the role of f/stops, shutter speeds, and sensor sensitivity in determining an exposure, you might want to skip to the next section, which explains how the T7i calculates exposure.

In the most basic sense, exposure is all about light. Exposure can make or break your photo. Correct exposure brings out the detail in the areas you want to picture, providing the range of tones and colors you need to create the desired image. Poor exposure can cloak important details in shadow, or wash them out in glare-filled featureless expanses of white. However, getting the perfect exposure requires some intelligence—either that built into the camera or the smarts in your head—because digital sensors can't capture all the tones we can see. If the range of tones in an image is extensive, embracing both inky black shadows and bright highlights, we often must settle for an exposure that renders most of those tones—but not all—in a way that best suits the photo we want to produce.

As the owner of a Canon T7i, you may be aware of the traditional "exposure triangle" of aperture (quantity of light, light passed by the lens), shutter speed (the amount of time the shutter is open), and the ISO sensitivity of the sensor—all working proportionately and reciprocally to produce an exposure.

Working with any of the three controls involves trade-offs. Larger f/stops provide less depth-of-field, while smaller f/stops increase depth-of-field (and potentially at the same time can *decrease* sharpness through a phenomenon called *diffraction*). Shorter shutter speeds do a better job of reducing the effects of camera/subject motion, while longer shutter speeds make that motion blur more likely. Higher ISO settings increase the amount of visual noise and artifacts in your image, while lower ISO settings reduce the effects of noise. (See Figure 4.1.)

Exposure determines the look, feel, and tone of an image, in more ways than one. Incorrect exposure can impair even the best-composed image by cloaking important tones in darkness, or by washing them out so they become featureless to the eye. On the other hand, correct exposure brings out the detail in the areas you want to picture, and provides the range of tones and colors you need to create the desired image. However, getting the perfect exposure can be tricky, because digital sensors can't capture all the tones we are able to see. If the range of tones in an image is extensive, embracing both inky black shadows and bright highlights, the sensor may not be able to capture them all. Sometimes, we must settle for an exposure that renders most of those tones—but not all—in a way that best suits the photo we want to produce. You'll often need to make choices about

Figure 4.1
The traditional exposure triangle includes aperture, shutter speed, and ISO setting.

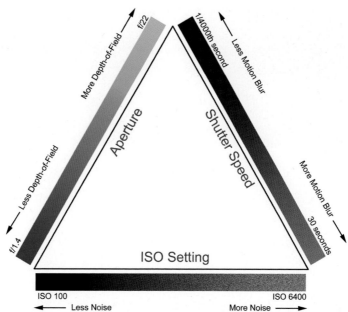

which details are important, and which are not, so that you can grab the tones that truly matter in your image. That's part of the creativity you bring to bear in realizing your photographic vision.

For example, look at two bracketed exposures presented at top in Figure 4.2. For the image at upper left, the highlights (chiefly the clouds at upper left and the top-left edge of the skyscraper) are well exposed, but everything else in the shot is seriously underexposed. The version on the upper right, taken an instant later with the tripod-mounted camera, shows detail in the shadow areas of the buildings, but the highlights are completely washed out. The camera's sensor simply can't capture detail in both dark areas and bright areas in a single shot.

With digital camera sensors, it's tricky to capture detail in both highlights and shadows in a single image, because the number of tones, the *dynamic range* of the sensor, is limited. The solution, in this case, was to resort to a technique called High Dynamic Range (HDR) photography, in which the two exposures from Figure 4.2 were combined in an image editor such as Photoshop, or a specialized HDR tool like Photomatix (about $100 from www.hdrsoft.com). The resulting shot is shown at bottom in Figure 4.2. I'll explain more about HDR photography later in this chapter. For now, though, I'm going to concentrate on showing you how to get the best exposures possible without resorting to such tools, using only the features of your Canon T7i.

To understand exposure, you need to understand the six aspects of light that combine to produce an image. Start with a light source—the sun, an interior lamp, or the glow from a campfire—and trace its path to your camera, through the lens, and finally to the sensor that captures the illumination.

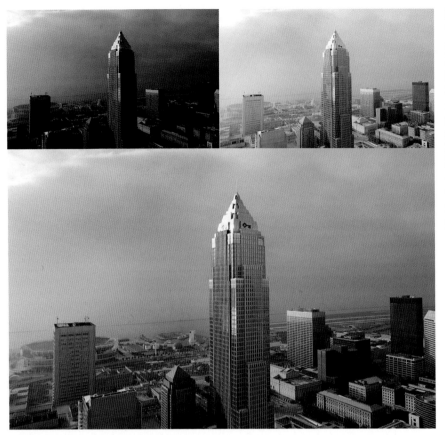

Figure 4.2
The image is exposed for the highlights, losing shadow detail (upper left). At upper right, the exposure captures detail in the shadows, but the background highlights are washed out. Combining the two exposures produces the best compromise image (bottom).

Here's a brief review of the things within our control that affect exposure.

- **Light at its source.** Our eyes and our cameras—film or digital—are most sensitive to that portion of the electromagnetic spectrum we call *visible light*. That light has several important aspects that are relevant to photography, such as color and harshness (which is determined primarily by the apparent size of the light source as it illuminates a subject). But, in terms of exposure, the important attribute of a light source is its *intensity*. We may have direct control over intensity, which might be the case with an interior light that can be brightened or dimmed. Or, we might have only indirect control over intensity, as with sunlight, which can be made to appear dimmer by introducing translucent light-absorbing or reflective materials in its path.

- **Light's duration.** We tend to think of most light sources as continuous. But, as you'll learn in Chapter 11, the duration of light can change quickly enough to modify the exposure, as when the main illumination in a photograph comes from an intermittent source, such as an electronic flash.

- **Light reflected, transmitted, or emitted.** Once light is produced by its source, either continuously or in a brief burst, we are able to see and photograph objects by the light that is reflected from our subjects toward the camera lens; transmitted (say, from translucent objects that are lit from behind); or emitted (by a candle or television screen). When more or less light reaches the lens from the subject, we need to adjust the exposure. This part of the equation is under our control to the extent we can increase the amount of light falling on or passing through the subject (by adding extra light sources or using reflectors), or by pumping up the light that's emitted (by increasing the brightness of the glowing object).

■ **Light passed by the lens.** Not all the illumination that reaches the front of the lens makes it all the way through. Filters can remove some of the light before it enters the lens. Inside the lens barrel is a variable-sized diaphragm that dilates and contracts to vary the size of the aperture and control the amount of light that enters the lens. You, or the T7i's autoexposure system, can control exposure by varying the size of the aperture. The relative size of the aperture is called the *f/stop*.

■ **Light passing through the shutter.** Once light passes through the lens, the amount of time the sensor receives it is determined by the T7i's shutter, which can remain open for as long as 30 seconds (or even longer if you use the Bulb setting) or as briefly as 1/4,000th second.

■ **Light captured by the sensor.** Not all the light falling onto the sensor is captured. If the number of photons reaching a particular photosite doesn't pass a set threshold, no information is recorded. Similarly, if too much light illuminates a pixel in the sensor, then the excess isn't recorded or, worse, spills over to contaminate adjacent pixels. We can modify the minimum and maximum number of pixels that contribute to image detail by adjusting the ISO setting. At higher ISOs, the incoming light is amplified to boost the effective sensitivity of the sensor.

These factors all work proportionately and reciprocally to produce an exposure. That is, if you double the amount of light that's available, increase the aperture by one stop, make the shutter speed twice as long, or boost the ISO setting 2X, you'll get twice as much exposure. Similarly, you can increase any of these factors while decreasing one of the others by a similar amount to keep the same exposure.

Most commonly, exposure settings are made using the aperture and shutter speed, followed by adjusting the ISO sensitivity if it's not possible to get the preferred exposure; that is, the one that uses the "best" f/stop or shutter speed for the depth-of-field (range of sharp focus) or action stopping we want (produced by short shutter speeds, as I'll explain later). Table 4.1 shows equivalent exposure settings using various shutter speeds and f/stops.

One of the most important aspects in this discussion is the concept of "equivalent exposure." This term means that exactly the same amount of light will reach the sensor at various combinations of aperture and shutter speed. Whether we use a small aperture (large f/number) with a long shutter speed or a wide aperture (small f/number) with a fast shutter speed, the amount of light reaching the sensor can be exactly the same. Table 4.1 shows equivalent exposure settings using various shutter speeds and f/stops; in other words, any of the combination of settings listed will produce the same exposure.

Table 4.1 Equivalent Exposures

Shutter Speed	f/stop	Shutter Speed	f/stop
1/30th second	f/22	1/500th second	f/5.6
1/60th second	f/16	1/1,000th second	f/4
1/125th second	f/11	1/2,000th second	f/2.8
1/250th second	f/8	1/4,000th second	f/2

F/STOPS AND SHUTTER SPEEDS

If you're *really* new to more advanced cameras (and I realize that many soon-to-be-ambitious photographers do purchase the T7i as their first digital SLR), you might need to know that the lens aperture, or f/stop, is a ratio, much like a fraction, which is why f/2 is larger than f/4, just as 1/2 is larger than 1/4. However, f/2 is actually *four times* as large as f/4. (If you remember your high school geometry, you'll know that to double the area of a circle, you multiply its diameter by the square root of two: 1.4.)

Lenses are usually marked with intermediate f/stops that represent a size that's twice as much/half as much as the previous aperture. So, a lens might be marked f/2, f/2.8, f/4, f/5.6, f/8, f/11, f/16, f/22, with each larger number representing an aperture that admits half as much light as the one before, as shown in Figure 4.3.

Shutter speeds are actual fractions (of a second), but the numerator is omitted, so that 60, 125, 250, 500, 1,000, and so forth represent 1/60th, 1/125th, 1/250th, 1/500th, and 1/1,000th second. To avoid confusion, Canon uses quotation marks to signify longer exposures: 2", 2"5, 4", and so forth representing 2.0-, 2.5-, and 4.0-second exposures, respectively.

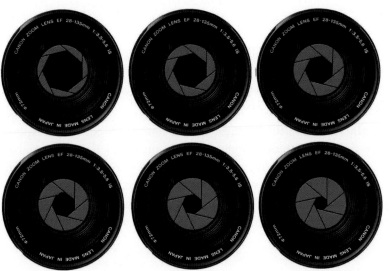

Figure 4.3

Top row (left to right): f/4, f/5.6, f/8; bottom row: f/11, f/16, f/22.

When the T7i is set for P (Program) mode, the metering system selects the correct exposure for you automatically, but you can change quickly to an equivalent exposure by locking the current exposure, and then spinning the Main Dial until the desired *equivalent* exposure combination is displayed. You can use this standard Program Shift feature more easily if you remember that you need to rotate the dial toward the *left* when you want to increase the amount of depth-of-field or use a slower shutter speed; rotate to the *right* when you want to reduce the depth-of-field or use a faster shutter speed. The need for more/less DOF and slower/faster shutter speed are the primary reasons you'd want to use Program Shift. I'll explain Program mode exposure shifting options in more detail later in this chapter.

In Aperture-priority (Av) and Shutter-priority (Tv) modes, you can change to an equivalent exposure using a different combination of shutter speed and aperture, but only by either adjusting the aperture in Aperture-priority mode (the camera then chooses the shutter speed) or shutter speed in Shutter-priority mode (the camera then selects the aperture). I'll cover all these exposure modes and their differences later in the chapter.

How the Rebel T7i Calculates Exposure

When using the optical viewfinder, your T7i calculates exposure by measuring the light that passes through the lens and is bounced up by the mirror to a 7,560-pixel RGB plus IR-sensitive metering sensor located near the focusing surface. (**Note:** In live view, the sensor image is used instead, as I'll explain later.) Light is evaluated using a pattern you can select (more on that later) and based on the assumption that each area being measured reflects about the same amount of light as a neutral gray card that reflects a "middle" gray reflectance. (The photographic "gray cards" you buy at a camera store have an 18-percent gray tone, which does represent middle gray; however, your camera is calibrated to interpret a somewhat darker 12-percent gray; I'll explain more about this later.) That "average" gray assumption is necessary, because different subjects reflect different amounts of light. In a photo containing, say, a white cat and a dark gray cat, the white cat might reflect five times as much light as the gray cat. An exposure based on the white cat will cause the gray cat to appear to be black, while an exposure based only on the gray cat will make the white cat appear washed out.

This is more easily understood if you look at some photos of subjects that are dark (they reflect little light), those that have predominantly middle tones, and subjects that are highly reflective. The next few figures show a simplified scale with a middle gray tone, plus black and white patches, along with a human figure (not a cat) to illustrate how different exposure measurements affect an exposure.

Correctly Exposed

The image shown in Figure 4.4 represents how a photograph might appear if you inserted the patches shown at bottom left into the scene, and then calculated exposure by measuring the light reflecting from the middle gray patch, which, for the sake of illustration, we'll assume reflects approximately 12 to 18 percent of the light that strikes it. The gray patch also happens to be similar in reflectance to the background behind the subject. The exposure meter in the T7i sees an object that it thinks is a middle gray, calculates an exposure based on that, and the patch in the center of the strip is rendered at its proper tonal value. Best of all, because the resulting exposure is correct, the black patch at left and white patch at right are rendered properly as well.

When you're shooting pictures with your T7i, and the meter happens to base its exposure on a subject that averages that "ideal" middle gray, you'll end up with similar (accurate) results. The camera's exposure algorithms are concocted to ensure this kind of result as often as possible, barring any unusual subjects (that is, those that are backlit, or have uneven illumination). The T7i has four different metering modes (described next), each of which is equipped to handle certain types of unusual subjects, as I'll outline.

Overexposed

Figure 4.5 shows what would happen if the exposure were calculated based on metering the left-most, black patch, which is roughly the same tonal value of the darkest areas of the subject's hair. The light meter sees less light reflecting from the black square than it would see from a gray middle-tone subject, and so figures, "Aha! I need to add exposure to brighten this subject up to a middle gray!" That lightens the "black" patch, so it now appears to be gray.

But now the patch in the middle that was *originally* middle gray is overexposed and becomes light gray. And the white square at right is now seriously overexposed and loses detail in the highlights, which have become a featureless white. Our human subject is similarly overexposed.

Underexposed

The third possibility in this simplified scenario is that the light meter might measure the illumination bouncing off the white patch, which roughly corresponds to the subject's blouse, and try to render *that* tone as a middle gray. A lot of light is reflected by the white square, so the exposure is *reduced*, bringing that patch closer to a middle gray tone. The patches that were originally gray and black are now rendered too dark. Clearly, measuring the gray card—or a substitute that reflects about the same amount of light—is the only way to ensure that the exposure is precisely correct. (See Figure 4.6.)

As you can see, the ideal way to measure exposure is to meter from a subject that reflects 12 to 18 percent of the light that reaches it. If you want the most precise exposure calculations, the solution is to use a stand-in, such as the evenly illuminated gray card I mentioned earlier. But, because the standard Kodak gray card reflects 18 percent of the light that reaches it and, as I said, your camera

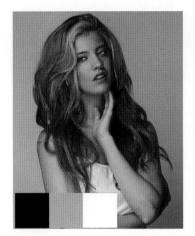
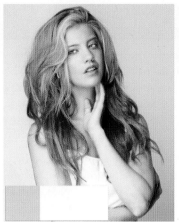
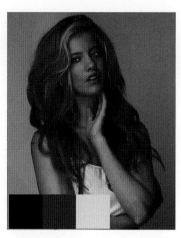

Figure 4.4 When exposure is calculated based on the middle-gray tone in the center of the card, the black and white patches are rendered accurately, too, and our model is properly exposed.

Figure 4.5 When exposure is calculated based on the black square at lower left, the black patch looks gray, the gray patch appears to be a light gray, and the white square is seriously overexposed.

Figure 4.6 When exposure is calculated based on the white patch on the right, the other two patches, and the photo, are underexposed.

is calibrated for a somewhat darker 12-percent tone, you would need to add about one-half stop *more* exposure than the value metered from the card.

In some very bright scenes (like a snowy landscape or a lava field), you won't have a mid-tone to meter. Another substitute for a gray card is the palm of a human hand (the backside of the hand is too variable). But a human palm, regardless of ethnic group, is even brighter than a standard gray card, so instead of one-half stop more exposure, you need to add one additional stop. That is, if your meter reading is 1/500th of a second at f/11, use 1/500th second at f/8 or 1/250th second at f/11 instead. (Both exposures are equivalent.)

Or, you might want to resort to using an evenly illuminated gray card mentioned earlier. Small versions are available that can be tucked in a camera bag. Place it in your frame near your main subject, facing the camera, and with the exact same even illumination falling on it that is falling on your subject. Then, use the Spot metering function (described in the next section) to calculate exposure.

But, the standard Kodak gray card reflects 18 percent of the light while, as I noted, your camera is calibrated for a somewhat darker 12-percent tone. If you insisted on getting a perfect exposure, you would need to add about one-half stop more exposure than the value provided by taking the light meter reading from the card. Of course, in most situations, it's not necessary to do this. Your camera's light meter will do a good job of calculating the right exposure, especially if you use the exposure tips in the next section. But, I felt that explaining exactly what is going on during exposure calculation would help you understand how your T7i's metering system works.

ORIGIN OF THE 18-PERCENT MYTH

Why are so many photographers under the impression that camera light meters are calibrated to the 18-percent "standard," rather than the true value, which may be 12 to 14 percent, depending on the vendor? You'll find this misinformation in an alarming number of places. I've seen the 18-percent "myth" taught in camera classes; I've found it in books, and even been given this wrong information from the technical staff of camera vendors. (They should know better—the same vendors' engineers who design and calibrate the cameras have the right figure.)

The most common explanation is that during a revision of Kodak's instructions for its gray cards in the 1970s, the advice to open up an extra half stop was omitted, and a whole generation of shooters grew up thinking that a measurement off a gray card could be used as-is. The proviso returned to the instructions by 1987, it's said, but by then it was too late. Next to me is a (c)2006 version of the instructions for KODAK Gray Cards, Publication R-27Q (still available in authorized versions from non-Kodak sources). The current directions read (with a bit of paraphrasing from me in italics):

- For subjects of normal reflectance increase the indicated exposure by 1/2 stop.
- For light subjects use the indicated exposure; for very light subjects, decrease the exposure by 1/2 stop. (*That is, you're measuring a subject that's lighter than middle gray.*)
- If the subject is dark to very dark, increase the indicated exposure by 1 to 1-1/2 stops. (*You're shooting a dark subject.*)

EXTERNAL METERS CAN BE CALIBRATED

The light meters built into your T7i are calibrated at the factory. But if you use a hand-held incident or reflective light meter, you *can* calibrate it, using the instructions supplied with your meter. Because a hand-held meter *can* be calibrated to the 18-percent gray standard (or any other value you choose), my rant about the myth of the 18-percent gray card doesn't apply.

Choosing a Metering Method

To calculate exposure automatically, you need to tell the T7i *where* in the frame to measure the light (this is called the *metering method*) and *what controls* should be used (aperture, shutter speed, or both) to set the exposure. That's called *exposure mode* (and includes Program (P), Shutter-priority (Tv), Aperture-priority (Av), or Manual (M) options, plus Auto and Creative Auto. I'll explain all these next.).

But first, I'm going to introduce you to the four metering methods used when shooting in conventional (non–live view) mode. You can select any of the four if you're working with P, Tv, Av, or M exposure modes; if you're using Auto or Creative Auto, Evaluative metering is selected automatically and cannot be changed.

1. Specify your metering method using one of these options:

   - Press the MENU button and navigate to the Shooting 3 menu, highlight the Metering Mode entry at the top of the screen, and tap the entry on the touch screen or press SET.

   - Use the Quick Control key (Q button) to access the Quick Control screen and navigate to the metering mode section, which is the third from the left in the bottom row. Tap the icon or press SET, and a screen pops up on the LCD offering four choices. (The screen was shown earlier in Chapters 2 and 3.)

2. Use the touch screen or left/right directional buttons to highlight Evaluative, Partial, Spot, or Center-weighted. Tap the icon of the method you want to use, or press SET when it is highlighted. Your choices include:

   - **Evaluative.** The T7i slices up the frame into 63 different zones, shown as yellow rectangles at left in Figure 4.7. The zones used are linked to the autofocus system (the 45 autofocus zones are also shown in the figure). The camera evaluates the measurements, giving extra emphasis to the metering zones that indicate sharp focus to make an educated guess about what kind of picture you're taking, based on examination of thousands of different real-world photos. For example, if the top sections of a picture are much lighter than the bottom portions, the algorithm can assume that the scene is a landscape photo with lots of sky. This mode is the best all-purpose metering method for most pictures. I'll explain how to choose an autofocus/exposure zone in the section on autofocus operation later in this chapter. See Figure 4.7, right, for an example of a scene that can be easily interpreted by the Evaluative metering mode.

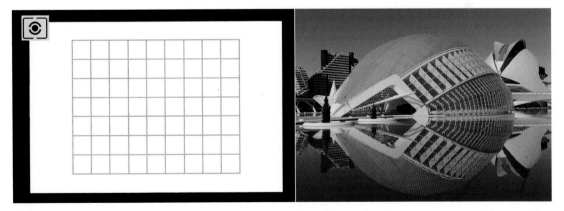

Figure 4.7 Left: Evaluative metering uses 63 zones marked by yellow rectangles. Right: An evenly lit scene like this one can be metered effectively using the Evaluative metering setting.

- **Partial.** This is a *faux* spot mode, using roughly 6 percent of the image area to calculate exposure, which, as you can see at left in Figure 4.8, is a rather large spot, represented by the larger yellow circle. The LCD icon is shown in the upper-left corner. Use this mode if the background is significantly brighter or darker than the subject, as at right in Figure 4.8.

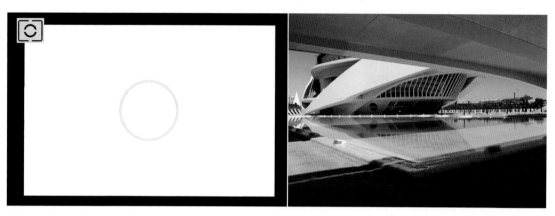

Figure 4.8 Left: Partial metering uses a center spot that's roughly six percent of the frame area. Right: Partial metering allowed measuring exposure from the central area of the image, while giving less emphasis to the darker areas at top and bottom.

- **Spot.** This mode confines the reading to a limited area in the center of the viewfinder, as shown at left in Figure 4.9, making up only 3.5 percent of the image. This mode is useful when you want to base exposure on a small area in the frame, such as the middle-gray area of the subject shown at right in Figure 4.9. If that area is in the center of the frame, so much the better. If not, you'll have to make your meter reading and then lock exposure by pressing the shutter release halfway, or by pressing the AE Lock button.

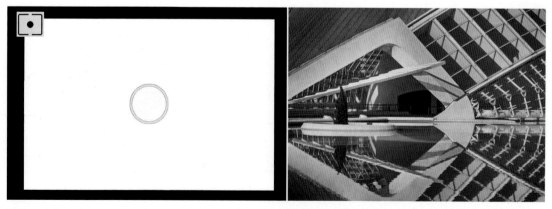

Figure 4.9 Left: Spot metering calculates exposure based on a center spot that's only 3.5 percent of the image area. Right: Spot metering was used to preserve the detail in the gray areas.

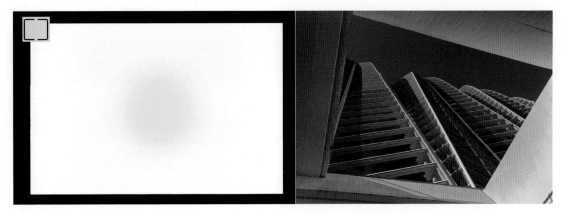

Figure 4.10 Left: Center-weighted metering calculates exposure based on the full frame, but emphasizes the center area. Right: Center-weighted metering calculated the exposure for this shot from the large area in the center of the frame, with less emphasis on the part of the structure framing the building beyond.

- **Center-weighted.** In this mode, the exposure meter emphasizes a zone in the center of the frame to calculate exposure, as shown at left in Figure 4.10, on the theory that, for most pictures, the main subject will be in the center. Center-weighting works best for portraits, architectural photos, and other pictures in which the most important subject is located in the middle of the frame, as at right in Figure 4.10. As the name suggests, the light reading is *weighted* toward the central portion, but information is also used from the rest of the frame. If your main subject is surrounded by very bright or very dark areas, partial might be a better choice. However, this scheme works well in many situations if you don't want to use one of the other modes.

3. Choose SET to confirm your choice.

Choosing an Exposure Method

You'll find four Creative Zone methods for choosing the appropriate shutter speed and aperture: Program (P), Shutter-priority (Tv), Aperture-priority (Av), and Manual (M). To select one of these modes, just spin the Mode Dial (located at the top-right side of the camera) to choose the method you want to use. You can also select from the Basic Zone exposure methods, which provide much less control.

Your choice of which exposure method is best for a given shooting situation will depend on things like your need for lots of (or less) depth-of-field, a desire to freeze action or allow motion blur, or how much noise you find acceptable in an image. Each of the Rebel T7i's exposure methods emphasizes one of those aspects of image capture or another. This section introduces you to all of them.

Basic Zone Exposure Methods

When using Basic Zone modes, you have little control over exposure. In any of these modes, the T7i sets Evaluative metering for you, and chooses the shutter speed and aperture automatically. Indeed, when using Special Scene modes, you can't change any of the other shooting settings (other than image quality).

In Scene Intelligent Auto mode, the T7i selects an appropriate ISO sensitivity setting, color (white) balance, Picture Style, color space, noise reduction features, and use of the Auto Lighting Optimizer. (All of these will be discussed in Chapter 8.)

In Creative Auto mode, the T7i makes most of the exposure decisions for you (just as in Scene Intelligent Auto mode), but allows you to make some adjustments, in a round-about way. In terms of exposure adjustments, what you can do is adjust the f/stop used by telling the T7i whether you want the background more blurred or less blurred. Because the Basic Zone modes don't provide extensive exposure control, I'll continue the description of the adjustments you *can* make at the end of this chapter.

Aperture-Priority

In Av mode, you specify the lens opening used, and the T7i selects the shutter speed. Aperture-priority is especially good when you want to use a particular lens opening to achieve a desired effect. Perhaps you'd like to use the smallest f/stop possible to maximize depth-of-field in a close-up picture. Or, you might want to use a large f/stop to throw everything except your main subject out of focus, as in Figure 4.11. Maybe you'd just like to "lock in" an f/stop smaller than the maximum aperture because it's the sharpest available aperture with that lens. Or, you might prefer to use, say, f/2.8 on a lens with a maximum aperture of f/1.4, because you want the best compromise between speed and sharpness.

Aperture-priority can even be used to specify a *range* of shutter speeds you want to use under varying lighting conditions, which seems almost contradictory. But think about it. You're shooting a soccer game outdoors with a telephoto lens and want a relatively high shutter speed, but you don't care if the speed changes a little should the sun duck behind a cloud. Set your T7i to Av, and adjust the aperture until a shutter speed of, say, 1/1,000th second is selected at your current ISO setting. (In bright sunlight at ISO 400, that aperture is likely to be around f/11.) Then, go ahead and shoot, knowing that your T7i will maintain that f/11 aperture (for sufficient DOF as the soccer players move about the field), but will drop down to 1/750th or 1/500th second if necessary should the lighting change a little.

A blinking 30 or 4000 shutter speed in the viewfinder indicates that the T7i is unable to select an appropriate shutter speed at the selected aperture and that over- and underexposure will occur at the current ISO setting. That's the major pitfall of using Av: you might select an f/stop that is too small or too large to allow an optimal exposure with the available shutter speeds. For example, if you choose f/2.8 as your aperture and the illumination is quite bright (say, at the beach or in snow),

Figure 4.11
Use Aperture-
priority to "lock in"
a large f/stop when
you want to blur the
background.

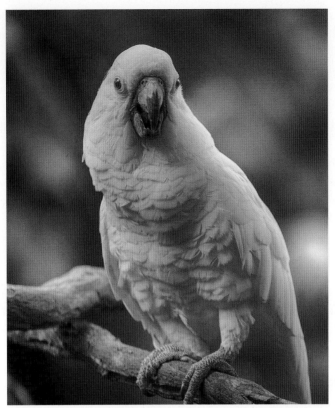

even your camera's fastest shutter speed might not be able to cut down the amount of light reaching the sensor to provide the right exposure. Or, if you select f/8 in a dimly lit room, you might find yourself shooting with a very slow shutter speed that can cause blurring from subject movement or camera shake. Aperture-priority is best used by those with a bit of experience in choosing settings. Many seasoned photographers leave their T7i set on Av all the time.

When to use Aperture-priority:

■ **General landscape photography.** The T7i is a great camera for landscape photography, of course, because its 24MP of resolution allows making huge, gorgeous prints, as well as smaller prints that are filled with eye-popping detail. Aperture-priority is a good tool for ensuring that your landscape is sharp from foreground to infinity, if you select an f/stop that provides maximum depth-of-field.

If you use Av mode and select an aperture like f/11 or f/16, it's your responsibility to make sure the shutter speed selected is fast enough to avoid losing detail to camera shake, or that the T7i is mounted on a tripod. One thing that new landscape photographers fail to account for is the movement of distant leaves and tree branches. When seeking the ultimate in sharpness, go ahead and use Aperture-priority, but boost ISO sensitivity a bit, if necessary, to provide a sufficiently fast shutter speed, whether shooting handheld or with a tripod.

- **Specific landscape situations.** Aperture-priority is also useful when you have no objection to using a long shutter speed, or, particularly, *want* the T7i to select one. Waterfalls are a perfect example. You can use A mode, set your camera to ISO 100, use a small f/stop, and let the camera select a longer shutter speed that will allow the water to blur as it flows. Indeed, you might need to use a neutral-density filter to get a sufficiently long shutter speed. But Aperture-priority mode is a good start.

- **Portrait photography.** Portraits are the most common applications of selective focus. A medium-large aperture (say, f/5.6 or f/8) with a longer lens/zoom setting (in the 85mm-135mm range) will allow the background behind your portrait subject to blur. A *very* large aperture (I frequently shoot wide open with my 85mm f/1.2 lens) lets you apply selective focus to your subject's *face*. With a three-quarters view of your subject, as long as their eyes are sharp, it's okay if the far ear or their hair is out of focus, as in Figure 4.12.

- **When you want to ensure optimal sharpness.** All lenses have an aperture or two at which they perform best, providing the level of sharpness you expect from a camera with the resolution of the T7i. That's usually about two stops down from wide open, and thus will vary depending on the maximum aperture of the lens. My 85mm f/1.2 is good wide open, but it's even sharper at f/2.8 or f/4; I shoot my 70-200mm f/2.8 wide open at concerts, but, if I can use f/4 instead, I'll get better results. Aperture-priority allows me to use each lens at its very best f/stop.

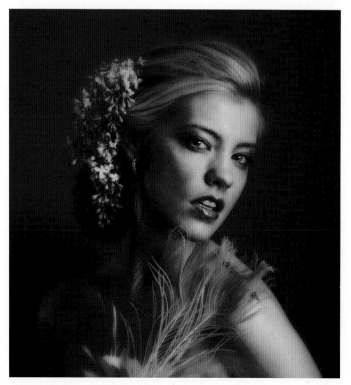

Figure 4.12
A large aperture is useful for portrait photography as long as the eyes are sharp.

■ **Close-up/Macro photography.** Depth-of-field is typically very shallow when shooting macro photos, and you'll want to choose your f/stop carefully. Perhaps you need the smallest aperture you can get away with to maximize DOF. Or, you might want to use a wider stop to emphasize your subject, as I did with the photo of the bird shown earlier in Figure 4.11. Av mode comes in very handy when shooting close-up pictures. Because macro work is frequently done with the T7i mounted on a tripod, and your close-up subjects, if not living creatures, may not be moving much, a longer shutter speed isn't a problem. Aperture-priority (Av mode) can be your preferred choice.

Shutter-Priority

Shutter-priority (Tv) is the inverse of Aperture-priority: you choose the shutter speed you'd like to use, and the camera's metering system selects the appropriate f/stop. Perhaps you're shooting action photos and you want to use the absolute fastest shutter speed available with your camera; in other cases, you might want to use a slow shutter speed to add some blur to a ballet photo that would be mundane if the action were completely frozen. Shutter-priority mode gives you some control over how much action-freezing capability your digital camera brings to bear in a situation.

Take care when using a slow shutter speed such as 1/8th second, because you'll get blurring from camera shake unless you're using a lens with vibration reduction (described in Chapter 7), or have mounted the T7i on a tripod or other firm support.

You'll also encounter the same problem as with Aperture-priority when you select a shutter speed that's too long or too short for correct exposure under some conditions. I've shot outdoor soccer games on sunny Fall evenings and used Shutter-priority mode to lock in a 1/1,000th second shutter speed, which triggered the blinking warning, even with the lens wide open.

Like Av mode, it's possible to choose an inappropriate shutter speed. If that's the case, the maximum aperture of your lens (to indicate underexposure) or the minimum aperture (to indicate overexposure) will blink.

When to use Shutter-priority:

■ **To reduce blur from subject motion.** Set the shutter speed of the T7i to a higher value to reduce the amount of blur from subjects that are moving. The exact speed will vary depending on how fast your subject is moving and how much blur is acceptable. You might want to freeze a basketball player in mid-dunk with a 1/1,000th second shutter speed, or use 1/250th second to allow the spinning wheels of a motocross racer to blur a tiny bit to add the feeling of motion.

■ **To add blur from subject motion.** There are times when you want a subject to blur, say, when shooting waterfalls with the camera set for a one- or two-second exposure in Shutter-priority mode.

■ **To add blur from camera motion when *you* are moving.** Say you're panning to follow a pair of relay runners. You might want to use Shutter-priority mode and set the T7i for 1/60th second, so that the background will blur as you pan with the runners. The shutter speed will be fast enough to provide a sharp image of the athletes, as shown in Figure 4.13.

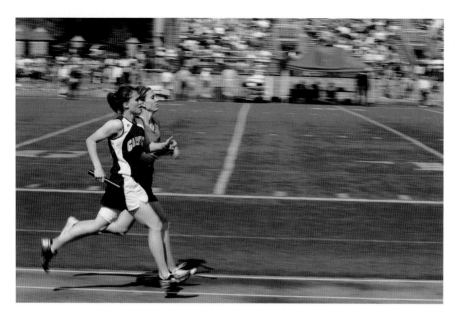

Figure 4.13
Shutter-priority allows you to specify a speed that will render a moving subject sharp as you pan.

- **To *reduce* blur from camera motion when *you* are moving.** In other situations, the camera may be in motion, say, because you're shooting from a moving train or auto, and you want to minimize the amount of blur caused by the motion of the camera. Shutter-priority is a good choice here, too.

- **Landscape photography handheld.** If you can't use a tripod for your landscape shots, you'll still probably want the sharpest image possible. Shutter-priority can allow you to specify a shutter speed that's fast enough to reduce or eliminate the effects of camera shake. Just make sure that your ISO setting is high enough that the T7i will select an aperture with sufficient depth-of-field, too.

- **Concerts, stage performances.** I shoot a lot of concerts with my 70-200mm f/2.8 lens, and have discovered that, when image stabilization is taken into account, a shutter speed of 1/180th second is fast enough to eliminate the effects of camera shake from handholding the T7i with this lens, and also to avoid blur from the movement of all but the most energetic performers. I use Shutter-priority and set the ISO so the camera will select an aperture in the f/4-5.6 range, which, for concert photography, I prefer for the right balance of background blur and adequate depth-of-field for the performers.

Program Mode

Program mode (P) uses the T7i's built-in smarts to select the correct f/stop and shutter speed using a database of picture information that tells it which combination of shutter speed and aperture will work best for a particular photo. If the correct exposure cannot be achieved at the current ISO setting, the shutter speed or aperture indicator in the viewfinder (or both) will blink, indicating under- or overexposure. You can then boost or reduce the ISO to increase or decrease sensitivity.

The T7i's recommended exposure can be overridden if you want. Use the EV setting feature (described later, because it also applies to Tv and Av modes) to add or subtract exposure from the metered value. And, as I mentioned earlier in this chapter, you can change from the recommended setting to an equivalent setting (as shown in Table 4.1) that produces the same exposure, but using a different combination of f/stop and shutter speed. To accomplish this:

1. Press the shutter release halfway to lock in the current base exposure, or press the AE Lock button (*) on the back of the camera (in which case the * indicator will illuminate in the viewfinder to show that the exposure has been locked).

2. Spin the Main Dial to change the shutter speed (the T7i will adjust the f/stop to match).

Your adjustment remains in force for a single exposure; if you want to change from the recommended settings for the next exposure, you'll need to repeat those steps.

When to use Program mode priority:

■ **When you're in a hurry to get a grab shot.** The T7i will do a pretty good job of calculating an appropriate exposure for you, without any input from you.

■ **When you hand your camera to a novice.** Set the T7i to P, hand the camera to your friend, relative, or trustworthy stranger you meet in front of the Eiffel Tower, point to the shutter release button and viewfinder, and say, "Look through here, and press this button."

■ **When no special shutter speed or aperture settings are needed.** If your subject doesn't require special anti- or pro-blur techniques, and depth-of-field or selective focus aren't important, use P as a general-purpose setting. You can still make adjustments to increase/decrease depth-of-field or add/reduce motion blur with a minimum of fuss.

Manual Exposure

Part of being an experienced photographer comes from knowing when to rely on your Rebel T7i's automation (including Scene Intelligent Auto, Creative Auto, or P mode), when to go semi-automatic (with Tv or Av), and when to set exposure manually (using M). Some photographers prefer to set their exposure manually, as the T7i will be happy to provide an indication of when its metering system judges your settings provide the proper exposure, using the analog exposure scale at the bottom of the viewfinder and on the status LCD.

Manual exposure can come in handy in some situations. You might be taking a silhouette photo and find that none of the exposure modes or EV correction features give you exactly the effect you want. For example, when I shot the ballet dancer in Figure 4.14 in front of a mostly dark background highlighted by an illuminated curtain off to the right, there was no way any of my Rebel T7i's exposure modes would be able to interpret the scene the way I wanted to shoot it, even with Spot metering, which didn't have a narrow enough field-of-view from my position. So, I took a couple test exposures, and set the exposure manually using the exact shutter speed and f/stop I needed. You might be working in a studio environment using multiple flash units. The additional flash are triggered by slave devices (gadgets that set off the flash when they sense the light from

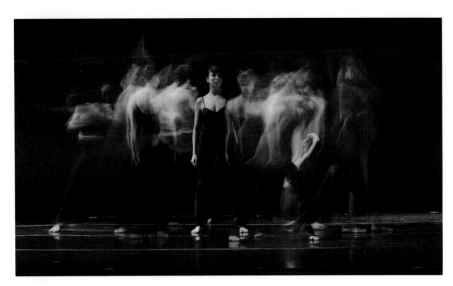

Figure 4.14
Manual exposure allows selecting both f/stop and shutter speed, especially useful when you're experimenting, as with this shot of ballet dancers.

another flash, or, perhaps from a radio or infrared remote control). Your camera's exposure meter doesn't compensate for the extra illumination, and can't interpret the flash exposure at all, so you need to set the aperture manually.

Because, depending on your proclivities, you might not need to set exposure manually very often, you should still make sure you understand how it works. Fortunately, the Rebel T7i makes setting exposure manually very easy. Just set the Mode Dial to M, turn the Main Dial to set the shutter speed, and hold down the Av button while rotating the Main Dial to adjust the aperture. Press the shutter release halfway or press the AE Lock button, and the exposure scale in the viewfinder shows you how far your chosen setting diverges from the metered exposure.

When to use Manual exposure:

- **When working in the studio.** If you're working in a studio environment, you generally have total control over the lighting and can set exposure exactly as you want. The last thing you need is for the T7i to interpret the scene and make adjustments of its own. Use M, and shutter speed, aperture, and (as long as you don't use ISO-Auto) the ISO setting are totally up to you.

- **When using non-dedicated flash.** External Canon dedicated flash units are cool, and can even be used to coordinate use of your T7i's internal flash. But if you're working with a non-compatible flash unit, particularly studio flash plugged into a PC/X sync adapter mounted on the hot shoe, the camera has no clue about the intensity of the flash, so you'll have to dial in the appropriate aperture manually.

- **If you're using a handheld light meter.** Determining that appropriate aperture, both for flash exposures and shots taken under continuous lighting, can be determined by a handheld light meter, flash meter, or combo meter that measures both kinds of illumination. With an external meter, you can measure highlights, shadows, backgrounds, or additional subjects separately, and use Manual exposure to make your settings.

■ **When you want to outsmart the metering system.** Your T7i's metering system is "trained" to react to unusual lighting situations, such as backlighting, extra-bright illumination, or low-key images with murky shadows. In many cases, it can counter these "problems" and produce a well-exposed image. But what if you don't *want* a well-exposed image? Manual exposure allows you to produce silhouettes in backlit situations, wash out all the middle tones to produce a luminous look, or underexpose to create a moody or ominous dark-toned photograph.

Adjusting Exposure with ISO Settings

Another way of adjusting exposures is by changing the ISO sensitivity setting. Sometimes photographers forget about this option, because the common practice is to set the ISO once for a particular shooting session (say, at ISO 100 or 200 for bright sunlight outdoors, or ISO 800 when shooting indoors) and then forget about ISO. ISOs higher than ISO 100 or 200 are seen as "bad" or "necessary evils." However, changing the ISO is a valid way of adjusting exposure settings, particularly with the Canon EOS Rebel T7i, which produces good results at ISO settings that create grainy, unusable pictures with some other camera models.

Indeed, I find myself using ISO adjustment as a convenient alternate way of adding or subtracting EV when shooting in Manual mode, and as a quick way of choosing equivalent exposures when in Auto or semi-automatic modes. For example, I've selected a Manual exposure with both f/stop and shutter speed suitable for my image using, say, ISO 200. I can change the exposure in full-stop increments by pressing the ISO button on top of the camera, and spinning the Main Dial one click at a time. The difference in image quality/noise at the base setting of ISO 200 is negligible if I dial in ISO 100 to reduce exposure a little, or change to ISO 400 to increase exposure. I keep my preferred f/stop and shutter speed, but still adjust the exposure.

Or, perhaps, I am using Tv mode and the metered exposure at ISO 200 is 1/500th second at f/11. If I decide on the spur of the moment I'd rather use 1/500th second at f/8, I can press the ISO button and spin the Main Dial to switch to ISO 100. Of course, it's a good idea to monitor your ISO changes, so you don't end up at ISO 1600 accidentally. ISO settings can, of course, also be used to boost or reduce sensitivity in particular shooting situations. The Rebel T7i can use ISO settings from ISO 100 up to 25600. When C.Fn-2: ISO Expansion is set to 1: On, then ISO can be set manually to H (ISO 52100 equivalent) for still photos. (In Movie shooting mode, the highest ISO that the T7i will use is 6400 when C.Fn-2 is set to OFF, and 25600 when C.Fn-2 is set to On.)

The camera can adjust the ISO automatically as appropriate for various lighting conditions. In Basic Zone modes, ISO is normally set between ISO 100 and ISO 12800. When you choose the Auto ISO setting, the T7i adjusts the sensitivity dynamically to suit the subject matter. In Basic Zone Scene Intelligent Auto, Landscape, Close-Up, Sports, Night Portrait, and Flash Off modes, the T7i adjusts ISO between ISO 100 and ISO 3200 as required. In Portrait mode, ISO is fixed at ISO 100, because the T7i attempts to use larger f/stops to blur the background, and the lower ISO setting lends itself to those larger stops.

When Auto ISO is chosen when using Creative Zone modes (P, Tv, Av, and M), sensitivity will be generally set within the range ISO 100 to ISO 12800 (ISO 25600 if ISO Expansion is activated), unless you've specified a lower maximum speed. Press the shutter release halfway to view the current ISO selected automatically by the camera on the LCD monitor or viewfinder.

When using flash, Auto ISO produces a setting of ISO 400 automatically, except when overexposure would occur (as when shooting subjects very close to the camera), in which case a lower setting (down to ISO 100) will be used. If you have an external dedicated flash attached and powered up, the T7i can set ISO in the range of 400 to 25600 automatically. That capability can be useful when shooting outdoor field sports at night and other "long distance" flash pictures, particularly with a telephoto lens, because you want to extend the "reach" of your external flash as far as possible (to dozens of feet or more), and boosting the ISO does that. Remember that if the Auto ISO ranges aren't suitable for you, individual ISO values can also be selected in any of the Creative Zone modes.

Tip

Find yourself locked out of ISO settings lower than 200 or higher than 25600? Check to see if a D+ symbol appears with your ISO setting display. That indicates that Check C.Fn-4: Highlight Tone Priority, located in the Set-up 4 menu, has been set to 1: Enable. When Highlight Tone Priority is active, only ISO 200 to 25600 can be selected.

Dealing with Visual Noise

Visual image noise is that random grainy effect that some like to use as a special effect, but which, most of the time, is objectionable because it robs your image of detail even as it adds that "interesting" texture. Noise is caused by two different phenomena: high ISO settings and long exposures.

High ISO noise commonly first appears when you raise your camera's sensitivity setting above ISO 800. With Canon cameras, which are renowned for their good ISO noise characteristics, noise may become visible at ISO 1600, and is usually fairly noticeable at ISO 3200. At the H setting (ISO 52100 equivalent), noise is usually quite bothersome, which is why that lofty sensitivity rating is disabled by default and must be activated with ISO expansion using C.Fn-2. This kind of noise appears as a result of the amplification needed to increase the sensitivity of the sensor. While higher ISOs do pull details out of dark areas, they also amplify non-signal information randomly, creating noise.

A similar noisy phenomenon occurs during long time exposures, which allow more photons to reach the sensor, increasing your ability to capture a picture under low-light conditions. However, the longer exposures also increase the likelihood that some pixels will register random phantom photons, often because the longer an imager is "hot," the warmer it gets, and that heat can be mistaken for photons. There's also a special kind of noise that CMOS sensors like the one used in the T7i are potentially susceptible to. With a CCD, the entire signal is conveyed off the chip and funneled through a single amplifier and analog-to-digital conversion circuit. Any noise introduced there is, at least, consistent. CMOS imagers, on the other hand, contain millions of individual amplifiers and A/D converters, all working in unison. Because all these circuits don't necessarily process in precisely the same way all the time, they can introduce something called fixed-pattern noise into the image data.

Fortunately, Canon's electronics geniuses have done an exceptional job minimizing noise from all causes in the T7i. Even so, you might still want to apply the optional long exposure noise reduction. This type of noise reduction involves the T7i taking a second, blank exposure, and comparing the random pixels in that image with the photograph you just took. Pixels that coincide in the two represent noise and can safely be suppressed. This noise reduction system, called *dark frame subtraction,* effectively doubles the amount of time required to take a picture, and is used only for exposures longer than one second. Noise reduction can reduce the amount of detail in your picture, as some image information may be removed along with the noise. So, you might want to use this feature with moderation. Some types of images don't require noise reduction, because the grainy pattern tends to blend into the overall scene. To activate your T7i's long exposure noise reduction features, go to the Shooting 4 menu, as explained further in Chapter 8.

You can also apply noise reduction to a lesser extent using Photoshop and other image editors, and when converting RAW files to some other format, using your favorite RAW converter, or an industrial-strength product like Noise Ninja (www.picturecode.com) to wipe out noise after you've already taken the picture.

Making EV Changes

Sometimes you'll want more or less exposure than indicated by the T7i's metering system. Perhaps you want to underexpose to create a silhouette effect, or overexpose to produce a high-key look. It's easy to use the T7i's Exposure Compensation system to override the exposure recommendations, available in any Creative Zone mode except Manual. There are two ways to make exposure value (EV) changes with the Rebel T7i. One method is fast and a bit clumsy to use, especially if your fingers aren't well coordinated. The other method takes a few seconds longer, but can be done smoothly by the most fumble-fingered among us.

Fast EV Changes

In Tv and Av modes, activate the exposure meters by tapping the shutter release button. Then just hold down the AV button (located on the back, next to the upper-right corner of the LCD) and rotate the Main Dial to the right to make the image brighter (add exposure), and to the left to make the image darker (subtract exposure).

The exposure scale in the viewfinder and on the LCD monitor indicates the EV change you've made. The EV change you've made remains for the exposures that follow, until you manually zero out the EV setting with the AV button + Main Dial. EV changes are ignored when using M or any of the Basic Zone modes.

Slower EV Changes

If you find yourself not turning the Main Dial quickly enough after you tap the shutter release button, try the second method for making EV changes with the T7i. It can be a little slower, but gives you more time to dial in your EV adjustment. You also have the option of setting exposure bracketing at the same time:

1. Press the MENU button and navigate to the Expo. Comp./AEB entry on the Shooting 2 menu.

2. When the screen appears, use the touch screen or press the left/right directional buttons to add or subtract EV adjustment. The screen has helpful labels (Darker on the left and Brighter on the right) to make sure you're adding/subtracting when you really want to. (See Figure 4.15.) Note that you can also set exposure bracketing by rotating the Main Dial while viewing this screen. (See Figure 4.16.)

3. Press/Tap SET to confirm your choice.

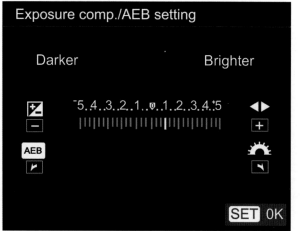

Figure 4.15
EV changes are displayed on the scale in the LCD when using the Shooting 2 menu.

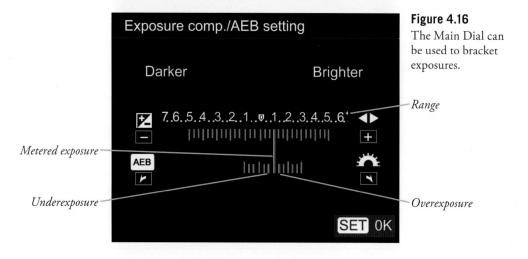

Figure 4.16
The Main Dial can be used to bracket exposures.

Range

Metered exposure

Underexposure

Overexposure

Bracketing

Bracketing is a method for shooting several consecutive exposures using different settings, as a way of improving the odds that one will be exactly right. Before digital cameras took over the universe, it was common to bracket exposures, shooting, say, a series of three photos at 1/125th second, but varying the f/stop from f/8 to f/11 to f/16. In practice, smaller than whole-stop increments were used for greater precision. Plus, it was just as common to keep the same aperture and vary the shutter speed, although in the days before electronic shutters, film cameras often had only whole increment shutter speeds available. Figure 4.17 shows a typical bracketed series.

Today, cameras like the T7i can bracket exposures much more precisely, and bracket white balance as well (using the WB Shift/Bkt entry found in the Shooting 3 menu and described in Chapter 8). While WB bracketing is sometimes used when getting color absolutely correct in the camera is important, autoexposure bracketing (AEB) is used much more often. When this feature is activated, the T7i takes three (and only three) consecutive photos: one at the metered "correct" exposure, one with less exposure, and one with more exposure, using an increment of your choice up to +/– 2 stops. (Choose between increments by setting C.Fn-1 to 0 [1/3 stop] or 1 [1/2 stop].) In Av mode, the shutter speed will change, while in Tv mode, the aperture speed will change.

Using AEB is trickier than it needs to be, but has been made more flexible than with some earlier Rebel models. With the T7i you can now choose to bracket only overexposures or underexposures— a very useful improvement!

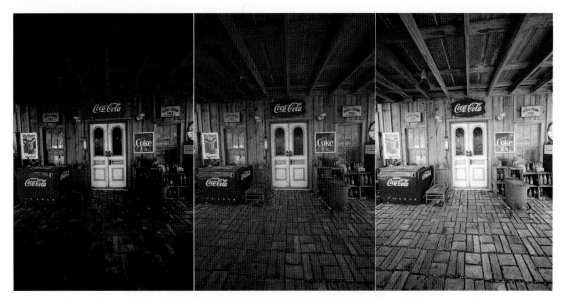

Figure 4.17 In this bracketed series, you can see underexposure (left), metered exposure (center), and overexposure (right).

Just follow these steps:

1. **Activate the Expo. Comp./AEB screen.** Press the MENU button and navigate to the Shooting 2 menu, where you'll find the Expo. Comp./AEB option. Choose SET to select this choice.

2. **Set the bracket range.** Rotate the Main Dial to spread out or contract the three bars to include the desired range you want to cover. For example, in Figure 4.18 (top), the red highlighted bars are separated from the center bar by a full f/stop, so the bracketing will produce one image at one stop *less* than the zero point (the large center bar), one at the zero point, and one at one stop more than that. Figure 4.18 (bottom) shows the bars more widely separated, for a bracketed set two stops under and two stops over the midpoint.

3. **Adjust zero point.** By default, the bracketing is zeroed around the center of the scale, which represents the correct exposure as metered by the T7i. But you might want to have your three bracketed shots all biased toward overexposure or underexposure. Perhaps you feel that the metered exposure will be too dark or too light, and you want the bracketed shots to lean in the other direction. Use the left/right directional buttons to move the bracket spread toward one end of the scale or the other. Figure 4.18 (top) shows the bracketing biased toward overexposure, whereas in 4.18 (bottom), the zero point is clustered around underexposure. (Actually, the exposure bar at left will be four stops under the metered exposure, the center bar two stops under, and the right bar at the metered value.)

NON-BRACKETING IS EXPOSURE COMPENSATION

When the three bracket indicators aren't separated, using the left/right directional buttons simply, in effect, adds or subtracts exposure compensation. You'll be shooting a "bracketed" set of one picture, with the zero point placed at the portion of the scale you indicated. Until you rotate the Main Dial to separate the three bracket indicators by at least one indicator, this screen just supplies EV adjustment. Also keep in mind that the increments shown will be either 1/3 stop or 1/2 stop, depending on how you've set C.Fn-1.

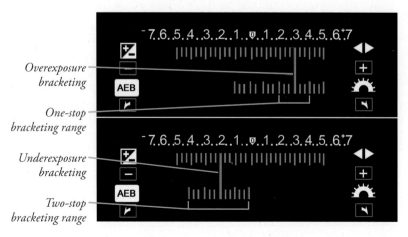

Overexposure bracketing

One-stop bracketing range

Underexposure bracketing

Two-stop bracketing range

Figure 4.18
Use the left/right directional buttons to bias the bracketing toward more or less exposure, and the Main Dial to set the bracket range.

4. **Confirm your choice.** Choose SET to enter the settings.

5. **Take your three photos.** You can use Single shooting mode to take the trio of pictures yourself, use the self-timer (which will expose all three pictures after the delay), or switch to Continuous shooting mode to take the three pictures in a burst.

6. **Monitor your shots.** As the images are captured, three indicators will appear on the exposure scale in the viewfinder, with one of them flashing for each bracketed photo, showing when the base exposure, underexposure, and overexposure are taken.

7. **Turn bracketing off when done.** Bracketing remains in effect when the set is taken so you can continue shooting bracketed exposures until you use the electronic flash, turn off the camera, or return to the menu to cancel bracketing. (Don't forget to press SET after you've zeroed out the bracketing parameters.)

> **NOTE**
>
> AEB is disabled when you're using Multi Shot Noise Reduction, taking long time exposures with the Bulb setting, or have enabled the Auto Lighting Optimizer in the Shooting 2 menu (in which case the optimizer will probably override and nullify bracketing).

Working with HDR

High dynamic range (HDR) photography is quite the rage these days, and entire books have been written on the subject. It's not really a new technique—film photographers have been combining multiple exposures for ages to produce a single image of, say, an interior room while maintaining detail in the scene visible through the windows.

Suppose you wanted to photograph a dimly lit room that had a bright window showing an outdoors scene. Proper exposure for the room might be on the order of 1/60th second at f/2.8 at ISO 200, while the outdoors scene probably would require f/11 at 1/400th second. That's almost a 7 EV step difference (approximately 7 f/stops) and well beyond the dynamic range of any digital camera, including the Canon T7i.

Until camera sensors gain much higher dynamic ranges (which may not be as far into the distant future as we think), special tricks like Active D-Lighting and HDR photography will remain basic tools. With the Canon T7i, you can create in-camera HDR exposures, or shoot HDR the old-fashioned way—with separate bracketed exposures that are later combined in a tool like Photomatix or Adobe's Merge to HDR Pro image-editing feature. I'm going to show you how to use both.

HDR Backlight Control

The T7i's in-camera HDR feature, available as a Special Scene option when the Mode Dial is in the SCN position, is simple, not particularly flexible, but still surprisingly effective in creating high dynamic range images. It's also remarkably easy to use. Although it combines only three images to create a single HDR photograph, and while it's not as good as the manual HDR method I'll describe in the section after this one, it's a *lot* faster. (You can also shoot HDR Movies, as I'll explain in Chapter 6.)

Figure 4.19 shows you a typical situation in which you might want to use this setting. In the original scene, it was impossible to capture both the interior of the covered bridge and the foliage that surrounded it. The HDR backlight control exposed three different images and combined them to produce the final shot in Figure 4.19. I'll show you how to use this mode next to preserve detail in both highlights and shadows.

Here are some tips for using this feature (these also apply to the Handheld Night Scene mode, which also merges multiple shots to create a single improved image):

- **Use a tripod if possible.** Because there may be some camera movement between the continuous shots, you'll get better results if you mount the T7i on a tripod.

- **Moving objects may produce ghosts.** In this case, there may be some *subject* motion between shots, producing "ghost" effects.

- **Misalignment.** If you *don't* use a tripod, this mode does a good job of realigning your multiple images when they are merged. However, it can't do a perfect job, particularly with repetitive patterns that are difficult for the camera's "brains" to sort out. Some misalignment is possible.

- **Unwanted cropping.** Because the processor needs to be able to shift each individual image slightly in any (or all) of four directions, it needs to crop the image slightly to trim out any non-image areas that result. Your final image will be slightly smaller than one shot in other modes.

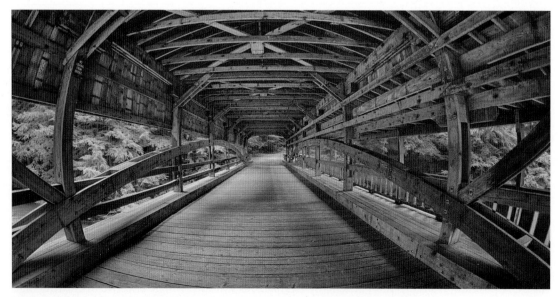

Figure 4.19 The T7i's HDR Backlight Control mode captures a full range of tones.

- **Can't use RAW or RAW+L.** Your image will be recorded as a Large JPEG only.
- **The process takes time.** Forget about firing off a large number of HDR Backlight Control shots in a row. After the T7i captures its three images, it takes a few seconds to process them and save your final image. Be patient.

In addition to the HDR Backlight Control Scene mode, the T7i also can produce HDR special effects when the Mode Dial is rotated to the Creative Filters position (see Figure 4.20):

- **Art Standard.** Offers a great deal of highlight and shadow detail, but with lower overall contrast and outlines accentuated, making the image look more like a painting. Saturation, bold outline, and brightness are adjusted to the default levels, and tonal range is lower in contrast.
- **Art Vivid.** Similar to Art Standard, but saturation is boosted to produce richer colors, and the bold outlines are not as strong, producing a poster-like effect.
- **Art Bold.** Even higher saturation than Art Vivid, with emphasized edge transitions, producing what Canon calls an "oil painting" effect.
- **Art Embossed.** Reduces saturation, darker tones, and lower contrast, and gives the image a faded, aged look. The edge transitions are brighter or darker to emphasize them.

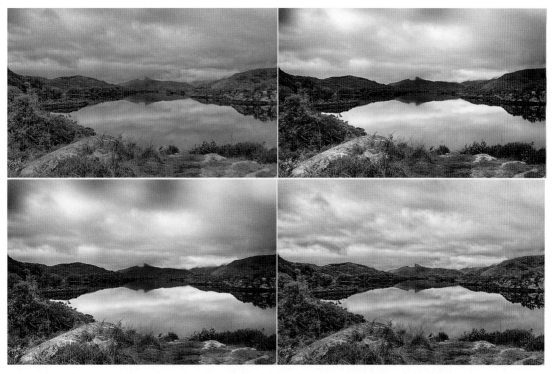

Figure 4.20 Top row (left to right): Art Standard, Art Vivid; bottom row: Art Bold, Art Embossed.

Bracketing and Merge to HDR

HDR (high dynamic range) photography was, for awhile, an incredibly popular fad. There are even entire books that do nothing but tell you how to shoot HDR images. Everywhere you looked there were overprocessed, garish HDR images that had little relationship to reality. I've been able to resist the temptation to overdo my landscape and travel photography (unlike the deliberately awful example I created for Figure 4.21). The phony-looking skies, the unnatural halos that appear at the edges of some objects, and the weird textures are usually a giveaway. My rule of thumb is that, if you can tell it's HDR, it's been done wrong—unless your intent was to show off what HDR can do.

The technique does have its uses, especially if done subtly, or as a special effect. That's what I was looking for when I shot Alastair Greene, guitarist for the Alan Parsons Project for Figure 4.22. I wanted an edgy, posterlike quality, and so applied HDR liberally, but with the hope that the effect might not be evident on first glance.

When you're using Merge to HDR Pro, a feature found in Adobe Photoshop (similar functions are available in other programs, including the Mac/PC utility Photomatix [www.hdrsoft.com; free to try, $99 to buy]), you'd take several pictures. As I mentioned earlier, one would be exposed for the shadows, one for the highlights, and perhaps one for the midtones. Then, you'd use the Merge to HDR command (or the equivalent in other software) to combine all the images into one HDR image that integrates the well-exposed sections of each version. You can use the EOS T7i's bracketing feature to produce those images.

The next steps show you how to combine the separate exposures into one merged high dynamic range image. The sample images at left in Figure 4.23 show the results you can get from a three-shot (manually) bracketed sequence.

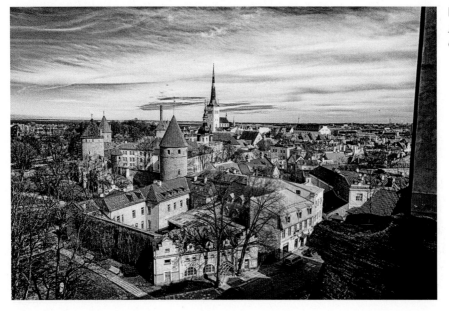

Figure 4.21
A deliberately over-cooked HDR photo.

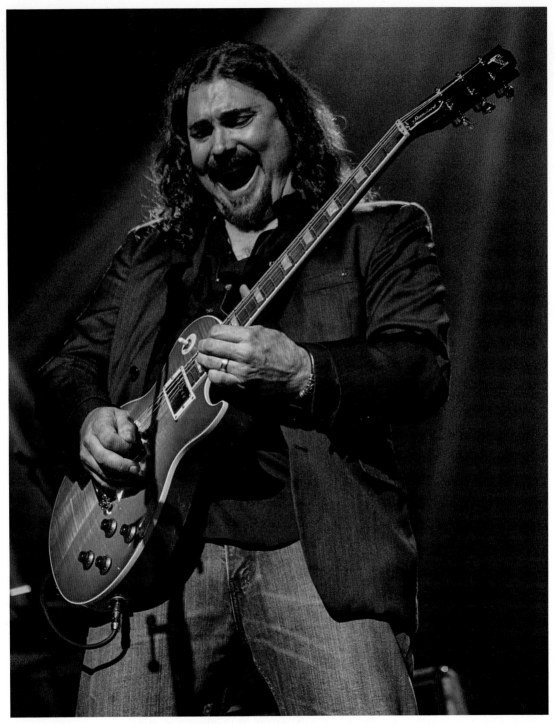

Figure 4.22 In this case, HDR added a desired posterlike effect.

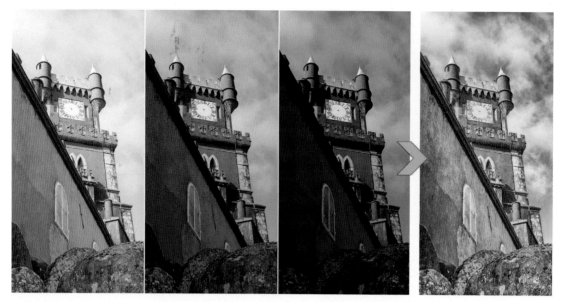

Figure 4.23 With three bracketed shots (left), you can end up with an extended dynamic range photo like the one at right.

The images should be as identical as possible, except for exposure. So, it's a good idea to mount the T7i on a tripod, use a remote release, and take all the exposures at once. Just follow these steps:

1. **Set up the camera.** Mount the T7i on a tripod.

2. **Choose an f/stop.** Set the camera for Manual exposure and select an aperture that will provide a correct exposure at your initial settings for the series of manually bracketed shots. *And then leave this adjustment alone!* You don't want the aperture to change for your series, as that would change the depth-of-field. You want the T7i to adjust exposure *only* using the shutter speed.

3. **Choose manual focus.** You don't want the focus to change between shots, so set the T7i to manual focus, and carefully focus your shot.

4. **Choose RAW exposures.** Set the camera to take RAW files, which will give you the widest range of tones in your images.

5. **Take your bracketed set.** If you use a remote control, press the button on the remote, or, carefully press the shutter release or use the self-timer and take the set of bracketed exposures, adjusting the shutter speed manually. Try spacing your four shots one f/stop apart.

6. **Continue with the Merge to HDR Pro steps listed next.** You can also use a different program, such as Photomatix, if you know how to use it.

The next steps show you how to combine the separate exposures into one merged high dynamic range image.

1. **Copy your images to your computer.** If you use an application to transfer the files to your computer, make sure it does not make any adjustments to brightness, contrast, or exposure. You want the real raw information for Merge to HDR Pro to work with.

2. **Activate Merge to HDR Pro.** Choose File > Automate > Merge to HDR Pro.

3. **Select the photos to be merged.** Use the Browse feature to locate and select your photos to be merged. You'll note a check box that can be used to automatically align the images if they were not taken with the camera mounted on a rock-steady support. This will adjust for any slight movement of the camera that might have occurred when you changed exposure settings.

4. **Choose parameters (optional).** The first time you use Merge to HDR Pro, you can let the program work with its default parameters. Once you've played with the feature a few times, you can read the Adobe help files and learn more about the options than I can present in this non-software-oriented camera guide.

5. **Click OK.** The merger begins.

6. **Save.** Once HDR merge has done its thing, save the file to your computer.

If you do everything correctly, you'll end up with a photo like the one shown at right in Figure 4.23.

What if you don't have the opportunity, inclination, or skills to create several images at different exposures, as described? If you shoot in RAW format, you can still use Merge to HDR, working with a *single* original image file. What you do is import the image into Photoshop several times, using Adobe Camera Raw to create multiple copies of the file at different exposure levels.

For example, you'd create one copy that's too dark, so the shadows lose detail, but the highlights are preserved. Create another copy with the shadows intact and allow the highlights to wash out. Then, you can use Merge to HDR to combine the two and end up with a finished image that has the extended dynamic range you're looking for. (This concludes the image-editing portion of the chapter. We now return you to our alternate sponsor: photography.)

Fixing Exposures with Histograms

Your T7i's histograms are a simplified display represented by the numbers of pixels at each of 256 brightness levels (although the camera actually captures many more levels in its 14-bit image files). The resulting graph produces an interesting mountain range effect. As I mentioned in Chapter 3, the T7i lets you designate either an RGB version or brightness only version of the histogram as your "main" histogram display, using the Histogram Display entry in the Playback 3 menu, and shown at left and right in Figure 4.24. Or, you can display both types at once, as seen in Figure 4.25, by scrolling down in the main histogram display screen using the up/down directional buttons. The T7i also provides a "live" histogram on the screen as you frame and shoot when using Live View mode.

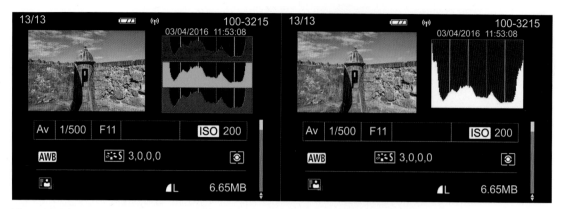

Figure 4.24 Shooting information display, with RGM histogram (left); Brightness Histogram display (right).

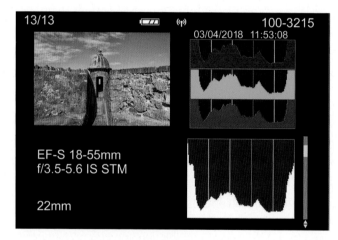

Figure 4.25
Both types of histograms can be viewed at once during playback.

Although your camera may offer separate charts for brightness and the red, green, and blue channels, when you first start using histograms, you'll want to concentrate on the brightness histogram, which represents a composite of all red, green, and blue tones using a white histogram. Each vertical line in the graph represents the proportionate number of pixels in the image for each brightness value, from 0 (black) on the left to 255 (white) on the right. The vertical axis measures that proportion of pixels at each level.

Tonal Range

Histograms help you adjust the tonal range of an image, the span of dark to light tones, from a complete absence of brightness (black) to the brightest possible tone (white), and all the middle tones in between. Because all values for tones fall into a continuous spectrum between black and white, it's easiest to think of a photo's tonality in terms of a black-and-white or grayscale image, even though you're capturing tones in three separate color layers of red, green, and blue.

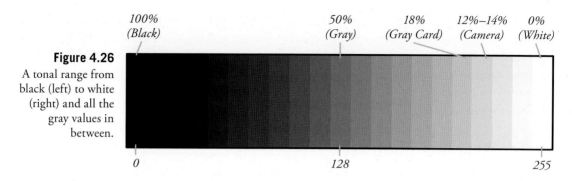

Figure 4.26

A tonal range from black (left) to white (right) and all the gray values in between.

Because your images are digital, the tonal "spectrum" isn't really continuous: it's divided into discrete steps that represent the different tones that can be captured. Figure 4.26 may help you understand this concept. The gray steps shown range from 100-percent gray (black) at the left, to 0-percent gray (white) at the right, with 20 gray steps in all (plus white).

Along the bottom of the chart are the digital values from 0 to 255 recorded by your sensor for an image with 8 bits per channel. (8 bits of red, 8 bits of green, and 8 bits of blue equal a 24-bit, full-color image.) Any black captured would be represented by a value of 0, the brightest white by 255, and the midtones would be clustered around the 128 marker.

Grayscale images (which we call black-and-white photos) are easy to understand. Or, at least, that's what we think. When we look at a black-and-white image, we think we're seeing a continuous range of tones from black to white, and all the grays in between. But, that's not exactly true. The blackest black in any photo isn't a true black, because *some* light is always reflected from the surface of the print, and if viewed on a screen, the deepest black is only as dark as the least-reflective area a computer monitor can produce. The whitest white isn't a true white, either, because even the lightest areas of a print absorb some light (only a mirror reflects close to all the light that strikes it), and, when viewing on a computer monitor, the whites are limited by the brightness of the display's LCD or LED picture elements. Lacking darker blacks and brighter, whiter whites, that continuous set of tones doesn't cover the full grayscale tonal range.

The full scale of tones becomes useful when you have an image that has large expanses of shades that change gradually from one level to the next, such as areas of sky, water, or walls. Think of a picture taken of a group of campers around a campfire. Since the light from the fire is striking them directly in the face, there aren't many shadows on the campers' faces. All the tones that make up the *features* of the people around the fire are compressed into one end of the brightness spectrum—the lighter end.

Yet, there's more to this scene than faces. Behind the campers are trees, rocks, and perhaps a few animals that have emerged from the shadows to see what is going on. These are illuminated by the softer light that bounces off the surrounding surfaces. If your eyes become accustomed to the reduced illumination, you'll find that there is a wealth of detail in these shadow images.

This campfire scene would be a nightmare to reproduce faithfully under any circumstances. If you are an experienced photographer, you are probably already wincing at what is called a *high-contrast* lighting situation. Some photos may be high in contrast when there are fewer tones and they are all bunched up at limited points in the scale. In a low-contrast image, there are more tones, but they are spread out so widely that the image looks flat. Your digital camera can show you the relationship between these tones using a *histogram.*

Histograms and Contrast

Although histograms are most often used to fine-tune exposure, you can glean other information from them, such as the relative contrast of the image. Figure 4.27 (top) shows a histogram representing an image having normal contrast. In such an image, most of the pixels are spread across the image, with a healthy distribution of tones throughout the midtone section of the graph. That large peak at the right side of the graph represents all those light tones in the sky. A normal-contrast image you shoot may have less sky area, and less of a peak at the right side, but notice that very few pixels hug the right edge of the histogram, indicating that the lightest tones are not being clipped because they are off the chart.

With a lower-contrast image, like the one shown in Figure 4.27 (center), the basic shape of the previous histogram will remain recognizable, but gradually will be compressed together to cover a smaller area of the gray spectrum. The squished shape of the histogram is caused by all the grays in the original image being represented by a limited number of gray tones in a smaller range of the scale.

Instead of the darkest tones of the image reaching into the black end of the spectrum and the whitest tones extending to the lightest end, there is a small gap at either end. Consequently, the blackest

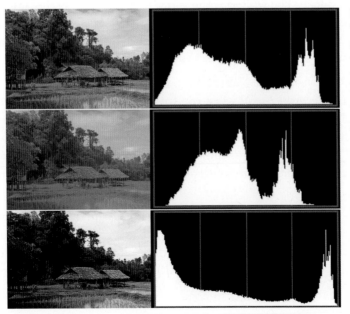

Figure 4.27
Top: The image has fairly normal contrast, even though there is a peak of light tones at the right side representing the sky. Center: The low-contrast image has all the tones squished into one section of the grayscale. Bottom: A high-contrast image produces a histogram in which the tones are spread out.

areas of the scene are now represented by a light gray, and the whites by a somewhat lighter gray. The overall contrast of the image is reduced. Because all the darker tones are actually a middle gray or lighter, the scene in this version of the photo appears lighter as well.

Going in the other direction, increasing the contrast of an image produces a histogram like the one shown in Figure 4.27 (bottom). In this case, the tonal range is now spread over the entire width of the chart, but, except for the bright sky (which you can see peaks at right), there is not much variation in the middle tones; the mountain "peaks" are not very high. When you stretch the grayscale in both directions like this, the darkest tones become darker (that may not be possible) and the lightest tones become lighter (ditto). In fact, shades that might have been gray before can change to black or white as they are moved toward either end of the scale.

The effect of increasing contrast may be to move some tones off either end of the scale altogether, while spreading the remaining grays over a smaller number of locations on the spectrum. That's exactly the case in the example shown. The number of possible tones is smaller and the image appears harsher.

Understanding Histograms

The important thing to remember when working with the histogram display in your T7i is that changing the exposure does *not* change the contrast of an image. The curves illustrated in the previous three examples remain exactly the same shape when you increase or decrease exposure. I repeat: The proportional distribution of grays shown in the histogram doesn't change when exposure changes; it is neither stretched nor compressed. However, the tones as a whole are moved toward one end of the scale or the other, depending on whether you're increasing or decreasing exposure. You'll be able to see that in some illustrations that follow.

So, as you reduce exposure, tones gradually move to the black end (and off the scale), while the reverse is true when you increase exposure. The contrast within the image is changed only to the extent that some of the tones can no longer be represented when they are moved off the scale.

To change the *contrast* of an image, you must do one of four things:

- **Change the T7i's contrast setting** using the menu system. You'll find these adjustments in your camera's Picture Styles, as explained in Chapter 8.

- **Use your camera's tone "booster."** The Highlight Tone Priority and Auto Lighting Optimizer features, described in Chapter 8, can also adjust contrast.

- **Alter the contrast of the scene itself,** for example, by using a fill light or reflectors to add illumination to shadows that are too dark.

- **Attempt to adjust contrast in post-processing** using your image editor or RAW file converter. You may use features such as Levels or Curves (in Photoshop, Photoshop Elements, and many other image editors), or work with HDR software to cherry-pick the best values in shadows and highlights from multiple images.

Of the four of these, the third—changing the contrast of the scene—is the most desirable, because attempting to fix contrast by fiddling with the tonal values is unlikely to be a perfect remedy. However, adding a little contrast can be successful because you can discard some tones to make the image more contrasty. However, the opposite is much more difficult. An overly contrasty image rarely can be fixed, because you can't add information that isn't there in the first place.

What you *can* do is adjust the exposure so that the tones *that are already present in the scene* are captured correctly. Figure 4.28 (top) shows the histogram for an image that is badly underexposed. You can guess from the shape of the histogram that many of the dark tones to the left of the graph have been clipped off. There's plenty of room on the right side for additional pixels to reside without having them become overexposed. So, you can increase the exposure (either by changing the f/stop or shutter speed, or by adding an EV value) to produce the corrected histogram shown in Figure 4.28 (center).

Conversely, if your histogram looks like the one shown in Figure 4.28 (bottom), with bright tones pushed off the right edge of the chart, you have an overexposed image, and you can correct it by reducing exposure. In addition to the histogram, the T7i has its Highlights feature, which shows areas that are overexposed with flashing tones (often called "blinkies") in the review screen. Depending on the importance of this "clipped" detail, you can adjust exposure or leave it alone. For example, if all the dark-coded areas in the review are in a background that you care little about, you can forget about them and not change the exposure, but if such areas appear in facial details of your subject, you may want to make some adjustments.

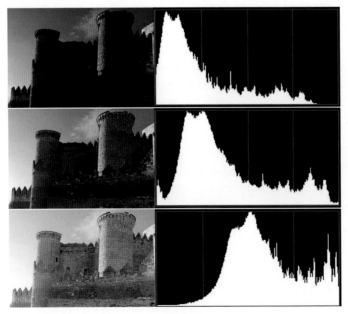

Figure 4.28

Top: A histogram of an underexposed image may look like this. Center: Adding exposure will produce a histogram like this one. Bottom: A histogram of an overexposed image will show clipping at the right side.

In working with histograms, your goal should be to have all the tones in an image spread out between the edges, with none clipped off at the left and right sides. Underexposing (to preserve highlights) should be done only as a last resort, because retrieving the underexposed shadows in your image editor will frequently increase the noise, even if you're working with RAW files. A better course of action is to expose for the highlights, but, when the subject matter makes it practical, fill in the shadows with additional light, using reflectors, fill flash, or other techniques rather than allowing them to be seriously underexposed.

The more you work with histograms, the more useful they become. One of the first things that histogram veterans notice is that it's possible to overexpose one channel even if the overall exposure appears to be correct. For example, flower photographers soon discover that it's really difficult to get a good picture of a rose. The exposure and luminance histogram may look okay—but there's no detail in the rose's petals, as you can see at left in Figure 4.29. Looking at the RGB histograms can show why: the red channel is probably blown out. If you look at the red histogram, you'll probably see a peak at the right edge that indicates that highlight information has been lost. In fact, the green channel may be blown, too, and so the green parts of the flower also lack detail. Only the blue channel's histogram would typically be entirely contained within the boundaries of the chart. (See Figure 4.29, right.)

Any of the primary channels (red, green, or blue) can blow out all by themselves, although bright reds seem to be the most common problem area. More difficult to diagnose are overexposed tones in one of the "in-between" hues on the color wheel. Overexposed yellows (which are very common) will be shown by blowouts in *both* the red and green channels. Too-bright cyans will manifest as excessive blue and green highlights, while overexposure in the red and blue channels reduces detail in magenta colors. As you gain experience, you'll be able to see exactly how anomalies in the RGB channels translate into poor highlights and murky shadows.

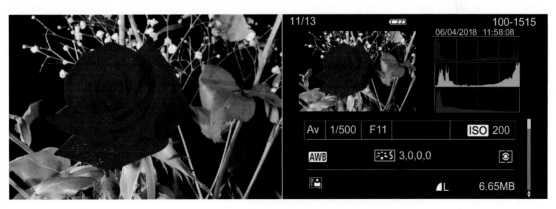

Figure 4.29 There is no detail in the rose's petals (left). Both the red and green channels are clipped on the right side of the histogram (right).

The only way to correct for color channel blowouts is to reduce exposure. As I mentioned earlier, you might want to consider filling in the shadows with additional light to keep them from becoming too dark when you decrease exposure. In practice, you'll want to monitor the red channel most closely, followed by the blue channel, and slightly decrease exposure to see if that helps. Because of the way our eyes perceive color, we are more sensitive to variations in green, so green channel blowouts are less of a problem, unless your main subject is heavily colored in that hue. If you plan on photographing a frog hopping around on your front lawn, you'll want to be extra careful to preserve detail in the green channel, using bracketing or other exposure techniques outlined in this chapter.

While you can often recover poorly exposed photos in your image editor, your best bet is to arrive at the correct exposure in the camera, minimizing the tweaks that you have to make in post-processing.

Basic Zone Modes

The final factor in the exposure equation is one that your T7i offers little control over: Basic Zone modes. Your Canon Rebel T7i includes Basic Zone shooting modes that can automatically make all the basic settings needed for certain types of shooting situations, such as Portraits, Landscapes, Close-ups, Sports, Night Portraits, and "No-Flash zone" pictures. They are especially useful when you suddenly encounter a picture-taking opportunity and don't have time to decide exactly which Creative Zone mode you want to use. Instead, you can spin the Mode Dial to the appropriate Basic Zone mode and fire away, knowing that, at least, you have a fighting chance of getting a good or usable photo.

Basic Zone modes are also helpful when you're just learning to use your T7i. Once you've learned how to operate your camera, you'll probably prefer one of the Creative Zone modes that provide more control over shooting options. The Basic Zone scene modes may give you few options or none at all. The AF mode, drive mode, and metering mode are all preset for you. However, you'll see a screen that shows you which of the settings you can change. I'll describe those options in the next section. For now, I'm going to tell you about each of the Basic Zone modes.

Here are the modes available directly from the Mode Dial:

- **Scene Intelligent Auto.** All the photographer has to do in this mode is press the shutter release button. Every other decision is made by the camera's electronics. The "Scene Intelligent" part comes from the T7i analysis of your scene so it can apply particular scene types, such as Portrait or Close-up (both described later) as appropriate to give you the best exposure/rendition of your image. The mode chosen is displayed in the upper-left corner of the LCD monitor as you shoot. It's not particularly important for you to note which mode is selected for you by Scene Intelligent Auto; it's supposed to be an *automatic* mode. If you do want to memorize the 29 different icons displayed, you'll find them on pages 196 and 206 of the T7i manuals, respectively.

- **Flash Off.** Absolutely prevents the flash from flipping up and firing, which you might want in some situations, such as religious ceremonies, museums, classical music concerts, and your double-naught spy activities.

- **Creative Auto.** Similar to Scene Intelligent Auto, Creative Auto, except that, like the scene modes described next, CA allows you to change some parameters. I'll describe Creative Auto in an upcoming section.

- **Portrait.** This mode tends to use wider f/stops and faster shutter speeds, providing blurred backgrounds and images with no camera shake. If you hold down the shutter release, the T7i will take a continuous sequence of photos, which can be useful in capturing fleeting expressions in portrait situations. Skin tones and hair are portrayed in a softer, more flattering way.

- **Landscape.** The T7i tries to use smaller f/stops for more depth-of-field, and boosts saturation slightly for richer colors. The built-in flash is disabled, but an attached and powered-up external Speedlite *will* fire.

- **Close-Up.** This mode is similar to the Portrait setting, with wider f/stops to isolate your close-up subjects, and high shutter speeds to eliminate the camera shake that's accentuated at close focusing distances. However, if you have your camera mounted on a tripod or are using an image-stabilized (IS) lens, you might want to use the Creative Zone Aperture-priority (Av) mode instead, so you can specify a smaller f/stop with additional depth-of-field.

- **Sports.** In this mode, the T7i tries to use high shutter speeds to freeze action, switches to continuous shooting to allow taking a quick sequence of pictures with one press of the shutter release, and uses AI Servo AF to continually refocus as your subject moves around in the frame. You can find more information on autofocus options in Chapter 5.

With the Mode Dial in the SCN position, you can also choose additional Special Scene modes. Rotate the Mode Dial to SCN, press the SET button, and then the left/right directional buttons to select any of these Special Scene modes:

- **Kids.** Applies continuous focusing to follow the movement of frenetic children, and continuous shooting to grab a continuous stream of still photos. Skin tones are adjusted to look vibrant and healthy. You can place the center AF point in the viewfinder over your main subject and press the shutter release halfway. The T7i will refocus as required to track the child's motion, and you'll hear a beep that indicates that refocusing is taking place. If the camera cannot achieve sharp focus, the focus confirmation indicator in the viewfinder will blink.

- **Food.** Rich colors and higher contrast in this mode make your food pictures look vivid and appetizing.

- **Candlelight.** This mode retains the warm tones typically seen in photos illuminated by candle-light. The built-in flash is disabled, but if you have an external Speedlite connected and powered up, it will fire anyway and spoil your picture. Turn it off!

- **Night Portrait.** Combines flash with ambient light to produce an image that is mainly illuminated by the flash, but the background is exposed by the available light. This mode uses longer exposures, so a tripod, monopod, or IS lens is a must.

■ **Handheld Night Scene.** The T7i takes four continuous shots and combines them to produce a well-exposed image with reduced camera shake.

■ **HDR Backlight Control.** The T7i takes three continuous shots at different exposures and combines them to produce a single image with improved detail in the highlights and shadows.

Making Changes in Basic Zone Modes

I've previously described how to use the Quick Control screen when working with Creative Zone modes to change many settings, such as ISO, shutter speed, aperture, and other parameters. When using Basic Zone modes, your options are different. In each case, you can activate the Quick Control screen by pressing the Quick Control button. Then, one of several different screens will appear on your LCD.

Scene Intelligent Auto/Auto (No Flash)

In either of these modes, autofocus, brightness, flash, and color tones are set for you based on the particular Scene mode the camera selects. Press the Q button, and a screen appears that allows you to navigate to the Drive mode and Flash Firing icons at the bottom to change these two parameters:

■ **Shooting mode.** In both Scene Intelligent Auto and Auto (No Flash) modes, Single Shooting is the default. You can also select High Speed Continuous Shooting, Low Speed Continuous Shooting, and 10-second, 2-second, or Continuous self-timers.

■ **Flash Firing.** In Scene Intelligent Auto mode, automatic firing is the default. You can also choose Built-In Flash On (Fires always), or Flash Off. In Auto (No Flash) mode, Flash Off is the default value and cannot be changed.

Creative Auto Mode

When the Mode Dial is set to Creative Auto, a screen like the one shown in Figure 4.30 appears. It shows the current settings for CA. The parameters include:

■ **Ambience.** Select ambience effects, plus Standard.

■ **Background blur.** Allows you to increase/decrease the blurriness of the background of your images by adjusting the aperture and depth-of-field.

■ **Drive mode.** You can select from any of the camera's Drive modes.

■ **Flash mode.** Choose the behavior of the electronic flash.

■ **Informational display.** Shows ISO setting, battery status, image quality, and number of exposures remaining.

■ **Q Button.** Tap this icon on the touch screen to produce the Quick Control menu. You can also press the physical Q button located to the right of the LCD monitor.

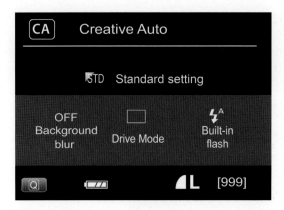

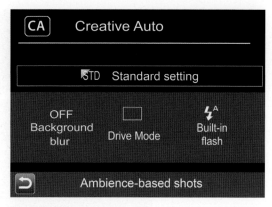

Figure 4.30 Creative Auto screen.

Figure 4.31 Quick Control screen in Creative Auto mode.

You can proceed from the main screen to the Quick Control menu for Creative Auto by pressing/tapping the Q button or Q icon. You'll then be presented with a screen like the one shown in Figure 4.31. Tap the touch screen or use the directional buttons to move from Ambience (STD Standard Setting is shown in the figure), to Background Blur, Drive Mode, or Flash Mode. As you highlight each of the four, you can press the SET button to make an adjustment.

■ **Ambience.** Highlight Ambience and press SET and a list of Ambience-based options appear. Use the up/down controls to select the "ambience" setting you want. Ambience is a type of picture style that adjusts parameters like sharpness or color richness to produce a particular look.

   • Select from among: Standard, Vivid, Soft, Warm, Intense, Cool, Brighter, Darker, or Monochrome.

   • If you've chosen something other than Standard (which cannot be modified), press the SET button to produce a screen like the one in Figure 4.32.

   • You can then rotate the Main Dial, use the left/right directional buttons to change the effect to Low, Standard, or Strong. With the Monochrome ambience setting, however, your choices are Blue, B/W, and Sepia. Press the SET button to confirm and exit.

■ **Background Blur.** When you highlight the Background Blur section, which is set to Off by default, you can rotate the Main Dial or use the left/right directional buttons to select blurred (the left side of the scale) or sharp (the right side). The T7i will try to use a larger f/stop to reduce depth-of-field and blur the background, or a smaller f/stop and increased depth-of-field to sharpen the background.

■ **Drive/Flash Modes.** Highlight either of these settings, and press the SET button to pop up their respective adjustment screens. In these screens, you can rotate the Main Dial to change among any of various drive modes or switch among the available flash modes (Flash On, Flash Off, and Auto Flash).

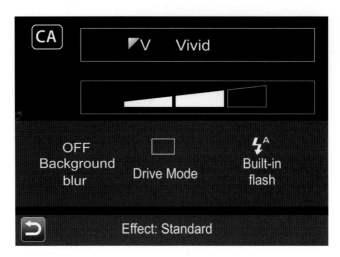

Figure 4.32
Adjusting ambience Vivid setting.

Find your desired ambience in Table 4.2 and set using a screen like the one shown in Figure 4.32.

Table 4.2 Selecting Ambience

Ambience Setting	Effect
Standard	This is the customized set of parameters for each Basic Zone mode, each tailored specifically for Portrait, Landscape, Close-Up, Sports, or other mode.
Vivid	Produces a look that is slightly sharper and with richer colors for the relevant Basic Zone mode.
Soft	Reduced sharpness for adult portraits, flowers, children, and pets.
Warm	Warmer, soft tones. An alternative setting for portraits and other subjects that you want to appear both soft and warm.
Intense	Darker tones with increased contrast to emphasize your subject. This setting is great for portraits of men.
Cool	Darker, cooler tones. Use with care on human subjects, which aren't always flattered by the icier look this setting can produce.
Brighter	Overall lighter image with less contrast.
Darker	Produces a darker image.
Monochrome	Choose from black-and-white, sepia, or blue (cyanotype) toning.

PREVIEW AMBIENCE

If you set ambience in Live View mode, the T7i will provide a preview image that simulates the effect your ambience setting will have on the finished image.

Other Basic Zone Modes

When you select one of the other Basic Zone modes, your choices may include the options listed in Table 4.3. When viewing the screen for a Basic Zone mode, the display lists the current settings for each of the parameters you can adjust. For example, the Kids and Sports screens indicate that High Speed Continuous drive mode is automatically activated (and you can change these to another drive mode, if you like). Other Scene mode screens will tell you when flash is deactivated. Food and Candlelight Scene modes allow adjusting color along a scale from cool to warm.

Table 4.3 Basic Zone Adjustments

Mode	Brightness	Drive Mode	Built-in Flash	Color Tone
Scene Modes				
Portrait	Yes	Yes	Yes	No
Landscape	Yes	Yes	No	No
Close-up	Yes	Yes	Yes	No
Sports	Yes	Yes	No	No
Special Scene Modes				
Group Photo	Yes	Yes	Yes	No
Kids	Yes	Yes	Yes	No
Food	Yes	Yes	Yes	Yes
Candlelight	Yes	Yes	No	Yes
Night Portrait	Yes	Yes	No	No
Handheld Night Scene	Yes	Yes	Yes	No
HDR Backlight Control	No	Yes	No	No

When the mode dial is set to Creative Filters, you can select special effects filters, which are similar to Scene modes (and have their own adjustable parameters). The available filters and their adjustments are listed in Table 4.4. The HDR Effects options are similar to those found in the HDR Backlight Control Scene mode.

Table 4.4 Special Effects Filters

Filter	Effect	Drive Mode	Built-in Flash	Other
Grainy B/W	Image converted to grainy black-and-white	Yes	Yes	Contrast: Low, Standard, High
Soft Focus	Blurring added	Yes	Yes	Soft Focus: Low, Standard, High
Fish-eye Effect	Extreme barrel distortion applied	Yes	Yes	Effect: Low, Standard, Strong
Water Painting	Watercolor art	Yes	Yes	Color Density: Light, Standard, Deep
Toy Camera	Vignetting and cheap plastic lens look	Yes	Yes	Color Tone: Cool, Standard, Warm
Miniature Effect	Scale model look	Yes	Yes	Focus area adjustable only in Live View mode
HDR Art Standard	Low contrast painting	Yes	No	
HDR Art Vivid	Increased saturation	Yes	No	
HDR Art Bold	Vivid oil painting effect	Yes	No	
HDR Art Embossed	Faded old picture effect	Yes	No	

Mastering the Mysteries of Autofocus

Capturing a compelling photograph involves a lot more than just correct exposure. The right tonal range, proper white balance, good color, and other factors all can help elevate your image from good to exceptional. But one of the most important and, sometimes, the most frustrating aspects of shooting with a highly automated—yet fully adjustable—camera like the T7i is achieving sharp focus. Your camera has lots of AF controls and options, and new users and veterans alike can quickly become confused. In this chapter, I'm going to clear up the mysteries of autofocus and show you exactly how to use your T7i's AF features to their fullest. I'll even tell you when to abandon the autofocus system and turn to the ancient art of manual focus, too.

Much of the material in this chapter applies to conventional shooting, using the optical viewfinder, with Creative Zone modes. Autofocus is selected for you automatically when using Scene or Creative Filters modes, and focus during live view shooting has some wrinkles of its own that I'll address in Chapter 6.

How Focus Works

This section describes the differences between contrast detection and phase detection autofocus, and details how linear and cross-type AF sensors work in the T7i's advanced focusing system. Even those who are familiar with these concepts should still read this section carefully, because Canon has made some revolutionary changes in AF with the introduction of its Dual Pixel CMOS AF sensor design in which every single pixel used for autofocus is split into two photodiodes that can be used to provide advanced autofocus features in Live View and Movie modes.

Although Canon added autofocus capabilities in the 1980s, back in the day of film cameras, prior to that focusing was always done manually. Honest. Even though viewfinders were bigger and brighter than they are today, special focusing screens, magnifiers, and other gadgets were often used to help the photographer achieve correct focus. Imagine what it must have been like to focus manually under demanding, fast-moving conditions such as sports photography.

Manual focusing was problematic because our eyes and brains have poor memory for correct focus, which is why your eye doctor must shift back and forth between sets of lenses and ask "Does that look sharper—or was it sharper before?" in determining your correct prescription. Similarly, manual focusing involves jogging the focus ring back and forth as you go from almost in focus, to sharp focus, to almost focused again. The little clockwise and counterclockwise arcs decrease in size until you've zeroed in on the point of correct focus. What you're looking for is the image with the most contrast between the edges of elements in the image.

The camera also looks for these contrast differences among pixels to determine relative sharpness. There are two ways that sharp focus is determined: phase detection and contrast detection. The camera also looks for these contrast differences among pixels to determine relative sharpness. To get the most from your camera, you really need to understand both. We'll start with the easier of the two: contrast detection.

Contrast Detection

Contrast detection is a slower mode and was used exclusively by Canon dSLRs in Live View and Movie modes until relatively recently, when Canon added a small number of special pixels to the sensor of its most recent cameras. That small number allowed a limited type of phase detection autofocus. The Dual Pixel CMOS AF used by the Canon T7i goes much further, as I'll explain later in this chapter. To appreciate the innovation, you need to understand traditional contrast detection first.

The relatively slow contrast detection method was necessary because, to allow live viewing of the sensor image, the camera's mirror has to be flipped up out of the way so that the illumination from the lens can continue through the open shutter to the sensor. Your view through the viewfinder is obstructed, of course, and there is no partially silvered mirror to reflect some light down to the autofocus sensors. So, an alternate means of autofocus must be used in Live View, and that method is *contrast detection*. That is, until CMOS AF was introduced, a new feature enabled by enhanced sensor technology which allows more robust on-sensor phase detection.

Contrast detection is a bit easier to understand and is illustrated by Figure 5.1, which uses an extreme enlargement of a shot of some wood siding (actually a 19th century outhouse). At top in the figure, the transitions between pixels are soft and blurred. When the image is brought into focus (bottom), the transitions are sharp and clear. Although this example is a bit exaggerated so you can see the results on the printed page, it's easy to understand that when maximum contrast in a subject is achieved, it can be deemed to be in sharp focus.

Figure 5.1
Focus in contrast detection mode evaluates the increase in contrast in the edges of subjects, starting with a blurry image (top) and producing a sharp, contrasty image (bottom).

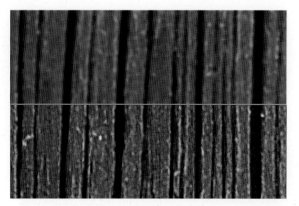

As I noted, contrast detection is used in Live View and Movie mode, even when Dual Pixel CMOS AF is also active. (In effect, you get two AF systems from one sensor.) Contrast detection works best and is very accurate with static subjects, but it is inherently slower and not well suited for tracking moving objects. Contrast detection works less well than phase detection in dim light, because its accuracy is determined by its ability to detect variations in brightness and contrast. You'll find that contrast detection works better with faster lenses, too, because larger lens openings admit more light that can be used by the sensor to measure contrast.

Phase Detection

Like all digital SLRs that use an optical viewfinder and mirror system to preview an image (that is, when not in Live View mode), the Canon T7i calculates focus using what is called a *passive phase detection* system. It's passive in the sense that the ambient illumination in a scene (or that illumination augmented with a focus-assist beam) is used to determine correct focus. (An *active* phase detection system might use a laser, sonar, or other special signal. In the photographic realm, only a few rare models—including one ancient system from Polaroid—resorted to such tactics.)

Parts of the image from two opposite sides of the lens are directed down to the floor of the camera's mirror box, where an autofocus sensor array resides; the rest of the illumination from the lens bounces upward toward the optical viewfinder system and the autoexposure sensors. Figure 5.2 is a wildly over-simplified illustration that may help you visualize what is happening.

SIMPLIFICATION MADE OVERLY SIMPLE

To reduce the complexity of the diagram, it doesn't show the actual path of the light passing through the lens, as it converges to the point of focus. That point is either the viewfinder screen when the mirror is down or the sensor plane when the mirror is flipped up and the shutter has opened. Nor does it show the path of the light directed to the autoexposure sensor. Only two of the pairs of autofocus microlenses are shown, and greatly enlarged so you can see their approximate position. All we're concerned about here is how light reaches the autofocus sensor.

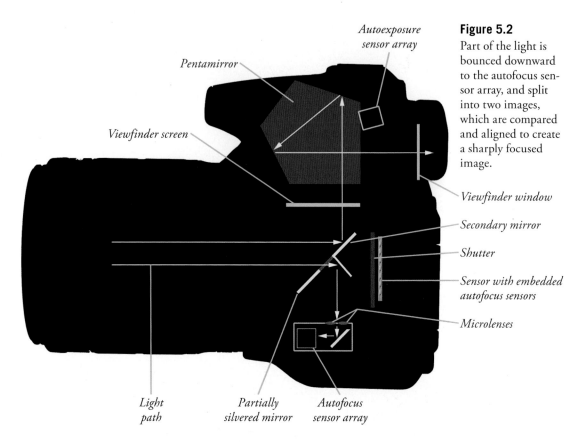

Figure 5.2

Part of the light is bounced downward to the autofocus sensor array, and split into two images, which are compared and aligned to create a sharply focused image.

Autoexposure sensor array

Pentamirror

Viewfinder screen

Viewfinder window

Secondary mirror

Shutter

Sensor with embedded autofocus sensors

Microlenses

Light path

Partially silvered mirror

Autofocus sensor array

As light emerges from the rear element of the lens, most of it is reflected upward toward the focusing screen, where the relative sharp focus (or lack of it) is displayed (and which can be used to evaluate manual focus). It then bounces off two more reflective surfaces in the pentamirror viewfinder (in the T7i; other cameras may use a *pentaprism* system instead) emerging at the optical viewfinder correctly oriented left/right and up/down. (The image emerges from the lens reversed.) Some of the illumination is directed to the autoexposure sensor at the top of the pentaprism housing.

A small portion of the illumination passes through the partially silvered center of the main mirror, and is directed downward to the autofocus sensor array, which includes 45 separate autofocus "detectors." Conceptually, these function as shown in Figure 5.3, another simplified illustration. The illumination arrives from opposite sides of the lens surface and is directed through separate microlenses, producing two half images. These images are compared with each other, much like (actually, *exactly* like) a two-window rangefinder used in surveying, weaponry, and non-SLR cameras like the venerable Leica M film models.

When the image is out of focus—or out of phase—as in Figure 5.4 (top), the two halves, each representing a slightly different view from opposite sides of the lens, don't line up. Sharp focus is achieved when the images are "in phase," and aligned, as in Figure 5.4 (bottom).

Figure 5.3

In phase detection, parts of an image are split in two and compared.

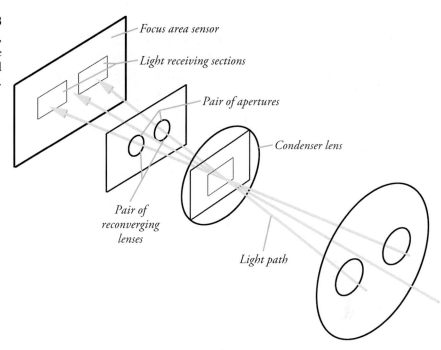

Focus area sensor

Light receiving sections

Pair of apertures

Condenser lens

Pair of reconverging lenses

Light path

Figure 5.4

When the image is in focus, the two halves of the image align, as with a rangefinder.

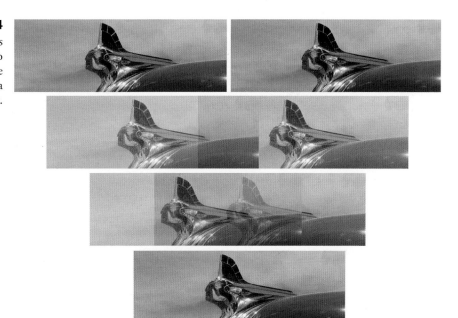

As with any rangefinder-like function, accuracy is better when the "base length" between the two images is larger. (Think back to your high school trigonometry; you could calculate a distance more accurately when the separation between the two points where the angles were measured was greater.) For that reason, phase detection autofocus is more accurate with larger (wider) lens openings than with smaller lens openings, and may not work at all when the f/stop is smaller than f/5.6 or f/8. Obviously, the "opposite" edges of the lens opening are farther apart with a lens having an f/2.8 maximum aperture than with one that has a smaller, f/5.6 maximum f/stop, and the base line is much longer. The T7i is able to perform these comparisons and then move the lens elements directly to the point of correct focus very quickly, in milliseconds.

Unfortunately, while the T7i's focus system finds it easy to measure degrees of apparent focus at each of the focus points in the viewfinder, it doesn't really know with any certainty *which* object should be in sharpest focus. Is it the closest object? The subject in the center? Something lurking *behind* the closest subject? A person standing over at the side of the picture? Many of the techniques for using autofocus effectively involve telling the T7i exactly what it should be focusing on, by choosing a focus zone or by allowing the camera to choose a focus zone for you. I'll address that topic shortly.

Dual Pixel CMOS AF

So far, we've explored how the T7i autofocuses when using the optical viewfinder. A completely different AF system comes into play when you're capturing stills or movies in live view. Understanding contrast and phase detection helps you appreciate the miracle that is Canon's Dual Pixel CMOS AF system. Used in Live View mode while shooting stills and movies, it works much more quickly than the camera's more traditional contrast detection system alone.

An array of special pixels, which cover 80 percent of the frame horizontally and vertically, provide the same type of split-image rangefinder phase detection AF that is available when using the optical viewfinder. The most important aspect of the system is that it doesn't rob the camera of any imaging resolution. It would have been possible to place AF sensors *between* the pixels used to capture the image, but that would leave the sensor with less area with which to capture light. Keep in mind that CMOS sensors, unlike earlier CCD sensors, have more on-board circuitry which already consumes some of the light-gathering area. Microlenses are placed above each photosensitive site to focus incoming illumination on the sensor and to correct for the oblique angles from which some photons may approach the imager. (Older lenses, designed for film, are the worst offenders in terms of emitting light at severely oblique angles; newer "digital" lenses do a better job of directing photons onto the sensor plane with a less "slanted" approach.)

With the Dual Pixel CMOS AF system, the same photosites capture both image and autofocus information. Each pixel is divided into two photodiodes, facing left and right when the camera is held in horizontal orientation (or above and below each other in vertical orientation; either works fine for autofocus purposes). Each pair functions as a separate AF sensor, allowing a special integrated circuit to process the raw autofocus information before sending it on to the T7i's digital image processor, which handles both AF and image capture. For the latter, the information grabbed by *both* photodiodes is combined, so that the full photosensitive area of the sensor pixel is used to capture the image.

While traditional contrast detection frequently involves frustrating "hunting" as the camera continually readjusts the focus plane trying to find the position of maximum contrast, adding Dual Pixel CMOS AF phase detection allows the T7i to focus smoothly, which is important for speed, and essential when shooting movies (where all that hunting is unfortunately captured for posterity). Movie Servo AF tracking is improved, allowing shooting movies of subjects in motion. The system works with (at this writing) 103 different lenses, both current and previously available optics, and works especially well with lenses that have speedy USM or STM motors. I'll explain the T7i's AF operation in live view and movie shooting in more detail in Chapter 6.

Cross-Type Focus Point

Returning to the optical viewfinder's AF system, we're going to explore one special aspect next. So far, we've only looked at focus sensors that calculate focus in a single direction. Figure 5.5 (top left and right) illustrates a horizontally oriented linear focus sensor evaluating a subject that is made up,

Figure 5.5
A horizontally oriented sensor handles vertical lines easily (top). A horizontal sensor has problems with subjects that have parallel horizontal lines (bottom left). A vertically oriented sensor is really needed for that type of subject (bottom right).

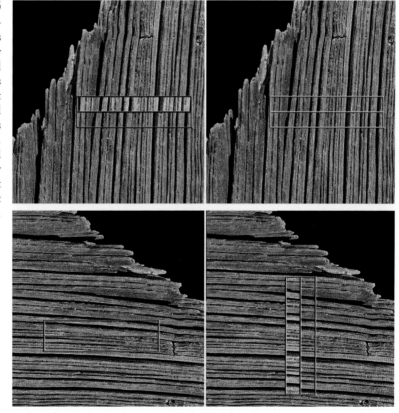

predominantly, of vertical lines. But what does such a sensor do when it encounters a subject that isn't conveniently aligned at right angles to the sensor array? You can see the problem in Figure 5.5 (bottom left), which pictures the same weathered wood siding rotated 90 degrees. The horizontal grain of the wood isn't divided as neatly by the split image, so focusing using phase detection is more difficult. The lines in the grain don't cross the AF sensor at right angles any more.

You can see the "solution" at bottom right in Figure 5.5, in the form of a vertical linear sensor, which does a better job of interpreting horizontal lines. By mixing both types in a focusing system, the vertical sensors could detect differences in horizontal lines, while the horizontal sensors took care of the vertical lines. Both varieties are equally adept at handling *diagonal* lines, which crossed each type of line sensor at a 45-degree angle.

However, a better solution is the use of a *cross-type* sensor, which is a merger of vertical and horizontal linear sensors, thus including sensitivity to horizontal, vertical, and lines at any diagonal angle. In lower light levels, with subjects that are moving, or with subjects that have no pattern and less contrast to begin with, the cross-type sensor not only works faster but can focus subjects that a horizontal- or vertical-only sensor can't handle at all.

In practice, these sensors consist of an *array* of lines and, in the T7i, none of them are strictly horizontal or vertical in orientation. Instead, the AF points are arranged as shown at left in Figure 5.6, using what are called *cross-type* sensors that form a plus-sign shape. All 45 AF points in the T7i are potentially cross sensors (the number available will depend on the aspect ratio you select (which can "crop out" some of the sensors) and the lens mounted on your camera (some AF points cannot function in cross mode with certain lenses, as I'll explain shortly).

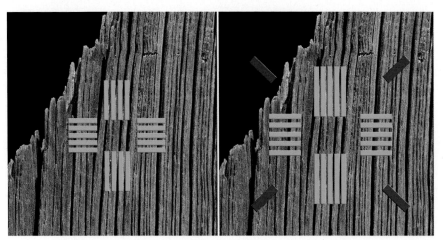

Figure 5.6
Cross-type sensors can achieve sharp focus with horizontal, vertical, and diagonal lines (left). The center focus point (right) has additional diagonal sensors (in red) that function with lenses with an f/2.8 or larger maximum aperture.

All of these 45 AF sensors function with lenses that have a maximum aperture of f/5.6 or larger (remember that smaller numbers equal larger apertures; f/4 is larger than f/5.6, for example). So, if you're using a lens with an f/stop from, say, f/1.2 through f/5.6, all 45 AF points will function as cross-type sensors. (Some may function in cross mode with a few f/8 lenses.) If your maximum aperture is even larger—f/2.8 or greater—the *center* AF point will also use a pair of diagonal sensors, represented in red at right in Figure 5.6. Note that the baseline of these diagonal AF points is much larger than that of the green vertically/horizontally oriented sensors. Coupled with the larger baseline of lenses with, say, f/1.2 to f/2.8 maximum apertures, the center AF sensors are significantly more accurate than those at the other 44 locations in the frame.

Usable AF Points and Lens Groups

The 45 AF points in your camera all function as cross-type sensors with the majority of lenses that you are likely to own. However, if you are using certain slower lenses, or use a teleconverter to multiply your lens's focal length, some of the focus points revert to line sensor behavior, or may become totally unavailable for autofocus.

Canon makes sorting out how usable AF points are affected by your choice of lenses and lens+ extender combinations easy, by classifying them in groups, labeled A through H. Pages 132 to 135 of Canon's T7i manual lists the lenses available *at the time the T7i was introduced,* and assigns a group to each. If you own lenses introduced in 2017 or later, I urge you to visit the Canon website for the definitive group for your particular optics.

The lens and lens/teleconverter combinations in the Group A and Group B categories all allow all 45 AF points to function as cross-type sensors, with Group A entries enabling the dual-cross center focus point. With Group C and Group D lenses, some or all of the AF points at the left and right flanks of the center array revert to horizontal line sensitive behavior. With Group E and Group F lenses, the two groups of five points at the far left and right edges of the array are not available, and Group G lens combinations disable the upper and lower row of points, leaving only 27 usable AF points. Group G lenses allow only one cross-type point in the center of the array.

Figure 5.7 provides a quick reference to the function of each AF sensor within a given lens grouping. Dual cross, cross-type, horizontal, and vertical sensors are all represented. If a particular AF point is grayed out in a particular group, that sensor is not used and is not displayed as you shoot. When you press either AF point selection button, the disabled points will blink, while the enabled points will stay lit. Here's a more detailed listing of the AF point behaviors you can expect:

■ **Group A.** Autofocusing with all 45 points is possible, so you can choose any of the AF area selection modes (described later in this chapter). However, with all lenses in this group, the center AF point functions as a high-precision dual cross sensor *if that lens has a maximum aperture of f/2.8 or larger.* The other 44 AF points are cross-type sensors. (See Figure 5.7, upper left.)

■ **Group B.** This group of lens/lens+extender combinations is virtually identical in function to Group A, except that the center AF point serves as a conventional cross-type sensor, rather than a dual cross sensor. Autofocusing with all 45 points is possible. (See Figure 5.7, upper center.)

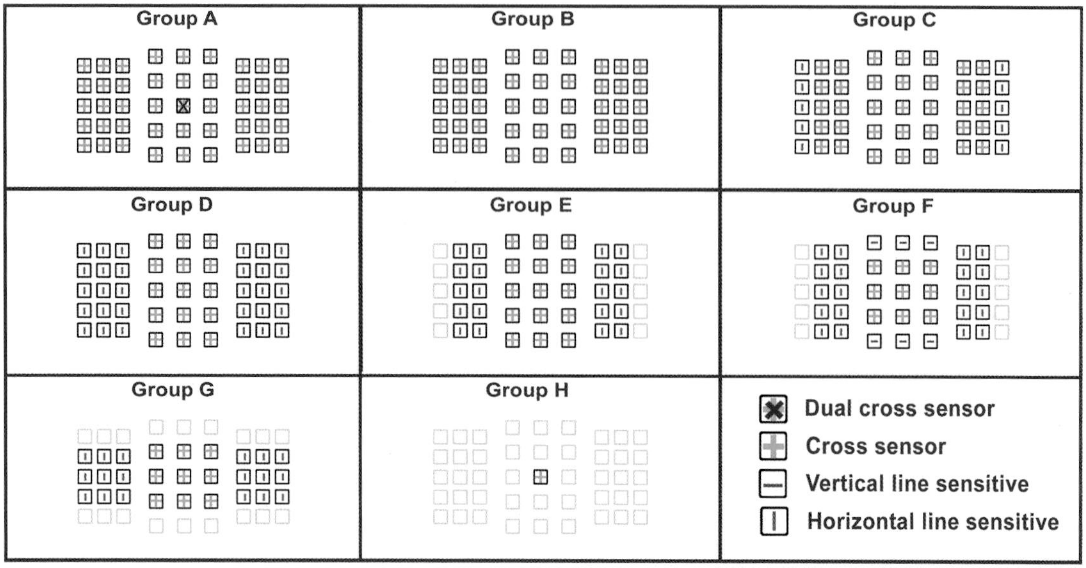

Figure 5.7 Dual cross, cross-type, horizontal, and vertical sensors.

- **Group C.** This group of lens/lens+extender combinations uses all 45 AF points, but the outermost 5 sensors on each side are sensitive only to horizontal lines, as you can see represented by orange lines in Figure 5.7, upper right.

- **Group D.** This fourth group uses all 45 AF points like the previous three, but only the 15 points in the center function as cross-type sensors. The outer sensors all are sensitive only to horizontal lines. (See Figure 5.7, center left.)

- **Group E.** Only 35 AF points are used with this group of lens/lens+extender combinations. The center 15 function as cross-type sensors, while two columns of sensors on either side of the center (20 in all) are sensitive only to horizontal lines. (See Figure 5.7 center.)

- **Group F.** Just 35 AF points are available with this next group of lens/lens+extender combinations. Only the 9 sensors at the very center are of the cross type. The rows above and below the center are sensitive to vertical lines, while the two columns on either side of the center are sensitive to horizontal lines. (See Figure 5.7, center right.)

- **Group G.** Only 27 AF points are available with this group. The nine center points function as cross-type sensors; the nine points to the left and nine to the right are sensitive to horizontal lines. The other points are disabled. (See Figure 5.7, lower left.)

- **Group H.** Only the center cross-type focus point can be used. (See Figure 5.7, bottom center.)

Focus Modes

Focus modes tell the camera *when* to evaluate and lock in focus. They don't determine *where* focus should be checked; that's the function of other autofocus features. Focus modes tell the camera whether to lock in focus once, say, when you press the shutter release halfway (or use some other control, such as the AE/AF Lock button), or whether, once activated, the camera should continue tracking your subject and, if it's moving, adjust focus to follow it.

The T7i has three AF modes: One-Shot AF (also known as single autofocus), AI Servo (continuous autofocus), and AI Focus AF (which switches between the two as appropriate). I'll explain all of these in more detail later in this section. But first, some confusion...

MANUAL FOCUS

With manual focus activated by sliding the AF/MF switch on the lens, your T7i lets you set the focus yourself. There are some advantages and disadvantages to this approach. While your batteries will last longer in manual focus mode, it will take you longer to focus the camera for each photo, a process that can be difficult. Modern digital cameras, even dSLRs, depend so much on autofocus that the viewfinders are no longer designed for optimum manual focus. Pick up any film camera and you'll see a bigger, brighter viewfinder with a focusing system that's a joy to focus on manually.

Adding Circles of Confusion

You know that increased depth-of-field brings more of your subject into focus. But more depth-of-field also makes autofocusing (or manual focusing) more difficult because the contrast is lower between objects at different distances. This is an added factor *beyond* the rangefinder aspects of lens opening size in phase detection. An image that's dimmer is more difficult to focus with any type of focus system, phase detection, contrast detection, or manual focus.

So, focus with a 200mm lens (or zoom setting) may be easier in some respects than at a 28mm focal length (or zoom setting) because the longer lens has less apparent depth-of-field. By the same token, a lens with a maximum aperture of f/1.8 will be easier to autofocus (or manually focus) than one of the same focal length with an f/4 maximum aperture, because the f/4 lens has more depth-of-field *and* a dimmer view. That's yet another reason why lenses with a maximum aperture smaller than f/5.6 can give your T7i's autofocus system fits—increased depth-of-field joins forces with a dimmer image that's more difficult to focus using phase detection.

To make things even more complicated, many subjects aren't polite enough to remain still. They move around in the frame, so that even if the T7i is sharply focused on your main subject, it may change position and require refocusing. An intervening subject may pop into the frame and pass between you and the subject you meant to photograph. You (or the T7i) have to decide whether to lock focus on this new subject, or remain focused on the original subject. Finally, there are some kinds of subjects that are difficult to bring into sharp focus because they lack enough contrast to allow the T7i's AF system (or our eyes) to lock in. Blank walls, a clear blue sky, or other subject matter may make focusing difficult.

If you find all these focus factors confusing, you're on the right track. Focus is, in fact, measured using something called a *circle of confusion*. An ideal image consists of zillions of tiny little points, which, like all points, theoretically have no height or width. There is perfect contrast between the point and its surroundings. You can think of each point as a pinpoint of light in a darkened room. When a given point is out of focus, its edges decrease in contrast and it changes from a perfect point to a tiny disc with blurry edges (remember, blur is the lack of contrast between boundaries in an image). (See Figure 5.8.)

If this blurry disc—the circle of confusion—is small enough, our eye still perceives it as a point. It's only when the disc grows large enough that we can see it as a blur rather than a sharp point that a given point is viewed as out of focus. You can see, then, that enlarging an image, either by displaying it larger on your computer monitor or by making a large print, also enlarges the size of each circle of confusion. Moving closer to the image does the same thing. So, parts of an image that may look perfectly sharp in a 5 × 7–inch print viewed at arm's length, might appear blurry when blown up to 11 × 14 and examined at the same distance. Take a few steps back, however, and it may look sharp again.

To a lesser extent, the viewer also affects the apparent size of these circles of confusion. Some people see details better at a given distance and may perceive smaller circles of confusion than someone standing next to them. For the most part, however, such differences are small. Truly blurry images will look blurry to just about everyone under the same conditions.

Technically, there is just one plane within your picture area, parallel to the back of the camera (or sensor, in the case of a digital camera), that is in sharp focus. That's the plane in which the points of the image are rendered as precise points. At every other plane in front of or behind the focus plane, the points show up as discs that range from slightly blurry to extremely blurry until the out-of-focus areas become one large blur that de-emphasizes the background.

In practice, the discs in many of these planes will still be so small that we see them as points, and that's where we get depth-of-field. Depth-of-field is just the range of planes that include discs that we perceive as points rather than blurred splotches. The size of this range increases as the aperture is reduced in size and is allocated roughly one-third in front of the plane of sharpest focus, and two-thirds behind it. The range of sharp focus is always greater behind your subject than in front of it.

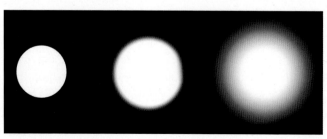

Figure 5.8
When a pinpoint of light (left) goes out of focus, its blurry edges form a circle of confusion (center and right).

Your Autofocus Mode Options

Choosing the right autofocus mode and the way in which focus points are selected is your key to success. Using the wrong mode for a particular type of photography can lead to a series of pictures that are all sharply focused—on the wrong subject. When I first started shooting sports with an autofocus SLR (back in the film camera days), I covered one game alternating between shots of base runners and outfielders with pictures of a promising young pitcher, all from a position next to the third-base dugout. The base runner and outfielder photos were great, because their backgrounds didn't distract the autofocus mechanism. But all my photos of the pitcher had the focus tightly zeroed in on the fans in the stands behind him. Because I was shooting film instead of a digital camera, I didn't know about my gaffe until the film was developed. A simple change, such as locking in focus or focus zone manually, or even manually focusing, would have done the trick.

To save battery power, unless Continuous Autofocus is activated, your T7i doesn't start to focus the lens until you partially depress either the shutter release or the AE/AF lock button (on the back of the camera and marked with an asterisk. (As you'll learn in Chapter 9, you can redefine this button to lock exposure and autofocus, or only autofocus, using the Custom Functions options.)

But, autofocus isn't some mindless beast out there snapping your pictures in and out of focus with no feedback from you after you press that button. There are several settings you can modify that return at least a modicum of control to you. Your first decision should be whether you set the T7i to One-Shot, AI Servo AF, or AI Focus AF. With the camera set for one of the Creative Zone modes, press the AF/right button and use the Main Dial to select the focus mode you want (see Figure 5.9). Press SET to confirm your choice. (The AF/M switch on the lens must be set to AF before you can change autofocus mode.)

Figure 5.9
Press the AF button and then rotate the Main Dial or Quick Control Dial until the AF choice you want is selected.

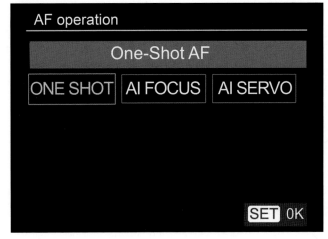

One-Shot AF

In this mode, also called *single autofocus*, focus is set once and remains at that setting until the button is fully depressed, taking the picture, or until you release the shutter button without taking a shot. For non-action photography, this setting is usually your best choice, as it minimizes out-of-focus pictures (at the expense of spontaneity). The drawback here is that you might not be able to take a picture at all while the camera is seeking focus; you're locked out until the autofocus mechanism is happy with the current setting. One-Shot AF/Single Autofocus is sometimes referred to as *focus priority* for that reason. Because of the small delay while the camera zeroes in on correct focus, you might experience slightly more shutter lag. This mode uses less battery power.

When sharp focus is achieved, the selected focus point will flash red in the viewfinder, and the focus confirmation light at the lower right will illuminate and remain lit as long as focus is maintained and you continue to hold down the shutter release. The exposure will be locked at the same time. By keeping the shutter button depressed halfway, you'll find you can reframe the image while retaining the focus (and exposure) that's been set. You can also use the AE Lock button to retain the exposure calculated from the center AF point while reframing.

AI Servo AF

This mode, also known as *continuous autofocus*, is the mode to use for sports and other fast-moving subjects. In this mode, once the shutter release is partially depressed, the camera sets the focus but continues to monitor the subject, so that if it moves or you move, the lens will be refocused to suit. Focus and exposure aren't really locked until you press the shutter release down all the way to take the picture. You'll often see continuous autofocus referred to as *release priority*. If you press the shutter release down all the way while the system is refining focus, the camera will go ahead and take a picture, even if the image is slightly out of focus. You'll find that AI Servo AF produces the least amount of shutter lag of any autofocus mode: press the button and the camera fires. It also uses the most battery power, because the autofocus system operates as long as the shutter release button is partially depressed.

AI Servo AF uses a technology called *predictive AF*, which allows the T7i to calculate the correct focus if the subject is moving toward or away from the camera at a constant rate. It uses either the automatically selected AF point or the point you select manually to set focus.

AI Focus AF

This setting is actually a combination of the first two. When selected, the camera focuses using One-Shot AF and locks in the focus setting. But, if the subject begins moving, it will switch automatically to AI Servo AF and change the focus to keep the subject sharp. AI Focus AF is a good choice when you're shooting a mixture of action pictures and less dynamic shots and want to use One-Shot AF when possible. The camera will default to that mode, yet switch automatically to AI Servo AF when it would be useful for subjects that might begin moving unexpectedly, such as children or pets.

Manual Focus

With manual focus activated by sliding the AF/MF switch on the lens, your T7i lets you set the focus yourself, both using the eye-level optical viewfinder and on the LCD monitor in Live View mode. There are some advantages and disadvantages to this approach. While your batteries will last longer in manual focus mode through the optical viewfinder, it will take you longer to focus the camera for each photo, a process that can be difficult. Modern digital cameras, even dSLRs, depend so much on autofocus that the viewfinders of models that have less than full-frame-sized sensors are no longer designed for optimum manual focus.

Selecting an AF Area Selection Mode

The Canon T7i uses 45 different focus points to calculate correct focus. In any of the Basic Zone shooting modes, the focus point is selected automatically by the camera. In the Creative Zone modes, you can allow the camera to select the focus point automatically, or you can specify which focus point should be used. There are three AF Area Selection modes. They are shown in Figure 5.10:

- **Single-point AF (Manual Selection).** You can choose one AF point for focus.
- **Zone AF (Manual Zone Selection).** Select any of nine different focus zones, each with a 3 × 3–point array.
- **Large Zone AF (Manual Selection of Zone).** You can choose the clusters of 15 focus points at left, right, or middle of the focus point array.
- **45-point Automatic Selection AF.** The camera will choose the focus point for you. This mode is always used in Basic Zone exposure modes.

To choose the AF Area, just follow these steps:

1. Make sure the lens AF/MF switch is set to AF.
2. Tap the shutter release to activate the focus system.
3. Press the AF Area Selection Mode button located southwest of the Main Dial. The current focus selection area will be highlighted in red on the viewfinder screen and the selection mode shown at the bottom.
4. Continue pressing, if necessary, until the method is shown in the viewfinder (or is highlighted on the LCD monitor).

When choosing a focus point manually, the viewfinder indicator will display **SEL [ ]** (for Single-point selection) or **[ ] AF** (for the other three modes) at the bottom of the frame.

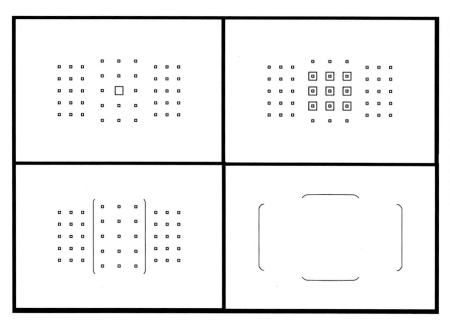

Figure 5.10
The three AF Area Selection modes are Single-point AF (Manual Selection), upper left; Zone AF (Manual Zone Selection), upper right; Large Zone AF, lower left; and 45-point Automatic Selection AF, lower right.

In the single-point manual selection mode, press the focus point selection button (in the upper-right corner of the back of the camera) or the focus point selection mode button. Then, use the directional buttons to move the active focus point around the frame. If you press SET, the AF center point will be selected. You can also rotate the Main Dial to move the focus point to the left or right in the middle row of sensors. In zone AF mode, rotating the Main Dial will switch from zone to zone in a loop.

While automatic point selection works well and is often best for moving subjects, manual point selection can be quite useful when you have time to zero in on a particular subject. This mode is certainly your best choice when you want to focus precisely on a subject that is surrounded by fine detail, as shown in Figure 5.11. The heron was not moving and my camera and 400mm lens were mounted on a sturdy tripod, so it was easy to place the focus spot exactly where I wanted it. Keep in mind that the portion of the sensor used to autofocus is not precisely represented by the rectangle shown in the viewfinder, so if you're focusing on, say, the near eye of a portrait subject turned at a 45-degree angle with a wide aperture, you might end up focusing on the bridge of their nose instead. You'll want to keep the actual focus area in mind in situations where focus is that critical.

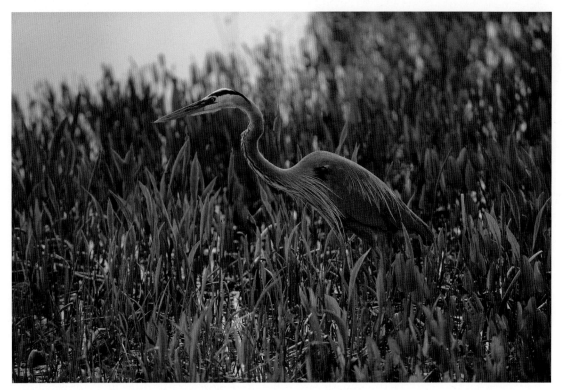

Figure 5.11 Manual point selection allowed focusing precisely on the heron, despite the surrounding detail.

AF with Color Tracking

The 7,560-pixel RGB+infrared exposure sensor mentioned in Chapter 4 can also be used to facilitate autofocus. The color information can recognize colors equivalent to skin tones, and thus enhance AF sensitivity when shooting still photos of human subjects. As I'll explain in Chapter 9, you can activate this feature using C.Fn II-7. The default is 0: Enable, which tells the T7i to select AF points representing skin tones automatically. It works well in One-Shot mode to lock in focus; in AI Servo AF mode, focusing on humans is enhanced (if no skin tones are detected, the camera will focus on the nearest object). As AI Servo AF continues to refocus as required until the shutter release is pressed down all the way, the T7i continues to select focus points representing the colors of the subject first focused on. Under lighting conditions dim enough to trigger the AF-assist beam, color information is not used. If you select 1: Disable, AF points are selected without regard to color information. Color tracking is not used in Landscape, Close-up, Food, Candlelight, Night Portrait, or Handheld Night Scene modes, nor in Fish-eye and Water Painting Effects modes.

Other Important AF Parameters

Several other parameters are used to fine-tune the T7i's AF behavior. The most important of these are available under Custom Functions II, include the following. Check Chapter 9 for instructions on how to select the options available with each of these features.

- **AF-Assist Beam Firing (C.Fn II-5).** Allows you to specify whether the AF-assist beam is enabled, disabled, fires only when an external flash is attached, or whether only an IR AF-assist beam is emitted by flashes having the IR feature.

- **AF Area Selection Method (C.Fn II-6).** Allows you to choose the AF Area Selection control—either presses of the AF selection/AF area selection buttons or a single press of those buttons followed by rotation of the Main Dial.

- **AF Point Display During Focus (C.Fn II-8).** Choose which AF points are displayed during focus.

- **Viewfinder Display Illumination (C.Fn II-9).** Select whether AF points in the viewfinder are illuminated in red once focus is achieved.

Back-Button Focus

Once you've been using your camera for a while, you'll invariably encounter the terms *back focus* and *back-button focus*, and wonder if they are good things or bad things. Actually, they are *two different things,* and are often confused with each other. *Back focus* is a bad thing, and occurs when a particular lens consistently autofocuses on a plane that's *behind* your desired subject. This malady may be found in some of your lenses, or all your optics may be free of the defect.

Back-button focus, on the other hand, is a tool you can use to separate two functions that are commonly locked together—exposure and autofocus—so that you can lock in exposure while allowing focus to be attained at a later point, or vice versa. It's a *good* thing, although using back-button focus effectively may require you to unlearn some habits and acquire new ways of coordinating the action of your fingers.

As you have learned, the default behavior of your Canon T7i is to set both exposure and focus (when AF is active) when you press the shutter release down halfway. When using One-Shot mode, that's that: both exposure and focus are locked and will not change until you release the shutter button, or press it all the way down to take a picture and then release it for the next shot. In AI Servo mode, exposure is locked and focus is set when you press the shutter release halfway, but the camera will continue to refocus if your subject moves for as long as you hold down the shutter button halfway. Focus isn't locked until you press the button down all the way to take the picture. In AI Focus AF mode, the camera will start out in One-Shot mode, but switch to AI Servo AF if your subject begins moving.

What back-button focus does is *decouple* or separate the two actions. You can retain the exposure lock feature when the shutter is pressed halfway, but assign autofocus *start* and/or autofocus *lock* to a different button. So, in practice, you can press the shutter button halfway, locking exposure, and reframe the image if you like (perhaps you're photographing a backlit subject and want to lock in exposure on the foreground, and then reframe to include a very bright background as well).

But, in this same scenario, you *don't* want autofocus locked at the same time. Indeed, you may not want to start AF until you're good and ready, say, at a sports venue as you wait for a ballplayer to streak into view in your viewfinder. With back-button focus, you can lock exposure on the spot where you expect the athlete to be, and activate AF at the moment your subject appears. The T7i gives you a great deal of flexibility, both in the choice of which button to use for AF, and the behavior of that button. You can *start* autofocus, *lock* autofocus at a button press, or *lock it while holding the button.* That's where the learning of new habits and mind-finger coordination comes in. You need to learn which back-button focus techniques work for you, and when to use them.

Back-button focus lets you avoid the need to switch from One-Shot to AI Servo AF when your subject begins moving unexpectedly. Nor do you need to use AI Focus AF mode and *hope* the camera switches from One-Shot to AI Servo appropriately. You retain complete control. It's great for sports photography when you want to activate autofocus precisely based on the action in front of you. It also works for static shots. You can press and release your designated focus button, and then take a series of shots using the same focus point. Focus will not change until you once again press your defined back button.

Want to focus on a spot that doesn't reside under one of the camera's 45 focus areas? Use back-button focus to zero in focus on that location, then reframe. Focus will not change. Don't want to miss an important shot at a wedding or a photojournalism assignment? With back-button focus, you can focus first, and wait until the decisive moment to press the shutter release and take your picture. The T7i will respond immediately and not bother with refocusing at all.

Back-button focus can also save battery power. Ordinarily, your IS lens will begin adjusting for camera shake as soon as you begin focusing. Constantly refocusing can consume a lot of power. With back-button focus, the IS isn't switched on until you actually decide to autofocus on your subject.

Activating Back-Button Focus

You'll find the key control for enabling back-button focus within the Custom Functions entry in the Set-up 4 menu. Just follow these steps:

1. **Access Custom Functions.** Press the MENU button and use the Main Dial to navigate to the Set-up 4 menu.
2. **Select Custom Functions.**
3. **Choose C.Fn IV: Operation/Others.** Select C.Fn.12 and press SET.

4. **Set AE/AF button to activate and lock autofocus.** You'll want option 2: AF/AF lock, No AE Lock.

5. **Exit.** Press SET to confirm, and the MENU button twice to exit (or just tap the shutter release button).

6. **Use back-button focus.** Henceforth, press the shutter release halfway to meter and lock exposure, and all the way to take a picture. AF will be (temporarily) locked at the same time. Keep the button partially depressed. When you want to lock in your final focus, press the AE/AF lock button (marked with the asterisk), and press the AF-ON button to activate autofocus. Then press the shutter release the rest of the way down to take the picture.

6

Movies and Live View

Cameras like the Canon EOS Rebel T7i are loaded with killer features. And, by killer, I mean that new capabilities found in digital SLRs have virtually killed off whole categories of cameras, such as high-end, point-and-shoot cameras that lack interchangeable lenses or superzoom optics, and, in the future, camcorders. Who needs a camcorder when your digital SLR can shoot full HD 1080p video *and* stills?

Live view has been around long enough that it's becoming old hat for some, but, we have learned, it was just a precursor to one of the T7i's deadliest killer features—full HD video shooting. Indeed, the opening montages of *Saturday Night Live* were all shot using Canon cameras, so you can see that movie shooting with your camera has a lot of potential. You can now buy fancy harnesses, rigs, and Steadycam setups for Canon digital cameras, turning the more ambitious among us into one-person motion picture studios, ready and able to shoot everything from family vacation movies suitable for broadcasting on PBS during pledge week to full-length feature films. It's mind-boggling to see how far movie-shooting dSLRs have progressed in the past several years.

Working with Live View

Of course, live view is tightly integrated with movie shooting, so we'll start with that. Live view (and to a lesser extent movie shooting) is one of those features that, despite increasing evidence to the contrary, experienced SLR users (especially those dating from the film era) sometimes think they don't need—until they try it. But live view and movie shooting have become a permanent fixture, even for latecomers to the party. Indeed, many point-and-shoot models don't even *have* optical viewfinders. So, we have an entire generation of amateur photographers who think the only way to frame and compose an image is to hold the camera out at arm's length so the back-panel LCD can be viewed more easily.

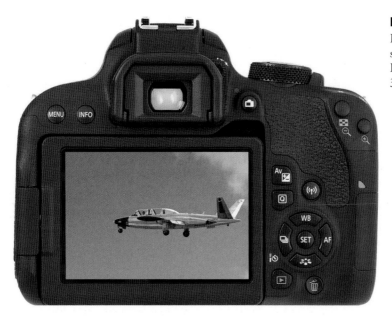

Figure 6.1
Live view really shines on the Canon EOS T7i's large 3-inch LCD.

Today the Canon EOS Rebel T7i has a gorgeous 3-inch LCD monitor that can be viewed under a variety of lighting conditions and from wide-ranging angles, so you don't have to be exactly behind the display to see it clearly. (See Figure 6.1.) It offers a 95-percent view of the sensor's capture area. The monitor is large enough to allow manual focusing. If you want to use automatic focus, you have several options that I'll describe in this chapter.

Live View Essentials

You may not have considered just what you can do with live view, because most of your shooting has been with a dSLR camera's optical viewfinder. But once you've played with it, you'll discover dozens of applications for this capability. Here's a list of things to think about.

- **Preview your images on a TV.** Connect your EOS T7i to a television or monitor with the optional HDMI cable HTC-100 and you can preview your image on a large screen.
- **Preview remotely.** Extend the cable between the camera and TV screen, and you can preview your images some distance away from the camera.
- **Shoot from your computer.** Canon gives you the software you need to control your camera from your computer, so you can preview images and take pictures or movies without physically touching the EOS T7i. You'll need to install the EOS Utility to do this.

- **Shoot from tripod or handheld.** Of course, holding the camera out at arm's length to preview an image is poor technique, and will introduce a lot of camera shake. If you want to use live view for handheld images, use an image-stabilized lens and/or a high shutter speed. A tripod is a better choice if you can use one.

- **Watch your power.** Live view uses a lot of juice and will deplete your battery rapidly. Canon estimates that you can get 310 to 350 shots per battery when using live view, depending on the temperature. Expect slightly fewer exposures when using flash. The optional AC adapter is a useful accessory.

Enabling Live View

You need to take some steps before using live view. This workflow prevents you from accidentally using live view when you don't mean to, thus potentially losing a shot, and it also helps ensure that you've made all the settings necessary to successfully use the feature efficiently. Here are the steps to follow:

1. **Choose a shooting mode.** Live view works with any exposure mode, including Scene Intelligent Auto and Creative Auto. You can even switch from one Basic Zone mode to another or from one Creative Zone mode to another while live view is activated. (If you change from Basic to Creative, or vice versa while live view is on, it will be deactivated and must be restarted.)

2. **Enable live view.** You'll need to activate live view by choosing the Live View Shoot. setting from the Shooting 5 menu (when the Mode Dial is set to a Creative Zone mode); if you're using a Basic Zone mode and are not currently using live view, you have only the Shooting 1 menu available. The last entry in that menu can enable or disable live view. Press SET and use the up/down directional buttons to select Enable and press the SET button again to exit.

> **TIP**
>
> Note that even if you've disabled live view, you can still flip the On/Off/Movie switch to Movie and shoot video.

3. **Choose other live view functions.** When you're using live view, the MENU button summons other live view options, with two screens in Basic Zone modes, and five screens in Creative Zone modes.

4. **Select live view or movie shooting.** Press the Live View/Movie button on the right side of the viewfinder to begin or end live view, or rotate the On/Off/Movie switch to the Movie position if you want to shoot video instead of stills.

There are four choices that pertain specially to live view in the Shooting 5 menu and are available *only* when live view is activated and you are using a Creative Zone mode. (See Figure 6.2.) Only the first three choices of those listed below are available when using a Basic Zone mode. The array of options include:

- **AF method (Face+Tracking, Smooth Zone, Live 1-Pt. AF).** This option lets you choose between AF with face recognition, manual zone selection, or single-point selection.

- **Touch Shutter (Enable/Disable).** In all Live View Shooting modes, when Touch Shutter is enabled, you can tap the subject on the screen to initiate focus on that subject and take a picture. The focus point will turn green and the image will be captured. If the T7i is unable to achieve focus, the point where you tapped will turn orange and the picture will not be taken. Tap the subject once more to try again. If you don't want to use this menu entry, the Touch Shutter can be enabled/disabled by tapping the Touch Shutter icon in the lower-left corner of the touch screen. If you don't see the icon on the screen, press the INFO. button until it appears.

- **Metering timer (4 sec. to 30 min.).** This option allows you to specify how long the EOS T7i's metering system will remain active before switching off. Tap the shutter release to start the timer again after it switches off. This choice is not available when using a Basic Zone mode.

- **Grid display (Off, Grid 1, Grid 2).** Overlays Grid 1, a "rule of thirds" grid, on the screen to help you compose your image and align vertical and horizontal lines; or Grid 2 (useful for architecture), which consists of four rows of six boxes, which allow finer control over placement of images in your frame. (See Figure 6.3.)

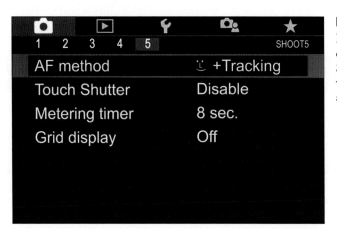

Figure 6.2

Live View settings can be found in the Shooting 5 menu when live view is active.

Figure 6.3
Two different grids
are available to help
you align vertical
and horizontal lines.

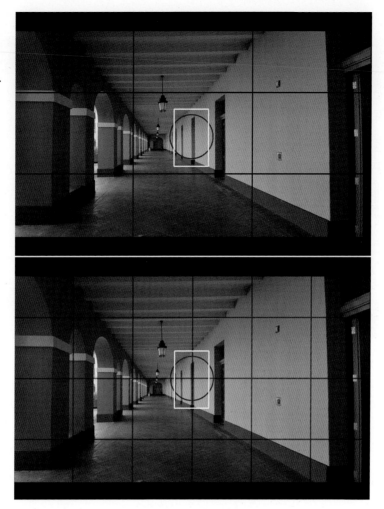

Activating Live View

Once you've enabled live view for later use, you can continue taking pictures normally through the T7i's viewfinder. When you're ready to activate live view, press the Live View/Movie button on the back of the camera, to the immediate right of the viewfinder window (and marked with a red dot). The mirror will flip up, and the sensor image will appear on the LCD. Press the INFO. button to cycle among a display that is blank (except for the image), one that contains basic shooting information, a full display with settings, and one that adds a live histogram. (See Figure 6.4 for the view with histogram.) Note that icons surrounded by a box can be tapped to make an adjustment for that value. Not all the icons shown appear at one time.

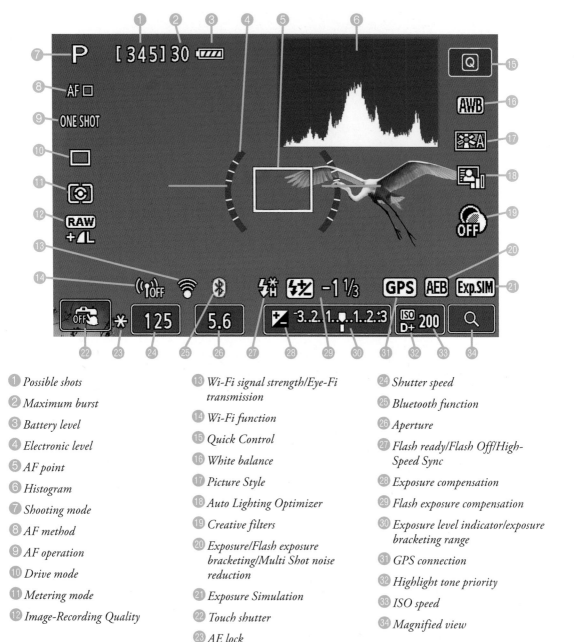

1 Possible shots

2 Maximum burst

3 Battery level

4 Electronic level

5 AF point

6 Histogram

7 Shooting mode

8 AF method

9 AF operation

10 Drive mode

11 Metering mode

12 Image-Recording Quality

13 Wi-Fi signal strength/Eye-Fi transmission

14 Wi-Fi function

15 Quick Control

16 White balance

17 Picture Style

18 Auto Lighting Optimizer

19 Creative filters

20 Exposure/Flash exposure bracketing/Multi Shot noise reduction

21 Exposure Simulation

22 Touch shutter

23 AE lock

24 Shutter speed

25 Bluetooth function

26 Aperture

27 Flash ready/Flash Off/High-Speed Sync

28 Exposure compensation

29 Flash exposure compensation

30 Exposure level indicator/exposure bracketing range

31 GPS connection

32 Highlight tone priority

33 ISO speed

34 Magnified view

Figure 6.4 Press the INFO. button to increase or decrease the amount of information shown on the LCD in Live View mode.

Here are the Live View options:

- **Shooting mode.** Shows which Creative Zone or Basic Zone mode you are using. Note that live view cannot be used in Candlelight scene mode.
- **AF method.** Shows whether you are using Face Detect+Tracking, Smooth Zone, or Live 1-point AF modes.
- **AF operation.** Displays either One-Shot or Servo focus modes.
- **Drive mode.** Indicates which drive mode will be used for live view images. You cannot use Single Shot Silent or Continuous Silent modes in live view.
- **Metering mode.** You can choose any of the metering modes. When you select Partial or Spot metering, a circle appears on the screen to indicate the metered area.
- **Image-Recording Quality.** Select RAW and JPEG image quality and size display parameters.
- **Bluetooth function.** Indicates Bluetooth is active.
- **Wi-Fi Function.** Status of the camera's Wi-Fi connection.
- **Touch shutter.** Tapping this icon enables or disables taking photos with a tap on the touch screen at the location you want in focus.
- **AE lock.** Indicates that exposure has been locked.
- **Shutter speed.** Shutter speed to be used. When a box appears around this icon, you can tap it to change the shutter speed. In Creative Auto mode, Background Blur control will be shown here and in the Aperture display area instead.
- **Aperture.** Shows the f/stop that will be used. If a box is shown around this icon, you can tap it to adjust the aperture.
- **Wi-Fi signal strength/Eye-Fi transmission.** Shows the strength of your Wi-Fi connection or that an Eye-Fi card is inserted in the camera.
- **Flash exposure compensation.** Displays how much flash exposure compensation will be applied.
- **Exposure compensation.** Displays how much ambient light exposure compensation will be applied.
- **Exposure level indicator/exposure bracketing range.** This scale shows exposure level and autoexposure bracketing range (represented by two extra dots flanking the center indicator dot). Tap the icon's box to make adjustments.
- **ISO speed.** Indicates current ISO setting. Tap the icon to change the ISO sensitivity.

- **Exposure/FEB/Multi Shot noise reduction.** These icons will appear next to the Exp. Sim. indicator when you're using autoexposure bracketing or flash exposure bracketing with an external flash unit.

- **Exposure Simulation.** Shows that the LCD monitor is displaying an approximation of the final image with many of your settings applied. See the sidebar that follows for a complete discussion of this feature.

- **Quick Control.** Tap to view the Quick Control menu, which allows you to change AF method, focus method, drive mode, metering method, image quality/size, white balance settings, Picture Style, auto lighting optimizer settings, or Creative Filter. (See Figure 6.5.)

- **White balance.** Shows current white balance settings.

- **Picture Style.** Displays current Picture Style.

- **Auto Lighting Optimizer.** Shows status of the auto lighting optimizer.

- **Creative filters.** Shows Creative Filter status.

- **Possible shots.** Indicates the approximate number of shots remaining on your memory card.

- **Maximum burst.** Displays how many continuous images can be captured before the buffer fills.

- **Battery level.** Remaining power in your battery.

- **AF point (Live 1-point AF).** Shows the area being used to calculate automatic focus. You can tap the touch screen to change the location of the focus point.

- **Flash ready/Flash Off/High-Speed Sync.** Shows flash status, and whether high-speed sync (with an attached external compatible Speedlite) is in use.

SIMULATED EXPOSURE

When Exp. Sim. is displayed in white on the live view screen, it indicates that the LCD screen image brightness is an approximation of the brightness of the image that will be captured. If the Exp. Sim. display is blinking, it shows that the screen image does *not* represent the appearance of the final image because the light level is too dim or too bright. The icon is grayed out when using Night Portrait or Handheld HDR, Multi Shot Noise Reduction, flash, or Bulb exposures, because the LCD image cannot accurately reflect the image you are going to capture.

The T7i applies any active Picture Style settings to the LCD image, so you can have a rough representation of the image as it will appear when modified. Sharpness, contrast, color saturation, and color tone will all be applied. In addition, the camera applies the following parameters to the live view image shown: White balance/white balance correction; Shoot by ambience/lighting/scene choices; Auto lighting optimization; Peripheral illumination/Chromatic aberration correction; Color tone; Metering mode; Highlight Tone Priority; Aspect ratio; and Depth-of-field when the DOF button is pressed.

- **Highlight Tone Priority.** If activated, a D+ will be shown next to the ISO indicator.
- **Magnified view.** Tap to zoom in on your image.
- **Histogram.** Shows a graph of the tones in your image, as discussed in Chapter 4. When the exposure simulation icon is grayed out, the histogram may not correctly represent the tonal range when shooting in extra low or bright scenes.

Quick Control

Press the Q button or tap the Q icon at the upper right of the touch screen while using a Creative Zone mode in live view, and you can adjust any of the values shown in the left- and right-hand columns. These include AF mode, Drive mode, White Balance, Picture Style, Auto Lighting Optimizer settings, Image quality settings, and Creative filters. Figure 6.5 shows the focus mode adjustment screen that appears. If you're using a Basic Zone mode, you can change AF mode, Drive mode, Creative filters, and several other settings, depending on the Basic Zone mode you are using.

CREATIVE FILTERS LIVE

Canon has added the ability to apply Creative Filters (described in Chapter 8) as you shoot images—and preview their looks before snapping a photo—when using live view. You'll find the Creative Filters options in the lower-right corner of the live Quick Control screen, as seen in Figure 6.5.

Figure 6.5
Focus mode adjustment within the Quick Control screen.

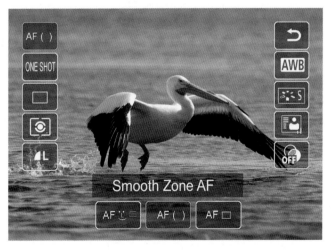

Focusing in Live View

Press the shutter button halfway to activate autofocus using the currently set live view autofocus mode. You can choose AF method: Face Detection+Tracking, Smooth Zone AF, or Live 1-Point AF. These determine how the T7i selects an area to focus on. You can also select AF operation: One-Shot or Servo, which control *when* focus is locked. Manual focus is also available if you prefer to set focus yourself.

To change the focus mode while using live view, you can access the Quick Control menu with the Q button or by tapping the Q icon on the touch screen, and navigating to the AF Method and AF operation options on the Quick Control menu. (See Figure 6.5.) AF Method is also available from the Shooting 5 menu when live view is active. I'll describe each of these separately.

Selecting an AF Method

As I mentioned, there are three AF methods: Face Detection+Tracking, Smooth Zone AF, or Live 1-Point AF. The last two are different from those found in earlier Canon Rebel models, replacing FlexiZone-Multi and FlexiZone-Single. The three current methods are described next.

Face Detection+Tracking Mode

The T7i will search the frame for a human face and attempt to focus on the face. Note that when using this mode, a magnified view of your image is not possible. To autofocus using Face Detection+Tracking mode, follow these steps:

1. **Set lens to autofocus.** Make sure the focus switch on the lens is set to AF.

2. **Activate live view.** Press the Live View/Movie button. Select Face Detection from the Quick Control menu or the Live View Shooting menu.

3. **Face detection.** A frame will appear around a face found in the image. If only one face is detected, the frame will be green; if more than one face is found, the frame will be white and have left/right triangles flanking it. (See Figure 6.6, left.) In that case, use the directional controls to move the frame to the face you want to use for focus. If no face is detected, the AF focus frame will be displayed and focus will be locked into the center.

4. **Focus.** Press the shutter button halfway to focus the camera on the face within the positioned Face Detection frame. When focus is locked in, the AF frame will turn green and the beeper, if activated, will chime. (See Figure 6.6, right.) If focus cannot be achieved, the AF frame will turn orange.

5. **Press and hold the shutter release to take the picture.** Press the shutter release all the way down to take the picture.

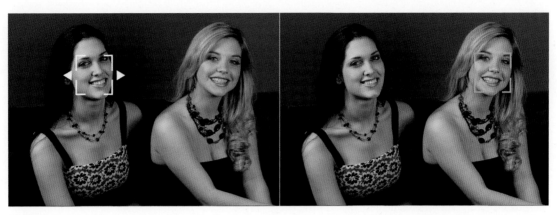

Figure 6.6 If multiple faces are found (left), the bracket can be moved among them. When focus is achieved (right), the bracket turns green.

Smooth Zone AF

This mode allows focusing over a wide area, using a zone that's roughly 9 percent of the total sensor area, and covering all but the outer edges of frame, as shown in Figure 6.7. You can use the directional buttons to move the frame to a zone you select—the AF area is 44 "clicks" wide and 31 "clicks" high, but it's much faster to just tap the touch screen. Follow these steps:

1. **Set lens to autofocus.** Make sure the focus switch on the lens is set to AF.
2. **Activate live view.** Press the Live View/Movie button.
3. **Select subject.** Compose the image on the LCD.

Figure 6.7
Choose your
focus zone.

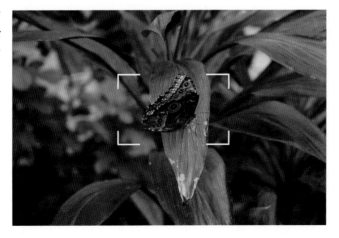

4. **Set zone.** Use the directional buttons to move the zone to your subject (the AF area is 44 "clicks" wide and 31 "clicks" high), or tap the touch screen on the area you want to focus on. To return the zone to the center of the frame, press SET or the Trash button.

5. **Press the shutter release button halfway.** When focus is achieved, the AF frame turns green, and you'll hear a beep. If the T7i is unable to focus, the AF point turns orange instead.

6. **Take picture.** Press the shutter release all the way down to take the picture.

Live 1-Point AF

This method uses a much smaller "zone" (Canon calls it "1-point," but it's larger than what we'd think of as a focus point). The focus area size is shown in Figure 6.8. When using Movie Servo AF (discussed later), the area is larger. Just follow these steps:

1. **Set lens to autofocus.** Make sure the focus switch on the lens is set to AF.

2. **Activate live view.** Press the Live View/Movie button.

3. **Choose AF point.** A focus point box will appear (as I noted, when using Movie Servo AF, the box will be larger). Use the directional controls to move the AF point anywhere you like on the screen, except for the edges. As always, it's usually faster to just tap the touch screen on the area you want to focus. Press the SET or Trash button to move it back to the center of the screen.

4. **Select subject.** Compose the image on the LCD so the selected focus point is on the subject.

5. **Press the shutter release button halfway.** When focus is achieved, the AF frame turns green, and you'll hear a beep. If the T7i is unable to focus, the AF point turns orange instead.

6. **Take picture.** Press the shutter release all the way down to take the picture.

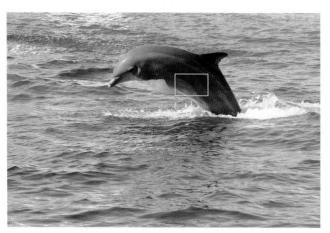

Figure 6.8
You can choose a focus area anywhere within the frame except the edges.

Magnified View

In Smooth Zone, Live 1-Point, or Manual Focus modes, you can see a magnified view that will help you determine focus. Magnified View is not available when using Face Detection. (To focus manually, you'll have to move the focus switch on the lens to the M position.) Focusing on an LCD screen isn't as difficult as you might think, but Canon has made the process even easier by providing this magnified view. Just follow these steps:

1. **Press the Magnify button or tap the Magnify icon at lower right on the touch screen.** Initially, a 1X magnification appears, showing the whole frame. Press/Tap again to enlarge by 5X, and another time to increase to 10X. If the Magnify icon, shown earlier in Figure 6.4, does not appear, press the INFO. button until it is visible. Another press will return you to the full-frame view.

2. **Move magnifying frame.** Use the directional controls to move the focus frame that's superimposed on the screen to the location where you want to focus, or tap the touch screen. You can press the SET or Trash button to center the focus frame in the middle of the screen. A reference box at lower right shows the relative position of the zoomed area to the full frame. (See Figure 6.9.)

3. **Focus.** If you're focusing manually, rotate the focus ring on the lens. The enlarged area is artificially sharpened to make it easier for you to see the contrast changes, and simplify focusing. In Smooth Zone and Live 1-Point AF, press the shutter release halfway to focus. If Servo AF (described next) is active, pressing the shutter release halfway in magnified view returns the camera to normal view for focusing.

Figure 6.9
You can use autofocus or manual focus when zoomed 5X or 10X.

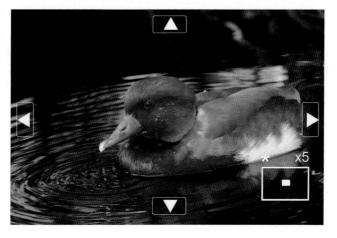

Focus Operation

Live view has two of the three focus operation modes available in still shooting: One-Shot and Servo (the equivalent of AI Servo). AI AF, which switches between One-Shot and Servo automatically in still mode, is not available when shooting with live view. Here's a recap to remind you of how these modes work.

One-Shot AF

In this mode, the T7i focuses once, and does not change focus until after you've depressed the shutter release all the way and taken a picture, or until you release the shutter button without taking a shot. It's great for shots without much action or subject movement. However, you might not be able to take a picture at all while the camera is seeking focus; you're locked out until the autofocus mechanism locks in. One-Shot AF is sometimes referred to as *focus priority* for that reason. Because of the small delay while the camera zeroes in on correct focus, you might experience slightly more shutter lag. This mode uses less battery power, which can be important in live view, which uses a lot of juice to power the LCD monitor all the time.

By keeping the shutter button depressed halfway, you'll find you can reframe the image while retaining the focus (and exposure) that's been set. You can also use the AE Lock button to retain the exposure calculated from the center AF point while reframing.

Servo AF

This mode, also known as *continuous autofocus*, is the mode to use for sports and other fast-moving subjects. In this mode, once the shutter release is partially depressed, the camera sets the focus but continues to monitor the subject, so that if it moves or you move, the lens will be refocused to suit the new composition. *Servo AF does not track your subject like Face Detection+Tracking.* Focus and exposure aren't really locked until you press the shutter release down all the way to take the picture. You'll often see continuous autofocus referred to as *release priority*. If you press the shutter release down all the way while the system is refining focus, the camera will go ahead and take a picture, even if the image is slightly out of focus. You'll find that Servo AF produces the least amount of shutter lag of any autofocus mode: press the button and the camera fires. It also uses the most battery power, because the autofocus system operates as long as the shutter release button is partially depressed.

Using the Touch Shutter

In Live View mode, you can activate/deactivate the Touch Shutter feature, which allows you to set focus and take a picture by tapping on your subject on the LCD monitor. It's a convenient way of activating focus and capturing an image with one gesture.

Touch Shutter can be enabled or disabled using the (logically named) Touch Shutter entry in the live view Shooting 5 menu, available when live view is enabled. You can also activate or deactivate the feature by tapping the touch shutter icon at the lower-left corner of the touch screen.

When disabled, you can still tap on the touch screen to specify where you want to focus, but you'll need to press the shutter release to actually take a picture. When touch shutter is enabled, all you need to do is tap your subject (most often, this will be a person's face). The T7i will focus using Face Detection+Tracking or Live 1-Point AF if you've selected either of those modes. If you've chosen Smooth Zone, the T7i switches to Live 1-Point instead.

When your subject is focused, the AF point will turn green and a picture will be taken automatically. If the camera was unable to focus, the AF point turns orange. In that case, try tapping again. You can press the SET or Trash buttons to move the focus point to the center of the frame and relocate it manually with the directional buttons, if you like, but I find that a screen tap works well.

Some notes from Canon: When Touch Shutter is active, Single Shooting is used even if Continuous Shooting has been selected. The Touch Shutter does not work in magnified view or when using the Miniature Effect Creative Filter. With the Fish-eye Creative Filter, the camera ignores your focus point and always uses the center point. (Both filters are described in Chapter 9.)

Bulb Exposures

With the camera set to Bulb in Manual exposure mode, you can tap the screen to start the exposure, and tap it again to stop the exposure. However, I don't recommend this technique. Unless you are very careful, these taps will cause the camera to vibrate, which can spoil your picture even if the camera is mounted on a tripod. Oddly enough, the effects are worst for "shorter" bulb exposures. For exposures longer than 15 seconds, the vibration is likely to subside within the first second or two, and have little effect on your final image.

Shooting Movies

The Canon EOS T7i can shoot full HD movies with stereo sound at 1920 × 1080 resolution, or Standard HD video at 1280 × 720 resolution. VGA movies can also be shot at 640 × 480 resolution.

In some ways, the camera's Movie mode is closely related to the T7i's Live View Still mode. In fact, the T7i uses live view-type imaging to show you the video clip on the LCD as it is captured. Many of the functions and setting options are the same, so the information in the previous sections will serve you well as you branch out into shooting movies with your camera. See Figure 6.10 for an atypical live view presented during movie shooting. It's *atypical* because, as always, not all the information shown in this reference image is displayed on the screen at the same time. Many of the icons represent features that are similar in live view; I'll explain the new ones as this chapter progresses.

To shoot in Movie mode, just rotate the On/Off/Movie switch to the Movie position. Press the Live View/Movie button to begin/end capture. That's quite simple, but there are some additional things you need to keep in mind before you start:

- **Choose your resolution.** The T7i can capture movies in Full High Definition (1920 × 1080 pixel) resolution at 60/50, 30/25, or 24 fps; Standard High Definition (1280 × 720 pixel) resolution at 60/50 and 30/25 fps; and VGA (640 × 480 pixel) resolution at 30/25 fps. I'll show you how to specify resolution in the next section.

- **Automatic auto.** The camera will adjust ISO value, shutter speed, and aperture automatically when using any Basic Zone mode or any Creative Zone mode other than Manual exposure. The sole exposure parameter you can control in Creative Zone modes other than Manual is the maximum ISO speed (from 6400, 12800, and 25600). If you want the capability of selecting your own shutter speed, aperture, or ISO sensitivity you must rotate the Mode Dial to the M position.

- **Use the right card.** You'll want to use a fast memory card, at least a Class 6 SDHC card; a Class 10 card is even better. Slower cards may not work properly. Choose a memory card with at least 4GB capacity (8GB or 16GB are preferable). If the card you are working with is too slow, a five-level thermometer-like "buffer" indicator may appear at the right side of the LCD, showing the status of your camera's internal memory. If the indicator reaches the top level because the buffer is full, movie shooting will stop automatically.

- **Use a fully charged battery.** Canon says that a fresh battery will allow about one hour of filming at normal (non-Winter) temperatures.

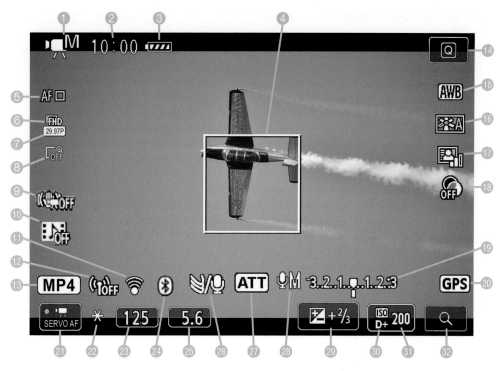

Figure 6.10 Live view during movie shooting.

① Movie Shooting mode

② Movie shooting remaining time/ Elapsed time

③ Battery level

④ AF point

⑤ AF method

⑥ Movie recording size

⑦ Frame rate

⑧ Digital zoom

⑨ Movie digital IS

⑩ Video snapshot

⑪ Wi-Fi signal strength/Eye-Fi card transmission status

⑫ Wi-Fi function

⑬ Movie recording format

⑭ Quick control

⑮ White balance

⑯ Picture style

⑰ Auto Lighting Optimizer

⑱ Creative Filters

⑲ Exposure level indicator

⑳ GPS connection

㉑ Movie servo AF

㉒ AE lock

㉓ Shutter speed

㉔ Bluetooth

㉕ Aperture

㉖ Wind filter

㉗ Attenuator

㉘ Recording level (Manual)

㉙ Exposure compensation

㉚ Highlight tone priority

㉛ ISO speed

㉜ Magnify/Digital Zoom

- **Image stabilizer uses extra power.** If your lens has an image stabilizer, it will operate at all times (not just when the shutter button is pressed halfway, which is the case with still photography) and use a considerable amount of power, reducing battery life. You can switch the IS feature off to conserve power. Mount your camera on a tripod, and you don't need IS anyway.

- **Silent running.** You can connect your T7i to a television or video monitor while shooting movies, and see the video portion on the bigger screen as you shoot. However, the sound will not play—that's a good idea, because, otherwise, you could likely get a feedback loop of sound going. The sound will be recorded properly and will magically appear during playback once shooting has concluded.

- **Final Image Simulation.** This feature, discussed earlier in the live view section, can also be used for movie-making. It displays the image during capture with a variety of settings already applied, including Picture Style, white balance, exposure, depth-of-field, Auto Lighting Optimizer, Peripheral Illumination/Chromatic Aberration correction, and Highlight Tone Priority adjustments. If you're using the HDR movie and Creative Filters movie options (described later), the T7i will show those effects, too, as you shoot.

Resolution and Frame Rates

Even intermediate movie shooters can be confused by the number of different choices for resolution and frame rates. This section will help clarify things for you. First, resolution:

- **1920 × 1080.** This resolution is so-called "full HD" and is the maximum resolution displayed when using the HDTV format. Many monitors and most HD televisions can display this resolution, and you'll have the best image quality when you use it. Use this resolution for your "professional" productions, especially those you'll be editing and converting to nifty-looking videos. However, the top-of-the-line resolution requires the most storage space, approximately 330 megabytes per minute, yielding about 44 minutes of "shooting time" on a 16GB memory card. (Of course, the maximum length of a single continuous clip is nearly 30 minutes.)

- **1280 × 720.** "Standard HD" provides less resolution, and can be displayed on any monitor or television that claims HDTV compatibility. If your production will appear only on computer monitors with 1280 × 720 resolution, or on HDTVs that max out at 720p, this resolution will be fine.

- **640 × 480.** This is so-called VGA resolution, suitable for display on computer monitors and, possibly, old standard-definition televisions. (Remember the ones with CRT tubes instead of LCD, LED, or plasma displays?) This lower-resolution format is less demanding of your storage, too, requiring about 82 megabytes per minute capture, and providing more than three hours of video clips on a single 16GB card. You'll use this resolution for productions destined for display on the Internet, and other similar uses.

Frame rates are a trickier proposition. Fortunately, one seemingly confusing set of alternatives can be dispensed with quickly: The 50 fps/25 fps and 60/30 fps options can be considered as pairs of *video*-oriented frame rates. The 60/30 fps rates are used only where the NTSC television standard is in place, such as North America, Japan, Korea, Mexico, and a few other places. The 50/25 frame rates are used where the PAL standard reigns, such as Europe, Russia, China, Africa, Australia, and other places. For simplicity, I'll refer just to the 60/30 frame rates in this section; if you're reading this in India, just convert to 50/25.

The third possibility is 24 fps, which is a standard frame rate used for motion pictures. Keep in mind that the rates are *nominal.* A 24 fps setting yields 23.976 frames per second; 30 fps gives you 29.97 actual "frames" per second; and 60 fps results in 59.94 "frames" per second. (The 25/60 fps values, however, are accurate.)

The difference lies in the two "worlds" of motion images: film and video. The standard frame rate for motion picture film is 24 fps, while the video rate, at least in the United States, Japan, and those other places using the NTSC standard is 30 fps (actually, 60 interlaced *fields* per second, which is why we can choose either 30 frames/fields per second or 60 frames/fields per second). Computer-editing software can handle either type, and convert between them. The choice between 24 fps and 30 fps is determined by what you plan to do with your video.

The short explanation is that, for technical reasons I won't go into here, shooting at 24 fps gives your movie a "film" look, excellent for showing fine detail. However, if your clip has moving subjects, or you pan the camera, 24 fps can produce a jerky effect called "judder." A 30 or 60 fps rate produces a home-video look that some feel is less desirable, but which is smoother and less jittery when displayed on an electronic monitor. I suggest you try both and use the frame rate that best suits your tastes and video-editing software.

Recording Time and File Size

When you choose a resolution and frame rate, you can also select either Standard or Light quality level. *Standard* provides the highest quality image at each resolution, but also puts the greatest demands on your memory card in terms of writing speed required and capacity. For example, at 1080p and Standard quality, an 8GB memory card can hold about 35 minutes of video, and must be able to receive the video stream at about 216 MB/minute. Drop down to Light quality (apparently, Canon wanted to avoid a more descriptive term, like Acceptable, Basic, or Rotten) and that same memory card can hold 86 minutes of video and only an 87 MB/minute write speed is required. At 720p resolution, Standard quality allows you to fit 40 minutes of video onto an 8GB card (not much of an improvement), but a whopping 4 hours and 10 minutes at Acceptable, I mean Light, quality. (And write speed requirements drop to a leisurely 30 MB/minute.) The Light quality is achieved by compressing multiple frames at a time, resulting in smaller files, and reduced quality.

In one sense, these figures are moot, because the Rebel is incapable of recording any single clip that is longer than 29 minutes, 59 seconds, or consume more than 4GB of memory card space when using an SD/SDHC memory card formatted in the camera. If you're saving to an SDXC memory card (one larger than 32GB) that has been formatted in the T7i, movie clips can be larger than 4GB, although the 29:59 time limit still applies.

When the (slightly less than) 30-minute limit is reached, movie shooting stops automatically. You can resume with a new clip by pressing the Live View/Movie button again. As the 4GB limit for SD/SDHC cards approaches, the elapsed time indicator on the LCD monitor begins blinking about 30 seconds ahead of time. Go ahead and keep shooting, as the camera will start a new movie file immediately. These are *separate* files, so they can't be played back automatically in consecutive order; you must select the following clips individually. You *can* stitch them together on your computer using a video-editing program, of course.

Also, remember that if your camera's internal temperature reaches what Canon considers to be the danger point, movie shooting may stop earlier. They haven't revealed what this temperature is, but, obviously the T7i will reach that temperature earlier when shooting in hot weather than in subzero climes.

Movie Settings

There are five Movie Settings menus that can be summoned by the MENU button only when the T7i has been set to Movie mode (rotate the On/Off/Movie switch to the Movie position). Some of these settings are identical to or similar to their counterparts for still shooting in Live View mode. I'm going to describe each of the five menus and detail how to set each of the available options.

Movie Shooting 1 Menu

In Creative Zone modes, this menu has five entries. The settings on the Movie Shooting 1 menu (see Figure 6.11) include:

- **Movie rec. size.** Choose 1920 × 1080 (Full HD) at 30 or 24 fps; 1280 × 720 (HD) at 60 or 30 fps; or 640 × 480 (Standard resolution) at 30 fps. Although there are only three actual recording sizes, you'll find six options in the menu; you can choose either Standard or Light quality for each resolution, as described earlier.

- **Digital zoom (T7i only).** Enable or Disable. This feature can be used when you're shooting 1080p (Full HD), with a digital (non-optical) zoom of roughly 3X to 10X. When active, you can press the up/down directional buttons to produce a sliding zoom scale at the right side of the LCD monitor screen. Up zooms in; down zooms back out.

  If you've used (and disliked) digital zoom features for still cameras because they come at a quality penalty, keep in mind that the eye is less sensitive to sharpness loss with video images that change 24 or more times per second, that digital zoom gives all your lenses a bit extra reach,

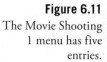

Figure 6.11
The Movie Shooting
1 menu has five
entries.

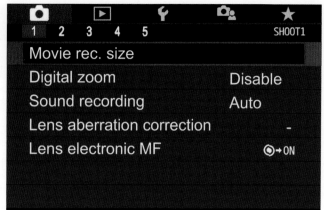

and that digital zooming *as you shoot* is much easier and more practical than trying to accomplish the same effect in an image editor. See the sidebar that follows for an explanation. My preference is to switch to a longer lens and not enable Digital Zoom, but many find it useful.

- **Sound recording.** Choose Auto, Manual, or Disable; plus enable or disable the wind filter.

  - **Auto.** The T7i sets the audio level for you.

  - **Manual.** Choose from 64 different sound levels. Select Rec Level and use the left/right directional buttons (or, with the T7i, rotate the QCD) while viewing the decibel meter at the bottom of the screen to choose a level that averages –12 dB for the loudest sounds.

  - **Disable.** Shoot silently, and add voice over, narration, music, or other sound later in your movie-editing software.

  You can use your T7i's built-in stereo microphone or plug a stereo microphone into the 3.5mm jack on the side of the camera. An external microphone is a good idea because the built-in microphone can easily pick up camera operation, such as the autofocus motor in a lens.

  - **Wind filter.** Enable to reduce the effects of wind noise on the microphone. This also reduces low tones in the sound recording. If wind is not a problem, you'll get better quality audio with this option disabled. Even better is to use an external microphone with a wind shield.

- **Lens aberration correction.** Lens corrections, described in detail in Chapter 8, can be made here.

- **Lens electronic manual focus.** Certain Canon lenses with USM or STM focus motors offer an electronic manual focus option when using the One-Shot AF mode. At the time I write this, there are nearly two-dozen lenses with this feature. Check page 122 of your T7i manual, or Canon's web page for the most up-to-date listing. I'll explain the difference between USM, STM, and other AF motors in Chapter 10.

  When this feature is enabled, you can use the electronic focus system of compatible lenses to fine-tune focus manually after autofocus has taken place. This capability can be used for both movies and still photography.

USEFUL DIGITAL ZOOM

Your EOS T7i's digital zoom feature is an exception to the rule (in still photography) that digital zooming is usually a bad thing. For movie shooting, it is a quite useful feature. Still cameras, mostly point-and-shoot models, with a digital zoom have justifiably received a bad rap. That's because, when shooting stills, digital zoom does nothing but crop the image, enlarging fewer pixels to fill the original frame.

However, when shooting movies, the 24 MP sensor view is *already* cropped to 1920 × 1080 pixels (2 MP). A center strip of the sensor's image is resampled *downward* to condense the information into an HD movie frame. Reducing available pixel data generally results in better image quality than blowing an image up by producing new pixels out of thin air with interpolation. So, the T7i's movie digital zoom will always be downsampling, because there is plenty of information in its APS-C frame to produce a decent 1920 × 1080–pixel frame even at 3X to 10X zooms. You'll still see noise and other artifacts at higher magnifications, but the results are quite usable.

Movie Shooting 2 Menu

This menu has four entries, which are generally very similar to their counterparts for still photography modes. Exposure compensation, ISO adjustments, and the Auto Lighting Optimizer were explained in Chapter 4, and I'll list the options for each in Chapter 8, and will not repeat that information here. To summarize, these entries, shown in Figure 6.12, include:

- **Exposure compensation.** This option operates very much like its still photography counterpart, except that bracket (by rotating the Main Dial) is not available. Add or subtract exposure using the touch screen or left/right directional buttons.

- **Movie ISO Speed.** This entry operates slightly differently than in still mode. When using Basic Zone, A, Tv, or P Zone settings, the T7i will automatically adjust the ISO speed for you in the range ISO 100 to ISO 12800. You can *only* choose a specific ISO speed when using Manual exposure mode.

- **Movie ISO Auto.** This option lets you choose a maximum limit for ISO Auto—either ISO 6400 or ISO 12800. If you have set C.Fn-2 (ISO Expansion) to 1: On, a maximum speed of ISO 25600 is available.

- **Auto Lighting Optimizer.** Entry functions like the still photography version.

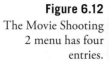

Figure 6.12
The Movie Shooting 2 menu has four entries.

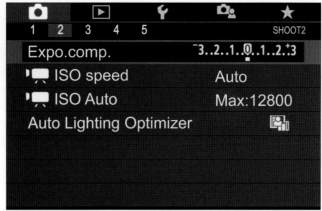

Movie Shooting 3 Menu

This menu has four entries. The settings on the Movie Shooting 3 menu (see Figure 6.13) include:

- **Picture Style.** You can select a Picture Style when using Creative Zone modes. You must make your selection before you start shooting, using either this menu entry, or the Quick Control screen. The Picture Style (down) button functions only as a focus frame directional button when Movie mode is active.

- **White balance.** You can adjust white balance from this entry in Creative Zone modes. You must either do it before you start shooting or from the Quick Control screen. The WB (up) button serves as a focus frame directional button in Movie mode.

- **Custom White Balance/White Balance Correction.** These two entries can be adjusted from the menu when using a Creative Zone mode.

Figure 6.13
The Movie Shooting 3 menu has four entries.

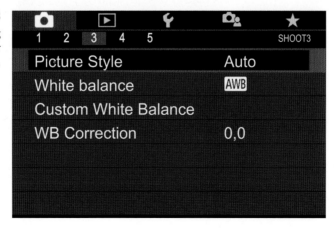

Movie Shooting 4 Menu

This menu has five entries. The settings on the Movie Shooting 4 menu (see Figure 6.14) include:

■ **Movie Servo AF.** When enabled, the camera will continually focus and refocus when in Movie mode, even when you are not pressing the shutter button halfway. Obviously, this continuous focusing will deplete your battery more quickly, and can produce annoying camera noise sounds on your video clip if you are using the T7i's internal microphones rather than an external unit. Some lenses are noisier than others while autofocusing, so STM optics, such as the EF-S 18-55mm STM and EF-S 18-135mm STM lenses are good choices for movie making.

You can *temporarily* disable Movie Servo mode if you want to lock focus at a given point, or want to avoid lens operation noise from being recorded on your soundtrack. Any of these steps will do the trick, listed in my order of preference:

• Press the Flash button on the left side of the viewfinder housing.

• Tap the Servo AF icon at lower left of the LCD monitor screen.

• In the Set-up 4 menu, select Custom Functions and set C.Fn-10 to 03: AF/Lock, No AE Lock. Then, you can pause Movie Servo AF by holding down the * button. It will resume when you release the button.

To re-enable Movie Servo mode after it's been temporarily stopped, press the Flash button a second time, tap the Servo AF icon on the LCD monitor, or press the MENU or Playback buttons twice.

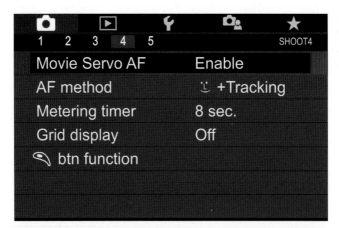

Figure 6.14
The Movie Shooting 4 menu has five entries.

- **AF method.** This option, explained earlier under live view, lets you choose between AF with Face Detection+Tracking, Smooth Zone, and Live 1-point AF.

- **Metering timer (4 sec. to 30 min.).** This option allows you to specify how long the EOS T7i's metering system will remain active before switching off.

- **Grid display.** You can select Off, Grid #1, or Grid #2, shown earlier in Figure 6.3.

- **AF w/shutter button during movie recording.** You can choose Enable to allow refocusing during movie shooting or Disable to prevent it. Refocusing after you've begun capturing a movie clip can be a good thing or a bad thing, so you want to be able to control when it happens. If you select Enable, then you can refocus during capture by pressing the shutter button. Refocusing will take place *only* when you press the shutter button; the T7i is not able to refocus continually as you shoot.

  Changing the focus during capture can be dangerous—your image is likely to go out of focus for a fraction of a second while the camera refocuses. That might not be bad if you plan on editing your movie and can remove the out-of-focus part of the clip. But refocusing during a shot can be disconcerting. Note that phase detection is used only at the beginning of the clip; subsequent refocusing will be performed using the live mode. Most of the time, I set this parameter to Disable to avoid accidentally refocusing during a shot.

Movie Shooting 5 Menu

This menu has four entries, each of which is used to enable or disable a specific movie-shooting capability. (See Figure 6.15.)

Figure 6.15
The Movie Shooting 5 menu has four entries.

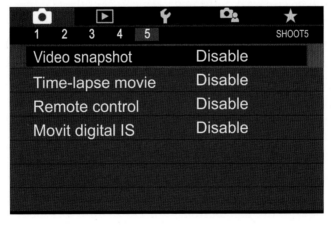

Your choices are as follows:

- **Video snapshot.** This is an easy way to create a set of movie clips, each lasting 2, 4, or 8 seconds. The T7i saves your snapshots to an album, each giving you a short movie that can be played back along with background music. I'll show you how to use this feature in an upcoming section.

- **Time-lapse movie.** Captures individual still images and stitches them together automatically to create a movie file. I'll explain Time-Lapse photography later in this chapter.

- **Remote control.** Enables or disables use of an optional remote control.

- **Movie Digital Image Stabilization.** Select Disable, Enable, or Enhanced. The T7i can stabilize your movie frames electronically, as described later. This feature is different from lens-based IS, and can function with lenses that don't have image stabilization, or which have had their IS turned off.

Capturing Video/Sound

To shoot movies with your camera, just follow these steps:

1. **Change to Movie mode.** Rotate the On/Off/Movie switch to the Movie setting.

2. **Select exposure mode.** Rotate the Mode Dial to the SCN, Creative Filters, or Manual exposure modes.

   - **Other Basic Zone modes.** If you choose a Basic Zone mode other than SCN or Creative Filters, the results will be the same as if you'd selected the green Scene Intelligent Auto mode. The A+ icon will be displayed in the upper-left corner of the LCD monitor, but will switch to one of the Scene mode icons if the camera detects an appropriate scene type.

   - **SCN/HDR Movie mode.** You *cannot* choose a Scene mode manually (the T7i applies Scene modes automatically when Basic Zone modes other than SCN or Creative Filters). Instead, when you rotate the dial to the SCN position, the camera switches to HDR Movie mode. I'll describe that feature shortly.

   - **Creative Filters.** When the Mode Dial is set to the Creative Filters position, you can press the INFO. button, followed by the Q button to select a specific creative filter. I'll explain your options shortly.

   - **Av, Tv, or P modes.** When the Mode Dial is set to any of these three positions, the T7i adjusts shutter speed, aperture, and ISO automatically for you. However, you can lock exposure by pressing the */Reduce button. Cancel exposure lock by pressing the AF Point Selection/Magnify button. You can add/subtract exposure compensation by holding down the EV button and rotating the Main Dial.

   - **Manual Exposure mode.** You can adjust shutter speed, aperture, and ISO speed manually.

3. **Focus.** Use the autofocus or manual focus techniques described in the preceding sections to achieve focus on your subject.

4. **Begin filming.** Press the Live View/Movie button to begin shooting. A red dot appears in the upper-right corner of the screen to show that video/sound are being captured. The access lamp also flashes during shooting.

5. **Changing shooting functions.** As with live view, you can change settings or review images normally when shooting video.

6. **Lock exposure.** You can lock in exposure by pressing the Reduce button on the upper-left corner of the back camera. Unlock exposure again by pressing the button once more.

7. **Stop filming.** Press the Live View/Movie button again to stop filming.

8. **View your clip.** Press the Playback button. You will see a still frame with the clip timing and a symbol telling you to press the SET button to see the clip. A series of video controls appear at the bottom of the frame. Press SET again and the clip begins. A thermometer bar progresses in the upper-left corner as the timing counts down. Press SET to stop at any time.

GETTING INFO

The information display shown on the LCD screen when shooting movies is almost identical to the one displayed during live view shooting. The settings icons in the left column show the same options, which can be changed in Movie mode, too, except that the Drive mode choice is replaced by an indicator that shows the current movie resolution and time remaining on your memory card.

Special Movie Modes

The T7i has three special movie modes: Video Snapshots, HDR Movies, and Time-Lapse Movies. This section explains each of them separately, along with tips for getting the most from these features.

Video Snapshots

Video snapshots are movie clips, all the same length, assembled into video albums as a single movie. You can choose a fixed length of 2, 4, or 8 seconds for all clips in an album. I use the 2-second length to compile mini-movies of fast-moving events, such as parades, giving me a lively album of clips that show all the things going on without lingering too long on a single scene. The 8-second length is ideal for landscapes and many travel clips, because the longer scenes give you time to absorb all the interesting things to see in such environments. The 4-second clips are an excellent way to show details of a single subject, such as a cathedral or monument when traveling, or an overview of the action at a sports event.

First, activate the video snapshot feature in the Movie 5 menu:

1. **Activate.** Select Video Snapshot from the Movie 5 menu.

2. **Enable Snapshots.** Highlight the Video Snapshot entry, press SET, select Enable, then press SET again to confirm. The screen shown in Figure 6.16 will appear.

3. **Select Album.** Next, highlight Album Settings and choose either Create a New Album or Add to Existing Album.

4. **Specify Snapshot Length.** If you choose to Create a New Album, a screen appears with the message "The next video snapshot will be added to a new album" along with the option to choose Snapshot Length. Highlight that option, press SET, and choose 2 Sec. Movie, 4 Sec. Movie, or 8 Sec. Movie. Press SET to confirm your choice.

5. **Confirm settings.** You'll be taken back to the previous screen. Highlight OK and tap OK or press SET.

6. **Enable/Disable Confirm Msg.** When enabled, a message will appear on the screen inviting you to Add to Album, Save As a New Album, Playback Video Snapshot, or Delete Without Saving to Album. If you select Disable, the camera *skips* this step, automatically saves your video snapshot, and is then ready to capture another. You'd want to disable the confirmation message if you planned to shoot several video snapshots one after the other and not have to respond to the confirmation message each time.

7. **Exit.** Press/Tap MENU to exit Video Snapshot setup. The next section will show you how to use the feature in a little more detail.

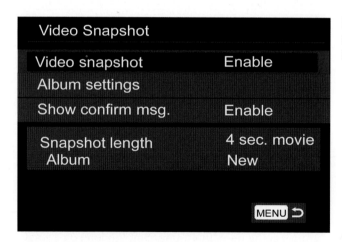

Figure 6.16
Select Video Snapshot options.

When Video Snapshot is enabled, conventional movie shooting is disabled. Instead, every time you press the Live View/Movie button, the T7i captures a clip of the length you've specified. The procedure goes something like this:

1. **Capture Video Snapshot.** In Movie mode, press the Live View/Movie button. The T7i will begin shooting a clip, and a blue bar appears showing you how much time remains before shooting stops automatically. (See Figure 6.17.)

2. **Save your clip as a video snapshot album.** If you've disabled the confirmation message, the clip will be saved to the current album, and you'll be returned to the screen shown in Figure 6.17, ready to capture another snapshot. Note that the confirmation message is overlaid on whichever Playback screen you've specified using the INFO. button. The figure illustrates the display when No Information is shown on playback.

3. **Choose confirmation option.** The screen shown in Figure 6.18 appears. You can use the left/right directional buttons or touch screen to select Save As Album/Add To Album (depending on whether this is the first clip for an album, or an additional clip), Save to New Album, Playback Video Snapshot (that you just took), or Do Not Save to Album/Delete Without Saving to Album (exit without adding to an album).

4. **Press SET.** Your first clip will be saved as the start of a new album.

5. **Shoot additional clips.** Press the Movie button to shoot more clips of the length you have chosen, and indicated by the blue bars at the bottom of the frame. At the end of the specified time, the confirmation screen will appear again.

Figure 6.17
Recording a video snapshot.

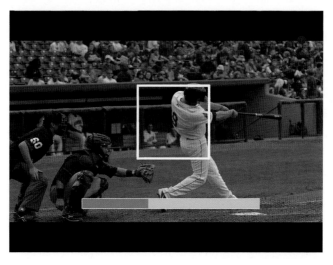

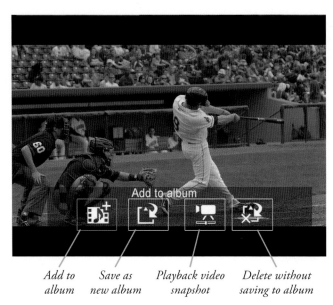

Figure 6.18
Video snapshot con-
firmation screen.

Add to   *Save as*   *Playback video*   *Delete without*
album   *new album*   *snapshot*   *saving to album*

6. **Add to album or create new album.** Select the left-most icon again if you want to add the most recent clip to the album you just started. Alternatively, you can press the left/right direc-tional buttons to choose the second icon from the left, Save as New Album. That will complete your previous album, and start a new one with the most recent clip.

   Or, if you'd like to review the most recent clip first to make sure it's worth adding to an album, select the Playback Video Snapshot icon (second from the right) and review the clip you just shot. You can then Add to Album, Create New Album, or Delete the Clip.

7. **Delete most recent clip.** If you decide the most recent clip is not one you'd like to add to your current album, you can select Do Not Save to Album/Delete without Saving to Album (the right-most icon).

8. **Switch from Video Snapshots to conventional movie clips.** If you want to stop shooting video snapshots and resume shooting regular movie clips (of a variable length), navigate to the Movie 5 menu again, and disable Video Snapshot.

   Note: Once you've set up the Video Snapshot feature, you can quickly enable or disable it using the Quick Control menu, which is illustrated later in this chapter. The Video Snapshot icon is the bottom icon in the left row of the Quick Control menu.

Shooting HDR Movies

HDR Movie extracts extra detail from your frames to provide more vibrant, extended dynamic range video clips. The chief limitation is that this mode works *only* if you have set the camera to the SCN position on the Mode Dial, which, as I mentioned earlier, shifts the camera into HDR Movie mode (and does not allow you to select a different SCN mode of any type).

When enabled, the T7i shoots movies at 1280 × 720, 30 fps (29.97) Standard quality (or 1280 × 720p, 25 fps Standard quality in countries using the PAL system). The feature reduces washed-out highlights in bright scenes, even if they are relatively high in contrast, using the camera's HDR Movies mode. The T7i merges multiple frames to achieve the HDR look, so a tripod is recommended to reduce (but not eliminate) noise caused by this additional processing.

Remember that HDR Movies can be shot only in Basic Zone SCN mode, and are not available if you're using Digital Zoom, Video Snapshot, or Time-Lapse options. Still photo shooting is disabled when you're using this feature.

Shooting Movies with Creative Filters

When the Mode Dial is set to the Creative Filters position, you can select one of five different cool special effects to apply to your video: Dream, Old Movies, Memory, Dramatic B&W, and Miniature Effect. Just follow these steps:

1. **Access Creative Filters.** Rotate the Mode Dial to the Creative Filters position.
2. **Activate Movie mode.** Rotate the power switch to the Movie position.
3. **Access the Quick Control menu.** Tap or press the Q button. The Quick Control menu appears.
4. **Highlight Creative Filters.** Select the top entry in the Quick Control menu and press SET.
5. **Select Movie Creative Filter.** Use the up/down buttons to make your choice and press SET. Your choices are Dream, Old Movies, Memory, Dramatic B&W, and Miniature Effect. I'll explain each in the sections that follow.
6. **Activate filter mode.** Press SET to activate your selected creative filter.
7. **Choose Filter Effect Level.** Back in the Quick Control menu, highlight the icon under the Creative Filters icon and choose Low, Standard, or High for the level of the effect. Then press SET or tap the Return icon to exit.

Dream

This gives your movies a blurry, high-key look that might be useful for dream sequences and other special looks. The edges of the frame are blurry. Choose the level you prefer, as described above.

Old Movies

We've all seen documentaries and such that feature old movies that have not been fully restored, and are complete with scratches and distortion. You'll even get some flicker, which, with actual old-time movies was a by-product of projecting film at today's standard of 24 frames per second, even though the film was moved through the camera by a hand crank, which produced variable frame rates. This option has no parameters to set other than the effect level, as detailed earlier.

Memory

Canon feels this effect evokes the mood of distant memories. Whether you agree or not, it is a useful effect that you should find some interesting applications for. The edges of the frame are lightened. Choose the level you prefer to adjust the richness of the colors and darkness of the areas along the edges.

Dramatic B&W

This is a great high-contrast, stark black-and-white look that you can use for cinéma vérité looks, documentaries, or your version of the monochrome movies that survived as B film flicks up until the early 1960s. You can choose a level for this effect, as well.

Miniature Effect

The Miniature Effect is also called the Tilt/Shift Effect, named after the (expensive!) Canon Tilt/Shift lenses that are required to dramatically change the plane of focus. You can shoot movies with a diorama effect, and have them play back at a herky-jerky high speed to enhance the toy-like look of your clip.

Unlike the other four Creative Filter effects, this one has a parameter. Just follow these steps.

1. **Evaluate area of focus.** When you activate Miniature Effect, you're taken to a screen with a band that shows the area that will remain in sharpest focus.
2. **Move focus point (optional).** If the current AF point is not within the effects' sharpest focus band, the icon at the bottom right of the screen will blink. Use the directional buttons so the focus frame is within the sharp focus band.
3. **Move sharp focus band.** To change the location of the focus band, press the Magnify button or tap the icon in the bottom right of the screen.
4. **The "sharp focus" screen will turn orange.** The sharp focus area is now moveable. (See Figure 6.19, left.)

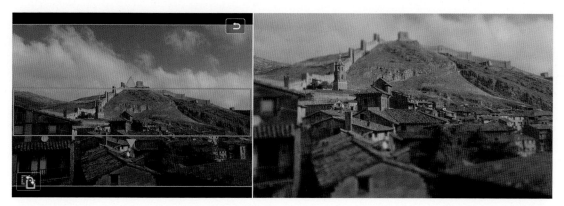

Figure 6.19 Move the frame over the area you want to remain in focus (left). Your miniature effect movie will be played back at 5X, 10X, or 20X normal speed (right).

5. **Change orientation (optional).** Press the INFO. button or press the icon at the bottom left of the screen to toggle the focus selection rectangle from horizontal and vertical mode. Then press SET.

6. **Change position of focus rectangle.** Use the up/down or left/right buttons (for horizontal and vertical frames, respectively) to move the sharp area to the location of your choice. You can press the Trash button to return the band to the center of the screen.

7. **Shoot your movie.** Press the Live View/Movie button to start/stop video capture. Your movie will look something like the example shown at right in Figure 6.19.

8. **Change playback speed (optional).** By default, your movie will play back at a speeded-up, herky-jerky rate of 5X normal speed. You can go to the Quick Control menu, where the Effect Level icon is replaced by one that can be used to select 5X, 10X, or 20X speed playback.

Time-Lapse Movies

The T7i's time-lapse movie facility is a still photography mode that shoots images at intervals you specify, and then stitches them together automatically to create a MOV-format movie in Full HD (1920 × 1080) at a playback rate of 30/25 fps. Some things to keep in mind when shooting time-lapse sequences:

■ **Battery limit.** Even with the LCD monitor turned off while shooting, a fully charged battery will accommodate only about 3.5 hours of time-lapse photography. Consider the optional AC Adapter AC-E6N/DC Coupler DR-E18.

■ **No autofocus or image stabilization.** Autofocus and image stabilization are disabled during shooting. This is a good thing, as refocusing between frames would be distracting and spoil the time-lapse effect, and IS is not needed when the camera is mounted on a tripod.

- **Silent running.** Your time-lapse movie will not have sound. If you think about it, that's a good thing, too.

- **Flash, auto power off, and other functions disabled.** You can't make camera adjustments using the menus or Quick Control screen during a time-lapse sequence.

- **Use a large, fast card.** Although the T7i will continue shooting when the memory card is full, the subsequent frames will not be recorded. If your card isn't fast enough to receive an image before the interval between frames elapses, a frame may be skipped.

- **Time-lapse disabled.** You cannot activate time-lapse photography when Movie Digital Zoom, Movie Digital IS, Video Snapshot, or a Creative Filter option has been set. Nor can you shoot these sequences when a Wi-Fi connection is active.

- **Forget about zooming.** Don't zoom during capture, even if you think it would be a cool special effect. Autofocus is disabled (see above), and proper exposure might change, along with lens aberration corrections, messing up your movie.

To create a time-lapse movie, just follow these steps:

1. **Set the Live View/Movie switch to the Movie position.** Even though time-lapse clips are a series of stills, you must be in Movie mode, and not using Scene or Creative Filter options to access the feature. While individual images are still photographs, no stills are stored; the camera converts them to a movie file even if you take only two shots in time-lapse mode.

2. **Navigate to the Movie Shooting 5 menu.** (Use the Movie Shooting 3 menu if the Mode Dial is set to Scene Intelligent Auto.) Select Time-Lapse Movie and press SET.

3. **Choose Enable.** A screen like the one shown in Figure 6.20 appears. Highlight Enable and press SET.

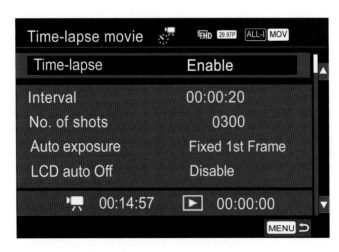

Figure 6.20
Enable/disable and make settings on this screen.

4. **Specify parameters.** Once Time-Lapse has been enabled, five parameters can be adjusted: Interval, Number of Shots, Auto Exposure, LCD Auto Off, and Beep as Image is Taken. You must scroll down with the directional buttons to view the last option. Make these adjustments:

   • **Interval.** Highlight hours, minutes, and seconds individually and choose the elapsed time between individual still shots. Press OK or SET to confirm each. You can select an interval up to 99 hours, 59 minutes, and 59 seconds.

   • **Number of shots.** Choose the number of shots to specify how long your time-lapse movie will be. You can select from two up to a total of 3,600 shots. When the interval and number of shots have been chosen, the amount of time the movie will cover and the playback time will be displayed on the bottom line of the screen. To choose an arbitrary (if far-fetched) example, if you selected an interval of one shot every 2 minutes, and a total of 2,000 shots, your time-lapse movie would require 167 consecutive days of shooting, and would play back in one minute, six seconds.

   • **Auto exposure.** Here you can select whether the camera should adjust exposure for each frame automatically, or should lock exposure at the settings calculated for the first frame. The latter would be your choice if you wanted to, say, record a typical outdoor scene from mid-day to sunset. With exposure locked at the first frame, changes in illumination would be shown— including cloudy periods and the gradual darkening of the scene at dusk. With Each Frame active, the camera would attempt to compensate for the changing lighting conditions to the extent it was able, nullifying the effect. Note that if Picture Style or White Balance are set to Auto, they, too will be adjusted in Each Frame mode.

   • **LCD Auto Off.** When enabled, the LCD monitor will turn off ten seconds after the first frame is shot and remain off, saving power (and allowing you to shoot longer sequences when not using an AC adapter). Disable, and the live view image will remain on the LCD until roughly 30 minutes after the first shot. I sometimes use this setting when I want to monitor the progress of my time-lapse shooting to make sure everything is proceeding as planned. Note that you can always manually turn the LCD monitor on or off using the INFO. button.

   • **Beep as Image Taken.** I usually enable this feature, which causes the camera to emit a reassuring beep each time an exposure is taken. The beep does not use much juice. However, no sound will be made if you've disabled Beep entirely in the Set-up 3 menu.

5. **Confirm.** When finished setting parameters, press MENU to confirm.

6. **Start time-lapse.** When ready to begin, press the shutter release halfway to check focus and exposure, and then press the Movie Start/Stop button to commence your time-lapse movie.

7. **Stop capture.** While the time-lapse movie is recording, you can press the Live View/Movie Start/Stop button to end capture, shutter release to start or stop capture, or the Start/Stop button to return to the exposure set-up screen. When time-lapse shooting ends, the settings are cleared and Time-Lapse is disabled until you activate it again.

Playback and Editing

You can play back your video snapshots from the confirmation screen. Or, you can exit Movie mode and review your stills and images and play any of them back by pressing the Playback button. A movie or album will be marked with an icon in the upper-left corner. If you're viewing thumbnails, the movies will be identified by a sprocket hole marking. Press the SET button to play back a movie or album when you see this icon.

As a movie or album is being played back, a screen of options appears at the bottom of the screen, as shown in Figure 6.21. When the icons are shown, use the left/right directional buttons to highlight one, and then press the SET button to activate that function:

- **Exit.** Exits playback mode.
- **Play.** Begins playback of the movie or album. To pause playback, press the SET button again. That restores the row of icons so you can choose a function.
- **Slow motion.** Displays the video in slow motion.
- **First frame.** Jumps to the first frame of the video, or the first scene of an album's first video snapshot.
- **Previous frame.** Press SET to view previous frame; hold down SET to rewind the movie.
- **Next frame.** Press SET to view the next frame; hold down SET to fast forward the movie.

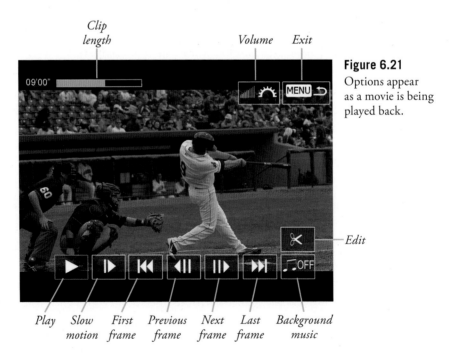

Figure 6.21
Options appear as a movie is being played back.

- **Last frame.** Jumps to last frame of the video, or the last scene of the album's last video snapshot.

- **Edit.** Summons an editing screen.

- **Background music/volume.** Select to turn recorded background music that you've copied to your memory card on/off. Rotate the Main Dial to adjust the volume of the background music.

While reviewing your video, you can trim from the beginning or end of your video clip by selecting the scissors symbol. The icons that appear have the following functions (see Figure 6.22):

- **Cut beginning.** Trims off all video prior to the current point.

- **Cut end.** Removes video after the current point.

- **Play video.** Play back your video to reach the point where you want to trim the beginning or end.

- **Save.** Saves your video to the memory card. A screen appears offering to save the clip as a New File, or to Overwrite the existing movie with your edited clip.

- **Exit.** Exits editing mode.

- **Adjust volume.** Modifies the volume of the background music.

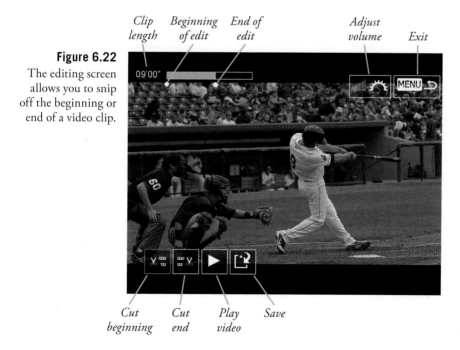

Figure 6.22
The editing screen allows you to snip off the beginning or end of a video clip.

Tips for Shooting Better Movies

Producing high-quality movies can be a real challenge for amateur photographers. After all, by comparison we're used to watching the best productions that television, video, and motion pictures can offer. Whether it's fair or not, our efforts are compared to what we're used to seeing produced by experts. While this chapter can't make you into a pro videographer, it can help you improve your efforts.

There are several things to consider when planning a video shoot, and when possible, a shooting script and storyboard can help you produce a higher-quality video.

Lens Craft

I cover the use of lenses with the T7i in more detail in Chapter 10, but a discussion of lens selection when shooting movies may be useful at this point. In the video world, not all lenses are created equal. The two most important considerations are depth-of-field, or the beneficial lack thereof, and zooming. I'll address each of these separately.

Depth-of-Field and Video

Have you wondered why professional videographers have gone nuts over still cameras that can also shoot video? As I mentioned, the producers of *Saturday Night Live* could afford to have Alex Buono, their director of photography, use the niftiest, most expensive high-resolution video cameras to shoot the opening sequences of the program. Instead, Buono opted for a pair of digital SLR cameras. One thing that makes digital still cameras so attractive for video is that they have relatively large sensors, which provides improved low-light performance and results in the attractive reduced depth-of-field, compared with most professional video cameras.

The roughly 24 million pixels used to *capture* the image are processed to create the 2,073,600 pixels of the final video frame. That's why the T7i gives you such great video quality, and why your video images retain roughly the same field of view and exact same depth-of-field you get with full-frame still images.

A larger sensor calls for the use of longer focal lengths to produce the same field of view, so, in effect, a larger sensor has reduced depth-of-field. And *that's* what makes cameras like the T7i attractive from a creative standpoint. Less depth-of-field means greater control over the range of what's in focus. Your T7i, with its larger sensor, has a distinct advantage over consumer camcorders in this regard, and even does a better job than many professional video cameras.

Zooming and Video

When shooting still photos, a zoom is a zoom is a zoom. The key considerations for a zoom lens used only for still photography are the maximum aperture available at each focal length ("How *fast* is this lens?"), the zoom range ("How far can I zoom in or out?"), and its sharpness at any given f/stop ("Do I lose sharpness when I shoot wide open?").

When shooting video, the priorities may change, and there are two additional parameters to consider. The first two I listed, lens speed and zoom range, have roughly the same importance in both still and video photography. Zoom range gains a bit of importance in videography, because you can always/usually move closer to shoot a still photograph, but when you're zooming during a shot most of us don't have that option (or the funds to buy/rent a dolly to smoothly move the camera during capture). But, oddly enough, overall sharpness may have slightly less importance under certain conditions when shooting video. That's because the image changes in some way many times per second, so any given frame doesn't hang around long enough for our eyes to pick out every single detail. You want a sharp image, of course, but your standards don't need to be quite as high when shooting video.

Here are the remaining considerations:

- **Zoom lens maximum aperture.** The speed of the lens matters in several ways. A zoom with a relatively large maximum aperture lets you shoot in lower light levels, and a big f/stop allows you to minimize depth-of-field for selective focus. Keep in mind that the maximum aperture may change during zooming. A lens that offers an f/3.5 maximum aperture at its widest focal length may provide only f/5.6 worth of light at the telephoto position.

- **Zoom range.** Use of zoom during actual capture should not be an everyday thing, unless you're shooting a kung-fu movie. However, there are effective uses for a zoom shot, particularly if it's a "long" one from extreme wide angle to extreme close-up (or vice versa). Most of the time, you'll use the zoom range to adjust the perspective of the camera *between* shots, and a longer zoom range can mean less trotting back and forth to adjust the field of view. Zoom range also comes into play when you're working with selective focus (longer focal lengths have less depth-of-field), or want to expand or compress the apparent distance between foreground and background subjects. A longer range gives you more flexibility.

- **Linearity.** Interchangeable lenses may have some drawbacks, as many photographers who have been using the video features of their digital SLRs have discovered. That's because, unless a lens is optimized for video shooting, zooming with a particular lens may not necessarily be linear. Rotating the zoom collar manually at a constant speed doesn't always produce a smooth zoom. There may be "jumps" as the elements of the lens shift around during the zoom. Keep that in mind if you plan to zoom during a shot, and are using a lens that has proved, from experience, to provide a non-linear zoom. (Unfortunately, there's no easy way to tell ahead of time whether you own a lens that is well suited for zooming during a shot.)

Keeping Things Stable and on the Level

Camera shake's enough of a problem with still photography, but it becomes even more of a nuisance when you're shooting video. The image-stabilization feature found in many lenses (and some third-party optics) can help minimize this. That's why these lenses make an excellent choice for video shooting if you're planning on going for the handheld cinema verité look.

Just realize that while handheld camera shots—even image stabilized—may be perfect if you're shooting a documentary or video that intentionally mimics traditional home movie-making, in other contexts it can be disconcerting or annoying. And even IS can't work miracles. As I'll point out in the next section, it's the camera movement itself that is distracting—not necessarily any blur in our subject matter.

If you want your video to look professional, putting the T7i on a tripod will give you smoother, steadier video clips to work with. It will be easier to intercut shots taken from different angles (or even at different times) if everything was shot on a tripod. Cutting from a tripod shot to a handheld shot, or even from one handheld shot to another one that has noticeably more (or less) camera movement can call attention to what otherwise might have been a smooth cut or transition.

Remember that telephoto lenses and telephoto zoom focal lengths magnify any camera shake, even with IS, so when you're using a longer focal length, that tripod becomes an even better idea. Tripods are essential if you want to pan from side to side during a shot, dolly in and out, or track from side to side (say, you want to shoot with the camera in your kid's coaster wagon). A tripod and (for panning) a fluid head built especially for smooth video movements can add a lot of production value to your movies.

Shooting Script

A shooting script is nothing more than a coordinated plan that covers both audio and video and provides order and structure for your video when you're in planned, storytelling mode. A detailed script will cover what types of shots you're going after, what dialogue you're going to use, audio effects, transitions, and graphics. A good script needn't constrain you: as the director, you are free to make changes on the spot during actual capture. But, before you change the route to your final destination, it's good to know where you were headed, and how you originally planned to get there.

When putting together your shooting script, plan for lots and lots of different shots, even if you don't think you'll need them. Only amateurish videos consist of a bunch of long, tedious shots. You'll want to vary the pace of your production by cutting among lots of different views, angles, and perspectives, so jot down your ideas for these variations when you put together your script.

If you're shooting a documentary rather than telling a story that's already been completely mapped out, the idea of using a shooting script needs to be applied more flexibly. Documentary filmmakers often have no shooting script at all. They go out, do their interviews, capture video of people, places, and events as they find them, and allow the structure of the story to take shape as they learn more about the subject of their documentary. In such cases, the movie is typically "created" during editing, as bits and pieces are assembled into the finished piece.

Storyboards

A storyboard makes a great adjunct to a detailed shooting script. It is a series of panels providing visuals of what each scene should look like. While the ones produced by Hollywood are generally of very high quality, there's nothing that says drawing skills are important for this step. Stick figures work just fine if that's the best you can do. The storyboard just helps you visualize locations, placement of actors/actresses, props and furniture, and also helps everyone involved get an idea of what you're trying to show. It also helps show how you want to frame or compose a shot. You can even shoot a series of still photos and transform them into a "storyboard" if you want, such as in Figure 6.23.

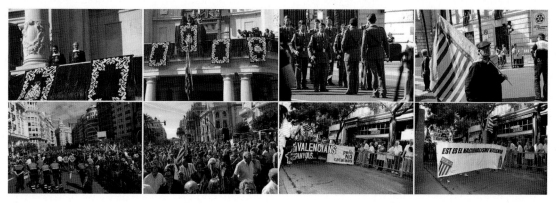

Figure 6.23 A storyboard is a series of simple sketches or photos to help visualize a segment of video.

Storytelling in Video

Today's audience is used to fast-paced, short-scene storytelling. In order to produce interesting video for such viewers, it's important to view video storytelling as a kind of shorthand code for the more leisurely efforts print media offers. Audio and video should always be advancing the story. While it's okay to let the camera linger from time to time, it should only be for a compelling reason and only briefly.

It only takes a second or two for an establishing shot to impart the necessary information. For example, many of the scenes for a video documenting a model being photographed in a Rock and Roll music setting might be close-ups and talking heads, but an establishing shot showing the studio where the video was captured helps set the scene.

Provide variety too. If you put your shooting script together correctly, you'll be changing camera angles and perspectives often and never leave a static scene on the screen for a long period of time. (You can record a static scene for a reasonably long period and then edit in other shots that cut away and back to the longer scene with close-ups that show each person talking.)

When editing, keep transitions basic! I can't stress this one enough. Watch a television program or movie. The action "jumps" from one scene or person to the next. Fancy transitions that involve exotic "wipes," dissolves, or cross fades take too long for the average viewer and make your video ponderous.

Composition

In movie shooting, several factors restrict your composition, and impose requirements you just don't always have in still photography (although other rules of good composition do apply). Here are some of the key differences to keep in mind when composing movie frames:

- **Horizontal compositions only.** Some subjects, such as basketball players and tall buildings, just lend themselves to vertical compositions. But movies are shown in horizontal format only. So, if you're interviewing a local basketball star, you can end up with a worst-case situation like the one shown in Figure 6.24. If you want to show how tall your subject is, it's often impractical to move back far enough to show him full-length. You really can't capture a vertical composition. Tricks like getting down on the floor and shooting up at your subject can exaggerate the perspective, but aren't a perfect solution.
- **Wasted space at the sides.** Moving in to frame the basketball player as outlined by the yellow box in Figure 6.24 means that you're still forced to leave a lot of empty space on either side. (Of course, you can fill that space with other people and/or interesting stuff, but that defeats your intent of concentrating on your main subject.) So, when faced with some types of subjects in a horizontal frame, you can be creative, or move in *really* tight. For example, if I was willing to give up the "height" aspect of my composition, I could have framed the shot as shown by the green box in the figure, and wasted less of the image area at either side.

- **Seamless (or seamed) transitions.** Unless you're telling a picture story with a photo essay, still pictures often stand alone. But with movies, each of your compositions must relate to the shot that preceded it, and the one that follows. It can be jarring to jump from a long shot to a tight close-up unless the director—you—is very creative. Another common error is the "jump cut" in which successive shots vary only slightly in camera angle, making it appear that the main subject has "jumped" from one place to another. (Although everyone from French New Wave director Jean-Luc Goddard to Guy Ritchie—Madonna's ex—have used jump cuts effectively in their films.) The rule of thumb is to vary the camera angle by at least 30 degrees between shots to make it appear to be seamless. Unless you prefer that your images flaunt convention and appear to be "seamy."

- **The time dimension.** Unlike still photography, with motion pictures there's a lot more emphasis on using a series of images to build on each other to tell a story. Static shots where the camera is mounted on a tripod and everything is shot from the same distance are a recipe for dull videos. Watch a television program sometime and notice how often camera shots change distances and directions. Viewers are used to this variety and have come to expect it. Professional video productions are often done with multiple cameras shooting from different angles and positions. But many professional productions are shot with just one camera and careful planning, and you can do just fine with your T7i.

Figure 6.24
Movie shooting requires you to fit all your subjects into a horizontally oriented frame.

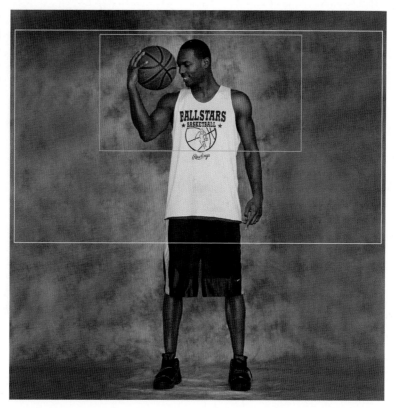

Here's a look at the different types of commonly used compositional tools:

■ **Establishing shot.** Much like it sounds, this type of composition, as shown in Figure 6.25, upper left, establishes the scene and tells the viewer where the action is taking place. Let's say you're shooting a video of your offspring's move to college; the establishing shot could be a wide shot of the campus with a sign welcoming you to the school in the foreground. Another example would be for a child's birthday party; the establishing shot could be the front of the house decorated with birthday signs and streamers or a shot of the dining room table decked out with party favors and a candle-covered birthday cake. Or, in Figure 6.25, upper left, I wanted to show the studio where the video was shot.

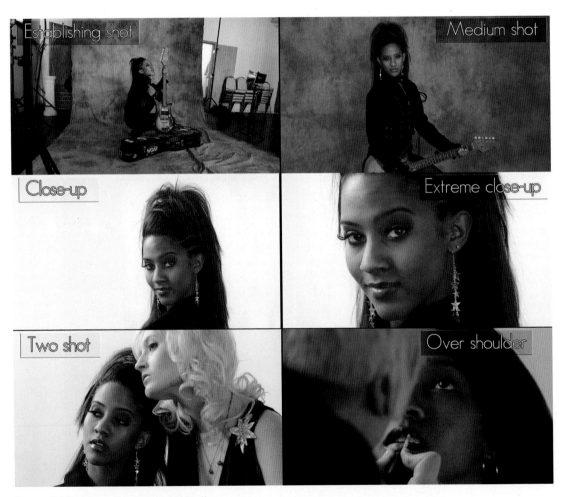

Figure 6.25 Mix your shots to help tell your story.

- **Medium shot.** This shot is composed from about waist to head room (some space above the subject's head). It's useful for providing variety from a series of close-ups and also makes for a useful first look at a speaker. (See Figure 6.25, upper right.)

- **Close-up.** The close-up, usually described as "from shirt pocket to head room," provides a good composition for someone talking directly to the camera. Although it's common to have your talking head centered in the shot, that's not a requirement. In Figure 6.25, center left, the subject was offset to the right. This would allow other images, especially graphics or titles, to be superimposed in the frame in a "real" (professional) production. But the compositional technique can be used with T7i videos, too, even if special effects are not going to be added.

- **Extreme close-up.** When I went through broadcast training back in the '70s, this shot was described as the "big talking face" shot and we were actively discouraged from employing it. Styles and tastes change over the years and now the big talking face is much more commonly used (maybe people are better looking these days?) and so this view may be appropriate. Just remember, the T7i is capable of shooting in high-definition video and you may be playing the video on a high-def TV; be careful that you use this composition on a face that can stand up to high definition. (See Figure 6.25, center right.)

- **"Two" shot.** A two shot shows a pair of subjects in one frame. They can be side by side or one in the foreground and one in the background. (See Figure 6.25, lower left.) This does not have to be a head-to-ground composition. Subjects can be standing or seated. A "three shot" is the same principle except that three people are in the frame.

- **Over-the-shoulder shot.** Long a composition of interview programs, the "over-the-shoulder shot" uses the rear of one person's head and shoulder to serve as a frame for the other person. This puts the viewer's perspective as that of the person facing away from the camera. (See Figure 6.25, lower right.)

Lighting for Video

Much like in still photography, how you handle light pretty much can make or break your videography. Lighting for video can be more complicated than lighting for still photography, since both subject and camera movement is often part of the process.

Lighting for video presents several concerns. First off, you want enough illumination to create a useable video. Beyond that, you want to use light to help tell your story or increase drama. Let's take a better look at both.

Illumination

You can significantly improve the quality of your video by increasing the light falling in the scene. This is true indoors or out, by the way. While it may seem like sunlight is more than enough, it depends on how much contrast you're dealing with. If your subject is in shadow (which can help them from squinting) or wearing a ball cap, a video light can help make them look a lot better.

Lighting choices for amateur videographers are a lot better these days than they were a decade or two ago. An inexpensive incandescent video light, which will easily fit in a camera bag, can be found for $15 or $20. You can even get a good-quality LED video light for less than $100. Work lights sold at many home improvement stores can also serve as video lights since you can set the camera's white balance to correct for any color casts. You'll need to mount these lights on a tripod or other support, or, perhaps, to a bracket that fastens to the tripod socket on the bottom of the camera.

Much of the challenge depends upon whether you're just trying to add some fill light on your subject versus trying to boost the light on an entire scene. A small video light will do just fine for the former. It won't handle the latter. Note that several Canon Speedlites, such as the Speedlite 320EX and new 430 EX II have their own built-in video lights.

Creative Lighting

While ramping up the light intensity will produce better technical quality in your video, it won't necessarily improve the artistic quality of it. Whether we're outdoors or indoors, we're used to seeing light come from above. Videographers need to consider how they position their lights to provide even illumination while up high enough to angle shadows down low and out of sight of the camera.

When considering lighting for video, there are several factors. One is the quality of the light. It can either be hard (direct) or soft (diffused). Hard light is good for showing detail, but can also be very harsh and unforgiving. "Softening" the light, but diffusing it somehow, can reduce the intensity of the light but make for a kinder, gentler light as well.

While mixing light sources isn't always a good idea, one approach is to combine window light with supplemental lighting. Position your subject with the window to one side and bring in either a supplemental light or a reflector to the other side for reasonably even lighting.

Lighting Styles

Some lighting styles are more heavily used than others. Some forms are used for special effects, while others are designed to be invisible. At its most basic, lighting just illuminates the scene, but when used properly it can also create drama. Let's look at some types of lighting styles:

- **Three-point lighting.** This is a basic lighting setup for one person. A main light illuminates the strong side of a person's face, while a fill light lights up the other side. A third light is then positioned above and behind the subject to light the back of the head and shoulders. (See Figure 6.26, left.)

- **Flat lighting.** Use this type of lighting to provide illumination and nothing more. It calls for a variety of lights and diffusers set to raise the light level in a space enough for good video reproduction, but not to create a particular mood or emphasize a particular scene or individual. With flat lighting, you're trying to create even lighting levels throughout the video space and minimize any shadows. Generally, the lights are placed up high and angled downward (or possibly pointed straight up to bounce off of a white ceiling). (See Figure 6.26, right.)

- **"Ghoul lighting."** This is the style of lighting used for old horror movies. The idea is to position the light down low, pointed upward. It's such an unnatural style of lighting that it makes its targets seem weird and "ghoulish."

- **Outdoor lighting.** While shooting outdoors may seem easier because the sun provides more light, it also presents its own problems. As a general rule, keep the sun behind you when you're shooting video outdoors, except when shooting faces (anything from a medium shot and closer) since the viewer won't want to see a squinting subject. When shooting another human this way, put the sun behind her and use a video light to balance light levels between the foreground and background. If the sun is simply too bright, position the subject in the shade and use the video light for your main illumination. Using reflectors (white board panels or aluminum foil-covered cardboard panels are cheap options) can also help balance light effectively.

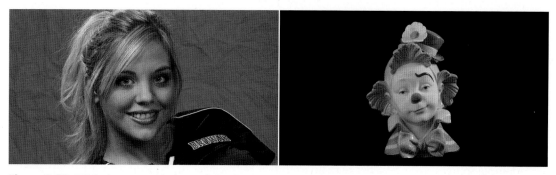

Figure 6.26 With three-point lighting (left); flat lighting is another approach for creating even illumination, lights can be bounced off of a white ceiling and walls to fill in shadows as much as possible (right).

Audio

When it comes to making a successful video, audio quality is one of those things that separates the professionals from the amateurs. We're used to watching top-quality productions on television and in the movies, yet the average person has no idea how much effort goes in to producing what seems to be "natural" sound. Much of the sound you hear in such productions is actually recorded on carefully controlled sound stages and "sweetened" with a variety of sound effects and other recordings of "natural" sound.

Tips for Better Audio

Since recording high-quality audio is such a challenge, it's a good idea to do everything possible to maximize recording quality. Here are some ideas for improving the quality of the audio your camera records:

- **Get the camera and its microphone close to the speaker.** The farther the microphone is from the audio source, the less effective it will be in picking up that sound. While having to position the camera and its built-in microphone closer to the subject affects your lens choices and lens perspective options, it will make the most of your audio source. Of course, if you're using a very wide-angle lens, getting too close to your subject can have unflattering results, so don't take this advice too far. It's important to think carefully about what sounds you want to capture. If you're shooting video of an acoustic combo that's not using a PA system, you'll want the microphone close to them, but not so close that, say, only the lead singer or instrumentalist is picked up, while the players at either side fade off into the background.

- **Use an external microphone.** You'll recall the description of the camera's external microphone port in Chapter 3. As noted, this port accepts a stereo mini-plug from a standard external microphone, allowing you to achieve considerably higher audio quality for your movies than is possible with the camera's built-in microphones (which are disabled when an external mic is plugged in). An external microphone reduces the amount of camera-induced noise that is picked up and recorded on your audio track. (The action of the lens as it focuses can be audible when the built-in microphones are active.)

  The external microphone port can provide plug-in power for microphones that can take their power from this sort of outlet rather than from a battery in the microphone. You may find suitable microphones from companies such as Shure and Audio-Technica.

- **Hide the microphone.** Combine the first few tips by using an external mic, and getting it as close to your subject as possible. If you're capturing a single person, you can always use a lapel microphone (described in the next section). But if you want a single mic to capture sound from multiple sources, your best bet may be to hide it somewhere in the shot. Put it behind a vase, using duct tape to fasten the microphone and fix the mic cable out of sight (if you're not using a wireless microphone).

■ **Turn off any sound makers you can.** Little things like fans and air handling units aren't obvious to the human ear, but will be picked up by the microphone. Turn off any machinery or devices that you can plus make sure cell phones are set to silent mode. Also, do what you can to minimize sounds such as wind, radio, television, or people talking in the background.

■ **Make sure to record some "natural" sound.** If you're shooting video at an event of some kind, make sure you get some background sound that you can add to your audio as desired in postproduction.

■ **Consider recording audio separately.** Lip-syncing is probably beyond most of the people you're going to be shooting, but there's nothing that says you can't record narration separately and add it later. It's relatively easy if you learn how to use simple software video-editing programs like iMovie (for the Macintosh) or Windows Movie Maker (for Windows PCs). Any time the speaker is off-camera, you can work with separately recorded narration rather than recording the speaker on-camera. This can produce much cleaner sound.

External Microphones

The single most important thing you can do to improve your audio quality is to use an external microphone. The T7i's internal stereo microphones mounted on the front of the camera will do a decent job, but have some significant drawbacks, partially spelled out in the previous section:

■ **Camera noise.** There are plenty of noise sources emanating from the camera, including your own breathing and rustling around as the camera shifts in your hand. Manual zooming is bound to affect your sound, and your fingers will fall directly in front of the built-in mics as you change focal lengths. An external microphone isolates the sound recording from camera noise.

■ **Distance.** Anytime your T7i is located more than 6 to 8 feet from your subjects or sound source, the audio will suffer. An external unit allows you to place the mic right next to your subject.

■ **Improved quality.** Obviously, Canon wasn't able to install a super-expensive, super-high-quality microphone. Not all owners of the T7i would be willing to pay the premium, especially if they didn't plan to shoot much video themselves. An external microphone will almost always be of better quality.

■ **Directionality.** The T7i's internal microphones generally record only sounds directly in front of them. An external microphone can be either of the directional type or omnidirectional, depending on whether you want to "shotgun" your sound or record more ambient sound.

You can choose from several different types of microphones, each of which has its own advantages and disadvantages. If you're serious about movie making with your T7i, you might want to own more than one. Common configurations include:

- **Shotgun microphones.** These can be mounted directly on your T7i. I prefer to use a bracket, which further isolates the microphone from any camera noise. One thing to keep in mind is that while the shotgun mic will generally ignore any sound coming from *behind* it, it will pick up any sound it is pointed at, even *behind* your subject. You may be capturing video and audio of someone you're interviewing in a restaurant, and not realize you're picking up the lunchtime conversation of the diners seated in the table behind your subject. Outdoors, you may record your speaker, as well as the traffic on a busy street or freeway in the background.

- **Lapel microphones.** Also called *lavalieres*, these microphones attach to the subject's clothing and pick up their voice with the best quality. You'll need a long enough cord or a wireless mic (described later). These are especially good for video interviews, so whether you're producing a documentary or grilling relatives for a family history, you'll want one of these.

- **Handheld microphones.** If you're capturing a singer crooning a tune, or want your subject to mimic famed faux newscaster Wally Ballou, a handheld mic may be your best choice. They serve much the same purpose as a lapel microphone, and they're more intrusive—but that may be the point. A handheld microphone can make a great prop for your fake newscast! The speaker can talk right into the microphone, point it at another person, or use it to record ambient sound. If your narrator is not going to appear on-camera, one of these can be an inexpensive way to improve sound.

- **Wired and wireless external microphones.** This option is the most expensive, but you get a receiver and a transmitter (both battery-powered, so you'll need to make sure you have enough batteries). The transmitter is connected to the microphone, and the receiver is connected to your T7i. In addition to being less klutzy and enabling you to avoid having wires on view in your scene, wireless mics let you record sounds that are physically located some distance from your camera. Of course, you need to keep in mind the range of your device, and be aware of possible signal interference from other electronic components in the vicinity.

WIND NOISE REDUCTION

Your Rebel has a wind cutoff option for the internal microphones, discussed earlier in this chapter. However, most microphones come with their own windscreen. Always use the windscreen provided with an external microphone to reduce the effect of noise produced by even light breezes blowing over the microphone. Many mics include a low-cut filter to further reduce wind noise. However, these can also affect other sounds. External mics often have their own low-cut filter switch.

7

Advanced Shooting

You can happily spend your entire shooting career using the techniques and features already explained in this book. Great exposures, sharp pictures, and creative compositions are all you really need to produce great shot after great shot. But, those with enough interest in getting the most out of their Canon EOS T7i will be interested in going beyond those basics to explore some of the more advanced techniques and capabilities of the camera. Capturing the briefest instant of time, transforming common scenes into the unusual with lengthy time exposures, and working with new tools like Wi-Fi are all tempting avenues for exploration. So, in this chapter, I'm going to offer longer discussions of some of the more advanced techniques and capabilities that I like to put to work.

Continuous Shooting

The Canon EOS T7i's Continuous shooting mode reminds me how far digital photography has brought us. The first accessory I purchased when I worked as a sports photographer some years ago was a motor drive for my film SLR. It enabled me to snap off a series of shots in rapid succession, which came in very handy when a fullback broke through the line and headed for the end zone. Even a seasoned action photographer can miss the decisive instant when a crucial block is made, or a baseball superstar's bat shatters and pieces of cork fly out. Continuous shooting simplifies taking a series of pictures, either to ensure that one has more or less the exact moment you want to capture or to capture a sequence that is interesting as a collection of successive images. (See Figure 7.1.)

Continuous shooting is available in any Creative Zone or Basic Zone mode (but *not* in Creative Filters mode). To use the T7i's Continuous shooting mode, press the Drive button (the left directional button) and use the touch screen or directional buttons to select either the Continuous Shooting High icon (to shoot at up to 6 fps) or Continuous Shooting Low (for shots at up to 3 fps).

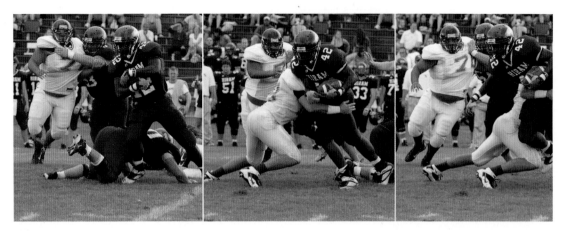

Figure 7.1 Continuous shooting allows you to capture an entire sequence of exciting moments as they unfold.

Alternatively, you can press the Q button to pop up the Quick Control screen and use the touch screen or physical controls to specify the drive mode. When you partially depress the shutter button, the viewfinder will display a number representing the maximum number of shots you can take at the current quality settings. (If your battery is low, this figure will be lower.)

Continuous shooting can be affected by the speed with which your T7i is able to focus. So, in AI Servo AF mode, the frames-per-second rate may be lower. Lenses that inherently focus more slowly (see Chapter 10 for information on the various types of autofocus motors built into Canon lenses), and scenes that are poorly lit can also affect the frame rate. The buffer in the T7i will generally allow you to take as many as 30 JPEG shots at 5 frames per second in a single burst (when using a UHS-I, or Ultra High Speed I compatible memory card), or 6 RAW photos at the 24MP resolution setting. To increase this number, reduce the image-quality setting by switching to JPEG only (from JPEG+RAW), to a lower JPEG quality setting, or by reducing the T7i's resolution from L to M or S.

The reason the size of your bursts is limited by the buffer is that continuous images are first shuttled into the T7i's internal memory, then doled out to the memory card as quickly as they can be written to the card. Technically, the T7i takes the RAW data received from the digital image processor and converts it to the output format you've selected—either JPG or CR2 (RAW) or both—and deposits it in the buffer ready to store on the card.

This internal "smart" buffer can suck up photos much more quickly than the memory card and, indeed, some memory cards are significantly faster or slower than others. You'll get the best results when using a shutter speed of 1/500th second, the widest lens opening of the lens, One-Shot auto-focus, and when image stabilization is turned off. However, when One-Shot AF is active, the T7i will focus only once at the beginning of the sequence, and then use that focus setting for the rest of the shots in the burst. If your subject is moving, you can use AI Servo AF instead, at a slightly slower continuous frame rate.

Setting High ISO Speed Noise Reduction to High or Multi Shot Noise Reduction in the Shooting 3 menu (in Creative Zone modes) also limits the length of your continuous burst. You'll also see a decrease if Chromatic Aberration is enabled in the Shooting 1 menu's Lens Aberration Correction entry, or you have the camera set to do white balance bracketing. (In such cases, the T7i stores three copies of each image snapped, slowing down the burst rate.) While you can use flash in Continuous mode, the camera will wait for the flash to recycle between shots, slowing down the continuous shooting rate.

When the buffer fills, you can't take any more continuous shots (a buSY indicator appears in the viewfinder) until the T7i has written some of them to the card, making more room in the buffer. (You should keep in mind that faster memory cards write images more quickly, freeing up buffer space faster.)

BURSTS NOT JUST FOR ACTION

I often use Continuous shooting mode even when I'm not busy shooting action. As I've mentioned before, bursts make sense when you're shooting HDR or bracketing. But here's a technique you might not have thought of—continuous shooting can give you sharper images!

When I'm photographing concerts, I most frequently use my 70-200mm f/2.8 IS zoom, handheld, with image stabilization turned on, and using the highest continuous frame rate at my disposal. I enjoy greater mobility by not using a monopod (and a tripod would be even more of a ball-and-chain, even if not forbidden by the venue). I'm generally shooting at around 1/180th second, which is usually fast enough to eliminate blur from the performers' motion. IS has no effect on stopping *their* movement, of course, and it does a fairly good job of eliminating camera/photographer shake. However, I invariably find that if I shoot in Continuous, one of the middle frames in a sequence will be sharpest. Even the most seasoned photographer will add a little bump to the camera when they squeeze (not stab) the shutter release.

More Exposure Options

In Chapter 4, you learned techniques for getting the *right* exposure, but I haven't explained all your exposure options just yet. You'll want to know about the *kind* of exposure settings that are available to you with the Canon EOS T7i. There are options that let you control when the exposure is made, or even how to make an exposure that's out of the ordinary in terms of length (time or bulb exposures). The sections that follow explain your camera's special exposure features, and even discuss a few it does not have (and why it doesn't).

A Tiny Slice of Time

Exposures that seem impossibly brief can reveal a world we didn't know existed. In the 1930s, Dr. Harold Edgerton, a professor of electrical engineering at MIT, pioneered high-speed photography using a repeating electronic flash unit he patented called the *stroboscope*. As the inventor of the electronic flash, he popularized its use to freeze objects in motion, and you've probably seen his photographs of bullets piercing balloons and drops of milk forming a coronet-shaped splash.

Electronic flash freezes action by virtue of its extremely short duration—as brief as 1/50,000th second or less. Although the EOS T7i's built-in flash unit can give you these ultra-quick glimpses of moving subjects, an external flash, such as one of the Canon Speedlites, offers even more versatility.

Of course, the T7i is fully capable of immobilizing all but the fastest movement using only its shutter speeds, which range all the way up to 1/4,000th second. Indeed, you'll rarely have need for such a brief shutter speed in ordinary shooting. If you wanted to use an aperture of f/2.8 at ISO 100 outdoors in bright sunlight, for some reason, a shutter speed of 1/4,000th second would more than do the job. You'd need a faster shutter speed only if you moved the ISO setting to a higher sensitivity (but why would you do that?). Under less than full sunlight, 1/4,000th second is more than fast enough for any conditions you're likely to encounter.

Most sports action can be frozen at 1/2,000th second or slower, and for many sports a slower shutter speed is actually preferable—for example, to allow the wheels of a racing automobile or motorcycle, or the propeller on a classic aircraft to blur realistically.

But if you want to do some exotic action-freezing photography without resorting to electronic flash, the T7i's top shutter speed is at your disposal. Here are some things to think about when exploring this type of high-speed photography:

- **You'll need a lot of light.** High shutter speeds cut very fine slices of time and sharply reduce the amount of illumination that reaches your sensor. To use 1/4,000th second at an aperture of f/6.3, you'd need an ISO setting of 800—even in full daylight. To use an f/stop smaller than f/6.3 or an ISO setting lower than 800, you'd need *more* light than full daylight provides. (That's why electronic flash units work so well for high-speed photography when used as the sole illumination; they provide both the effect of a brief shutter speed and the high levels of illumination needed.)

- **Forget about reciprocity failure.** If you're an old-time film shooter, you might recall that very brief shutter speeds (as well as very high light levels and very *long* exposures) produced an effect called *reciprocity failure,* in which given exposures ended up providing less than the calculated value because of the way film responded to very short, very intense, or very long exposures of light. Solid-state sensors don't suffer from this defect, so you don't need to make an adjustment when using high shutter speeds (or brief flash bursts).

■ **Don't combine high shutter speeds with electronic flash.** You might be tempted to use an electronic flash with a high shutter speed. Perhaps you want to stop some action in daylight with a brief shutter speed and use electronic flash only as supplemental illumination to fill in the shadows. Unfortunately, under most conditions you can't use flash in subdued illumination with your T7i at any shutter speed faster than 1/200th second. That's the fastest speed at which the camera's focal plane shutter is fully open: at shorter speeds, the "slit" comes into play, so that the flash will expose only the small portion of the sensor exposed by the slit during its duration. (Check out "Avoiding Sync Speed Problems" in Chapter 11 if you want to see how you *can* use shutter speeds shorter than 1/200th second with certain Canon Speedlites, albeit at much-reduced effective power levels.)

Working with Short Exposures

You can have a lot of fun exploring the kinds of pictures you can take using very brief exposure times, whether you decide to take advantage of the action-stopping capabilities of your built-in or external electronic flash or work with the Canon EOS T7i's faster shutter speeds. Here are a few ideas to get you started:

■ **Take revealing images.** Fast shutter speeds can help you reveal the real subject behind the façade, by freezing constant motion to capture an enlightening moment in time. Legendary fashion/portrait photographer Philippe Halsman used leaping photos of famous people, such as the Duke and Duchess of Windsor, Richard Nixon, and Salvador Dali to illuminate their real selves. Halsman said, *"When you ask a person to jump, his attention is mostly directed toward the act of jumping and the mask falls so that the real person appears."* Try some high-speed portraits of people you know in motion to see how they appear when concentrating on something other than the portrait. (See Figure 7.2.)

■ **Create unreal images.** High-speed photography can also produce photographs that show your subjects in ways that are quite unreal. A helicopter in mid-air with its rotors frozen makes for an unusual picture. Figure 7.3 shows a pair of pictures. At top, a shutter speed of 1/1,000th second virtually stopped the rotation of the chopper's rotors, while the bottom image, shot at 1/250th second, provides a more realistic view of the blurry blades as they appeared to the eye.

■ **Capture unseen perspectives.** Some things are *never* seen in real life, except when viewed in a stop-action photograph. MIT scientist Dr. Harold Edgerton's balloon bursts were only a starting point. Freeze a hummingbird in flight for a view of wings that never seem to stop. Or, capture the splashes as liquid falls into a bowl, as shown in Figure 7.4. No electronic flash was required for this image (and wouldn't have illuminated the water in the bowl as evenly). Instead, a clutch of high-intensity lamps and an ISO setting of 1600 allowed the EOS T7i to capture this image at 1/2,000th second.

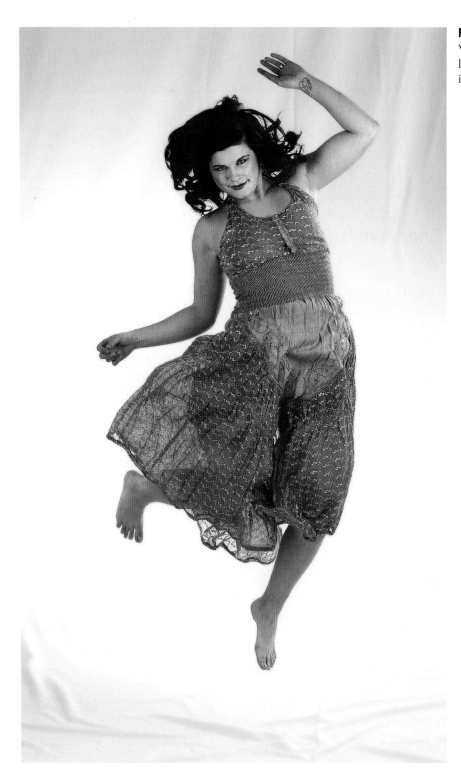

Figure 7.2
When your subjects leap, the real person inside emerges.

Figure 7.3

Top: the chopper's blades are frozen at 1/1,000th second; bottom: a more realistic blurry rendition at 1/250th second shutter speed.

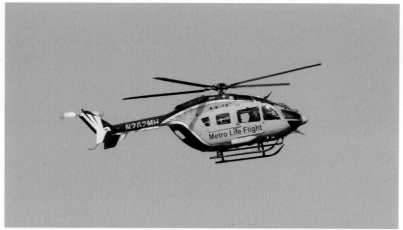

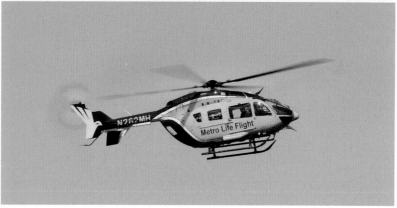

■ **Vanquish camera shake and gain new angles.** Here's an idea that's so obvious it isn't always explored to its fullest extent. A high enough shutter speed can free you from the tyranny of a tripod, making it easier to capture new angles, or to shoot quickly while moving around, especially with longer lenses. I tend to use a monopod or tripod for almost everything when I'm not using an image-stabilized lens, and I end up missing some shots because of a reluctance to adjust my camera support to get a higher, lower, or different angle. If you have enough light and can use an f/stop wide enough to permit a high shutter speed, you'll find a new freedom to choose your shots. I have a favored 170mm-500mm lens that I use for sports and wildlife photography, almost invariably with a tripod, as I don't find the "reciprocal of the focal length" rule particularly helpful in most cases. (I would *not* handhold this hefty lens at its 500mm setting with a 1/500th second shutter speed under most circumstances.) However, at 1/2,000th second or faster, and with a sufficiently high ISO setting (I recommend ISO 800-1600) to allow such a speed, it's entirely possible for a steady hand to use this lens without a tripod or monopod's extra support, and I've found that my whole approach to shooting animals and other elusive subjects changes in high-speed mode. Selective focus allows dramatically isolating my prey wide open at f/6.3, too.

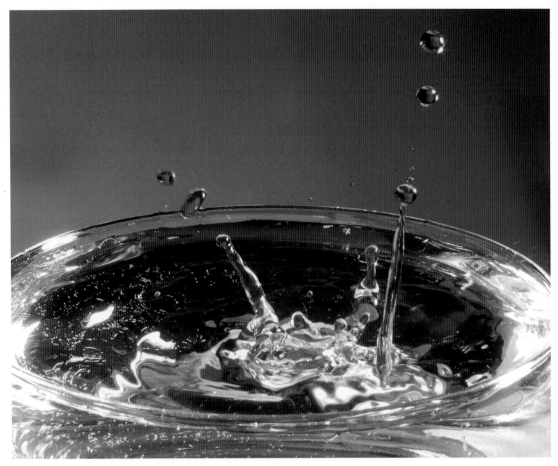

Figure 7.4 A large amount of artificial illumination and an ISO 1600 sensitivity setting allowed capturing this shot at 1/2,000th second without use of an electronic flash.

Long Exposures

Longer exposures are a doorway into another world, showing us how even familiar scenes can look much different when photographed over periods measured in seconds. At night, long exposures produce streaks of light from moving, illuminated subjects like automobiles or amusement park rides. Extra-long exposures of seemingly pitch-dark subjects can reveal interesting views using light levels barely bright enough to see by. At any time of day, including daytime (in which case you'll often need the help of neutral-density filters, which reduce the amount of light passing through the lens, to make the long exposure practical), long exposures can cause moving objects to vanish entirely, because they don't remain stationary long enough to register in a photograph.

Three Ways to Take Long Exposures

There are actually three common types of lengthy exposures: *timed exposures*, *bulb exposures*, and *time exposures*. The EOS T7i offers only the first two, but once you understand all three, you'll see why Canon made the choices it did. Because of the length of the exposure, all the following techniques should be used with a tripod to hold the camera steady.

- **Timed exposures.** These are long exposures from 1 second to 30 seconds, measured by the camera itself. To take a picture in this range, simply use Manual or Tv modes and use the Main Dial to set the shutter speed to the length of time you want, choosing from preset speeds of 1.0, 1.5, 2.0, 3.0, 4.0, 6.0, 8.0, 10.0, 15.0, 20.0, or 30.0 seconds (if you've specified 1/2-stop increments for exposure adjustments), or 1.0, 1.3, 1.6, 2.0, 2.5, 3.2, 4.0, 5.0, 6.0, 8.0, 10.0, 13.0, 15.0, 20.0, 25.0, and 30.0 seconds (if you're using 1/3-stop increments). The advantage of timed exposures is that the camera does all the calculating for you. There's no need for a stopwatch. If you review your image on the LCD and decide to try again with the exposure doubled or halved, you can dial in the correct exposure with precision. The disadvantage of timed exposures is that you can't take a photo for longer than 30 seconds.

- **Bulb exposures.** This type of exposure is so-called because in the olden days the photographer squeezed and held an air bulb attached to a tube that provided the force necessary to keep the shutter open. Traditionally, a bulb exposure is one that lasts as long as the shutter release button is pressed; when you release the button, the exposure ends. To make a bulb exposure with the T7i, set the camera on M using the Mode Dial, then rotate the Main Dial all the way past the longest available shutter speeds to the Bulb position. Then, press the shutter to start the exposure, and press it again to close the shutter.

- **Time exposures.** This is a setting found on some cameras to produce longer exposures. With cameras that implement this option, the shutter opens when you press the shutter release button, and remains open until you press the button again. Usually, you'll be able to close the shutter using a mechanical cable release or, more commonly, an electronic release cable. The advantage of this approach is that you can take an exposure of virtually any duration without the need for special equipment (the tethered release is optional). You can press the shutter release button, go off for a few minutes, and come back to close the shutter (assuming your camera is still there). The disadvantages of this mode are exposures must be timed manually, and with shorter exposures, it's possible for the vibration of manually opening and closing the shutter to register in the photo. For longer exposures, the period of vibration is relatively brief and not usually a problem—and there is always the release cable option to eliminate photographer-caused camera shake entirely. While the T7i does not have a built-in time exposure capability, you can simulate it with the bulb exposure technique, described previously, or use a remote control with the facility.

Working with Long Exposures

Because the EOS T7i produces such good images at longer exposures, and there are so many creative things you can do with long-exposure techniques, you'll want to do some experimenting. Get yourself a tripod or another firm support and take some test shots with long exposure noise reduction both enabled and disabled using the entry in the Shooting 4 menu, as explained in Chapter 8 (to see whether you prefer low noise or high detail) and get started. Here are some things to try:

- **Make people invisible.** One very cool thing about long exposures is that objects that move rapidly enough won't register at all in a photograph, while the subjects that remain stationary are portrayed in the normal way. That makes it easy to produce people-free landscape photos and architectural photos at night or, even, in full daylight if you use a neutral-density filter (or two or three) to allow an exposure of at least a few seconds. At ISO 100, f/22, and a pair of 8X (three-stop) neutral-density filters, you can use exposures of nearly two seconds; overcast days and/or more neutral-density filtration would work even better if daylight people-vanishing is your goal. They'll have to be walking *very* briskly and across the field of view (rather than directly toward the camera) for this to work. At night, it's much easier to achieve this effect with the 20- to 30-second exposures that are possible, as you can see in Figure 7.5.

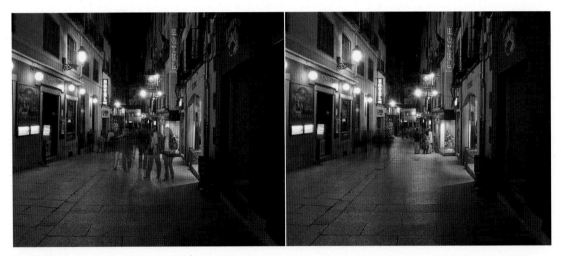

Figure 7.5 This alleyway is thronged with people, as you can see in this two-second exposure using only the available illumination (left). With the camera still on a tripod, a 30-second exposure rendered the passersby almost invisible (right).

■ **Create streaks.** If you aren't shooting for total invisibility, long exposures with the camera on a tripod or monopod can produce some interesting streaky effects, as you can see in Figure 7.6. You don't need to limit yourself to indoor photography, however. Even a single 8X ND (neutral-density) filter will let you shoot at f/22 and 1/6th second in full daylight at ISO 100.

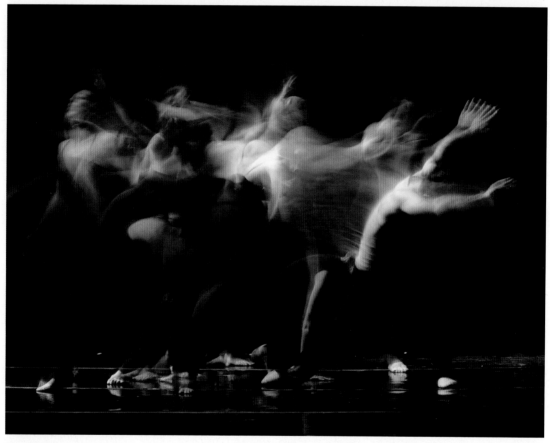

Figure 7.6 These dancers produced a swirl of movement during the 1/8th second exposure.

■ **Produce light trails.** At night, car headlights and taillights and other moving sources of illumination can generate interesting light trails. Your camera doesn't even need to be mounted on a tripod; handholding the T7i for longer exposures adds movement and patterns to your trails. If you're shooting fireworks, a longer exposure of several seconds may allow you to combine several bursts into one picture, as shown in Figure 7.7, which was shot with a tripod-mounted camera.

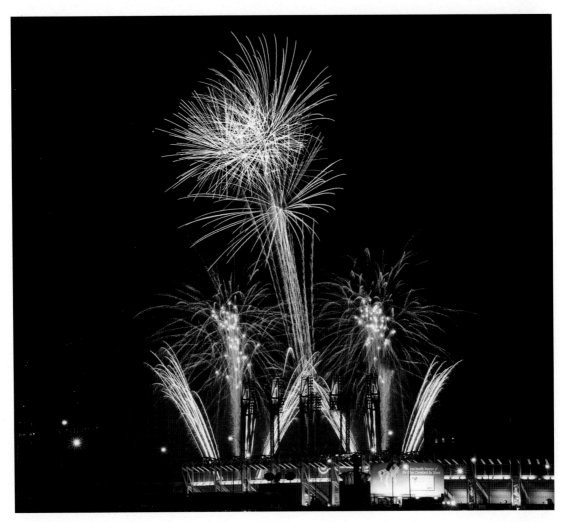

Figure 7.7 A long exposure and a tripod allows capturing several bursts of fireworks in one image.

- **Blur moving water, etc.** You'll find that waterfalls and other sources of moving liquid produce a special type of long exposure blur, because the water from the cascade merges into a fantasy-like veil that looks different at different exposure times, and with different waterfalls. Watery torrents with turbulent flow produce a rougher look at a given longer exposure than falls that flow smoothly. Although blurred waterfalls have become almost a cliché, there are still plenty of other water scenes that benefit from long exposures. Figure 7.8, for example, is *not* a frozen lake. It's the Gulf of Mexico off Horseshoe Key, Florida, captured using a two-minute exposure and stacked neutral-density filters.

- **Show total darkness in new ways.** Even on the darkest nights, there is enough starlight or glow from distant illumination sources to see by, and, if you use a long exposure, there is enough light to take a picture, too. Figure 7.9 shows San Juan, Puerto Rico late at night.

TIP

Long exposures in daylight almost always require using the smallest f/stop available with your lens, such as f/22. When stopping down that far, you may find that sensor dust, unexpectedly brought into sharp focus, has infected areas with solid tones, such as the sky. A little retouching in your image editor may be in order.

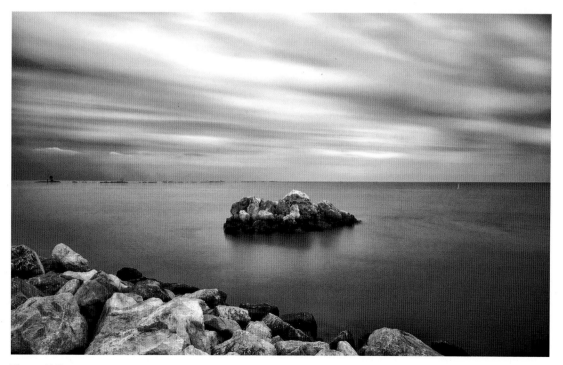

Figure 7.8 A two-minute exposure gave the Gulf of Mexico an otherworldly sheen.

Figure 7.9 A 20-second exposure revealed this view of San Juan, Puerto Rico.

Delayed Exposures

Sometimes it's desirable to have a delay of some sort before a picture is actually taken. Perhaps you'd like to get in the picture yourself, and would appreciate it if the camera waited 10 seconds after you press the shutter release to take the picture. Maybe you want to give a tripod-mounted camera time to settle down and damp any residual vibration after the release is pressed to improve sharpness for an exposure with a relatively slow shutter speed. It's possible you want to explore the world of time-lapse photography. The next sections present your delayed exposure options.

Self-Timer

The EOS T7i has a built-in self-timer with 10-second and 2-second delays. Activate the timer by pressing the Drive button and press the left directional buttons until the drive modes appear on the LCD monitor. Press the shutter release button halfway to lock in focus on your subjects (if you're taking a self-portrait, focus on an object at a similar distance and use focus lock). When you're ready to take the photo, continue pressing the shutter release the rest of the way. The lamp on the front of the camera will blink slowly for eight seconds (when using the 10-second timer) and the beeper will chirp (if you haven't disabled it in the Shooting menu, as described in Chapter 8). During the final two seconds, the beeper sounds more rapidly and the lamp remains on until the picture is taken. The top-panel LCD displays a countdown while all this is going on.

Another way to use the self-timer is with the mirror lockup feature (which can be enabled using C.Fn-10, as explained in Chapter 9). This is something you might want to do if you're shooting close-ups, landscapes, or other types of pictures using the self-timer, to trip the shutter in the most vibration-free way possible. Forget to bring along your tripod, but still want to take a close-up picture with a precise focus setting? Set your digital camera to the self-timer function, then put the camera on any reasonably steady support, such as a fence post or a rock. When you're ready to take the picture, press the shutter release. The camera might teeter back and forth for a second or two, but it will settle back to its original position before the self-timer activates the shutter. The self-timer remains active until you turn it off—even if you power down the T7i, so remember to turn it off when finished.

Using Wi-Fi/NFC and Bluetooth

Your T7i can communicate using Bluetooth, standard Wi-Fi communications or, with Android devices, NFC (Near Field Communications). The latter is a radio protocol similar to Bluetooth that makes automatic connections simply by touching the NFC indicator located between the port covers on the side of the camera to the NFC indicator on the Android phone or tablet.

The various permutations and features are complex, to the extent that Canon offers a separate exhaustive (and exhausting) 170-page Wireless Communication Function Instruction Manual. This book concentrates on still photography rather than information technology or local area networks, and, obviously, I can't devote 170 pages just to Wi-Fi topics. However, I think you'll find enough information in the following sections to get you started.

First, here is a list of the connections you can make with the T7i's wireless features:

- **Phones and tablets.** You can connect to a smartphone or tablet and use an app on the device to operate the camera remotely or review images on your memory card. Both Android and iOS are supported. Quick connection with Android devices using NFC (Near Field Communications) is available, but, to date, Apple's iOS supports NFC only for Apple Pay. That may change while this book is in print.

- **Connect Station.** Canon offers the Connect Station, a 1TB storage device that can download images from the T7i over a wireless connection, or transfer them directly using its memory card slot. The transferred images can be viewed using a web browser, or directed to an HDMI-compatible monitor/HDTV over a cable connection. An included remote control allows you to display the images in slide-show fashion.

- **Remote control.** The T7i can be operated remotely using a computer with EOS Utility software installed.
- **Direct printing.** If you have a Wi-Fi-compatible printer that supports PictBridge, you can make hard copies of your images with a wireless connection.
- **Web upload.** The free Canon iMage Gateway can be used to share your images with colleagues, family, or friends over the Internet.

I'll explain all of these in the next sections, but first you need to consider some general guidelines for the T7i's built-in wireless functions:

General Wi-Fi Guidelines

Here are some general tips for using the EOS T7i's built-in Wi-Fi functions:

- **Conserve processing power.** Wi-Fi uses some of your camera's internal CPU's processing muscle, so when the T7i is busy communicating with another device, give Wi-Fi top priority. Don't press the shutter release, rotate the Mode Dial, or review images with the Playback button. If you do, Wi-Fi functions may be interrupted.
- **Some functions are disabled.** When Wi-Fi is enabled the T7i cannot communicate with a computer, printer, external monitor, GPS, or other device with a direct (cable) connection, USB, or HDMI cable link. For example, if you're viewing your camera's output on a monitor using an HDMI connection, the monitor will go dark during communication. In addition, you can't use an Eye-Fi card (an SD card with its own built-in Wi-Fi functions) and the internal wireless functions simultaneously; if you've set the T7i's Wi-Fi functions to Enable, any Eye-Fi card is automatically disabled. The camera cannot be connected to other NFC devices, including printers, when you're using the NFC function.
- **No auto shutoff.** When using wireless communications, the camera's power-saving shutdown feature is disabled.
- **Monitor connection status.** Wireless status can be seen within the information display on the camera's LCD monitor. When Wi-Fi is disabled, or enabled but no connection is available, an OFF indicator is shown. A green wireless LED on the left shoulder of the camera will illuminate when wireless functions are active.

Connecting to Your Camera

Although you can connect your camera to your smart device manually using the T7i's menu commands, the latest version of Canon's software for your smart device also includes a wizard with step-by-step instructions that potentially make connection even easier. The procedure is basically identical whether you use the menu commands or Easy Connection wizard, but the wizard prompts you to take each step. You can link your camera and device using Bluetooth, Near Field Connection (NFC, if you have an Android device), or conventional Wi-Fi. The description that follows shows the steps to initially connect using Bluetooth; the option to connect using Wi-Fi/NFC instead is mentioned in Step 6.

EASY CONNECTION

Due to page constraints, I'm going to stick to a detailed description of the connection wizard and then proceed directly to sections that tell you what you can do with your wireless capabilities. If you want to use some of the more advanced connectivity features, such as connecting to network access points manually or using WPS, and various authentication and encryption schemes, you'll need to consult Canon's manual.

---

1. **Download App.** If you plan to link your T7i to an Android or iOS smart device, visit your device's store and download the Canon Camera Connect app to your smartphone or tablet. Launch the app and the screen shown in Figure 7.10 appears. Tap the Easy Connection box to launch the wizard.

Figure 7.10
The Canon Camera Connect app for your phone or tablet.

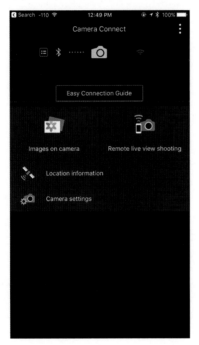

2. **Select camera.** The first screen (Figure 7.11, far left) invites you to select a camera/camcorder to connect. If you have previously connected your smart device to a Canon camera, that device will be shown as an option (Figure 7.11, center left). Otherwise, tap Connect a Camera/Camcorder for the First Time or Connect Another Camera/Camcorder (if that second screen appears).

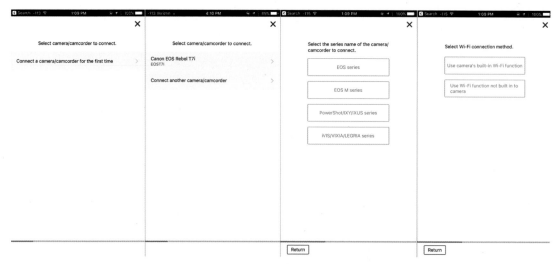

Figure 7.11 Choose your T7i camera using these four screens in the wizard.

3. **Specify your camera series.** Choose EOS series, shown at the top in Figure 7.11, center right. The wizard will then ask you which type of Wi-Fi connection method you want to use. Tap Use Camera's Built-in Wi-Fi Function (Figure 7.11, far right).

4. **Authorize Bluetooth.** The screen that follows, shown at far left in Figure 7.12, asks if your camera supports Bluetooth. The T7i does, so tap Yes, It Does to proceed.

5. **Turn camera on.** At this point it's time to start working with your camera's menu options. The wizard's screens will tell you what to do. Power up your T7i and press the MENU button, and navigate to the Wireless Communication entry at the bottom of the Set-up 1 page, as directed by the wizard in Figure 7.12, center left and center right. Press SET to enter the Wireless Communication Settings menu. That menu is displayed later in this section.

TIP

You can instantly jump to the Wireless Communication Settings menu by pressing the Wi-Fi button, located to the immediate right of the Av and Q buttons on the back of the camera.

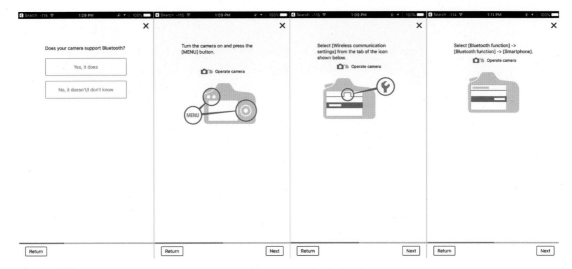

Figure 7.12 These screens ask you to activate Bluetooth using the T7i's menus.

6. **Enable communications.** Conventional Wi-Fi/NFC, and Bluetooth can be enabled separately.

   • **Wi-Fi/NFC (optional).** You do not need to enable Wi-Fi/NFC to connect using Bluetooth, but if you are unable to make a Bluetooth connection, the wizard will offer to use Wi-Fi/NFC instead. You can enable those features using the Wi-Fi Settings entry at the top of the menu. When you enable Wi-Fi/NFC, additional settings become available allowing you to activate NFC (if you have an Android device), set a password, and so forth. Enabling Wi-Fi/NFC does not interfere with Bluetooth communications; however, you can only use one or the other at a time, not both simultaneously.

   • **Bluetooth function.** Select this T7i menu entry, and press SET. From the options that appear, choose Smartphone, as directed by the prompt in the Easy Connection wizard (Figure 7.12, far right).

7. **Pair camera and smart device.** The wizard will next direct you to choose Pairing in the Bluetooth Function menu on the camera (Figure 7.13, far left). Ignore the Connect Via Wi-Fi option, unless your Bluetooth connection fails. When you press SET on the camera, a message will appear asking you whether to display a QR code. Choose Do Not Display and press SET again. (If you capture the QR code with your phone/tablet you're whisked away to the iOS or Android app store to download the Canon Camera Connect app. I asked you to do this already in Step 1, so you can ignore this entreaty.)

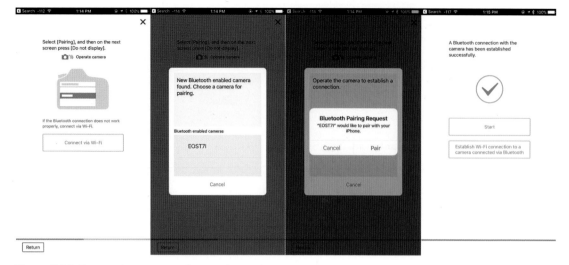

Figure 7.13 Pairing the camera and smart device.

8. **Bluetooth connects.** A message appears on the T7i's LCD monitor: "Pairing in Progress Use Canon app/software on the smartphone to finish pairing." Simultaneously, the two screens shown in Figure 7.13 center left and center right are shown. When your camera's nickname appears, tap Pair to complete the connection. When successful, the screen shown at far right in the figure appears. Tap Start to begin using your connection, or tap the box below it if the connection was not successful and you want to try to connect using Wi-Fi/NFC instead.

NICKNAME

The first time you connect a given camera you may be offered the option of changing the default nickname (EOST7I) to something else. You can also access this option from the Wireless Communications menu (see Figure 7.14) to specify a different nickname.

The entry screen has two sections, the entered text area, and an alphabetical character selection area. (See Figure 7.15.) Press the Q button to toggle between the two. In the selection area, navigate to the character you want to add and press SET. Access uppercase, lowercase, numbers, and symbols by tapping the Aa1@ box at lower right on the virtual keyboard, and enter a space using the box at lower left.

You can enter up to 8 characters in your nickname, such as "BuschT7i". You cannot have a nickname with no characters at all. If Touch Control is enabled, you'll find all the available characters on multiple screens; when disabled, all are available on a single screen. Press the Trash button to erase a character, the INFO. button to cancel text entry, and MENU to finish and confirm your nickname by selecting OK on the screen that pops up. If you later want to change the nickname, return to this menu entry in the Wireless Communications screen.

Figure 7.14
The Nickname option is near the bottom of the Wireless Communication Settings menu.

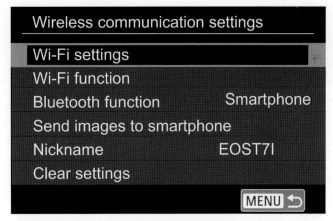

Figure 7.15
Enter a nickname.

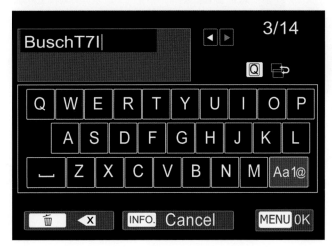

Changing to Wi-Fi

If your Bluetooth connection fails or is unreliable, you can use the Easy Connection wizard to set up a Wi-Fi/NFC connection instead. When the T7i's conventional Wi-Fi connection is enabled, you'll need to use your device's Setttings screen to select that hotspot. Figure 7.16 shows the typical steps for an iOS device. Android connection is similar.

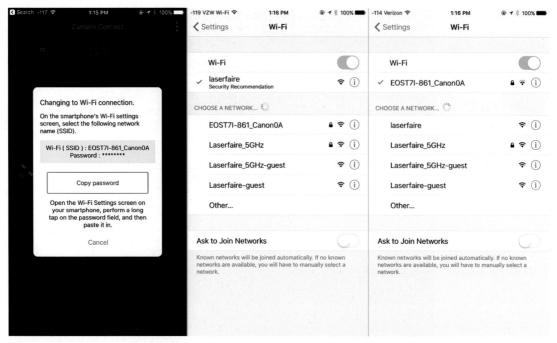

Figure 7.16 Connecting via Wi-Fi.

Using Your Connection

Once you've connected your camera to your smartphone or tablet, there are five different things you can do using the Canon Camera Connect app on your device. I'll describe each of them in the following sections.

READ THE FUNNY MANUAL

As I noted earlier, it's impossible to cover all the connection permutations and possible errors you might encounter when connecting your camera to your smart device. The Canon Wi-Fi manual is very thorough, and the troubleshooting and other instructions are easy to follow once you've absorbed the basics I'm providing in this chapter.

Transferring Images Between Cameras

You can easily transfer JPEG images and movie files between Canon cameras introduced in 2012 or later that have *built-in* wireless functions (your T7i cannot communicate with earlier cameras that have Wi-Fi capabilities solely through an Eye-Fi card). Note that the destination camera must support a transmitted video file's movie format to display it. Your T7i can connect to only one other Canon camera at a time.

To exchange images with another camera, one at a time, just follow these steps:

1. **Turn on Wi-Fi/Bluetooth connectivity.** Press the Wi-Fi button on the camera, located to the right of the Av and Q buttons.

2. **Connect camera and device (optional).** You may see one of two initial screens:

   • **Setup.** If the Wireless Communication Setting screen appears, it means you haven't yet set up a wireless connection. Use the steps listed earlier to set up the connection.

   • **Select device.** If you have set up multiple devices, a history screen showing the devices you have established a connection with may appear. Highlight the one you want and press SET to select. Then use the left/right directional buttons to navigate to the screen shown in Figure 7.17.

3. **Highlight Transfer Images Between Cameras.** It's the icon at left in the top row in the figure. Press SET to continue.

4. **Register second camera.** You'll need to register the second camera you'd like to communicate with. Choose the Register a Device for Connection entry and press SET.

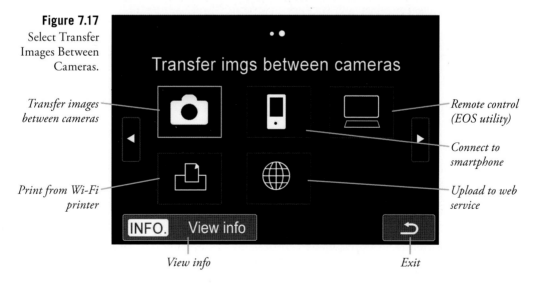

Figure 7.17
Select Transfer Images Between Cameras.

Transfer images between cameras

Print from Wi-Fi printer

Remote control (EOS utility)

Connect to smartphone

Upload to web service

View info

Exit

5. **Make connection.** A screen appears that says "Start connection on target camera." Switch to the other camera and activate the connection there. (Refer to the instructions for the destination camera if necessary to carry out this step.) The process may take a few seconds.

6. **Connection established.** If a connection cannot be established, a warning "Could not establish connection" (Err 101) appears. Otherwise, as soon as the connection is made, the T7i registers the nickname of the target camera and connection information for re-use to pair the two cameras in the future.

7. **Files displayed.** The image files on your camera are displayed so you can select which images to transmit.

8. **Specify image file.** Scroll among the available images, and press the SET button to select one. You can press the Index/Reduce button and rotate the Main Dial to the left to switch to an index/thumbnail display, or to the right to return to single-image display.

9. **Resize (optional).** You can transmit the image shown on the screen, but you don't need to transmit the full-resolution image. You can choose Resize Image.

10. **Start transfer.** When the size of the image to be sent is shown, select Send Img Shown and press SET to start the transfer. A progress screen is displayed during the transmission.

11. **Send additional images.** Repeat Steps 5 to 9 to send additional images.

12. **Terminate connection.** Press the Wi-Fi button to display the transfer confirmation screen, select OK, and press SET to end the transfer connection.

You can also select a batch of up to 50 individual files and send them in one group. (Don't worry: automatic power off is disabled during transmission.) The steps are similar to those listed above, except when you reach Step 7, choose Resize Image, followed by Send Selected. Then choose additional images, which are marked with a check mark in the upper-left corner of the display. When finished choosing images to transmit, press the Q button. You can then resize the selected images in a batch and choose Send to transmit all the selected images.

Communicating with your Smart Device

The center icon in the top row of the screen shown in Figure 7.17 allows you to connect your camera to your phone or tablet and carry out a variety of useful functions. Some functions require using Wi-Fi instead of Bluetooth, so you may see the Switching to Wi-Fi screen shown earlier in Figure 7.16. Just follow the prompts to switch to a Wi-Fi connection instead.

Once you're connected, you'll see a screen in the Canon Camera Connect app similar to the one shown in Figure 7.18, left. You can tap icons to access screens that let you view and transmit images on your T7i; shoot remotely in live view; activate and log location data provided by your smart device; and change camera settings (see Figure 7.18, center and right).

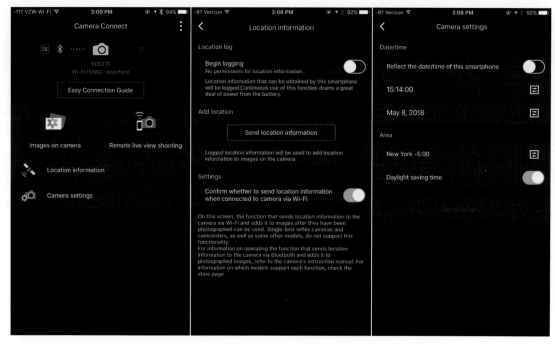

Figure 7.18 Camera Connect app (left); activate and log location data (center and right).

Figure 7.19
Live view and
picture review.

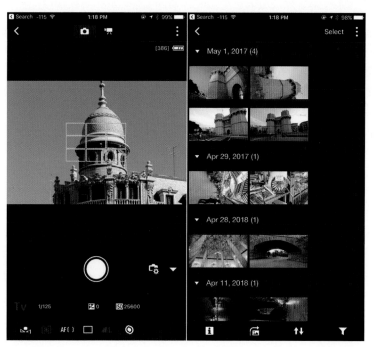

The remote shooting capability is very powerful. It automatically switches the T7i to Live View mode, and displays exactly what the sensor sees on your device's screen (Figure 7.19). You can control shutter speed and/or aperture in Tv, Av, and M shooting modes (which you set on the camera using the Mode Dial); adjust ISO sensitivity; and select white balance, autofocus method, drive mode, and touch shutter—all from your phone or tablet. Then, when you're ready to take a picture, tap the large shutter button icon on your device and take the picture. It will be stored on the camera and can be downloaded to your device, too.

One especially cool feature is being able to tap your device screen (or the T7i's LCD monitor) to locate the AF area/zone within the frame. The camera settings icon (superimposed with a gear icon at lower right) allows you to set various live view parameters, including magnification and rotation.

Save Images to Connect Station

Canon offers the Connect Station, a 1TB storage device that can download images from the T7i over a wireless Wi-Fi or NFC connection, or transfer them directly using its two memory card slots. The transferred images can be viewed using a web browser, or directed to an HDMI-compatible monitor/HDTV over a cable connection. The $260 device includes a remote control that allows you to display the images in slide-show fashion.

Remote Control with EOS Utility

While you can control your T7i using the Camera Connect app on your smartphone as described above, you can also use a laptop or desktop computer to wirelessly operate your camera using the free EOS Utility that can be downloaded from the Canon website. Connection is done in a similar way:

1. Choose Remote Control (EOS Utility) from the Wi-Fi Function screen shown earlier in Figure 7.17. (It's the desktop computer icon.)

2. Select Easy Connection on the camera as described earlier to display the SSID and encryption key (password) on the T7i's LCD monitor.

3. Access your computer/operating system's wireless settings. Keep in mind that while virtually all laptops have wireless built-in, not all desktop computers do.

4. Select the camera's SSID from the list and enter the password/encryption/network security key.

5. Start the EOS Utility 3 on your computer, and select Pairing Over Wi-Fi/LAN.

6. Choose OK when the Start Pairing Device notice shows up on the T7i.

7. When pairing is accomplished, you will be able to access the camera wirelessly using the EOS Utility.

Printing from a Wi-Fi Printer

Many (perhaps most) printers today have built-in wireless capabilities, allowing you to print out directly from your computer without a physical link between the computer and printer. The EOS T7i adds the same function to your camera/printer setup, so you can make hard copies of your images from files in your camera without the bother of transferring them to a computer first. All you need is your T7i and a PictBridge-compatible printer that conforms to the DPS over IP standard. (More alphabet soup: *Digital Photo Solutions* and *Internet Protocol*.)

To use this feature, you must:

- **Configure your printer for wireless printing.** The instructions vary from printer to printer, so you should consult your printer manual for the procedures. Once you've done this, you'll be able to print photos from your camera, plus files from your computer and other compatible devices, such as smartphones. Wireless printing is *not* limited to camera-to-printer communications.

- **Link your camera to the printer.** The procedures are the same as those mentioned earlier. You can use your camera's built-in access point or connect to your local area network (*infrastructure network*). A list of detected printers is displayed, and, as before, you can save the camera-printer connection to a setting for re-use later. Multiple printer connections can be registered.

    If your printer *does not* connect wirelessly, you can still connect to the camera using your LAN, as described previously.

- **Printing images.** Once linked, you can print by pressing the Playback button and scrolling to the image you want to output. Select printing parameters, number of prints, and other settings just as you would for printing over a wired connection to a PictBridge printer.

Uploading to a Web Service

This wireless option allows you to select images and upload them to the Canon Image Gateway, which is a free-of-charge service. You can register online through your computer and through this entry. Once you've become a member, you can upload photos, create photo albums, and use other Canon Image Gateway services. The site also can interface with other web services you have an account with, including e-mail, Twitter, YouTube, and Facebook.

All you need is your EOS T7i and a computer with the EOS Utility installed. Before you can interface with the Canon gateway wirelessly, you must connect your camera and computer using the conventional digital/USB connection, log onto the Gateway through the "globe" icon, and configure the camera's settings to allow access to the web services. (Remember that Wireless capabilities must be set to Disable any time you want to use a wired connection between your camera and computer.)

Then, you can remove the direct link, turn wireless features back on, and connect to your computer through the wireless access methods described earlier in this chapter. Still images can be uploaded to the Gateway, and movies to YouTube. Images can be uploaded directly to Facebook, or shared with Facebook and Twitter users by posting a link back to the Canon Image Gateway location of the files. As with the image transfer features described earlier, you can resize images before uploading, and send photos one by one or in batches.

8

Customizing with the Shooting and Playback Menus

Your Rebel T7i is undoubtedly one of the most customizable, tweakable, fine-tunable cameras Canon has offered non-professional users. In fact, this versatility has made the T7i surprisingly popular among professional photographers as well. If your camera doesn't behave in exactly the way you'd like, chances are you can make a small change in the Shooting, Playback, and Set-up menus that will tailor the T7i to your needs. In fact, if you don't like the *menus*, you can create your own using the clever My Menu system.

This chapter and the next will help you sort out the settings you can make to customize how your Canon Rebel T7i uses its features, shoots photos, displays images, and processes the pictures after they've been taken. As I've mentioned before, this book isn't intended to replace the manual you received with your T7i, nor have I any interest in rehashing its contents. You'll still find the original manual useful as a standby reference if, for example, you want to look up autofocus lens groupings (as mentioned in Chapter 5). There is, however, some unavoidable duplication between the Canon manual and this chapter, because I'm going to explain the key menu choices and the options you may have in using them. You should find, though, that this chapter gives you the information you need in a much more helpful format, with plenty of detail on why you should make some settings that are particularly cryptic.

I'm not going to waste a lot of space on some of the more obvious menu choices. For example, you can probably figure out that the Beep option in the Shooting 3 menu deals with the solid-state beeper in your camera that sounds off during various activities (such as the self-timer countdown). You can certainly decipher the import of the two options available for the Red-Eye Reduc. entry (Enable, Disable), assuming you know what red-eye reduction is. (I'll explain it if you don't.) So, in this chapter, I'll devote no more than a sentence or two to the blatantly obvious settings and concentrate on the more confusing aspects of T7i setup, such as Automatic Exposure Bracketing. I'll cover the Shooting menus (including Live View and Movie shooting) and Playback menus in this chapter, and turn to the Set-up, Custom Functions, and My Menu options in Chapter 9. The Live View and Movie Shooting menus were covered in Chapter 6 and will not be repeated here.

Let's start off with an overview of the T7i's menus themselves.

Anatomy of the Rebel T7i's Menus

If you've used another EOS model, you'll find the T7i's menu system familiar. Some menu items have been moved around and/or renamed. With the current system, just press the MENU button, spin the Main Dial to highlight the menu tab you want to access, and then scroll up and down within a menu with the directional buttons. If you have small enough fingers, you can use the touch screen, too. What could be easier? Different menu tabs are provided, depending on the shooting mode. Note that while Movie and Live View modes provide menu tabs with the same numbers as those in Creative Zone modes, the menu choices differ somewhat.

Table 8.1 Available Menus	
Modes	**Available Menus tabs**
M, Tv, Av, P	Shooting 1, Shooting 2, Shooting 3, Shooting 4, Shooting 5, Playback 1, Playback 2, Playback 3, Set-up 1, Set-up 2, Set-up 3, Set-up 4, Display Level, My Menu 1, My Menu 2, My Menu 3
Scene, Scene Intelligent Auto, Flash Off, Creative Auto, Creative Filters	Shooting 1, Playback 1, Playback 2, Playback 3, Set-up 1, Set-up 2, Set-up 3, Set-up 4, Display Level
Movie, Live View	Shooting 1, Shooting 2, Shooting 3, Shooting 4, Shooting 5, Playback 1, Playback 2, Playback 3, Set-up 1, Set-up 2, Set-up 3, Set-up 4, Display Level, My Menu 1, My Menu 2, My Menu 3

MENU NAVIGATION

Remember: you can use the touch screen to move from menu to menu, or, alternatively, you can work with the Main Dial and the directional buttons to highlight a menu entry. Press/tap SET to select a menu item. That procedure is probably the best way to start out, because those controls are used to make so many settings with the Rebel T7i that they quickly become almost intuitive.

You can jump from tab to tab even if you've highlighted a menu setting on another tab—and the T7i will remember which menu entry you've highlighted when you return to that menu. The memorization works even if you leave the menu system or turn off your camera. The T7i always remembers the last menu entry you used with a tab. So, if you generally use the Format Card command each time you access the Set-up 1 menu, that's the entry that will be highlighted when you choose that tab. The camera remembers which tab was last used, too, so, potentially, formatting your memory card might take just a couple presses (the MENU button, SET to select the highlighted Format command, then a tap, or a click of the directional buttons to choose OK, and another SET to start the format process).

In this chapter, I'm going to explain all the tabs and all the menu entries, and not take the time to mention which of those are *not* available when using scene and other modes. The automatic modes are intended for situations when you don't want full control over your T7i's operation, anyway, and menu limitations go with the territory. The T7i's tabs are color-coded: red for Shooting menus; blue for Playback menus; amber for Set-up menus; teal for Display Level; and green for the My Menu tab. The currently selected menu's icon is white within a background corresponding to its color code. All the inactive menus are dimmed.

Here are the things to watch for as you navigate the menus: (See Figure 8.1.)

- **Main menu tabs.** In the top row of the menu screen, the menu that is currently active will be highlighted as described earlier. Immediately below it a digit representing the menu tab's number and the name of the tab appear. Just remember that the red camera icons stand for still, live view, and movie shooting options; the blue right-pointing triangles represent playback options; the yellow wrench icons stand for set-up options; teal stands for display level; and the green star stands for personalized menus defined for the star of the show—you.

- **Selected menu item.** The currently selected menu entry within a given tab will have a black background and will be surrounded by a box the same hue as its color code.

- **Other menu choices.** The other menu items visible on the screen will have a dark gray background.

- **Current setting.** The current settings for visible menu items are shown in the right-hand column, until one menu item is selected (by choosing SET). At that point, all the settings vanish from the screen except for those dealing with the active menu choice.

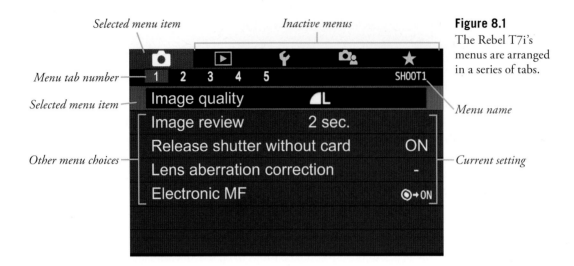

Selected menu item   Inactive menus

Figure 8.1
The Rebel T7i's menus are arranged in a series of tabs.

Menu tab number

Selected menu item

Menu name

Other menu choices

Current setting

When you've moved the menu highlighting to the menu item you want to work with, choose the SET button to select it. The current settings for the other menu items in the list will be hidden, and a list of options for the selected menu item (or a submenu screen) will appear. Within the menu choices, you can scroll up or down with the touch screen or directional buttons; choose SET to select the choice you've made; and choose MENU again to exit.

Shooting Menu Options

The various direct setting buttons on the back panel of the camera for white balance (the up directional button), Picture Styles (down directional button), drive mode (left directional button), AF mode (right directional button), and ISO (the top-panel button south of the Main Dial) are likely to be the most common settings changes you make, with changes during a session fairly common. You'll find that the Shooting menu options are those that you access second most frequently when you're using your Rebel T7i. You might make such adjustments as you begin a shooting session, or when you move from one type of subject to another. Canon makes accessing these changes very easy.

This section explains the options of the five Shooting menus for still photography available in Creative Zone modes, and how to use them.

The options you'll find in these red-coded menus include:

- Image Quality
- Image Review
- Release Shutter without Card
- Lens Aberration Correction
- Electronic Manual Focus
- Exposure Compensation/AEB (Automatic Exposure Bracketing)
- Flash Control
- Red-Eye Reduction
- ISO Speed
- ISO Auto
- Auto Lighting Optimizer

- Metering Mode
- Color Space
- Picture Style
- White Balance
- Custom White Balance
- WB Shift/BKT
- Long Exposure Noise Reduction
- High ISO Speed Noise Reduction
- Dust Delete Data
- Anti-Flicker Shooting
- Aspect Ratio
- Live View Shooting

Image Quality

Options: Resolution: Large (default), Medium, Small 1, Small 2, Small 3; JPEG Compression: Fine (default), Standard; JPEG (default), RAW, or RAW+JPEG

My preference: Resolution: Large; JPEG Compression: Fine; RAW+JPEG

You can choose the image quality settings used by the T7i to store its files. You have three choices when selecting a quality setting:

- **Resolution.** The number of pixels captured determines the absolute resolution of the photos you shoot with your T7i. Your choices range from 24 megapixels (Large or L), measuring 6000 × 4000 pixels; 11 megapixels (Medium or M), measuring 3984 × 2656 pixels; 5.9 megapixels (Small 1 or S1), measuring 2976 × 1984 pixels; and 2.5 megapixels (Small 2 or S2).

- **JPEG compression.** To reduce the size of your image files and allow more photos to be stored on a given memory card, the T7i uses JPEG compression to squeeze the images down to a smaller size. This compacting reduces the image quality a little, so you're offered your choice of Fine compression and Normal compression. The symbols help you remember that Fine compression (represented by a quarter-circle) provides the smoothest results, while Normal compression (signified by a stair-step icon) provides "jaggier" images.

■ **JPEG, RAW, or both.** You can elect to store only JPEG versions of the images you shoot (7.6MB each at the Large Fine resolution setting) or you can save your photos as uncompressed, loss-free RAW files, which consume about four times as much space on your memory card (up to 28MB per file). Or, you can store both at once as you shoot. Many photographers elect to save *both* a JPEG and a RAW file, so they'll have a JPEG version that might be usable as-is, as well as the original "digital negative" RAW file in case they want to do some processing of the image later. You'll end up with two different versions of the same file: one with a JPG extension, and one with the CR2 extension that signifies a Canon RAW file.

To choose the combination you want, access the menus, scroll to Quality, and choose SET. A screen similar to the one shown in Figure 8.2 will appear with two rows of choices. The top row and first two entries on the second row are for JPEG-only settings, two Large and Medium options (at Fine and Normal compression), and four Small choices, representing S1 Fine, S1 Normal, and S2 at the resolutions listed above. A red box appears around the currently selected choice. You can also select RAW+JPEG Large Fine and RAW only. Both produce full-resolution versions of the image.

Why so many choices? There are some limited advantages to using the Medium and Small resolution settings, Normal JPEG compression setting, and the two lower resolution RAW formats. They all allow stretching the capacity of your memory card so you can shoehorn quite a few more pictures onto a single memory card. That can come in useful when on vacation and you're running out of storage, or when you're shooting non-critical work that doesn't require full resolution. The Small 2 setting can be useful for photos taken for real estate listings, web page display, photo ID cards, or similar non-critical applications.

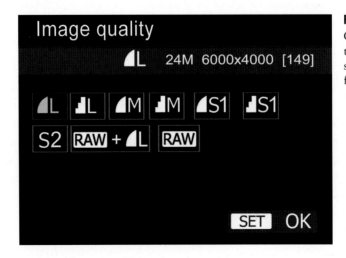

Figure 8.2
Choose your resolution, JPEG compression, and file format from this screen.

For most work, using lower resolution and extra compression is often false economy. You never know when you might actually need that extra bit of picture detail. Your best bet is to have enough memory cards to handle all the shooting you want to do until you have the chance to transfer your photos to your computer or a personal storage device.

However, reduced image quality can sometimes be beneficial if you're shooting sequences of photos rapidly, as the T7i is able to hold more of them in its internal memory buffer before transferring to the memory card. Still, for most sports and other applications, you'd probably rather have better, sharper pictures than longer periods of continuous shooting.

JPEG vs. RAW

You'll sometimes be told that RAW files are the "unprocessed" image information your camera produces, before it's been modified. That's nonsense. RAW files are no more unprocessed than your camera film is after it's been through the chemicals to produce a negative or transparency. A lot can happen in the developer that can affect the quality of a film image—positively and negatively— and, similarly, your digital image undergoes a significant amount of processing before it is saved as a RAW file. Canon even applies a name (DIGIC 7) to the digital image processing (DIP) chip used to perform this magic.

A RAW file is more similar to a film camera's processed negative. It contains all the information, captured in 14-bit channels per color (and stored in a 16-bit space), with no compression, no sharpening, and no application of any special filters or other settings you might have specified when you took the picture. Those settings are *stored* with the RAW file so they can be applied when the image is converted to a form compatible with your favorite image editor. However, using RAW conversion software such as Adobe Camera Raw or Canon's Digital Photo Professional, you can override those settings and apply settings of your own. You can select essentially the same changes there that you might have specified in your camera's picture-taking options.

RAW exists because sometimes we want to have access to all the information captured by the camera, before the camera's internal logic has processed it and converted the image to a standard file format. RAW doesn't save as much space as JPEG. What it does do is preserve all the information captured by your camera after it's been converted from analog to digital form. Of course, the T7i's RAW format preserves the *settings* information.

So, why don't we always use RAW? Although some photographers do save only in RAW format, it's more common to use either RAW plus one of the JPEG options or just shoot JPEG and avoid RAW altogether. That's because having only RAW files to work with can significantly slow down your workflow. While RAW is overwhelmingly helpful when an image needs to be fine-tuned, in other situations working with a RAW file (when all you really need is a good quality, un-tweaked JPEG image) consumes time that you may not want to waste. For example, RAW images take longer to store on the memory card, and require more post-processing effort, whether you elect to go with the default settings in force when the picture was taken, or just make minor adjustments.

As a result, those who depend on speedy access to images or who shoot large numbers of photos at once may prefer JPEG over RAW. Wedding photographers, for example, might expose several thousand photos during a bridal affair and offer hundreds to clients as electronic proofs for possible inclusion in an album or transfer to a CD or DVD. These wedding shooters, who want JPEG images as their final product, take the time to make sure that their in-camera settings are correct, minimizing the need to post-process photos after the event. Given that their JPEGs are so good (in most cases thanks, in large part, to the pro photographer's extensive experience), there is little need to get bogged down shooting RAW.

Sports photographers also eschew RAW files. I visited a local Division III college one sunny September afternoon and managed to cover a football game, trot down a hill to shoot a women's soccer match later that afternoon, and ended up in the adjacent field house shooting a volleyball invitational tournament an hour later. I managed to shoot 1,920 photos, most of them at a 6 fps clip, in about four hours. I certainly didn't have any plans to do post-processing on very many of those shots, and firing the T7i at its maximum frame rate didn't allow RAW shooting, so carefully exposed and precisely focused JPEG images were my file format of choice that day.

JPEG was invented as a more compact file format that can store most of the information in a digital image, but in a much smaller size. JPEG predates most digital SLRs, and was initially used to squeeze down files for transmission over slow dial-up connections. Even if you were using an early dSLR with 1.3 megapixel files for news photography, you didn't want to send them back to the office over a modem (Google it) at 1,200 bps.

But, as I noted, JPEG provides smaller files by compressing the information in a way that loses some image data. JPEG remains a viable alternative because it offers several different quality levels. At the highest quality Fine level, you might not be able to tell the difference between the original RAW file and the JPEG version, even though the 24-megapixel RAW file occupies, by Canon's estimate, 28.1MB on your memory card, while the Fine JPEG at the same resolution takes up only 7.6MB of space. You've squeezed the image significantly without losing much visual information at all.

In my case, I shoot virtually everything at RAW+JPEG Fine. Most of the time, I'm not concerned about filling up my memory cards, as I usually have a minimum of five fast 8GB memory cards with me. I also have some 32GB SD cards that are a little slower (so I don't use them for sports), but with even more capacity. If I think I may fill up all those cards, I have Apple's Camera Connection Kit for my iPad, and can transfer photos to that device. As I mentioned earlier, when shooting sports, I'll shift to JPEG Fine (with no RAW file) to squeeze a little extra speed out of my T7i's Continuous High shooting mode, and to reduce the need to wade through eight-photo bursts taken in RAW format. On the other hand, on my last trip to Europe, I took only RAW (instead of my customary RAW+JPEG) photos to fit more images onto my iPad, as I planned on doing at least some post-processing on many of the images for a travel book I was working on.

Image Review

Options: Off, 2 sec. (default), 4 sec., 8 sec., Hold

My preference: 2 sec.

You can adjust the amount of time an image is displayed for review on the LCD after each shot is taken. You can elect to disable this review entirely (Off), or choose display times of 2, 4, or 8 seconds. You can also select Hold, an indefinite display, which will keep your image on the screen until you use one of the other controls, such as the shutter button, Main Dial, or directional buttons. Turning the review display off or choosing a brief duration can help preserve battery power. However, the T7i will always override the review display when the shutter button is partially or fully depressed, so you'll never miss a shot because a previous image was on the screen. Choose Image Review from the Shooting 1 menu, and select Off, 2 sec., 4 sec., 8 sec., or Hold. If you want to retain an image on the screen for a longer period, but don't want to use Hold as your default, press the Erase button under the LCD monitor. The image will display until you choose Cancel or Erase from the menu that pops up at the bottom of the screen. A longer review time gives you an opportunity to delete a non-keeper without a visit to the menu system.

Release Shutter without Card

Options: Enable/On (Default), Disable/Off

My preference: Disable/Off

This entry in the Shooting 1 menu gives you the ability to snap off "pictures" without a memory card installed—or to lock the camera shutter release if that is the case. It is sometimes called Play mode, because you can experiment with your camera's features or even hand your T7i to friends to let them fool around, without any danger of pictures being taken. Back in our film days, we'd sometimes finish a roll, rewind the film back into its cassette surreptitiously, and then hand the camera to a child to take a few pictures—without wasting any film. It's hard to waste digital film, but Release Shutter without Card mode is still appreciated by some, especially camera vendors who want to be able to demo a camera at a store or trade show, but don't want to have to equip every demonstrator model with a memory card. Choose this menu item, invoke SET, select Enable or Disable, and SET again to turn this capability on or off.

Lens Aberration Correction

Options: Peripheral illumination correction: Enable (default)/Disable; Chromatic Aberration correction: Enable (default)/Disable; Distortion correction: Enable/Disable (default)

My preference: Use the default values

The T7i can automatically partially correct for lens aberrations in four different ways, as long as you are using a lens for which correction data is available. Previously, several of these corrections were available only when post-processing the image in Digital Photo Professional or another utility.

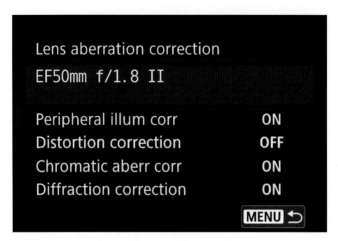

Figure 8.3
The Lens Aberration Correction screen.

The four choices (see Figure 8.3), all described in detail in the section that follows, are:

■ **Peripheral illumination correction.** Fixes light fall-off at the edges of an image.

■ **Distortion correction.** Adjusts for barrel and pincushion distortion.

■ **Chromatic aberration correction.** Reduces color fringes around the edges of subjects.

■ **Diffraction correction.** Corrects for moiré effects produced when shooting at a very small aperture.

I'll explain what each of these components do one at a time, and include some examples of those aspects that can be easily illustrated. When you select this menu option from the Shooting 1 menu, the screen shown in Figure 8.3 appears. The lens currently attached to the camera is shown, along with a notation whether correction data needed to brighten the corners is already registered in the camera. (Information about 25 of the most popular lenses is included in the T7i's firmware.) If so, you can choose Enable to activate the feature, or Disable to turn it off. Press the SET button to confirm your choice. Note that in-camera correction must be specified *before* you take the photo, so that the magical DIGIC 7 processing engine can correct your photo before it is saved to the memory card.

Peripheral Illumination Correction

One defect is caused by a phenomenon called *vignetting*, which is a darkening of the four corners of the frame because of a slight amount of fall-off in illumination at those nether regions. This menu option allows you to activate Peripheral Illumination Correction, a clever feature built in to the T7i that partially (or fully) compensates for this effect for any lens included in the camera's internal, updateable (through firmware upgrades) database. Depending on the f/stop you use, the lens mounted on the camera, and the focal length setting, vignetting can be non-existent, slight, or may be so strong that it appears you've used a too-small hood on your camera. (Indeed, the wrong lens hood can produce a vignette effect of its own.) Vignetting can be affected by the use of a telephoto converter (more on those in Chapter 10, too).

Peripheral illumination drop-off, even if pronounced, may not be much of a problem. I actually *add* vignetting, sometimes, when shooting portraits and some other subjects. Slightly dark corners tend to focus attention on a subject in the middle of the frame. On the other hand, vignetting with subjects that are supposed to be evenly illuminated, such as landscapes, is seldom a benefit.

To minimize the effects of corner light fall-off, you can process RAW files using Digital Photo Professional or, if you want your JPEG files fixed as you shoot them, by using this menu option. Figure 8.4 shows an image at top left without peripheral illumination correction, and a corrected image at bottom left. I've exaggerated the vignetting a little to make it more evident on the printed page. Keep in mind that the amount of correction available with Digital Photo Pro can be a little more intense than that applied in the camera. In addition, the higher the ISO speed, the less correction is applied. If you see severe vignetting with a particular lens, focal length, or ISO setting, you might want to turn off this feature, shoot RAW, and apply correction using DPP instead.

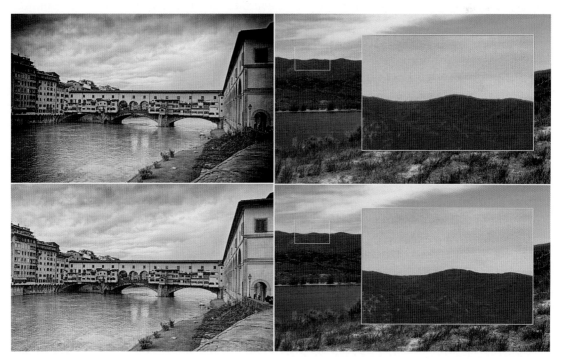

Figure 8.4 Left: Vignetting (top) is undesirable. You can correct this defect in the camera (bottom). Right: Color fringes can be corrected using the lens aberration correction feature (right top and bottom).

Distortion Correction

This option makes adjustments to correct barrel and pincushion distortion, based on information in the camera's database.

Barrel distortion is found in some wide-angle lenses, and causes straight lines to bow outward, with the strongest effect at the edges. In fisheye (or *curvilinear*) lenses, this defect is a feature. When distortion is not desired, you'll need to use a lens that has corrected barrel distortion. Manufacturers like Canon do their best to minimize or eliminate it (producing a *rectilinear* lens), often using *aspherical* lens elements (which are not cross-sections of a sphere). You can also minimize less severe barrel distortion simply by framing your photo with some extra space all around, so the edges where the defect is most obvious can be cropped out of the picture. If none of the above work, you can apply this feature, which is disabled by default, to "undistort" your image with some bending of its own.

Pincushion distortion is a trait of many telephoto lenses, producing lines that curve inward toward the center of the frame. You might find after a bit of testing that it is worse at certain focal lengths with your particular zoom lens. Like chromatic aberration, it can be partially corrected using tools like Photoshop's Lens Correction filter and Photoshop Elements' Correct Camera Distortion filter, Digital Photo Professional, or this in-camera feature.

Chromatic Aberration

Another defect involves fringes of color around backlit objects, produced by *chromatic aberration*, which comes in two forms: *longitudinal/axial*, in which all the colors of light don't focus in the same plane, and *lateral/transverse*, in which the colors are shifted in one direction. (See Figure 8.4, top right.) When this feature is enabled, the camera will automatically correct images taken with one of the supported lenses to reduce or eliminate the amount of color fringing seen in the final photograph. (See Figure 8.4, bottom right.)

Diffraction Correction

Diffraction is a phenomenon that can cause a reduction in the apparent sharpness of your image due to scattering and interference of photons as they pass through smaller lens openings. In effect, the edges of your lens aperture affects proportionately more photons as the f/stop grows smaller. The relative amount of space available to pass freely decreases, and the amount of edge surface that can collide with incoming light increases.

The best analogy I can think of is a pond with two floating docks sticking out into the water, as shown in Figure 8.5. Throw a big rock in the pond, and the ripples pass between the docks relatively smoothly if the structures are relatively far apart (top). Move them closer together (bottom), and some ripples rebound off each dock to interfere with the incoming wavelets. In a lens, smaller apertures produce the same effect.

Figure 8.5
Diffraction interference can be visualized as ripples on a lake.

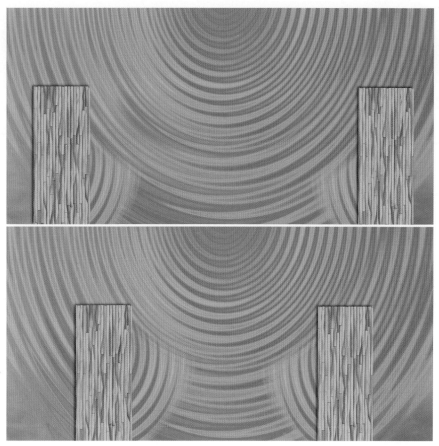

With the T7i, Canon has greatly expanded the list of lens data included within the camera itself. However, if lens aberration correction information for your lens is not registered in the camera, you can often remedy that deficit using the most recent version of the EOS Utility. Just follow these steps:

1. **Link up your camera.** Connect your T7i to your computer using a USB cable.
2. **Launch the EOS utility.** Load the utility and click on Camera Settings/Remote Shooting from the splash screen that appears.
3. **Select the Shooting menu.** It's located on the menu bar located about midway in the control panel that appears on your computer display. The Shooting menu icon is the white camera on a red background.
4. **Click on the Lens Aberration Correction choice.** The selection screen will appear.

5. **Choose your lens.** Select the category containing the lens you want to register from the panels at the top of the new screen; then place a check mark next to all the lenses you'd like to register in the camera.

6. **Confirm your choice.** Click OK to send the data from your computer to the T7i and register your lenses.

7. **Activate correction.** When a newly registered lens is mounted on the camera, you will be able to activate the anti-vignetting feature for that lens from the Set-up 1 menu.

Electronic Manual Focus

Options: Disable after One-Shot AF (default), Enable after One-Shot AF

My preference: Disable

Certain Canon lenses with USM or STM focus motors offer an electronic manual focus option when using the One-Shot AF mode. When enabled, you can continue to adjust the focus already achieved by the AF system as long as you hold the shutter button down halfway. If you release the button, the T7i will refocus the next time you press the shutter release.

At the time I write this, there are nearly two-dozen lenses with this feature. Check page 122 of your T7i manual, or Canon's web page for the most up-to-date listing. I'll explain the difference between USM, STM, and other AF motors in Chapter 10. When this feature is enabled, you can fine-tune focus using the electronic focus system, which is also called "focus-by-wire" because the focus motor is used to make the adjustment rather than mechanical gearing. It works with compatible lenses to fine-tune focus manually after autofocus has taken place. This capability can be used for both movies and still photography.

Exposure Compensation/Automatic Exposure Bracketing

Options: Exposure Comp/Auto Exposure Bracketing

My preference: N/A

The first entry on the Shooting 2 menu is Expo. Comp./AEB, or exposure compensation and automatic exposure bracketing. (See Figure 8.6.) As you learned in Chapter 4, exposure compensation (added/subtracted by pressing the directional buttons while this menu screen is visible) increases or decreases exposure from the metered value.

Exposure bracketing using the T7i's AEB feature is a way to shoot several consecutive exposures using different settings, to improve the odds that one will be exactly right. Automatic exposure bracketing is also an excellent way of creating the base exposures you'll need when you want to combine several shots to create a high dynamic range (HDR) image. (You'll find a discussion of HDR photography—one of the latest rages—in Chapter 4, too.)

To activate automatic exposure bracketing, select this menu choice, then rotate the Main Dial to spread or contract the three dots beneath the scale until you've defined the range you want the bracket to cover, shown as full-stop jumps in Figure 8.7. Then, use the touch screen or directional buttons to move the brackets right or left, biasing the bracketing toward underexposure (move left) or overexposure (move right).

When AEB is activated, the three bracketed shots will be exposed in this sequence: metered exposure, decreased exposure, increased exposure. You'll find more information about exposure bracketing in Chapter 4.

Figure 8.6
Exposure compensation/exposure bracketing is the first entry in the Shooting 2 menu.

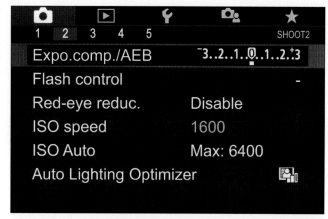

Figure 8.7
Set the range of the three bracketed exposures.

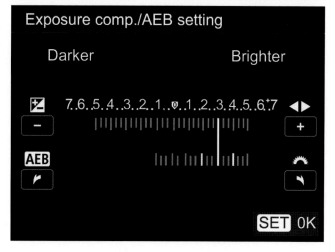

Flash Control

Options: Flash Firing, E-TTL II Metering, Flash Sync. Speed in Av Mode, Built-in Flash Settings, External Flash Function Settings, External Flash Custom Function Settings, Clear Settings

My preference: Varies

This multi-level menu entry includes six settings for controlling the Canon Rebel T7i's built-in, pop-up electronic flash unit, as well as accessory flash units you can attach to the camera (see Figure 8.8). I'll provide in-depth coverage of how you can use these options in Chapter 11, but will list the main options here for reference.

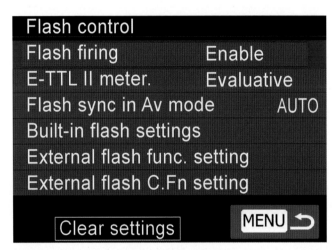

Figure 8.8
The Flash Control menu entry has six setting submenus.

Flash Firing

Use this option to enable or disable the built-in electronic flash. You might want to totally disable the T7i's flash (both built-in and accessory flash) when shooting in sensitive environments, such as concerts, in museums, or during religious ceremonies. When disabled, the flash cannot fire even if you accidentally elevate it, or have an accessory flash attached and turned on. If you turn off the flash here, it is disabled in any exposure mode. You can also select Auto/Flash Off from the Mode Dial, if you don't want to use another exposure mode.

E-TTL II Metering

You can choose Evaluative (Matrix) or Average metering modes for the electronic flash exposure meter. Evaluative looks at selected areas in the scene to calculate exposure, and is the best choice for most images because it attempts to interpret the type of scene being shot; Average calculates flash exposure by reading the entire scene, and it is possibly a good option if you want exposure to be calculated for the overall scene.

Flash Sync in AV Mode

You can select the flash synchronization speed that will be used when working in Aperture-priority mode; choose from Auto (the T7i selects the shutter speed from 30 seconds to 1/200th second), to a range embracing only the speeds from 1/200th to 1/60th second, or fixed at 1/200th second.

Normally, in Aperture-priority mode when using flash, you specify the f/stop to be locked in. The exposure is then adjusted by varying the output of the electronic flash. Because the primary exposure comes from the flash, the main effect of the shutter speed selected is on the secondary exposure from the ambient light on the scene.

As I'll explain in Chapter 11, Auto is your best choice under most conditions. The T7i will choose a shutter speed that balances the flash exposure and available, ambient light. The 1/200th to 1/60th second setting locks out slower shutter speeds, preventing blur from camera/subject movement in the secondary ("ghost") exposure. However, the background may be rendered dark if the flash is not strong enough to illuminate it. The 1/200th second (fixed) setting further reduces the chance of getting those blurry ghosts, but there is more of a chance the background will be dark. You'll find a more detailed explanation of these options in Chapter 11.

Built-in Flash Settings

There are five possible main choices for this menu screen. There are additional options that are not shown or are grayed out unless you're working in Easy Wireless or Custom Wireless flash mode. All these advanced modes are explained in Chapters 11 and 12.

- **Built-in flash.** Your choices here are Normal Firing, Easy Wireless, and Custom Wireless. The first choice is used when you're working with the built-in flash only; the two other options are used when you are syncing your camera with a wireless external flash, as explained in detail in Chapters 11 and 12.

- **Flash mode.** This entry is available only if you've selected Custom Wireless (above), and allows you to choose from automatic exposure calculation (E-TTL II) or manual flash exposure.

- **Shutter sync.** Available only in Normal Firing mode, you can choose 1st curtain sync, which fires the pre-flash used to calculate the exposure before the shutter opens, followed by the main flash as soon as the shutter is completely open. This is the default mode, and you'll generally perceive the pre-flash and main flash as a single burst. Alternatively, you can select 2nd curtain sync, which fires the pre-flash as soon as the shutter opens, and then triggers the main flash in a second burst at the end of the exposure, just before the shutter starts to close. (If the shutter speed is slow enough, you may clearly see both the pre-flash and main flash as separate bursts of light.) This action allows photographing a blurred trail of light of moving objects with sharp flash exposures at the beginning and the end of the exposure. This type of flash exposure is slightly different from what some other cameras produce using 2nd curtain sync. I'll explain how it works in Chapter 11.

If you have an external compatible Speedlite attached, you can also choose Hi-speed sync, which allows you to use shutter speeds faster than 1/200th second, using the External Flash Function Setting menu, described next and explained in Chapter 11.

■ **Flash exposure compensation.** If you'd rather adjust flash exposure using a menu than with the ISO/Flash exposure compensation button, you can do that here. Select this option with the SET button, then dial in the amount of flash EV compensation you want using the directional buttons. The EV that was in place before you started to make your adjustment is shown as a blue indicator, so you can return to that value quickly. Use SET again to confirm your change, then tap MENU or press the MENU button twice to exit.

■ **Wireless functions.** As I mentioned earlier, these choices appear only when you've selected Custom Wireless, and include Mode, Channel, Firing Group, and other options used only when you're working in wireless mode to control an external flash. If you've disabled wireless functions, the other options don't appear on the menu. I'm going to leave the explanation of these options for Chapter 12, which is an entire chapter dedicated to using the Rebel T7i's wireless shooting capabilities.

External Flash Function Setting

You can access this menu only when you have a compatible electronic flash attached and switched on. If you press the INFO. button while adjusting flash settings, both the changes made to the settings of an attached external flash and to the built-in flash will be cleared. These options are quite complex, so I'm going to save the description of them for Chapters 11 and 12.

External Flash Custom Function Setting

Many external Speedlites from Canon include their own list of Custom Functions, which can be used to specify things like flash metering mode and flash bracketing sequences, as well as more sophisticated features, such as modeling light/flash (if available), use of external power sources (if attached), and functions of any slave unit attached to the external flash. This menu entry allows you to set an external flash unit's Custom Functions from your T7i's menu.

Clear Settings

This entry produces a menu screen that allows you to zero-out any changes you've made to your built-in flash settings, external flash settings, or external flash's Custom Function settings.

Red-Eye Reduction

Options: Enable, Disable (default)

My preference: Disable

Your Rebel T7i has a slightly effective Red-Eye Reduction flash mode. Unfortunately, your camera is unable, on its own, to totally *eliminate* the red-eye effects that occur when an electronic flash (or, rarely, illumination from other sources) bounces off the retinas of the eye and into the camera lens. Animals seem to suffer from yellow or green glowing pupils, instead; the effect is equally undesirable. The effect is worst under low-light conditions (exactly when you might be using a flash) as the pupils expand to allow more light to reach the retinas. The most you can hope for is to *reduce* or minimize the red-eye effect.

The best way to truly eliminate red-eye is to raise the flash up off the camera so its illumination approaches the eye from an angle that won't reflect directly back to the retina and into the lens. The extra height of the built-in flash may not be sufficient, however. That alone is a good reason for using an external flash. If you're working with your T7i's built-in flash, your only recourse may be to switch on the Red-Eye Reduction feature with the menu choice. It causes a lamp on the front of the camera to illuminate with a half-press of the shutter release button, which may cause your subjects' pupils to contract, decreasing the amount of the red-eye effect. (You may have to ask your subject to look at the lamp to gain maximum effect.)

ISO Speed

Options: Auto, ISO settings from 100 to 25600, H (ISO 51200 equivalent)

My preference: N/A

This menu choice allows you to select individual ISO settings in one-stop increments (that is, 100, 200, 400…) or Auto (in which case the T7i will choose an appropriate ISO sensitivity for you), with a maximum determined by the ISO Auto entry (which follows this one). You can quickly set Auto when this screen is available by pressing the INFO. button. You can also access this menu entry by pressing the ISO button on the top-right surface of the camera. You can also make ISO settings from the Quick Control screen using the touch screen. The range available has the following limitations:

- **Default range.** If neither C.Fn-2 or C.Fn-4 (described next) are enabled, your selectable settings are ISO 100 to ISO 25600.
- **When ISO Expansion is active.** If C.Fn-2 is enabled, an ISO setting of H (51200 equivalent) becomes available.

- **When Highlight Tone Priority is active.** If you have enabled C.Fn-4 (as described in Chapter 9), your ISO range is limited to ISO 200 to ISO 25600. (Even if ISO expansion is set.)
- **Whole stop increments.** *You* can select ISO values only in whole stop increments, but ISO Auto does not have this limitation. It may select an intermediate value, such as ISO 160 or ISO 640, and will display that value in the viewfinder or on the LCD monitor when you press the shutter release halfway.

ISO Auto

Options: Max 400, 800, 1600, 3200, 6400, 12800, 25600

My preference: Max: 3200, which gives the camera some flexibility in choosing an ISO sensitivity, but avoids invoking the most noise-prone settings.

When you choose Auto (as described above), the T7i can adjust the ISO setting to suit your scene. Fortunately, if you do select Auto, that doesn't necessarily mean that ISO settings are totally beyond your control. With this menu entry, you can choose the *maximum* ISO setting that will be used when working in Auto ISO mode. That will help you avoid unpleasant surprises, which can happen when the T7i opts for an ISO setting that's high enough to produce more visual noise than you might find acceptable.

You can choose a maximum ISO of 400, 800, 1600, 3200, 6400, 12800, or 25600, and the camera will honor your wishes. When you've chosen ISO 25600 as the max rating, though, that doesn't mean that the T7i will necessarily adjust sensitivity all the way up to that lofty level. Instead, it will choose an ISO appropriate for the amount of illumination available; that is, a higher ISO in dimmer conditions, and a lower ISO for brighter scenes. As I noted earlier, the actual ISO in use will be displayed on the top-panel LCD when you press the shutter button halfway, so you aren't necessarily in the dark (so to speak) about the ISO setting being applied. The range used depends on the shooting mode you're working with, and the maximum you set using this menu entry.

Auto Lighting Optimizer

Options: Disable/Off, Low, Standard, High

My preference: Disable/Off

The Auto Lighting Optimizer provides a partial fix for images that are too dark or flat. Such photos typically have low contrast, and the Auto Lighting Optimizer improves them—as you shoot—by increasing both the brightness and contrast as required. The feature can be activated in Program, Aperture-priority, and Shutter-priority modes. You can select from four settings: Standard (the default value, which is always selected when using Scene Intelligent Auto and Creative Auto modes, and used for Figure 8.9), plus Low, Strong, and Disable. Press the INFO. button to add/remove a

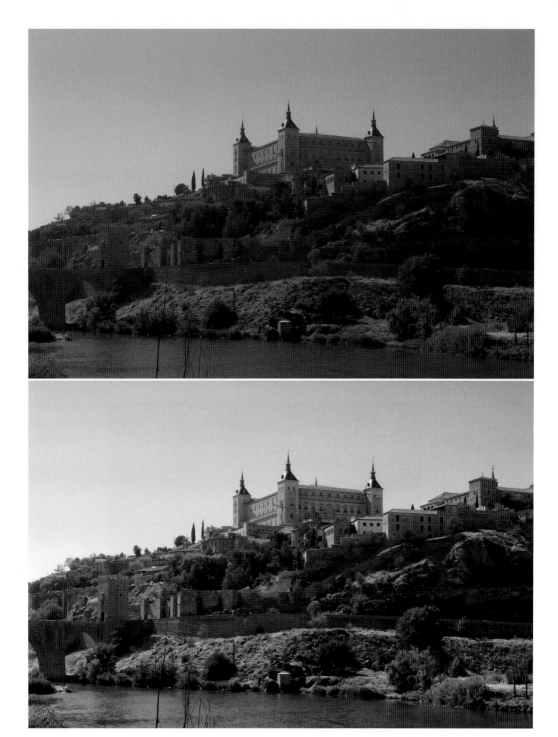

Figure 8.9 Auto Lighting Optimizer can brighten dark, low-contrast images (top), giving them a little extra snap and brightness (bottom).

check mark icon that indicates the Auto Lighting Optimizer is disabled during manual exposure. Since you're likely to be specifying a particular exposure in Manual mode, you probably don't want the optimizer to interfere with your settings, so disabling the feature is the default.

This setting doesn't always work well when you're using Exposure Compensation (or Flash Exposure Compensation). Your images may still be too bright. In such cases, disable Auto Lighting Optimizer and use Exposure Compensation to get the tonal values you want.

Note that when you've enabled Highlight Tone Priority (using C.Fn-4 in the Set-up 4 menu, described in Chapter 9), the Rebel will automatically try to preserve detail in the brightest areas of your image, and Auto Lighting Optimizer is disabled.

Metering Mode

Options: Evaluative (default), Partial, Spot, Averaging

My preference: I most often stick with Evaluative, unless I encounter a subject that lends itself to one of the other modes.

This menu entry, the first in the Shooting 3 menu (see Figure 8.10), is simply an alternate way to choose between Evaluative, Partial, Spot, and Averaging metering, which were explained in detail in Chapter 4. You can also set metering mode using the Quick Control menu (select the icon that's third from the left in the bottom row).

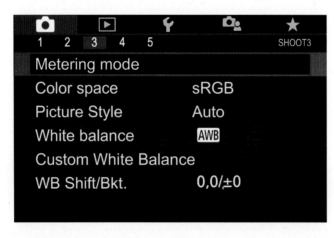

Figure 8.10
Metering Mode is the first entry in the Shooting 3 menu.

Color Space

Options: sRGB (default), Adobe RGB

My preference: I use the expanded Adobe RGB color space.

When you are using one of the Creative Zone modes, you can select one of two different color spaces (also called *color gamuts*) using this menu entry, shown previously among the other menu choices in Figure 8.10. One color space is named *Adobe RGB* (because it was developed by Adobe Systems in 1998), while the other is called *sRGB* (supposedly because it is the *standard* RGB color space). These two color gamuts define a specific set of colors that can be applied to the images your T7i captures.

The Color Space menu choice applies directly to JPEG images shot using P, Tv, Av, and M exposure modes. When you're using Scene Intelligent Auto or Creative Auto modes, the T7i uses the sRGB color space for all the JPEG images you take. RAW images are a special case. They have the information for *both* sRGB and Adobe RGB, but when you load such photos into your image editor, it will default to sRGB (with Scene Intelligent Auto or Creative Auto shots) or the color space specified here unless you change that setting while importing the photos. (See the "Best of Both Worlds" sidebar that follows for more information.)

Figure 8.11
The outer figure shows all the colors we can see; the two inner outlines show the boundaries of Adobe RGB (black triangle) and sRGB (white triangle).

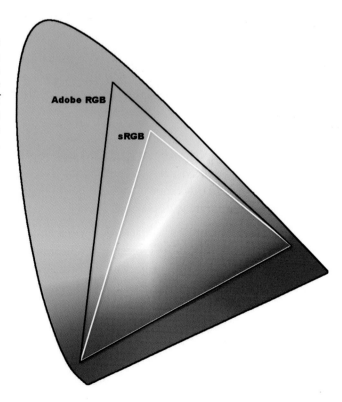

You may be surprised to learn that the Rebel T7i doesn't automatically capture *all* the colors we see. Unfortunately, that's impossible because of the limitations of the sensor and the filters used to capture the fundamental red, green, and blue colors, as well as that of the elements used to display those colors on your camera and computer monitors. Nor is it possible to *print* every color our eyes detect, because the inks or pigments used don't absorb and reflect colors perfectly. In short, your sensor doesn't capture all the colors that we can see, your monitor can't display all the colors that the sensor captures, and your printer outputs yet another version.

On the other hand, the T7i does capture quite a few more colors than we need. The original 14-bit RAW image contains a possible 4.4 *trillion* different hues, which are condensed down to a mere 16.8 million possible colors when converted to a 24-bit (eight bits per channel) image. While 16.8 million colors may seem like a lot, it's a small subset of 4.4 trillion captured, and an even smaller subset of all the possible colors we can see. The set of colors, or gamut, that can be reproduced or captured by a given device (scanner, digital camera, monitor, printer, or some other piece of equipment) is represented as a color space that exists within the larger full range of colors.

That full range is represented by the odd-shaped splotch of color shown in Figure 8.11, as defined by scientists at an international organization called the International Commission on Illumination (usually known as the CIE for its French name *Commission internationale de l'éclairage*) back in 1931. The colors possible with Adobe RGB are represented by the larger, black triangle in the figure, while the sRGB gamut is represented by the smaller white triangle.

Regardless of which triangle—or color space—is used by the T7i, you end up with some combination of 16.8 million different colors that can be used in your photograph. (No one image will contain all 16.8 million! If every pixel in a 15-megapixel photo were a different color—which is extremely unlikely—you'd need only 15 million different colors.) But, as you can see from the figure, the colors available will be *different.*

Adobe RGB is what is often called an *expanded* color space, because it can reproduce a range of colors that is spread over a wider range of the visual spectrum. Adobe RGB is useful for commercial and professional printing. You don't need this range of colors if your images will be displayed primarily on your computer screen or output by your personal printer.

The other color space, sRGB, is recommended for images that will be output locally on the user's own printer, as this color space matches that of the typical inkjet printer fairly closely. While both Adobe RGB and sRGB can reproduce the exact same 16.8 million absolute colors, Adobe RGB spreads those colors over a larger portion of the visible spectrum, as you can see in the figure. Think of a box of crayons (the jumbo 16.8 million crayon variety). Some of the basic crayons from the original sRGB set have been removed and replaced with new hues not contained in the original box. Your "new" box contains colors that can't be reproduced by your computer monitor, but which work just fine with a commercial printing press.

BEST OF BOTH WORLDS

As I mentioned, if you're using a Basic Zone mode, the T7i selects the sRGB color space automatically. In addition, you may choose to set the sRGB color space with this menu entry to apply that gamut to all your other photos as well. But, in either case, you can still easily obtain Adobe RGB versions of your photos if you need them. Just shoot using RAW+JPEG. You'll end up with sRGB JPEGs suitable for output on your own printer, but you can still extract an Adobe RGB version from the RAW file at any time. It's like capturing two different color spaces at once—sRGB and Adobe RGB—and getting the best of both worlds.

Of course, choosing the right color space doesn't solve the problems that result from having each device in the image chain manipulating or producing a slightly different set of colors. To that end, you'll need to investigate the wonderful world of *color management*, which uses hardware and software tools to match or *calibrate* all your devices, as closely as possible, so that what you see more closely resembles what you capture, what you see on your computer display, and what ends up on a printed hardcopy. Entire books have been devoted to color management, and most of what you need to know doesn't directly involve your Canon Rebel T7i, so I won't detail the nuts and bolts here.

To manage your color, you'll need, at the bare minimum, some sort of calibration system for your computer display, so that your monitor can be adjusted to show a standardized set of colors that is repeatable over time. (What you see on the screen can vary as the monitor ages, or even when the room light changes.) I use the Spyder5 Pro monitor color correction system from Datacolor (www.datacolor.com) for my computer's three 26-inch wide screen LCD displays. The Spyder sensor checks room light levels every five minutes, and reminds me to recalibrate every week or two using a small device that attaches temporarily to the front of the screen and interprets test patches that the software displays during calibration. The rest of the time, the sensor sits in its stand, measuring the room illumination, and adjusting my monitors for higher or lower ambient light levels.

If you're willing to make a serious investment in equipment to help you produce the most accurate color and make prints, you'll want a more advanced system (up to $500) like the various other Spyder products from Datacolor or Colormunki from X-Rite (www.colormunki.com).

Picture Style

Options: Auto, Standard, Portrait, Landscape, Fine Detail, Neutral, Faithful, Monochrome, three User Styles

My preference: Auto

This feature is one of the most important tools for customizing the way your Canon T7i renders its photos. Picture Styles are a type of fine-tuning you can apply to your photos to change certain characteristics of each image taken using a particular Picture Style setting. The parameters you can specify for full-color images include the amount of sharpness, degree of contrast, the richness of the color, and the hue of skin tones. For black-and-white images, you can tweak the sharpness and contrast, but the two color adjustments (meaningless in a monochrome image) are replaced by controls for filter effects (which I'll explain shortly), and sepia, blue, purple, or green tone overlays.

The Canon T7i has six preset color Picture Styles, for Standard, Portrait, Landscape, Fine Detail, Neutral, and Faithful pictures, plus Auto, and three user-definable settings called User Def. 1, User Def. 2, and User Def. 3, which you can define to apply to any sort of shooting situation you want, such as sports, architecture, or baby pictures. There is also a seventh, Monochrome, Picture Style that allows you to adjust filter effects or add color toning to your black-and-white images. See Figure 8.12 for the main Picture Style menu.

Picture Styles are extremely flexible. Canon has set the parameters for Auto and the six predefined color Picture Styles and the single monochrome Picture Style to suit the needs of most photographers. But you can adjust any of those "canned" Picture Styles to settings you prefer. Better yet, you

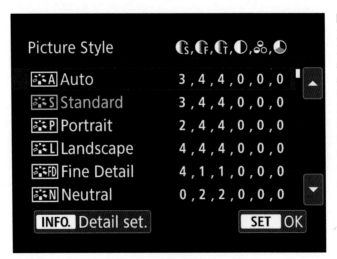

Figure 8.12
Eleven different Picture Styles are available from this scrolling menu; these six, plus Faithful, Monochrome and three User Def. styles that become visible when you scroll down the list.

can use those three User Definition files to create brand-new styles that are all your own. If you want rich, bright colors to emulate Velvia film or the work of legendary photographer Pete Turner, you can build your own color-soaked style. If you want soft, muted colors and less sharpness to create a romantic look, you can do that, too. Perhaps you'd like a setting with extra contrast for shooting outdoors on hazy or cloudy days.

The current settings for each are arrayed along the top in Figure 8.12 as icons: left to right, S (sharpness strength), F (sharpness fineness), T (sharpness threshold), Contrast (a half white/half black circle), Saturation (a triangle composed of three circles), and Color Tone (a circle divided into thirds). When you scroll down within the Monochrome Picture Style, Filter Effect (overlapping circles) and Toning Effect (paintbrush tip) appear. These parameters applied when using Picture Styles are described next.

- **Sharpness.** This parameter determines the apparent contrast between the outlines or edges in an image, which we perceive as image sharpness. When adjusting sharpness, remember that more is not always a good thing. A little softness is necessary (and is introduced by a blurring "anti-alias" filter in front of the sensor) to reduce or eliminate the moiré effects that can result when details in your image form a pattern that is too close to the pattern, or frequency, of the sensor itself. The default levels of sharpening (for most Picture Styles) were chosen by Canon to allow most moiré interference to be safely blurred to invisibility, at the cost of a little sharpness. As you boost sharpness (either using a Picture Style or in your image editor), moiré can become a problem, plus, you may end up with those noxious "halos" that appear around the edges of images that have been oversharpened. Use this adjustment with care. You have three individual parameters within this setting that you can adjust individually:

  - **Strength.** Set the intensity of the sharpening on an eight-step scale from 0 (weak outline emphasis) to 7 (strong outline emphasis). Adding too much strength can result in a halo and excess detail around the edges within your image.

  - **Fineness.** This determines which edges will be emphasized, on a scale of 1 (sharpens the finest lines in your image) to 5 (sharpens only larger, coarser lines). Use a lower number if you anticipate your image will have a wealth of fine detail that you want to emphasize, such as a heavily textured subject. A larger number might be better for portraits, so that eyes and hair might be sharpened, but not skin defects. Changes in Fineness and Threshold (which follows) do not apply when shooting movies.

  - **Threshold.** This setting uses contrast between the edges being sharpened and the surrounding areas, to determine the degree of sharpening applied to the outlines. It uses a scale from 1 to 5, with lower numbers allowing sharpening when there is less contrast between the edge and surroundings. There is an increase in noise when a low threshold is set. Higher numbers produce sharpening only when the contrast between edge and adjacent pixels is already high. The highest numbers can produce excessive contrast and a posterlike effect.

- **Contrast.** Use this control, with values from −4 (low contrast) to +4 (higher contrast), to change the number of middle tones between the deepest blacks and brightest whites. Low-contrast settings produce a flatter-looking photo, while high-contrast adjustments may improve the tonal rendition while possibly losing detail in the shadows or highlights.

- **Saturation.** This parameter, adjustable from −4 (low saturation) to +4 (high saturation) controls the richness of the color, making, say, a red tone appear to be deeper and fuller when you increase saturation, and tend more toward lighter, pinkish hues when you decrease saturation of the reds. Boosting the saturation too much can mean that detail may be lost in one or more of the color channels, producing what is called "clipping." You can detect this phenomenon when using the RGB histograms, as described in Chapter 4.

- **Color tone.** This adjustment has the most effect on skin tones, making them either redder (0 to −4) or yellower (0 to +4).

- **Filter effect (Monochrome only).** Filter effects do not add any color to a black-and-white image. Instead, they change the rendition of gray tones as if the picture were taken through a color filter. I'll explain this distinction more completely in the sidebar "Filters vs. Toning" later in this section.

- **Toning effect (Monochrome only).** Using toning effects preserves the monochrome tonal values in your image, but adds a color overlay that gives the photo a sepia, blue, purple, or green cast.

The predefined Picture Styles are as follows:

- **Auto.** Adjusts the color to make outdoor scenes look more vivid, with richer colors.

- **Standard.** This Picture Style applies a set of parameters, including boosted sharpness, that are useful for most picture taking, and which are applied automatically when using Basic Zone modes other than Portrait or Landscape.

- **Portrait.** This style boosts saturation for richer colors when shooting portraits, which is particularly beneficial for women and children, while reducing sharpness slightly to provide more flattering skin texture. The Basic Mode Portrait setting uses this Picture Style. You might prefer the Faithful style for portraits of men when you want a more rugged or masculine look, or when you want to emphasize character lines in the faces of older subjects of either gender.

- **Landscape.** This style increases the saturation of blues and greens, and increases both color saturation and sharpness for more vivid landscape images. The Basic Zone Landscape mode uses this setting.

- **Fine Detail.** As you might expect, this setting uses sharpening and contrast to produce an image with optimum detail, at the expense of possibly adding some visual noise.

- **Neutral.** This Picture Style is a less-saturated and lower-contrast version of the Standard style. Use it when you want a more muted look to your images, or when the photos you are taking seem too bright and contrasty (say, at the beach on a sunny day).

- **Faithful.** The goal of this style is to render the colors of your image as accurately as possible, roughly in the same relationships as seen by the eye.

- **Monochrome.** Use this Picture Style to create black-and-white photos in the camera. If you're shooting JPEG only, the colors are gone forever. But if you're shooting JPEG+RAW you can convert the RAW files to color as you import them into your image editor, even if you've shot using the Monochrome Picture Style. Your T7i displays the images in black-and-white on the screen during playback, but the colors are there in the RAW file for later retrieval.

Tip

You can use the Monochrome Picture Style even if you are using one of the RAW formats alone, without a JPEG version. The T7i displays your images on the screen in black-and-white, and marks the RAW image as monochrome so it will *default* to that style when you import it into your image editor. However, the color information is still present in the RAW file and can be retrieved, at your option, when importing the image.

Selecting Picture Styles

Canon makes selecting a Picture Style for use very easy, and, to prevent you from accidentally changing an existing style when you don't mean to, divides *selection* and *modification* functions into two separate tasks. There are several different ways to choose from among your existing Picture Styles:

- **Picture Styles menu.** Use this menu entry and scroll down the list shown in Figure 8.12 with the directional buttons until the style you want to use is highlighted. Then press SET.

- **Quick Control screen.** Press the Q button and navigate to the Picture Styles icon at center left of the Quick Control screen with the directional buttons. Press SET, then highlight the Style you want to use and press SET again.

- **Picture Style button.** The down directional button produces a screen that allows you to choose a Picture Style, as seen in Figure 8.13. (This screen is similar to the one produced by the Quick Control screen.)

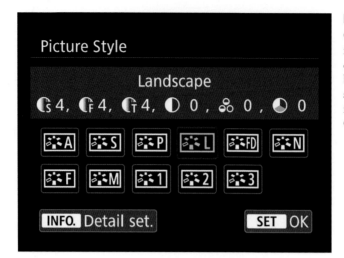

Figure 8.13
Choose Picture Style from the screen produced by the down button (a similar screen is summoned from the Quick Control menu).

Defining Picture Styles

Canon makes interpreting current Picture Style settings and applying changes very easy. As you saw in Figure 8.12, the current settings of the visible Picture Style options are shown as numeric values on the menu screen. You can change one of the existing Picture Styles or define your own whenever the Picture Styles menu is visible. Just press the INFO. button and follow these steps:

1. **Choose a style to modify.** Use the Quick Control Dial to highlight the style you'd like to adjust.

2. **Activate adjustment mode.** Press the INFO. button to choose Detail Set. The screen that appears next will be similar to the one shown at left in Figure 8.14 for the six color styles or three User Def. styles. The Monochrome screen looks like the one at right in Figure 8.14. In either case, you must scroll down to view all the options.

3. **Choose a parameter to change.** Use the directional buttons to scroll among the parameters, plus Default Set. at the bottom of the screen, which restores the values to the preset numbers.

4. **Activate changes.** Press SET to change the values of a highlighted parameter.

5. **Adjust values.** Use the directional buttons to move the triangle to the value you want to use. Note that the previous value remains on the scale, represented by a gray triangle. This makes it easy to return to the original setting if you want.

6. **Confirm changes.** Press the SET button to lock in that value, then press the MENU button three times to back out of the menu system.

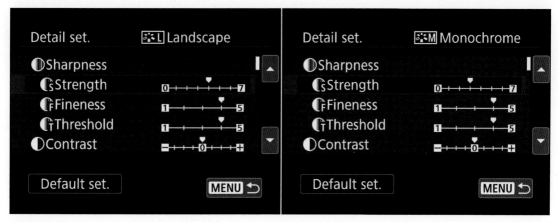

Figure 8.14 Each parameter can be changed separately for color Picture Styles (left), and Monochrome (right).

Any Picture Style that has been changed from its defaults will be shown in the Picture Style menu with blue highlighting the altered parameter. You don't have to worry about changing a Picture Style and then forgetting that you've modified it. A quick glance at the Picture Style menu will show you which styles and parameters have been changed.

Making changes in the Monochrome Picture Style is slightly different, as the Saturation and Color Tone parameters are replaced with Filter Effect and Toning Effect options. (Keep in mind that once you've taken a JPEG photo using a Monochrome Picture Style, you can't convert the image back to full color.) You can choose from Yellow, Orange, Red, Green filters, or None, and specify Sepia, Blue, Purple, or Green toning, or None. You can still set the Sharpness and Contrast parameters that are available with the other Picture Styles.

Adjusting Styles with the Picture Style Editor

If you'd rather edit Picture Styles in your computer, the Picture Style Editor supplied for your camera in versions for both Windows and Macs, allows you to create your own custom Picture Styles, or edit existing styles, including the Standard, Landscape, Faithful, and other predefined settings already present in your T7i. You can change sharpness, contrast, color saturation, and color tone—and a lot more—and then save the modifications as a PF2 file that can be uploaded to the camera, or used by Digital Photo Professional to modify a RAW image as it is imported.

FILTERS VS. TONING

Although some of the color choices overlap, you'll get very different looks when choosing between Filter Effects and Toning Effects. Filter Effects add no color to the monochrome image. Instead, they reproduce the look of black-and-white film that has been shot through a color filter. That is, Yellow will make the sky darker and the clouds will stand out more, whereas Orange makes the sky even darker and sunsets more full of detail. The Red filter produces the darkest sky of all and darkens green objects, such as leaves. Human skin may appear lighter than normal. The Green filter has the opposite effect on leaves, making them appear lighter in tone. Figure 8.15, left, shows the same scene shot with no filter, then Yellow, Green, and Red filters.

The Sepia, Blue, Purple, and Green Toning Effects, on the other hand, all add a color cast to your monochrome image. Use these when you want an old-time look or a special effect, without bothering to recolor your shots in an image editor. Figure 8.15, right, shows the various Toning Effects available.

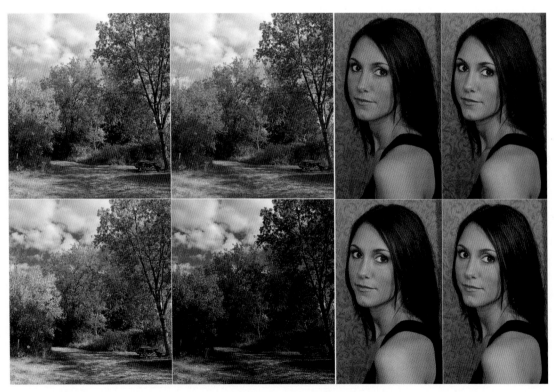

Figure 8.15 Left: Applying color filters: No filter (upper left); Yellow filter (upper right); Green filter (lower left); and Red filter (lower right). Right: Toning: Sepia (top left); Blue (top right); Purple (lower left); and Green (lower right).

To create and load your own Picture Style, just follow these steps:

1. **Load the editor.** Launch the Picture Style Editor (PSE, not to be confused with the *other* PSE, Photoshop Elements).

2. **Access a RAW file.** Load a RAW CR2 image you'd like to use as a reference into PSE. You can drag a file from a folder into the editor's main window, or use the Open command in the File menu.

3. **Choose an existing style to base your new style on.** Select any of the base styles except for Standard. Your new style will begin with all the attributes of the base style you choose, so start with one that already is fairly close to the look you want to achieve ("tweaking" is easier than building a style from the ground up).

4. **Split the screen.** You can compare the appearance of your new style with the base style you are working from. Near the lower-left edge of the display pane are three buttons you can click to split the old/new styles vertically, horizontally, or return to a single image.

5. **Dial in basic changes.** Click the Advanced button in the Tool palette to pop up the Advanced Picture Style Settings dialog box. These are the same parameters you can change in the camera. Click OK when you're finished.

6. **Make advanced changes.** The Tool palette has additional functions for adjusting hue, tonal range, and curves. Use of these tools is beyond the scope of a single chapter, let alone a notation in a list, but if you're familiar with the advanced tools in Photoshop, Photoshop Elements, Digital Photo Pro, or another image editor, you can experiment to your heart's content. Note that these modifications go way beyond what you can do with Picture Styles in the camera itself, so learning how to work with them is worth the effort.

7. **Save your Picture Style.** When you're finished, choose Save Picture Style File from the File menu to store your new style as a PF2 file on your hard disk. Add a caption and copyright information to your style in the boxes provided. If you click Disable Subsequent Editing, your style will be "locked" and protected from further changes, and the modifications you did make will be hidden from view (just in case you dream up your own personal, "secret" style). But you'll be unable to edit that style later on. If you think you might want to change your custom Picture Style, save a second copy without marking the Disable Subsequent Editing box.

Uploading a Picture Style to the Camera

Now it's time to upload your new style to your Canon T7i into one of your three User Def. slots in the Picture Style array. Just follow these steps:

1. **Link your camera for upload.** Connect your camera to your computer using the USB cable, turn the T7i on, launch the EOS Utility, and click the Camera Settings/Remote Shooting choice in the splash screen.

2. **Choose the Shooting menu.** It's marked with an icon of a white camera on a red background, from the menu bar located about midway in the control panel that appears on your computer display.

3. **Select Register User Defined Style.** Click on the box, outlined in red in the figure, to produce the Register Picture Style dialog box.

4. **Choose a User Def. tab.** Click on one of the three tabs, labeled User Def. 1, User Def. 2, or User Def. 3. Each tab will include the name of the current Picture Style active in that tab.

5. **Click the Open File button and choose the Picture Style file to load.** The Picture Styles you've saved (or downloaded from another source) will appear with a PF2 extension. Click on the one you want to use, and then click the Open button in the Open dialog box.

6. **Upload Picture Style to the camera.** The Register Picture Style File dialog box will return. Click OK and the Picture Style will be uploaded to the camera in the User Def. "slot" represented by the tab you've chosen. The name of the Picture Style will appear in the T7i's menu in place of User Def. 1 (or User Def. 2/User Def. 3).

Changing a Picture Style's Settings from the EOS Utility

You can modify the settings of a Picture Style that's already loaded into your camera from the EOS Utility when your camera is linked to your computer. Just follow these steps:

1. **Link your camera to the computer.** Connect your camera to your computer using the USB cable, turn the T7i on, launch the EOS Utility, and click the Camera Settings/Remote Shooting choice in the splash screen.

2. **Choose the Shooting menu.** It's marked with an icon of a white camera on a red background, from the menu bar located about midway in the control panel that appears on your computer display.

3. **Access the Picture Style.** Click on the Picture Style choice. The currently active Picture Style in the camera will be shown, along with its detail settings.

4. **Choose a Picture Style to modify.** Click the Picture Style box to produce a listing of all the available Picture Styles.

5. **Click Detail Set**. At lower left, Landscape is now highlighted. When you click on Detail Set., a dialog box appears. You can move the sliders to change the settings, as described earlier. You can also click the Default Set. button to return the settings to their original values.

6. **Confirm choice.** Click Return when you've finished making changes, and the Picture Style you've modified will be changed in the camera.

7. **Exit EOS Utility.** Disconnect your camera from your computer, and your modified style is ready to use.

White Balance

Options: Auto, Daylight, Shade, Cloudy, White Fluorescent, Custom
My preference: N/A

Allows you to choose from among the available white balance presets: Auto, Daylight, Shade, Cloudy, Tungsten, Fluorescent, Color Temperature, and Custom. When Auto White Balance is set, pressing the INFO. button allows you to choose between Auto: Ambience Priority (which retains warm tones under tungsten illumination) and Auto: White Priority (which preserves neutral white tones under tungsten illumination).

Custom White Balance

Options: White balance setting
My preference: N/A

If automatic white balance or one of the six other preset settings available (Daylight, Shade, Cloudy, Tungsten, White Fluorescent, or Flash) aren't suitable, you can set a custom white balance using this menu option. The custom setting you establish will then be applied whenever you select Custom using the White Balance menu that pops up when you press the WB button (the up directional button). (See Figure 8.16.)

To set the white balance to an appropriate color temperature under the current ambient lighting conditions, focus manually (with the lens set on MF) on a plain white or gray object, such as a card or wall, making sure the object fills the spot metering circle in the center of the viewfinder. Then, take a photo. Next press the MENU button and select Custom WB from the Shooting 3 menu. Use the directional buttons until the reference image you just took appears and choose SET to store the white balance of the image as your Custom setting. Only compatible images that can be used to specify a custom white balance will be shown on the screen. Custom white balance images are marked with a custom icon, and cannot be removed (although they can be replaced with a new custom white balance image).

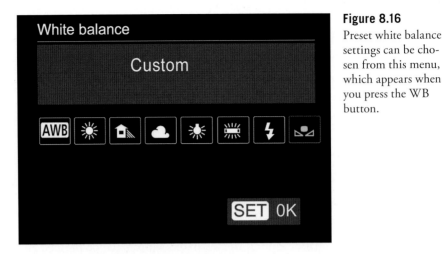

Figure 8.16

Preset white balance settings can be chosen from this menu, which appears when you press the WB button.

A WHITE BALANCE LIBRARY

Shoot a selection of blank-card images under a variety of lighting conditions on a spare memory card. If you want to "recycle" one of the color temperatures you've stored, insert the card and set the Custom white balance to that of one of the images in your white balance library, as described above.

White Balance Shift and Bracketing

Options: WB bias and WB bracketing

My preference: N/A

White balance shift allows you to dial in a white balance color bias along the blue/yellow-amber dimensions, and/or green-magenta scale. In other words, you can set your color balance so that it is a little bluer or yellower (only), a little more magenta or green (only), or a combination of the two bias dimensions. You can also bracket exposures, taking several consecutive pictures each with a slightly different color balance biased in the directions you specify.

The process is a little easier to visualize if you look at Figure 8.17, which shows the screen for the T7i. The center intersection of lines BA and GM (remember high school geometry!) is the point of zero bias. Move the point at that intersection using the directional buttons to locate it at any point on the graph using the blue/yellow-amber and green-magenta coordinates. The amount of shift will be displayed in the SHIFT box to the right of the graph. White balance bracketing is like white balance shifting, only the bracketed changes occur along the bias axis you specify.

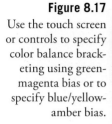

Figure 8.17
Use the touch screen or controls to specify color balance bracketing using green-magenta bias or to specify blue/yellow-amber bias.

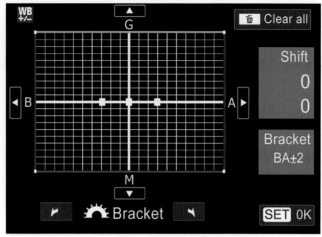

Your controls are as follows:

- **To change the white balance bias:** Use the up/down/left right buttons to move the balance point to any position or axes at once.
- **White balance bracketing:** Rotate the Main Dial to the left, to change the single point to three points that can be moved along the green-magenta axis. Rotating the Main Dial to the right relocates the three points along the blue-amber axis. (See Figure 8.17.)
- **Clear all settings:** Press the Trash button to clear all settings and return to the default shift/bracketing settings.

Bias bracketing can be performed in any JPEG-only mode. You can't use any RAW format or RAW+JPEG format because the RAW files already contain the information needed to fine-tune the white balance and white balance bias.

In most cases, it's fairly easy to determine if you want your image to be more green, more magenta, more blue, or more yellow, although judging your current shots on the LCD screen can be tricky unless you view the screen in a darkened location so it will be bright and easy to see. Bracketing is covered in Chapter 4.

Long Exposure Noise Reduction

Options: Off, Auto, On

My preference: Auto

This menu choice is the first entry in the Shooting 4 menu. (See Figure 8.18.) It allows you to enable or disable long exposure noise reduction, or allow the T7i to evaluate your scene and decide whether to use this noise-canceling adjustment. Visual noise is that graininess that shows up as multicolored specks in images, and this setting helps you manage it. In some ways, noise is like the excessive grain found in some high-speed photographic films. However, while photographic grain is sometimes used as a special effect, it's rarely desirable in a digital photograph.

The visual noise-producing process is something like listening to a CD in your car, and then rolling down all the windows. You're adding sonic noise to the audio signal, and while increasing the CD player's volume may help a bit, you're still contending with an unfavorable signal-to-noise ratio that probably mutes tones (especially higher treble notes) that you really want to hear.

The same thing happens when the analog signal is amplified: You're increasing the image information in the signal, but boosting the background fuzziness at the same time. Tune in a very faint or distant AM radio station on your car stereo. Then turn up the volume. After a certain point, turning up the volume further no longer helps you hear better. There's a similar point of diminishing returns for digital sensor ISO increases and signal amplification as well.

These processes create several different kinds of noise. Noise can be produced from high ISO settings. As the captured information is amplified to produce higher ISO sensitivities, some random noise in the signal is amplified along with the photon information. Increasing the ISO setting of your camera raises the threshold of sensitivity so that fewer and fewer photons are needed to register

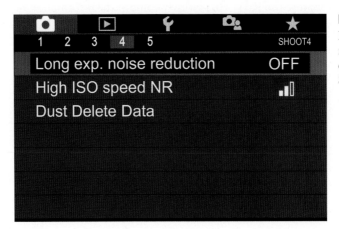

Figure 8.18

Long exposure noise reduction is the first entry in the Shooting 4 menu.

as an exposed pixel. Yet, that also increases the chances of one of those phantom photons being counted among the real-life light particles, too.

Fortunately, the Rebel T7i's sensor and its digital processing chip are optimized to produce the low noise levels, so ratings as high as ISO 800 can be used routinely (although there will be some noise, of course), and even ISO 3200 can generate good results.

A second way noise is created is through longer exposures. Extended exposure times allow more photons to reach the sensor, but increase the likelihood that some photosites will react randomly even though not struck by a particle of light. Moreover, as the sensor remains switched on for the longer exposure, it heats, and this heat can be mistakenly recorded as if it were a barrage of photons. This entry can be used to tailor the amount of noise-canceling performed by the digital signal processor.

■ **Off.** Disables long exposure noise reduction. Use this setting when you want the maximum amount of detail present in your photograph, even though higher noise levels will result. This setting also eliminates the extra time needed to take a picture caused by the noise reduction process. If you plan to use only lower ISO settings (thereby reducing the noise caused by ISO amplification), the noise levels produced by longer exposures may be acceptable. For example, you might be shooting a river spilling over rocks at ISO 100 with the camera mounted on a tripod, using a neutral-density filter and long exposure to cause the pounding water to blur slightly. To maximize detail in the non-moving portions of your photos, you can switch off long exposure noise reduction. Because the noise-reduction process used with Auto and On can effectively double the time required to take a picture, Off is a good setting to use when you want to avoid this delay when possible.

■ **Auto.** The Rebel T7i examines your photo taken with an exposure of one second or longer, and if long exposure noise is detected, a second, blank exposure is made and compared to the first image. Noise found in the "dark frame" image is subtracted from your original picture, and only the noise-corrected image is saved to your memory card.

■ **On.** When this setting is activated, the T7i applies dark frame subtraction to all exposures longer than one second. You might want to use this option when you're working with high ISO settings (which will already have noise boosted a bit) and want to make sure that any additional noise from long exposures is eliminated, too. Noise reduction will be applied to some exposures that would not have caused it to kick in using the Auto setting.

Tip

While the "dark frame" is being exposed, the LCD screen will be blank during Live View mode, and the number of shots you can take in Continuous shooting mode will be reduced. White balance bracketing is disabled during this process.

High ISO Speed Noise Reduction

Options: Disable/Off, Low, Standard, High, Multi Shot Noise Reduction

My preference: Low, with further noise reduction as required in an image editor

The other type of noise results from using higher ISO settings. This entry allows you to specify just how much or how little of this noise reduction to apply, which can be a valuable option because noise reduction does eliminate detail while blurring the amount of noise. The default is Standard noise reduction, but you can specify Low or High noise reduction, or disable noise reduction entirely. At lower ISO values, noise reduction improves the appearance of shadow areas without affecting highlights; at higher ISO settings, noise reduction is applied to the entire photo. Note that when the Strong option is selected, the maximum number of continuous shots that can be taken will decrease significantly, because of the additional processing time for the images.

- **Off/Disable.** No additional noise reduction will be applied.

- **Low.** A smaller amount of noise reduction is used. This will increase the grainy appearance, but preserve more fine image detail.

- **Standard.** At lower ISO values, noise reduction is applied primarily to shadow areas; at higher ISO settings, noise reduction affects the entire image.

- **High.** More aggressive noise reduction is used, at the cost of some image detail, adding a "mushy" appearance that may be noticeable and objectionable. Because of the image processing applied by this setting, your continuous shooting maximum burst will decrease significantly.

- **Multi Shot Noise Reduction.** The camera takes four shots continuously, aligns them (to compensate for slight camera movement during the sequence), and merges them into a single image with reduced noise. The camera can perform this magic because *most* of the pixels in all the images will be identical (except for those that differ because of camera movement), and pixels that are much different among the four shots can be considered to be caused by random noise.

  Note that if there is a great deal of camera shake (not compensated for by your lens's image stabilization), there will be fewer pixels that can be safely considered noise, so the overall reduction may be less. Therefore, you should hold the camera as steady as possible when using this mode. Repetitive patterns and moving subjects also can confuse the image processing, and the manipulation takes some time, so you may not be able to shoot another image for a brief period while the BUSY indicator is visible. You cannot use this feature with RAW or RAW+JPEG image quality settings, while using autoexposure or white balance bracketing, nor when using flash. Your Distortion setting (discussed earlier in this chapter) will be set to Disable.

Dust Delete Data

Options: Obtain data

My preference: N/A

This feature lets you "take a picture" of any dust or other particles that may be adhering to your sensor. The T7i will then append information about the location of this dust to your photos, so that the Digital Photo Professional software can use this reference information to identify dust in your images and remove it automatically. You should capture a Dust Delete Data photo from time to time as your final line of defense against sensor dust.

To use this feature, select Dust Delete Data to produce the screen shown in Figure 8.19. Select OK and choose SET. The camera will first perform a self-cleaning operation by applying ultrasonic vibration to the low-pass filter that resides on top of the sensor. Then, a screen will appear asking you to press the shutter button. Point the T7i at a solid-white card with the lens set on manual focus and rotate the focus ring to infinity. When you press the shutter release, the camera takes a photo of the card using Aperture-priority and f/22 (which provides enough depth-of-field [actually, in this case, *depth-of-focus*] to image the dust sharply). The "picture" is not saved to your memory card but, rather, is stored in a special memory area in the camera. Finally, a "Data obtained" screen appears.

The Dust Delete Data information is retained in the camera until you update it by taking a new "picture." The T7i adds the information to each image file automatically.

Figure 8.19

Capture updated dust data for your sensor to allow Digital Photo Professional to remove it automatically.

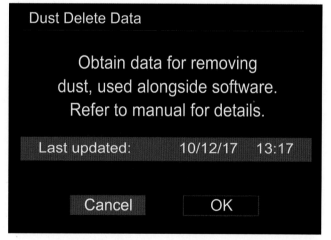

Dust Delete Data

Obtain data for removing
dust, used alongside software.
Refer to manual for details.

Last updated: 10/12/17   13:17

Cancel   OK

Anti-Flicker Shooting

Options: Enable, Disable (default)

My preference: Disable, unless shooting under flickering light source

This is the first of three entries in the Shooting 5 menu. (See Figure 8.20.) Novice sports photographers often ask me why shots they take in certain gymnasiums or arenas have inconsistent exposure, wildly varying color, or banding. The answer is that certain types of artificial lighting actually have a blinking cycle that is imperceptible to the eye, but which the camera can capture. This setting, when enabled, detects the frequency (it's optimized for 100 to 120 Hz illumination) of the light source that is blinking, and takes the picture at the moment when the flicker has the least effect on the final image. It cannot be used in live view or movie shooting.

You may experience a slight shutter release time lag as the camera "waits" for the proper instant, and your continuous shooting speed may be reduced, which makes this setting a necessary evil for sports and other activities involving action. Your results may vary when using P or Av modes, because the shutter speed can change between shots as proper exposure requires. You're better off using Tv or M mode, so the shutter speed remains constant.

A handy Flicker! warning will appear in the viewfinder, alerting you that the feature is enabled, as long as you've set Viewfinder Display in the Set-up 2 menu to include that alert. (Don't worry, I'll explain Viewfinder Display completely in Chapter 9.) Anti-Flicker is disabled when using Mirror Lockup (C.Fn-10, also explained in Chapter 9), and may not work as well with dark backgrounds, a bright light within the image area, when using wireless flash, and under other shooting conditions. Canon recommends taking test shots to see how effective the feature is under the light source you are working with.

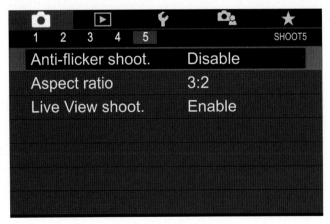

Figure 8.20
Anti-Flicker Shooting is the first entry in the Shooting 5 menu.

Aspect Ratio

Options: 3:2 (default), 4:3, 16:9, 1:1
My preference: 3:2

Allows you to choose an aspect ratio, or proportions of your image, from 3:2, 4:3, 16:9, or 1:1 when working in PSAM exposure modes. Selecting proportions other than the 3:2 default results in a cropped image, and the live view display provides a black border on the LCD to show the limits of the image area (see Figure 8.21). At the Large or RAW size setting, you end up with images that measure 5184 × 3456 pixels/24 MP (3:2 ratio); 4608 × 3456 pixels/16 MP (4:3 ratio); 5184 × 2912 pixels/15.1 MP (16:9 ratio); and 3456 × 3456 pixels/11.9 MP (1:1 ratio). At Medium (M), Small 1 (S1), and Small 2 (S2), the images are proportionately smaller. This choice is not available when using a Basic Zone mode.

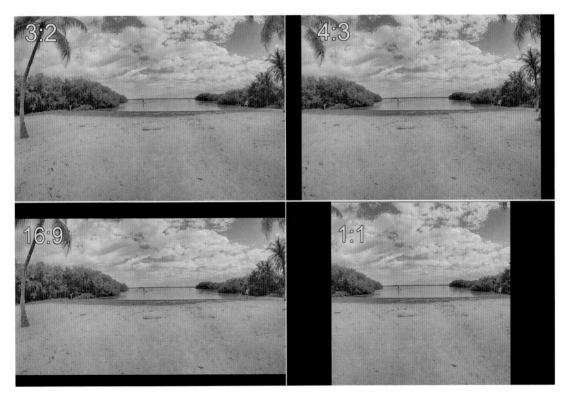

Figure 8.21 You can choose the proportions of your image.

Live View Shooting

Options: Enable, Disable

My preference: Enable

This menu entry enables/disables live view shooting and the Live View button. Disabling live view does not affect movie shooting, which is activated by rotating the On/Off/Movie switch to the Movie position. You might want to disable live view when you want to be sure it doesn't kick in when you press the Live View button, for example, when at a concert or religious ceremony at which the illuminated LCD screen might be distracting. Live view is not available when using Candlelight Scene mode.

Playback Menu Options

The three blue-coded Playback menus are where you select options related to the display, review, and printing of the photos you've taken. The choices you'll find include:

- Protect Images
- Rotate Images
- Erase Images
- Print Order
- Photobook Set-up
- Creative Filters
- Cropping
- Resize

- Rating
- Slide Show
- Set Image Search Conditions
- Image Jump with Main Dial
- AF Point Display
- Histogram Display
- Ctrl over HDMI

Protect Images

Options: Select Images, Select Range, All Images in Folder, Unprotect All Images in Folder, All Images on Card, Unprotect All Images on Card

My preference: N/A

This is the first of six entries in the Playback 1 menu (see Figure 8.22). If you want to keep an image from being accidentally erased (either with the Erase button or by using the Erase Images menu entry), you can mark that image for protection. To protect one or more images, press the MENU button while viewing an image and choose Protect.

Figure 8.22
The Playback 1
menu.

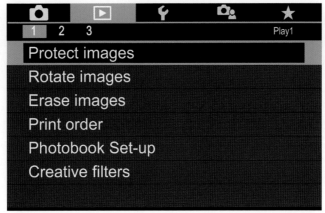

Then, select from the following options:

■ Select Images

■ Select Range

■ All Images in Folder

■ Unprotect All Images in Folder

■ All Images on Card

■ Unprotect All Images on Card

If you choose the first option, you can view and select individual images with the left/right directional controls, Main Dial, or touch screen, followed by pressing the SET button when the image you want to protect is displayed on the screen. A key icon will appear at the upper edge of the information display while still in the protection screen, and when reviewing that image later. Choose Select Range and you can mark the first of a string of images by highlighting it and pressing SET. Then navigate to the last image to be protected and press SET again.

To remove protection, repeat the process. You can scroll among the other images on your memory card and protect/unprotect them in the same way. Image protection will not save your images from removal when the card is reformatted.

Rotate Images

Options: Rotates image

My preference: N/A

While you can set the Rebel T7i to automatically rotate images taken in a vertical orientation using the Auto Rotate option in the Set-up 1 menu (as described in Chapter 9), you can manually rotate an image during playback using this menu selection. Select Rotate from the Playback 1 menu, use the touch screen or directional buttons to page through the available images on your memory card until the one you want to rotate appears, then choose SET. The image will appear on the screen rotated 90 degrees, as shown in Figure 8.23. Select SET again, and the image will be rotated 270 degrees.

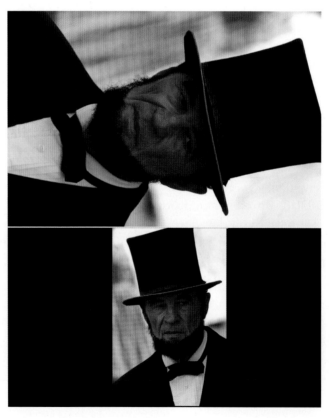

Figure 8.23
A vertically oriented image that isn't rotated appears larger on the LCD, but rotation allows viewing the photo without turning the camera.

Erase Images

Options: Select and Erase Images, Select Range, All Images in Folder, All Images on Card
My preference: N/A

Choose this menu entry and you'll be given four choices: Select and Erase Images, Select Range, All Images in Folder, and All Images on Card. You can use the first three to selectively remove images, while the third option deletes all the pictures on a card. But, using the Format command is usually faster and more thorough.

- **Select and Erase Images.** View the images on your card by pressing the left/right directional buttons to scroll through them. To mark an image for deletion or to remove a check mark, press the SET button. When you're finished selecting, press the Trash button (to the lower right of the LCD) and you'll be asked to confirm. Choose Cancel or OK and SET to finish.

- **Select Range.** Operates similarly to the range protect option listed earlier. Choose Select Range and you can mark the first of a string of images by highlighting it and pressing SET. Then navigate to the last image to be erased and press SET again.

- **All Images in Folder.** You'll be shown a list of the available folders on your memory card. Select SET, and a prompt will appear asking you to confirm, and reminding you that Protected images will not be removed.

- **All Images on Card.** A prompt will ask you to confirm this step. The All Images on Card choice removes all the pictures on the card, except for those you've marked with the Protect command, and does not reformat the memory card.

Print Order

Options: Select Image; By Folder; All Images; Set Up: Print type (Standard, Index, Both); Date (On/Off); File Number (On/Off)
My preference: N/A

The Rebel T7i supports the DPOF (Digital Print Order Format) that is now almost universally used by digital cameras to specify which images on your memory card should be printed, and the number of prints desired of each image. This information is recorded on the memory card, and can be interpreted by a compatible printer when the camera is linked to the printer using the USB cable, or when the memory card is inserted into a card reader slot on the printer itself. Photo labs are also equipped to read this data and make prints when you supply your memory card to them.

Once marked for DPOF printing, you can print the selected images, or take your memory card to a digital lab or kiosk, which is equipped to read the print order and make the copies you've specified. (You can't "order" prints of RAW images or movies.)

To create a DPOF print order, just follow these steps:

1. **Access Print Order screen.** In the Playback 1 menu, navigate to Print Order. Press SET.
2. **Access Set up.** The Print Order screen will appear. (See Figure 8.24.) Use the directional buttons to highlight Set Up. Press SET.
3. **Select Print type.** Choose Print Type (Standard, Index/Thumbnails print, or Both), and specify whether Date or File Number imprinting should be turned on or off. (You can turn one or the other on, but not both Date and File Number imprinting.) You cannot set print type individually; all images in the print order will use the same print type. Press MENU to return to the Print Order screen.
4. **Choose selection method.** Highlight Sel. Image (choose individual images) or Multiple.
   - **Select individual images.** With Sel. Image, use the directional buttons to view the images, and press SET to mark or unmark an image for printing. If you'd rather view thumbnails of images, press the Thumbnail/Zoom In button. Press the Magnify/Zoom Out button to return to single-image view.
   - **Multiple.** Allows you to select Range, Mark All in Folder, Clear All in Folder, Mark All on Card, Clear All on Card., By Folder (to select/deselect all images in a folder), or All Image (to mark/unmark all the images on your memory card). Press SET to choose a range or folder, and MENU to return to the print order screen.

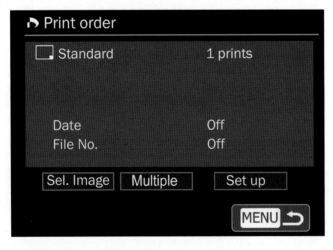

Figure 8.24
Select the images to be printed individually, by folder, or all the images on your memory card.

5. **Choose number of prints.** If you've selected individual images (rather than a range, folder, or card) as an image is selected, you can press the up/down directional buttons to specify 1 to 99 prints for that image. (For Index prints, you can only specify whether the selected image is included in the index print, not the number of copies.) Press SET to confirm. You can then use the up/down buttons to select additional images. Press MENU when finished selecting to return to the Print Order screen.

6. **Output your hardcopies.** If the camera is linked to a PictBridge-compatible printer, an additional option appears on the Print Order screen—Print. You can select that; optionally, adjust Paper Settings as described in the previous section, and start the printing process. Alternately, you can exit the Print Order screen by tapping the shutter release button. Then turn off the camera and printer, remove the memory card, and insert it in the memory card slot of a compatible printer, retailer kiosk, or digital minilab.

Photobook Set-up

Options: Select Images, Multiple

My preference: N/A

You can select up to 998 images on your memory card, and then use the EOS Utility to copy them all to a specific folder on your computer. This is a handy way to transfer only specific images to a particular folder, and is especially useful when you're collecting photos to assemble in a photobook. Your choices include:

- **Select images.** You can mark individual images from any folder on your memory card.
- **Multiple.** You can choose Select Range, All images in folder, Clear all in folder, All images on card, Clear all on card.

Once you marked the images you want to transfer to the specified folder, use the EOS Utility to copy them.

Creative Filters

Options: Grainy B/W, Soft Focus, Fish-Eye, Art Bold, Water Painting, Toy Camera, Miniature

My preference: N/A

One new feature of the T7i is the ability to apply Creative Filters to images as you take the picture, and preview their effect before shooting during live view. However, the original method of applying interesting effects to images you've already taken remains available. You can process an image using one of these filters, and save a copy alongside the original. When you select this menu entry, you'll be taken to a screen that allows you to choose an image to modify. You can scroll through the available images with the touch screen or directional buttons or press the Thumbnail/Reduce Image button to view thumbnails and select from those. Only images that can be edited are shown. Then, select SET, and choose the filter you want to apply from a list at the bottom of the screen using the left/right directional buttons. Choose SET to activate the filter, then use the touch screen or left/right directional buttons again to adjust the amount of the effect (or select the area to be adjusted using the miniature effect). Choose SET once more to save your new image.

The seven effects include the following. Four of them (Grainy B/W, Soft Focus, Fish-Eye Effect, Toy Camera Effect) are shown in Figure 8.25, and the Miniature Effect is shown in Figure 8.26.

- **Grainy B/W.** Creates a grainy monochrome image. You can adjust contrast among Low, Normal, and Strong settings.
- **Soft Focus.** Blur your image using Low, Normal, and Strong options.
- **Fish-eye Effect.** Creates a distorted, curved image.

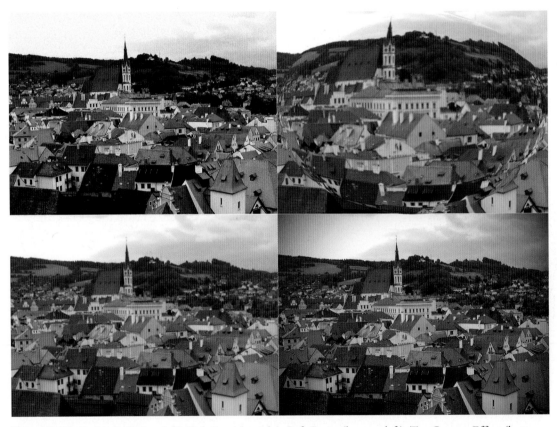

Figure 8.25 Grainy B/W (top left), Fish-Eye (top right), Soft Focus (bottom left), Toy Camera Effect (bottom right).

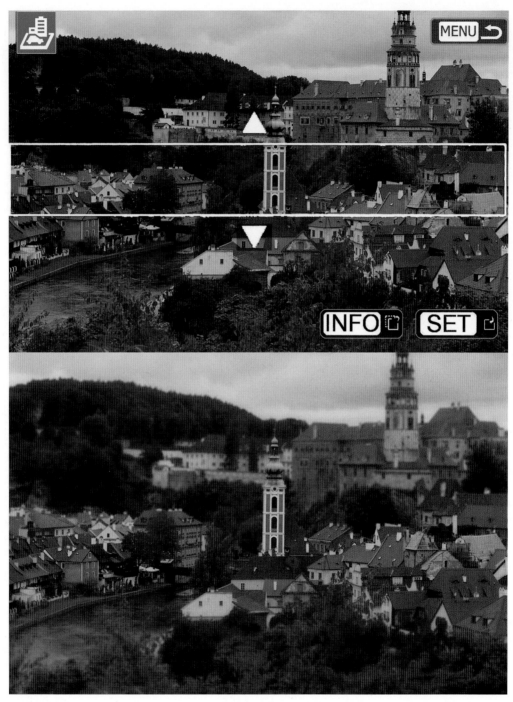

Figure 8.26 Specify the sharp area of your image (top). The resulting Miniature Effect image looks like a tiny town, perhaps for a toy train layout (bottom).

- **Art Bold Effect.** Produces a three-dimensional oil painting effect. You can adjust contrast and saturation.

- **Water Painting Effect.** Gives you soft colors like a watercolor painting, and allows you to adjust color density.

- **Toy Camera Effect.** Darkens the corners of an image, much as a toy camera does, and adds a warm or cool tone (or none), as you wish.

- **Miniature Effect.** This is a clever effect, and it's hampered by a misleading name and the fact that its properties are hard to visualize (which is not a great attribute for a visual effect). This tool doesn't create a "miniature" picture, as you might expect. What it does is mimic tilt/shift lens effects that angle the lens off the axis of the sensor plane to drastically change the plane of focus, producing the sort of look you get when viewing some photographs of a diorama, or miniature scene. Confused yet? All you need to do is specify the area of the image that you want to remain sharp (see Figure 8.26, top) and you'll end up with a version like the one shown in Figure 8.26, bottom.

Cropping

Options: Aspect Ratio, Orientation, Magnification

My preference: N/A

This is the first entry on the Playback 2 menu. (See Figure 8.27.) Sometimes images contain extraneous material, and you want to crop them before, say, sending via e-mail to a friend or colleague. You can crop JPEG images but not RAW files, and save as a new image in a trimmed size.

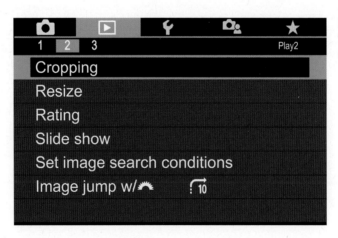

Figure 8.27
The Playback 2 menu.

Just follow these steps:

1. Select Cropping and press SET.

2. Select your image, either by paging through available full-size images, or through Index thumbnails (press the Reduce button to view thumbnails).

3. Press SET to display the green cropping frame.

4. Use the Magnify and Reduce buttons to increase or decrease the size of the cropping frame.

5. Change the Aspect Ratio of the cropping frame among 3:2, 4:3, 16:9, or 1:1 ratios by turning the Main Dial.

6. Move the cropping frame around in your image using the left/right/up/down directional buttons, or drag using the touch screen.

7. Correct tilt (plus or minus 10 degrees in 0.1-degree increments) using a displayed grid by pressing the INFO. button and rotating the Main Dial. You can also tap the left/right icons at the upper left of the screen to quickly fix tilt in 0.5-degree increments.

8. View the cropped image in full view by pressing the Quick Control (Q) button.

9. When satisfied, press the SET button to save the cropped image.

Resize

Options: Medium, Small 1, Small 2

My preference: N/A

If you've already taken an image and would like to create a smaller version (say, to send by e-mail), you can create one from this menu entry. Just follow these steps:

1. **Choose Resize.** Select this menu entry from the Playback 2 menu.

2. **View images to resize.** You can scroll through the available images with the touch screen or directional buttons, or press the Thumbnail/Reduce Image button to view thumbnails and select from those. Only images that can be resized are shown. They include JPEG Large, Medium, Small 1, and Small 2 images. RAW images of any type cannot be resized.

3. **Select an image.** Choose SET to select an image to resize. A pop-up menu will appear on the screen offering the choice of reduced-size images. These include M (Medium: 10.6MP, 3984 × 2656 pixels); S1 (Small 1: 5.9MP, 2976 × 1984 pixels); or S2 (Small 2: 2.5MP, 1920 × 1280 pixels). You cannot resize an image to a size that is larger than its current size; that is, you cannot save a JPEG Medium image as JPEG Large.

4. **Resize and save.** Choose SET to save as a new file, and confirm your choice by selecting OK from the screen that pops up, or cancel to exit without saving a new version. The old version of the image is untouched.

Rating

Options: One to Five Stars

My preference: N/A

If you want to apply a quality rating to images or movies you've shot (or use the rating system to represent some other criteria), you can use this entry to give images one, two, three, four, or five stars, or turn the rating system off. The Image Jump function can display only images with a given rating. Suppose you were photographing a track meet with multiple events. You could apply a one-star rating to jumping events, two stars to relays, three stars to throwing events, four stars to hurdles, and five stars to dashes. Then, using the Image Jump feature, you could review only images of one particular type.

With a little imagination, you can apply the rating system to all sorts of categories. At a wedding, you could classify pictures of the bride, the groom, guests, attendants, and parents of the couple. If you were shooting school portraits, one rating could apply to First Grade, another to Second Grade, and so on. Given a little thought, this feature has many more applications than you might think. To use it, just follow these steps:

1. Choose the Rating menu item.
2. Use the touch screen or directional buttons to select an image or movie. Press the Thumbnail/Reduce Image/Zoom Out button to display three images at once. Press the AF point/Magnify/Zoom In button to return to a single image.
3. When an image or movie is visible, press the up/down buttons to apply a one- to five-star rating. The display shows how many images have been assigned each rating so far.
4. When finished rating, choose MENU to exit.

Slide Show

Options: Display Time, Repeat, Transitional Effect, Background Music

My preference: N/A

Slide Show is a convenient way to review images one after another, without the need to manually switch between them. To activate, just choose Slide Show from the Playback 2 menu. During playback, you can press the SET button to pause the "slide show" (in case you want to examine an image more closely), or the INFO. button to change the amount of information displayed on the screen with each image. For example, you might want to review a set of images and their histograms to judge the exposure of the group of pictures. By default, all images on the card are shown one after another. To limit your show to certain images only, use the Set Image Search feature, described next.

To set up your slide show, follow these steps:

1. **Begin set up.** Choose Slide Show from the Playback 2 menu, choosing SET to display the screen shown in Figure 8.28.

2. **Choose Display Time.** Choose to show each image for 1, 2, 3, 5, 10, or 20 seconds.

3. **Select Repeat.** You can have your slide show repeat when it's finished. This would be an excellent choice if you have connected the output of your T7i to an HDTV, monitor, or digital projector through the HDMI port and want to use your camera to continuously show a demo or other presentation.

4. **Specify Transition Effect.** Add a professional look to your slide show by specifying any of five different transition effects, including three types of fades.

5. **Enable/Disable Background Music.** You can enable or disable background music. However, you must first copy the background music to your memory card, using the procedure in the section that follows.

6. **Start the show.** Highlight Start and choose SET to begin your show. (If you'd rather cancel the show you've just set up, select MENU.)

7. **Use show options during display.** Press SET to pause/restart; INFO. to cycle among the playback information displays; MENU to stop the show.

Figure 8.28
Set up your slide show using this screen.

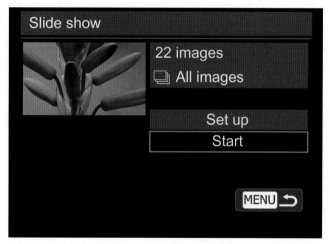

Adding Music

Use the EOS Utility to add music files to your memory card, so you can play them back during your slide shows. Just follow these steps:

1. **Connect.** Link your T7i to your computer and then launch the EOS Utility application.
2. **Choose Register Background Music.** When the Camera Settings screen appears, select Register Background Music to view the Background Music window.
3. **Add tunes (optional).** The EOS Utility includes several background music files with themes like sports, memories, and travel. You can also add your own music files in .WAV format to the catalog, using the Add button or by dragging and dropping the files. Up to a total of 20 different background tracks can be stored, each up to 29 minutes, 59 seconds long.
4. **Register to card.** Select the music files you want to include and click Register. They will be copied to your memory card, overwriting any music files already stored there.

Set Image Search Conditions

Options: Filter by: Rating, Date, Folder, Protection, or File Type
My preference: N/A

You don't need to see every image on your memory card as you play them back. This entry allows you to specify which images are shown during image review, available in a slide show, or subject to the Protect and Erase features. Just follow these steps:

1. **Choose Set Image Search Conditions.** Highlight the entry and press SET.
2. **Select condition.** A vertical column at left appears with the conditions available, listed, from top to bottom: Rating, Date, Folder, Protection, or File Type. Use the up/down buttons to highlight a condition.
3. **Enter parameter.** Use the left/right buttons to set the parameter for a particular condition:
   - **Rating.** You can choose one to five stars.
   - **Date.** Select specific dates *that include photos taken.* (That is, you cannot select a date on which no images where taken with this card.)
   - **Folder.** Select from among the various folders on your card. If only one folder is available, that is chosen by default.
   - **Protected.** Choose Protected or Unprotected images.
   - **Type of File.** Choose to show only stills, various combinations of RAW, RAW+JPEG, and JPEG, plus movie files.

4. **Set condition.** When parameters are set for a condition, press INFO. to add it to your conditions. You can press INFO. again to unselect it. Mix and match conditions, choosing any one, or any combination of the five parameters. Press Trash to remove all conditions.

5. **Confirm.** Press SET to exit. An informational screen will appear. Press OK to confirm.

Image Jump with Main Dial

Options: 1 Image, 10 Images, Specified Number, Date, Folder, Movies, Stills, Protected, Rating
My preference: 10 Images

As first described in Chapter 2, you can leap ahead or back during picture review by swiping across the touch screen with two fingers, or by rotating the Main Dial. You can select from a variety of increments that will be used with this menu entry. The Jump method is shown briefly on the screen as you leap ahead to the next image displayed, as shown in Figure 8.29. Your options are as follows:

- **1 image.** Rotating the Main Dial one click or swiping jumps forward or back 1 image.
- **10 images.** Rotating the Main Dial one click or swiping jumps forward or back 10 images.
- **Specified number.** When this option is highlighted, rotate the Main Dial to choose the increment between jumps, from one image to 100.
- **Date.** Rotating the Main Dial one click or swiping jumps forward or back to the first image taken on the next or previous calendar date.
- **Folder.** Rotating the Main Dial one click or swiping jumps forward or back to the first image in the next folder available on your memory card (if one exists).

Figure 8.29
The Jump method is shown on the LCD briefly when you leap forward or back using the Main Dial or a two-fingered touch screen swipe.

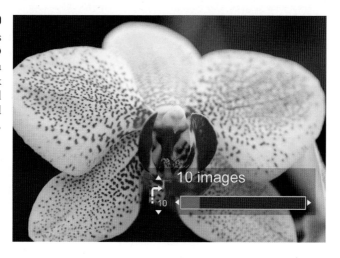

■ **Movies.** Rotating the Main Dial one click or swiping jumps forward or back, displaying movies you captured only.

■ **Stills.** Rotating the Main Dial one click or swiping jumps forward or back, displaying still images only.

■ **Protected.** Rotating the main dial jumps between Protected images only. This is a good way to review images you deemed worthy of protection, or which you have marked with the protected attribute for some other reason (say, you wanted to group some favorite shots for review, but not apply a specific star rating).

■ **Rating.** Rotating the Main Dial one click or swiping jumps forward or back, displaying images by the ratings you've applied (as described earlier). Tap the touch screen or rotate the Main Dial to choose the rating parameter.

AF Point Display

Options: Enable, Disable

My preference: Enable

This is the first entry in the Playback 3 menu (see Figure 8.30). It specifies whether the autofocus points used to determine focus are displayed on the playback image. I always like to have this information, both as confirmation that focus was achieved using the best AF point, and as a way of troubleshooting out-of-focus conditions caused by the camera or my bad judgment.

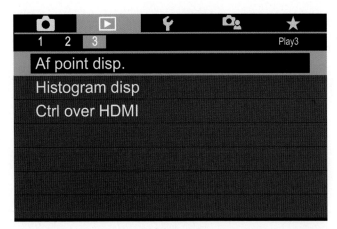

Figure 8.30
AF Point Display is the first entry in the Playback 3 menu.

Histogram Display

Options: Brightness, RGB

My preference: RGB

As you learned in Chapter 4, the T7i can show either a brightness histogram or set of three separate Red, Green, and Blue histograms in the full information display during picture review, or, it can show you both types of histogram in the partial information display. This entry gives you the option of choosing the mode you prefer.

Brightness histograms give you information about the overall tonal values present in the image. The RGB histograms can show more advanced users valuable data about specific channels that might be "clipped" (details are lost in the shadows or highlights). This menu choice determines only how they are displayed during picture review. The amount of information displayed cycles as you repeatedly press the INFO. button in Playback mode.

Ctrl over HDMI

Options: Enable, Disable

My preference: N/A

When your camera is connected to a TV that is compatible with the HDMI CEC standard, you can use the remote control to activate playback functions. You'll need a compatible TV, remote control, and an HDMI cable to connect your camera to the television. Then, choose Enable in this menu entry and follow the directions that came with your television and remote for selecting still photo and movie playback features. If your TV does not allow use of the remote, return to the menu selection and chose Disable to give the camera control of playback.

9

Customizing with the Set-up Menu, Display Level Menu, and My Menu

In the last chapter, I introduced you to the layout and general functions of the Canon EOS T7i's menu system, In this chapter, you'll learn how to work with the four Set-up menus, choose the amount of hand-holding you need with the Display Level menu, and how to assemble your own roster of favorite menu listings with the My Menu feature.

If you're jumping directly to this chapter and need some guidance in how to navigate the T7i's menu system, review the first few pages of Chapter 8. Otherwise, you're welcome to dive right in.

Set-up Menu Options

There are four amber-coded set-up menus where you make adjustments on how your camera *behaves* during your shooting session, as differentiated from the Shooting menu, which adjusts how the pictures are actually taken.

Your choices include:

- Select Folder
- File Numbering
- Auto Rotate
- Format Card
- Wireless Communication Settings
- Eye-Fi Settings
- Auto Power Off
- LCD Brightness
- LCD Off/On Button
- Date/Time/Zone
- Language
- Viewfinder display

- GPS Device Settings
- Video System
- Touch Control
- Beep
- Battery Info.
- Sensor Cleaning
- Custom Functions (C.Fn)
- Clear Settings
- Copyright Information
- Manual/Software URL
- Certification Logo Display
- Firmware Version

Select Folder

Options: Select Folder, Create Folder

My preference: N/A

Choose this menu option, the first on the Set-up 1 menu (see Figure 9.1), to create a folder where the images you capture will be stored on your memory card, or to switch between existing folders. Just follow these steps:

1. **Choose Select Folder.** Access the option from the Set-up 1 menu.
2. **View list of available folders.** The Select Folder screen pops up with a list of the available folders on your memory card, with names like 100CANON, 101CANON, etc.
3. **Choose a different folder.** To store subsequent images in a different existing folder, use the touch screen or directional buttons to highlight the label for the folder you want to use. When a folder that already has photos is selected, two thumbnails representing images in that folder are displayed at the right side of the screen.
4. **Confirm the folder.** Choose SET to confirm your choice of an existing folder.
5. **Create new folder.** If you'd rather create a new folder, highlight Create Folder in the Select Folder screen and choose SET. The name of the folder that will be created is displayed, along with a choice to Cancel or OK creating the folder. Choose SET to confirm your choice.
6. **Exit.** Press MENU to return to the Set-up 1 menu.

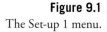

Figure 9.1
The Set-up 1 menu.

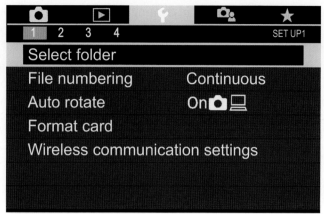

The folders your T7i create always follow the *nnn*CANON convention. You can also use your computer to create folders with names that depart from this arrangement, as long as you adhere to the camera's general rules for memory card folder names. Here's how to create folders with personalized names:

1. **Access the memory card from your computer.** There are two ways to do this.

   a. **USB link.** Plug the USB cable into the port on the left side of the T7i and connect to a USB connector on your computer. In Windows, the T7i will appear as a generic digital camera icon. A similar icon will appear on the Mac OS X desktop.

   b. **Use a card reader.** Remove the card from the T7i and insert it in a card reader attached to your computer.

2. **Open the camera/memory card in your computer.** A folder called DCIM will appear at the top level. All the folders your T7i can access must be located inside the DCIM folder.

3. **Create a new folder within the DCIM folder.** Although you're not limited to the *nnn*CANON arrangement, you must adhere to the rules in the steps that follow.

4. **Type in a three-digit folder number.** You can use any three numbers from 100 to 999, as long as those numbers are not already in use on that memory card. In other words, you can't have folders named 101CANON and 101SPAIN.

5. **Add a five-character description of your choice.** You can use any uppercase or lowercase letters from A to z, plus the underscore character (to represent a space). You cannot use an actual space, nor any other characters, even if your computer allows them in a file name. An invalid folder name will end up being "invisible" to the T7i, even if it actually exists on your memory card.

With a little imagination (and caution, to avoid creating "bad" folder names), you can develop some useful folder names, and switch among them at will. I find this capability especially useful when working with very large (32GB or 64GB) cards, because I can do a great deal of organizing right on the card itself. Perhaps I have some images in a particular folder that I use as a "slide show" for display on my T7i's back-panel LCD. Or, I might want to sort images by location or date. For example, I could use 104_USA_, 105SPAIN, 106FRANC, or 107GBRIT to indicate the location where the images were shot.

File Numbering

Options: Continuous (default), Auto Reset, Manual Reset

My preference: N/A

The EOS T7i will automatically apply a file number to each picture you take, using consecutive numbering for all your photos over a long period of time, spanning many different memory cards, starting over from scratch when you insert a new card, or when you manually reset the numbers. Numbers are applied from 0001 to 9999, at which time the camera creates a new folder on the card (100, 101, 102, and so forth), so you can have 0001 to 9999 in folder 100, then numbering will start over in folder 101.

The camera keeps track of the last number used in its internal memory. That can lead to a few quirks you should be aware of. For example, if you insert a memory card that had been used with a different camera, the T7i may start numbering with the next number after the highest number used by the previous camera. (I once had a brand-new Canon camera start numbering files in the 8,000 range.) I'll explain how this can happen next.

On the surface, the numbering system seems simple enough: In the menu, you can choose Continuous, Automatic Reset, or Manual Reset. Here is how each works:

- **Continuous.** If you're using a blank/reformatted memory card, the T7i will apply a number that is one greater than the number stored in the camera's internal memory. If the card is not blank and contains images, then the next number will be one greater than the highest number on the card *or* in internal memory. (In other words, if you want to use continuous file numbering consistently, you must always use a card that is blank or freshly formatted.) Here are some examples.

  - You've taken 4,235 shots with the camera, and you insert a blank/reformatted memory card. The next number assigned will be 4,236, based on the value stored in internal memory.

  - You've taken 4,235 shots with the camera, and you insert a memory card with a picture numbered 2,728. The next picture will be numbered 4,236.

  - You've taken 4,235 shots with the camera, and you insert a memory card with a picture numbered 8,281. The next picture will be numbered 8,282, and that value will be stored in the camera's menu as the "high" shot number (and will be applied when you next insert a blank card).

- **Automatic reset.** If you're using a blank/reformatted memory card, the next photo taken will be numbered 0001. If you use a card that is not blank, the next number will be one greater than the highest number found on the memory card. Each time you insert a memory card, the next number will either be 0001 or one higher than the highest already on the card.

- **Manual reset.** The T7i creates a new folder numbered one higher than the last folder created, and restarts the file numbers at 0001. Then, the camera uses the numbering scheme that was previously set, either Continuous or Automatic Reset, each time you subsequently insert a blank or non-blank memory card.

Auto Rotate

Options: On: Camera, Computer (default); On: Computer Only; Off

My preference: N/A

You can turn this feature On or Off. When activated, the EOS T7i rotates pictures taken in vertical orientation on the LCD screen so you don't have to turn the camera to view them comfortably. However, this orientation also means that the longest dimension of the image is shown using the shortest dimension of the LCD, so the picture is reduced in size. (You have three options, shown in Figure 9.2.) The image can be autorotated when viewing in the camera *and* on your computer screen using your image editing/viewing software. The image can be marked to autorotate *only* when reviewing your image in your image editor or viewing software. This option allows you to have rotation applied when using your computer, while retaining the ability to maximize the image on your LCD in the camera. The third choice is Off. The image will not be rotated when displayed in the camera or with your computer. Note that if you switch Auto Rotate off, any pictures shot while the feature is disabled will not be automatically rotated when you turn Auto Rotate back on; information embedded in the image file when the photo *is taken* is used to determine whether autorotation is applied.

Figure 9.2

Choose auto rotation both in the camera and on your computer display (top); only on your computer display (middle); or no automatic rotation (bottom).

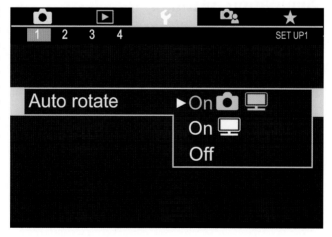

Format Card

Options: Format, Low-Level Format

My preference: N/A

Use this item to erase everything on your memory card and set up a fresh file system ready for use. When you select Format, you'll see a display like Figure 9.3, showing the capacity of the card, how much of that space is currently in use, and two choices at the bottom of the screen to Cancel or OK (proceed with the format). Press the Trash button if you'd like to do a low-level format. That's a more basic format that removes all sectors from the card and creates new ones, which can help speed up a card that seems to be slow (because the camera must skip over "bad" sectors left behind from previous uses). An orange bar appears on the screen to show the progress of the formatting step.

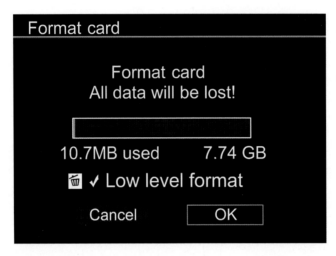

Figure 9.3
You must confirm the format step before the camera will erase a memory card.

Wireless Communication Settings

Options: Wi-Fi Settings, Wi-Fi Function, Bluetooth Function, Send Images to Smartphone, Nickname, Clear Settings

My preference: N/A

These options were covered in detail in Chapter 7 and won't be repeated here.

Eye-Fi Settings

Options: Enable/Disable (default), Connection information

My preference: N/A

This menu item appears when you have an Eye-Fi card inserted in the camera. You can enable and disable Eye-Fi wireless functions, and view connection information. I no longer recommend use of Eye-Fi cards, because the T7i has better built-in Wi-Fi/Bluetooth capabilities. In addition, Eye-Fi has changed support for older menu cards, and reduced the number of features available. If you do want to use an Eye-Fi card, remember that because the card draws power from the camera even when it's switched off, you might want to Disable the card (or remove it from the camera) when you don't need to use its features.

Auto Power Off

Options: 10/30 sec. (default), 30 sec., 1 min., 2 min., 4 min., 8 min., 15 min., Disable

My preference: 1 min.; 4 min. when shooting sports

This setting, the first in the Set-up 2 menu (see Figure 9.4), allows you to determine how long the EOS T7i remains active before shutting itself off. The default setting is 10/30 seconds, which turns an idle camera off after about 10 seconds when using the optical viewfinder, and 30 seconds in live view, movie, and playback modes. You can also select specific limits: 30 seconds, 1, 2, 4, 8, or 15 minutes, or Disable, which leaves the camera turned on indefinitely. However, even if the camera has shut itself off, if the power switch remains in the On position, you can bring the camera back to life by pressing the shutter button. I like a longer timeout when I am shooting sports, so that my camera is always ready to shoot.

Figure 9.4
The Set-up 2 menu has six options.

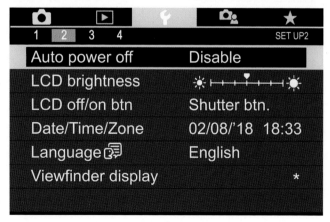

LCD Brightness

Options: Adjust LCD monitor brightness

My preference: N/A

Choose this menu option and a thumbnail image with a grayscale strip appears on the LCD, as shown in Figure 9.5. You can use the touch screen, directional buttons, or the Main Dial to adjust the brightness to a comfortable viewing level. Use the gray bars as a guide; you want to be able to see both the lightest and darkest steps at top and bottom, and not lose any of the steps in the middle. Brighter settings use more battery power, but can allow you to view an image on the LCD outdoors in bright sunlight. When you have the brightness you want, select SET to lock it in and return to the menu.

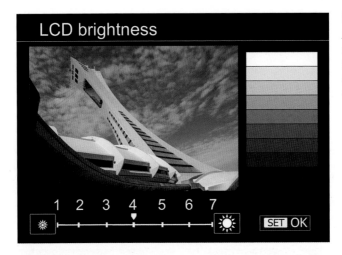

Figure 9.5
Adjust LCD brightness for easier viewing under varying ambient lighting conditions.

LCD Off/On Button

Options: Shutter Btn (default), Shutter/DISP, Remains On

My preference: Remains On

The T7i offers an option to set the camera so that the shooting display on the LCD monitor does not turn off under certain circumstances. Your options include:

- **Shutter btn.** The LCD monitor display turns off when you press the shutter release halfway, as when you are locking focus/exposure, or beginning to take a picture. If you release the shutter button without taking a picture, the LCD display returns.

- **Shutter/DISP.** As with the previous option, pressing the shutter release halfway turns off the LCD monitor display, but when you release the button, the display does not return. To restore the LCD display, press the DISP button. This provides a handy way to turn the LCD monitor display off quickly: just tap the shutter button.

■ **Remains on.** The LCD monitor display remains on when the shutter release is pressed halfway. You can turn it on or off by pressing the DISP button. I prefer this mode so I can rely on the LCD display to review my current exposure settings as I shoot.

Date/Time/Zone

Options: Date, Time, Date Format, Time Zone

My preference: N/A

Use this menu entry to set the current time zone used by the camera. Canon assigned a separate menu item to this setting so that you can quickly change time zones with no risk of adjusting any of the other date/time settings by accident.

When the screen appears, highlight the time zone and choose SET, and then press the up/down directional buttons to switch to a different zone, represented by a major city name within that time zone (e.g., New York, London, Moscow). Choose SET again to lock it in. Use the left/right directional buttons to switch between time zone and the Daylight Savings fields. You can specify whether the camera honors Daylight Savings Time. When you're finished adjusting the time zone information, press the right directional button to advance to the bottom row, and then choose OK to confirm or Cancel to return to the last settings specified.

Use this option to set the date and time, which will be embedded in the image file along with exposure information and other data. As first outlined in Chapter 1, you can set the date and time by following these steps:

1. Access this menu entry from the Set-up 2 menu.

2. Use the directional buttons to move the highlighting down to the entries, as seen in Figure 9.6.

Figure 9.6
Adjust the
time and date.

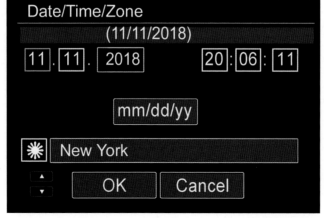

3. Use the directional buttons to select the value you want to change. When the gold box highlights the month, day, year, hour, minute, or second format you want to adjust, or the daylight savings time setting, press the SET button to activate that value. A pair of up-down-pointing triangles appears above the value.

4. Use the directional buttons to adjust the value up or down. Press SET to confirm the value you've entered.

5. Repeat steps 3 and 4 for each of the other values you want to change. The date format can be switched from the default mm/dd/yy to yy/mm/dd or dd/mm/yy.

6. When finished, use the touch screen or directional buttons to select either OK (if you're satisfied with your changes) or Cancel (if you'd like to return to the Set-up 2 menu without making any changes). Choose SET to confirm your choice.

7. When finished setting the date and time, press MENU to exit, or just tap the shutter release.

Language

Options: 25 languages
My preference: English

Choose from 25 languages for menu display, rotating the directional buttons until the language you want to select is highlighted. Press the SET button to activate. Your choices include English, German, French, Dutch, Danish, Portuguese, Finnish, Italian, Ukrainian, Norwegian, Swedish, Spanish, Greek, Russian, Polish, Czech, Magyar, Romanian, Turkish, Arabic, Thai, Simplified Chinese, Traditional Chinese, Korean, and Japanese.

Viewfinder Display

Options: Electronic Level, Grid Display, Flicker Detection
My preference: N/A

You can show or hide several optical viewfinder overlays. You can choose any or all from a list that includes Electronic Level, Grid Display, and Flicker Detection warning. Note that the Anti-Flicker feature is enabled or disabled using the entry in the Shooting 5 menu, as described in Chapter 8.

GPS Device Settings

Options: Enable/Disable (default), GPS Functions

My preference: N/A

Although this menu item appears in the Set-up 3 menu all the time (see Figure 9.7), its adjustments can be displayed only if the optional Canon GPS Receiver GP-E2 (less than $250) is attached. To use the device:

1. **Attach to the hot shoe of the camera,** then turn the switch on top to either Log or On. The red BATT. lamp will blink every five seconds if the device has a fresh AA battery. Three rapid blinks indicate a low battery.

2. **Acquire signal.** The red GPS lamp will blink rapidly while the unit is acquiring satellite signals, usually for 30 to 60 seconds. When the signal is locked in the lamp will blink slowly, every 3 to 6 seconds. A status indicator will appear in the camera's viewfinder.

3. **Record GPS information.** The GPS data is embedded in your image files as you shoot whenever the GPS Device Settings entry is set to Enable.

4. **Activate digital compass.** Once enabled, you can select GPS Device Settings/Digital Compass to activate the GP-E2's digital compass feature. View the direction the camera is pointing by pressing the INFO. button.

5. **Log.** When the GPS button is set to the Log position, the receiver will record your route information internally. It does not have to be attached to the camera to perform this function. If the GP-E2 is attached to the hot shoe, it will also embed geotag information in your image files. Location logs are recorded daily, using the intervals you select. Choose shorter intervals for routes that change direction frequently, and longer intervals for less twisty routes. Log files can be saved with the Map Utility, and converted to the standard .KMZ file format compatible with Google Earth and other applications.

Figure 9.7
The Set-up 3 menu.

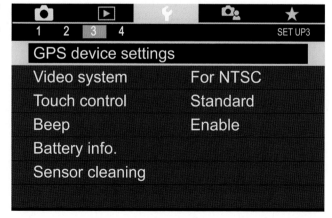

6. **Time settings.** Choose Auto Time Setting to specify whether the GPS device should use your camera's internal clock to set time, or use satellite data.

- **Set Now.** Your camera's time will be set using the GPS signal.

- **Auto Update.** Your camera's time will be updated each time the GP-E2 is attached and receiving a signal.

- **Disable.** Your camera's internal clock is not updated from satellite data.

Video System

Options: NTSC/PAL

My preference: N/A

This setting controls the output of the T7i through the AV cable when you're displaying images on an external monitor. You can select either NTSC, used in the United States, Canada, Mexico, many Central, South American, and Caribbean countries, much of Asia, and other countries, or PAL, which is used in the UK, much of Europe, Africa, India, China, and parts of the Middle East.

VIEWING ON A TELEVISION

Canon makes it quite easy to view your images on a standard television screen, and not much more difficult on a high-definition television (HDTV).

For HDTV display, purchase the optional HDMI Cable HTC-100 and connect it to the HDMI OUT terminal just below AV Out/USB port on the left side of the camera.

Connect the other end to an HDMI input port on your television or monitor (my 42-inch HDTV has three of them; my 26-inch monitor has just two). Then turn on the camera and press the Playback button. The image will appear on the external TV/HDTV/monitor and will not be displayed on the camera's LCD. HDTV systems automatically show your images at the appropriate resolution for that set.

Touch Control

Options: Standard (default), Sensitive, Disable

My preference: N/A

Use this entry to set standard sensitivity, a more sensitive response, or to totally disable the LCD touch screen feature. If you find yourself accidentally triggering commands by touching the screen or frequently touch the wrong settings and want to turn it off, you can do so. I often disable touch screen control when I am wearing gloves.

Beep

Options: Enable (default), Touch Screen, Disable

My preference: Disable

The Rebel T7i's internal beeper provides a helpful chirp to signify various functions, such as the countdown of your camera's self-timer. You can switch it off if you want to avoid the beep because it's annoying, impolite, or distracting (at a concert or museum), or undesired for any other reason. It's one of the few ways to make the T7i a bit quieter, other than Silent Single Shooting and Silent Continuous Shooting, which are *less noisey* rather than truly silent. (I've actually had new dSLR owners ask me how to turn off the "shutter sound" the camera makes; such an option was available in the point-and-shoot camera they'd used previously.) Select Beep from the menu, choose SET, and use the touch screen or directional buttons to choose Enable or Disable, or Touch Screen (which silences the beep only during touch screen operations), as you prefer. Use SET again to activate your choice.

Battery Info.

Options: Information display of battery capacity, battery life

My preference: N/A

This is an informational display only, showing the remaining capacity of your battery, and estimated lifetime of the battery. When one or two green bars are displayed, your battery is still in good shape; when a single red bar is shown, it's time to get a new battery.

Sensor Cleaning

Options: Auto Cleaning: Enable/Disable; Clean Now, Clean Manually

My preference: Auto Cleaning: Enable

One of the Canon EOS T7i's most useful features is the automatic sensor cleaning system that reduces or eliminates the need to clean your camera's sensor manually. Canon has applied anti-static coatings to the sensor and other portions of the camera body interior to counter charge build-ups that attract dust. A separate filter over the sensor vibrates ultrasonically each time the T7i is powered on or off, shaking loose any dust, which is captured by a sticky strip beneath the sensor.

Use this menu entry (see Figure 9.8) to enable or disable automatic sensor cleaning on power up (select Auto Cleaning to choose) or to activate automatic cleaning during a shooting session (select Clean Now). You can also choose the Clean Manually option to flip up the mirror and clean the sensor yourself with a blower, brush, or swab. If the battery level is too low to safely carry out the cleaning operation, the T7i will let you know and refuse to proceed, unless you use the optional AC-E6N/DR-18 adapter/coupler combination.

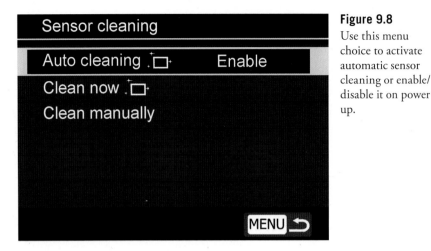

Figure 9.8
Use this menu choice to activate automatic sensor cleaning or enable/disable it on power up.

Custom Functions

Options: 15 Custom Functions

My preference: N/A

Custom Functions, which lead off the fourth page of the Set-up menu (see Figure 9.9), let you customize the behavior of your camera in more than a dozen different ways. If you don't like the default way the camera carries out certain tasks, you just may be able to do something about it. You can find the Custom Functions in their own screen, divided into four groups of settings: Exposure (I, C.Fn-1 to C.Fn-3); Image (II, C.Fn-4); Autofocus/Drive (III, C.Fn-5 to C.Fn-10); and Operation/Others (IV, C.Fn-11 to C.Fn-15). Each of the Custom Functions is set in exactly the same way, so

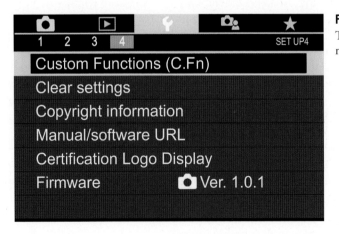

Figure 9.9
The fourth Set-up menu page.

I'm not going to bog you down with a bunch of illustrations showing how to make this setting or that. One quick run-through using Figure 9.10 should be enough. Here are the key parts of the Custom Functions screen. Note that in all cases, the default for each Custom Function is 0.

- **Custom Functions category.** At the top of the settings screen is a label that tells you which category that screen represents.

- **Current Function name.** Use the touch screen or left/right directional buttons to select the function you want to adjust. The name of the function currently selected appears at the top of the screen, and its number is marked with an overscore in the row of numbers at the bottom of the screen. You don't need to memorize the function numbers.

- **Function currently selected.** The function number appears in two places. In the upper-right corner you'll find a box with the current function clearly designated. In the lower half of the screen are two lines of numbers. The top row has numbers from 1 to 15, representing the Custom Function. The second row shows the number of the current setting. If the setting is other than the default value (a zero), it will be colored blue, so you can quickly see which Custom Functions have been modified. The currently selected function will have a gold line above it.

- **Available settings.** Within the alternating medium gray/dark gray blocks appear numbered setting options. The current setting is highlighted in blue. You can use the up/down directional buttons to scroll to the option you want and then choose SET to select it; then press MENU to back out of the Custom Functions menus.

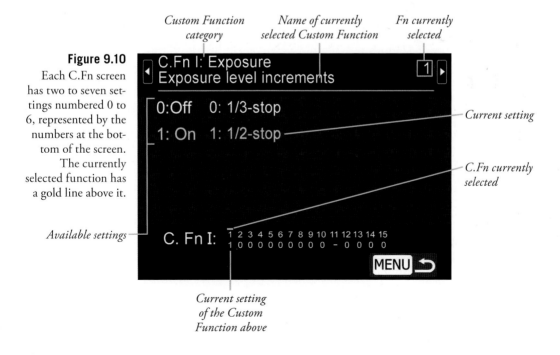

Figure 9.10
Each C.Fn screen has two to seven settings numbered 0 to 6, represented by the numbers at the bottom of the screen. The currently selected function has a gold line above it.

Custom Function category

Name of currently selected Custom Function

Fn currently selected

Current setting

C.Fn currently selected

Available settings

Current setting of the Custom Function above

- **Current setting.** Underneath each Custom Function is a number from 0 to 6 that represents the current setting for that function.
- **Option selection.** When a function is selected, the currently selected option appears in a highlighted box. As you scroll up and down the option list, the setting in the box changes to indicate an alternate value.

In the listings that follow, I'm going to depart from the sometimes-cryptic labels Canon assigns to each Custom Function in the menu, and instead categorize them by what they actually do. I'm also going to provide you with a great deal more information on each option and what it means to your photography.

C.Fn-1: Size of Exposure Adjustments

Options: 0: 1/3 stop, 1: 1/2 stop
My Preference: 0: 1/3 stop

Exposure level increments. This setting tells the Rebel T7i the size of the "jumps" it should use when making exposure adjustments—either one-third or one-half stop. The increment you specify here applies to f/stops, shutter speeds, EV changes, and autoexposure bracketing.

- **0: 1/3 stop.** Choose this setting when you want the finest increments between shutter speeds and/or f/stops. For example, the T7i will use shutter speeds such as 1/60th, 1/80th, 1/100th, and 1/125th second, and f/stops such as f/5.6, f/6.3, f/7.1, and f/8, giving you (and the autoexposure system) maximum control.
- **1: 1/2 stop.** Use this setting when you want larger and more noticeable changes between increments, as when you're shooting HDR images. The T7i will apply shutter speeds such as 1/60th, 1/125th, 1/250th, and 1/500th second, and f/stops including f/5.6, f/6.7, f/8, f/9.5, and f/11. These coarser adjustments are useful when you want more dramatic changes between different exposures.

C.Fn-2: Whether ISO 52100 Is Available or Disabled

Options: 0: Off, 1: On
My Preference: 0: Off

ISO expansion. Ordinarily, only ISO settings from 100 to 25600 are available (ISO 200–25600 if Highlight Tone Priority [C.Fn-4] is enabled). The ISO Expansion function is disabled by default to prevent you from unintentionally using ISO settings higher than ISO 25600. If you want to use the H (ISO 52100; ISO 25600 for movies) setting, it must be activated using this Custom Function. I've found the noise produced at the ISO 12800 setting on my EOS T7i to be quite acceptable under certain situations, and ISO 25600/52100 can sometimes be useable. That's particularly so with images of subjects that have a texture of their own that tends to hide or mask the noise.

CAUTION

Be aware that if you've activated Highlight Tone Priority (described later), the H setting (and ISO values less than ISO 200) will not be available even if you have enabled ISO expansion.

- **0: Off.** The H (ISO 52100 still images/25600 for movies) setting is locked out and not available when using the ISO button or menu options.
- **1: On.** The H settings can be selected.

C.Fn-3: Canceling Exposure Compensation Automatically

Options: 0: Enable, 1: Disable
My Preference: 0: Enable

Exposure Compensation Auto Cancel. When enabled, helps you avoid incorrect exposures by turning off any exposure compensation you've dialed in when the camera is turned off. Your options are as follows:

- **0: Enable.** Each time you power down the camera, exposure compensation settings you've made are cancelled. That avoids situations where you forgot you'd made an EV adjustment, and can't figure out why your pictures are now over- or underexposed. This is the safest setting.
- **1: Disable.** Exposure compensation remains in effect even after you turn the camera on. I use this option during long shooting sessions in which I turn off the camera from time to time, either to save juice or because I am taking a break. I don't have to remember to dial in my preferred EV setting for that session; it's still there until I zero it out or change to another exposure compensation setting.

C.Fn-4: Improving Detail in Highlights

Options: 0: Disable, 1: Enable
My Preference: 0: Disable

Highlight Tone Priority. This setting concentrates the available tones in an image from the middle grays up to the brightest highlights, in effect expanding the dynamic range of the image at the expense of shadow detail. You'd want to activate this option when shooting subjects in which there is lots of important detail in the highlights, and less detail in shadow areas. Highlight tones will be preserved, while shadows will be allowed to go dark more readily (and may exhibit an increase in noise levels). Bright beach or snow scenes, especially those with few shadows (think high noon, when the shadows are smaller) can benefit from using Highlight Tone Priority. The D+ indicator is shown in the viewfinder and the LCD monitor when this feature is active.

Your options are:

- **0: Disable.** The Rebel T7i's normal dynamic range is applied.
- **1: Enable.** Highlight areas are given expanded tonal values, while the tones available for shadow areas are reduced. The ISO 100 sensitivity setting is disabled and only ISO 200 to ISO 25600 are available. You can tell that this restriction is in effect by viewing the D+ icon shown in the viewfinder, on the ISO Selection screen, and in the shooting information display for a particular image.

C.Fn-5: Activation of the Autofocus Assist Lamp

Options: 0: Enable, 1: Disable, 2: Enable External Flash Only, 3: IR AF-Assist Beam Only

My Preference: 1: Disable

Autofocus assist beam. This setting determines when the built-in flash or an external flash is activated to emit a pulse of light prior to the main exposure that helps provide enough contrast for the Rebel T7i to focus on a subject.

- **0: Enable.** The AF-assist light is emitted by the camera's built-in flash whenever light levels are too low for accurate focusing using the ambient light.
- **1: Disable.** The AF-assist illumination is disabled. You might want to use this setting when shooting at concerts, weddings, or darkened locations where the light might prove distracting or discourteous. I find the AF-assist light not very useful except when photographing objects fairly close to the camera, so I choose this setting most of the time.
- **2: Enable external flash only.** The built-in AF-assist light is disabled, but if a Canon EX dedicated flash unit is attached to the camera, its AF-assist feature (a flash pulse) will be used when needed. Because the flash unit's AF-assist is more powerful, you'll find this option useful when you're using flash and are photographing objects in dim light that are more than a few feet away from the camera (and thus not likely to be illuminated usefully by the Rebel T7i's built-in light source). Note that if AF-assist beam firing is disabled within the flash unit's own Custom Functions, this setting will not override that.
- **3: IR AF-assist beam only.** Canon dedicated Speedlites with an infrared assist beam can be set to use only the IR assist burst. That will keep other flash bursts from triggering the AF-assist beam.

C.Fn-6: Select AF Area Selection Method

Options: 0: AF Area Selection/AF Area Selection Mode buttons, 1: Main Dial

My Preference: 0: AF Area Selection/AF Area Selection Mode buttons

AF Area selection:

This setting allows you to choose the control used for changing the AF Area Selection method.

- ■ **0: AF Area Selection button→AF Area Selection Mode button.** Press the AF Area Selection button (at the upper-right corner of the back panel of the camera) *or* the AF Area Selection Mode button (located just northwest of the Main Dial). Subsequently, pressing the AF Area Selection Mode button changes the AF area selection mode.

- ■ **1: AF Area Selection button→Main Dial.** Press the AF Area Selection button (at the upper-right corner of the back panel of the camera) *or* the AF Area Selection Mode button (located just northwest of the Main Dial). Subsequently, rotating the Main Dial changes the AF area selection mode. When the Main Dial's behavior is defined this way, use the directional keys to adjust the AF point horizontally.

C.Fn-7: Use Colors to Recognize Skin Tones while Autofocusing

Options: 0: Enable, 1: Disable

My Preference: 0: Enable

Auto AF Point Selection: Color Tracking. When using Zone AF, Large Zone AF, or Automatic Selection AF (as described in Chapter 5), the T7i can use skin tone colors as a cue to select appropriate autofocus points, making focusing on people faster and more accurate. Disable if you find that non-human hues in an image are present and misleading the autofocus system, or if you want to give AF a slight speed boost (searching for skin tones takes time).

C.Fn-8: AF Point Display During Focus

Options: 0: Selected (constant), 1: All (constant), 2: Selected (pre-AF, focused), 3: Selected (focused), 4: Disable display

My Preference: 0: Selected (constant)

This setting simply allows you to specify whether you want the selected AF point to be highlighted in red.

- ■ **0: Selected (constant).** The AF point selected by you or the camera is always displayed. You'll use this default setting most of the time, as I do, because it's useful to be able to see exactly which part of the frame is being used to calculate focus.

- ■ **1: All (constant).** All 45 AF points are displayed, all the time. Use if you want to be able to see the location of all the AF points as you frame and shoot.

- **2: Selected (pre-AF, focused).** Selected AF points are displayed only when selecting AF points, when the camera is ready to shoot before AF operation, and when focus is achieved (except when AI Servo AF is being used). This is a slightly less distracting mode.

- **3: Selected (focused).** The selected AF points are displayed only when selecting AF points or when focus is achieved (except when AI Servo AF is being used).

- **4: Disable display.** I often use this setting when the AF point highlighting is distracting, or when I'm photographing a scene with lots of red and the highlighting won't be readily visible, anyway.

C.Fn-9: VF Display Illumination

Options: 0: Auto, 1: Enable, 2: Disable

My Preference: 0: Auto

Tells the T7i to highlight the AF points and alignment grid in red in the viewfinder when focus is achieved. With all three options, there is no illumination when AI Servo AF is used. In addition, pressing the AF Area Selection Button or AF Area Selection Mode button illuminates the AF points and grid regardless of which of these options you have chosen. Select the option that suits your preference for when the AF points and grid are displayed.

- **0: Auto.** AF points and grid are illuminated under low light when focus is achieved.

- **1: Enable.** AF points and grid are illuminated when focus is achieved under all lighting conditions.

- **2: Disable.** AF points and grid are not illuminated when focus is achieved.

C.Fn-10: Whether It Is Possible to Lock Up the Viewing Mirror Prior to an Exposure

Options: 0: Disable, 1: Enable

My Preference: 0: Disable

Mirror lockup. The Mirror Lockup function determines whether the reflex viewing mirror will be flipped up out of the way in advance of taking a picture, thereby eliminating any residual blurring effects caused by the minuscule amount of camera shake that can be produced if (as is the case normally) the mirror is automatically flipped up an instant before the actual exposure. When shooting telephoto pictures with a very long lens, or close-up photography at extreme magnifications, even this tiny amount of vibration can have an impact.

You'll want to make this adjustment immediately prior to needing the mirror lockup function, because once it's been enabled, the mirror *always* flips up, and picture taking becomes a two-press operation. That is, you press the shutter release once to lock exposure and focus, and to swing the mirror out of the way. Your viewfinder goes blank (of course, the mirror's blocking it). Press the shutter release a second time to actually take the picture. Because the goal of mirror lockup is to produce the sharpest picture possible, and because of the viewfinder blackout, you can see that the camera should be mounted on a tripod prior to taking the picture, and, to avoid accidentally shaking the camera yourself, using an off-camera shutter release mechanism is a good idea.

- **0: Disable.** Mirror lockup is not possible.
- **1: Enable.** Mirror lockup is activated and will be used for every shot until disabled.

Canon lists some important warnings and techniques related to using mirror lockup in the Rebel T7i manual, and I want to emphasize them here and add a few of my own, even if it means a bit of duplication. Better safe than sorry!

- **Don't use ML for sensor cleaning.** Though locked up, the mirror will flip down again automatically after 30 seconds, which you don't want to happen while you're poking around the sensor with a brush, swab, or air jet. There's a separate Set-up 3 menu item—Sensor Cleaning—for sensor housekeeping.

- **Avoid long exposure to extra-bright scenes.** The shutter curtain, normally shielded from incoming light by the mirror, is fully exposed to the light being focused on the focal plane by the lens mounted on the T7i. When the mirror is locked up, you certainly don't want to point the camera at the sun, and even beach or snow scenes may be unsafe if the shutter curtain is exposed to their illumination for long periods. (This advice also applies to Live View, of course, because the sensor is similarly exposed while you're previewing the image on the LCD.)

- **ML can't be used in continuous shooting modes.** The Rebel T7i will use single shooting mode for mirror lockup exposures, regardless of the sequence mode you've selected.

- **Use self-timer to eliminate second button press.** If you've activated the self-timer, the mirror will flip up when you press the shutter button down all the way, and then the picture will be taken two seconds later. This technique can help reduce camera shake further if you don't have a remote release available and have to use a finger to press the shutter button. You can also use the Remote Controller RC-5 or RC-6. With the RC-5, press the transmit button to lock up the mirror; the shot will be taken automatically two seconds later. With the RC-6, set the remote for a two-second delay to produce the same effect.

C.Fn-11: Viewfinder Warnings

Options: Monochrome Picture Style, WB correction, Multi-shot noise reduction

My Preference: Enable all three

This useful function lets you individually enable or disable three different viewfinder warnings, allowing you to reduce the amount of clutter in your field of view as you frame an image, while retaining the warnings that you really, really want to remain in effect. Mark any or all with a check mark by highlighting the option and pressing SET.

Your choices include warnings for the following:

- **Monochrome Picture Style.** If you shoot JPEG most of the time, you might want a tip-off that you've set the camera in black-and-white mode, because color information cannot be added in post-processing. If you generally shoot RAW or RAW+JPEG, you won't care, because the RAW image retains the color information.

- **WB correction.** It's easy to dial in some white balance correction, and easier to forget that you've done so. This warning will let you know—again, very important when shooting JPEG only.

- **Multi-shot noise reduction.** When High-Speed Noise Reduction is set to Multi-Shot Noise Reduction, you'll receive a warning. While the availability of this extreme setting isn't normally a problem, if you feel you're likely to need a tip-off, you can activate this warning.

C.Fn-12: What Happens When You Partially Depress the Shutter Release/Press the AE Lock Button

Options: 0: AF/AE Lock, 1: AE Lock/AF, 2: AF/AF Lock, no AE Lock, 3: AE/AF, no AE Lock
My Preference: 0: AF/AE Lock

Shutter button/AE Lock button (*). This setting controls the behavior of the shutter release and the AE Lock button (*) when you are using Creative Zone exposure modes. With Basic Zone modes, the Rebel T7i always behaves as if it has been set to Option 0, described below. Options 1, 2, and 3 are designed to work with AI Servo mode, which locks focus as it is activated, but refocuses if the subject begins to move. The options allow you to control exactly when focus and exposure are locked when using AI Servo mode.

In the options list, the first action in the pair represents what happens when you press the shutter release; the second action says what happens when the AE Lock button is pressed.

- **0: AF/AE Lock.** With this option, pressing the shutter release halfway locks in focus; pressing the * button locks exposure. Use this when you want to control each of these actions separately.

- **1: AE Lock/AF.** Pressing the shutter release halfway locks exposure; pressing the * button locks autofocus. This setting swaps the action of the two buttons compared to the default 0 option.

- **2: AF/AF Lock, no AE Lock.** Pressing the AE Lock button interrupts the autofocus and locks focus in AI Servo mode. Exposure is not locked at all until the actual moment of exposure when you press the shutter release all the way. This mode is handy when moving objects may pass in front of the camera (say, a tight end crosses your field of view as you focus on the quarterback) and you want to be able to avoid change of focus. Note that you can't lock in exposure using this option.

- **3: AE/AF, no AE Lock.** Pressing the shutter release halfway locks in autofocus, except in AI Servo mode, in which you can use the * button to start or stop autofocus. Exposure is always determined at the moment the picture is taken, and cannot be locked.

C.Fn-13: Using the SET Button as a Function Key

Options: 0: Normal (disabled), 1: Image Quality, 2: Flash Exposure Compensation, 3: LCD monitor On/Off, 4: Menu display, 5: ISO speed, 6: Flash Function Settings

My Preference: 1: Image Quality

Assign SET button. You already know that the physical SET button can be used to select a choice or option when navigating the menus. However, when you're taking photos, the button has no function at all. You can easily remedy that with this setting. This setting allows you to assign one of five different actions to the SET key. Because the button is within easy reach of your right thumb, that makes it quite convenient for accessing a frequently used function.

CAUTION

One thing to keep in mind when redefining the behavior of controls (including other controls that can be modified within the Custom Functions menus) is that any non-standard customization you do will definitely be confusing to others who use your camera, and may even confuse you if you've forgotten that you've changed a control from its default function.

- **0: Normal (disabled).** This is the default during shooting; no action is taken.
- **1: Image quality.** Pressing the SET button produces the Shooting 1 menu's Quality menu screen on the color LCD. You can cycle among the various quality options with the up/down and left/right directional buttons. Choose SET again to lock in your choice. I prefer this setting, as the camera does not have a dedicated quick-access button for this function.
- **2: Flash exposure comp.** The SET button summons the flash exposure compensation screen. Use the left/right directional buttons to adjust flash exposure plus or minus two stops. If you're using an external flash unit, its internal flash exposure compensation settings override those set from the camera. Choose SET to confirm your choice.
- **3: LCD monitor On/Off.** Assigns to the SET button the same functions as the DISP. button. Because the SET button can be accessed with the thumb, you may find it easier to use when turning the LCD monitor on or off.
- **4: Menu display.** Pressing SET produces the T7i's menu screen on the LCD, with the last menu entry you used highlighted. Choose SET again to work with that menu normally, or press the MENU button to cancel and back out of the menus. This setting duplicates the MENU button's function, but some find it easier to locate the SET button with their thumb.
- **5: ISO speed.** This assigns the SET button the same function as the ISO button. Use it if you'd rather not grope for the ISO button on top of the camera.
- **6: Flash Function settings.** Adjust function settings of the built-in flash, or any external flash that is attached and powered up.

C.Fn-14: LCD Display When Power On

Options: 0: Display On, 1: Previous Display Status

My Preference: 0: Display On

LCD display when power on. Controls the behavior of the LCD when the Rebel T7i is switched on. There are two options:

- **0: Display on.** When the T7i is powered on, the shooting settings screen will be shown. You can turn this screen on and off by pressing the INFO./DISP. button. Use this option if you always want the settings screen to be displayed when the camera is turned on.

- **1: Previous display status.** When the Rebel T7i is turned on, the LCD monitor will display the shooting settings screen if it was turned on when the camera was last powered down. If the screen had been turned off (by pressing the INFO. button), it will not be displayed when the camera is next powered up. Use this option if you frequently turn off the settings screen, and want the camera to "remember" whether the screen was on display when the T7i was last powered down.

C.Fn-15: Retract Lens on Power Off

Options: 0: Enable, 1: Disable

My Preference: 1: Disable

If you own a gear-driven STM lens such as the EF40 f/2.8 STM optic, use this setting to have the camera retract the lens to its smallest form factor when the camera is powered down. I leave it off, because I often turn off the camera for a few minutes and would prefer to have it set the way it was when the camera was powered down.

Clear Settings

Options: Clear All Camera Settings, Clear All Custom Functions

My preference: N/A

This menu choice has provisions for resetting all the settings to their default values. Regardless of how you've set up your EOS T7i, it will be adjusted for One-Shot AF mode, Automatic AF point selection, Evaluative metering, JPEG Fine Large image quality, Automatic ISO, sRGB color mode, Automatic white balance, and Standard Picture Style. Any changes you've made to exposure compensation, flash exposure compensation, and white balance will be canceled, and any bracketing for exposure or white balance nullified. Custom white balances and Dust Delete Data will be erased. The Clear Setting screen has two options: Clear All Camera Settings, and Clear All Custom Func (C.Fn).

Table 9.1 shows the settings defaults after using this menu option.

Table 9.1 Camera Setting Defaults

Shooting Settings	Default Value
SCN Mode	Group Photo
Creative Filters	Grainy B/W
AF operation	One-Shot AF
AF area selection mode	Auto selection
Drive mode	Single shooting
Metering mode	Evaluative
ISO speed	Auto
ISO Auto	Maximum 6400
Exposure Compensation /AEB	Canceled
Flash exposure compensation	Canceled
Red-eye reduction	Disable
Anti-flicker shooting	Disable
Aspect Ratio	3:2
Viewfinder display	Display only flicker detection
Custom Functions	**Unchanged**
Flash Control	**Default Value**
Flash firing	Enable
E-TTL II flash metering	Evaluative flash metering
Flash sync. speed in Av mode	Auto
Display Level Settings	Guided for all four
Image-Recording Settings	**Default Value**
Image Quality	JPEG Large/Fine
Aspect Ratio	3:2
Picture Style	Auto
Auto Lighting Optimizer	Standard
Peripheral illumination correction	Enable/Correction data retained

Table 9.1 Camera Setting Defaults (continued)

Image-Recording Settings (continued)	Default Value
Chromatic aberration correction	Enable/Correction data retained
Distortion correction	Disable
Diffraction correction	Enable
Lens electronic manual focus	Disable after One-Shot AF
White balance	Auto: Ambience Priority
Custom white balance	Canceled
White balance correction	Canceled
WB-BKT	Canceled
Long exposure NR	Disable
High ISO NR	Standard
File numbering	Continuous
Auto cleaning	Enable
Dust Delete Data	Erased

Camera Settings	Default Value
Auto power off	10/30 seconds
Beep	Enable
Release shutter without card	Enable
Image Review	2 seconds
AF Point display	Disable
Histogram	Brightness
Image jump with Main Dial	10 images
Auto rotate	On/Camera/Computer
LCD brightness	Centered
LCD off/on button	Shutter button
Date/Time/Zone	Unchanged
Language	Unchanged

Table 9.1 Camera Setting Defaults (continued)

Camera Settings (continued)	Default Value
Video system	Unchanged
Touch control	Standard
Copyright information	Unchanged
Control over HDMI	Disable
Eye-Fi transmission	Disable
My Menu settings	Unchanged
My Menu Display	Normal display
Wi-Fi	Disable
Bluetooth function	Disable

Live View Settings	Default
Live view shooting	Enable
AF Method	Face+Tracking
AF operation	One-Shot
Touch Shutter	Disable
Metering timer	8 seconds
Grid display	Off
Creative filters	Disable

Movie Shooting	Default
Creative filters	Dream
AF Method	Face+Tracking
Movie Servo AF	Enable
Movie recording size	FHD:29.97p
Digital zoom	Disable
Movie ISO Speed	Auto
Movie ISO Auto	Maximum 12800
Sound recording	Auto; Wind filter, Auto; Attenuator, Disable

Table 9.1 Camera Setting Defaults (continued)

Movie Shooting (continued)	Default Value
Grid Display	Off
AF with shutter button during movie recording	One-Shot AF
Video Snapshot	Disable
Time-lapse movie	Disable
Remote control shooting	Disable
Movie digital image stabilization	Disable
Creative filters	Disable

Copyright Information

Options: Display Copyright Info, Enter Author's Name, Enter Copyright Details, Delete Copyright Information

My preference: N/A

You can embed your name (as "author" or *auteur* of the image) and copyright information in the Exif (Exchangeable Image File format) data appended to each photo that you take. When you choose this menu entry (see Figure 9.11), you have four options:

- **Display Copyright Info.** Shows the current author and copyright data.
- **Enter Author's Name.** Produces a text entry screen, which can be operated using the touch screen (my recommendation) or with the T7i's buttons, as described earlier.
- **Enter Copyright Details.** Produces the same text entry screen, allowing you to enter copyright details. Oddly enough, no copyright symbol is available (although the @ sign is provided so you can type in your e-mail address!). Many just use the parentheses and a lowercase c: (c). However, you should know that this is, strictly speaking, not legal. The legit substitute for the actual copyright symbol are the characters *Copr.* or the full term *Copyright*.
- **Delete Copyright Information.** Removes the current copyright information (both author and copyright data). Once you delete the data, or if you haven't entered it yet, this option and the Display Copyright Info. option are grayed out and unavailable.

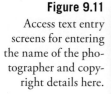

Figure 9.11
Access text entry screens for entering the name of the photographer and copyright details here.

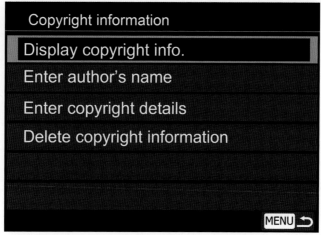

Copyright information

Display copyright info.

Enter author's name

Enter copyright details

Delete copyright information

MENU ↰

Manual/Software URL

Options: None

My preference: N/A

Displays a QR code you can snap with your smart device to jump to a web page where software and PDF manuals for your T7i can be downloaded.

Certification Logo Display

Options: None

My preference: N/A

This cryptic entry is used by Canon to display the logos of some of the certification organizations that have approved the T7i's specifications. You'll find others on the bottom of the camera itself. As a camera user, you don't really care about certifications, but Canon added this entry as a way of updating any new credentials through a firmware update, thus avoiding the need to change the labels/engravings on the camera body itself. So now you know.

Firmware Version

Options: Display Only

My preference: N/A

You can see the current firmware release in use in the menu listing. If you want to update to a new firmware version for either the camera or a lens, press the SET button to select which type of firmware you want to upgrade. Then insert a memory card containing the binary file, and press the SET button to begin the process.

Display Level

Options: Shooting Screen, Menu Display, Mode Guide, Feature Guide

My preference: Disable or turn off guides.

As I explained early in this book, the guided menus and displays are useful when you first start using your T7i, but add extra steps and clutter once you've learned your camera. Turn them off when you no longer need training wheels.

My Menu

Options: Add My Menu tab, Delete all My Menu tabs, Delete all items, Menu display

My preference: N/A

The Canon EOS Rebel T7i has a great feature that allows you to define your own menu with multiple tabs, each with just the items listed that you want. Remember that the T7i always returns to the last menu and menu entry accessed when you press the MENU button. So, you can set up My Menu to include just the items you want, and jump to those items instantly by pressing the MENU button. Or, you can set your camera so that My Menu appears when the MENU button has been pressed, regardless of what other menu entry you accessed last.

Initially, the My Menu tab will have one page. You can add more pages using the Add My Menu Tab entry, shown in Figure 9.12. That screen also allows you to delete all tabs, delete all items on your existing tabs, and change the menu display:

- **Add another My Menu tab.** Each time you do, you must use Configure to add at least one entry to the new menu. Your new menus will be assigned names, like MY MENU1, MY MENU2, etc. The original MY MENU: Set up tab will move to the farthest position in the tab lineup. You can have a maximum of five new tabs, plus the sixth Set up tab.

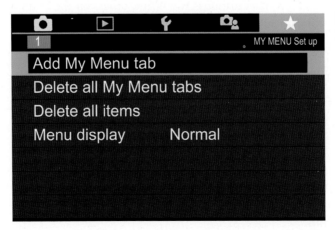

Figure 9.12
My Menu setup tab.

■ **Delete all My Menu tabs.** If you want to start over, you can delete all your tabs.

■ **Delete All items.** This deletes all the registered items on all the tabs you have added. The options in the MY MENU: Set up tab remain. When you delete all items, each will still contain a Configure choice, which allows you to register more entries. The tabs themselves are not removed.

■ **Menu display.** This determines which menu screen appears first when the MENU button is pressed. You can choose:

• **Normal display (default).** Shows the *most recently displayed* menu tab from the Shooting, AF, Playback, Set-up, Custom Settings, and My Menu choices. You'd want this if you prefer to jump back to whichever menu you were working with recently.

• **Display from My Menu tab.** Shows the My Menu tab only. Use this if you want to bypass the conventional menus and make your menu choices only from your custom My Menu tabs. The other menu tabs are still shown and can be selected.

• **Display only My Menu tab.** Only the My Menu tabs are available. The others are hidden. Use this only if you do not need to use the conventional menus as you work. You can return to this entry and restore Normal display at any time.

To customize one of the My Menu tabs, you have to *register* the menu items you want to include. Just follow these steps:

1. Press the MENU button and use the Main Dial to select the My Menu tab. In the setup screen, choose Add My Menu tab to create a new tab. The new tab will have a single entry: Configure.

2. Select Configure and press SET. The configure choices will appear. (See Figure 9.13.)

3. Choose Select Items to register. Press SET to view a screen of available menu choices you can add to My Menu.

Figure 9.13
Configuration choices.

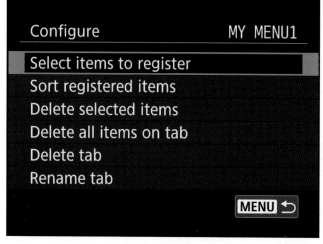

Configure   MY MENU1

Select items to register
Sort registered items
Delete selected items
Delete all items on tab
Delete tab
Rename tab

MENU ↩

4. Scroll through the list and highlight the menu item you want to register and press SET.

5. Confirm your choice by selecting OK in the next screen and pressing SET again.

6. Continue to select more entries for your My Menu tab. You can add up to six for each tab.

7. When you're finished, press the MENU button twice to return to the My Menu screen to see your customized menu, which might look like my example in Figure 9.14.

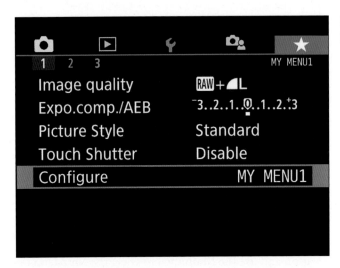

Figure 9.14
Example menu.

The Configure screen has other options you can use to customize your My Menu screens:

■ **Sort registered items.** Choose this entry to reorder the items in each My Menu tab. Select the menu item and press the SET button. Rotate the Quick Control Dial to move the item up and down within the menu list. When you've placed it where you'd like it, press the MENU button to lock in your selection and return to the previous screen. When finished, press MENU again to exit.

■ **Delete selected items, Delete all items on tab, Delete tab.** Use these to remove an individual menu item or all menu items on a tab, or to delete the entire tab itself.

■ **Rename tab.** You're not stuck with the MY MENU1, MY MENU2… monikers. This entry allows you to apply a new name for a tab with up to 16 characters. For example, if you created customized Shooting or Autofocus settings, you could name them My Shooting and My Autofocus, respectively. As with any of the T7i's text-entry screens, this is one example of when the touch screen is highly preferable.

10

Working with Lenses

In September 2016, Canon announced that it had produced its 110 millionth EF-series lens. Considering that it took 11 years for Canon to sell its first 10 million copies of its EF lens line, but only nine months to peddle its most recent 10 million lenses, it's easy to see that the digital photography revolution can take credit for the most recent explosion.

With more than six dozen lenses in its current lineup, Canon is catering to the wide-ranging needs of a broad user base, from novice photo enthusiasts to advanced amateur and professional photographers. It's this mind-bending assortment of high-quality lenses available to enhance the capabilities of cameras like the Canon EOS T7i that make the product line so appealing. Thousands of current and older lenses introduced by Canon and third-party vendors since 1987 can be used to give you a wider view, bring distant subjects closer, let you focus closer, shoot under lower-light conditions, or provide a more detailed, sharper image for critical work. Other than the sensor itself, the lens you choose for your dSLR is the most important component in determining image quality and perspective of your images.

The most exciting development in recent years has been the introduction of lenses especially well-suited for videography, including an upgraded 18-135mm f/3.5-5.6 IS USM lens (around $600). Featuring a new "Nano USM" motor, it's compatible with the Canon PZ-E1 Power Zoom Adapter for the lens (an affordable $150). The adapter is a detachable device that silently and smoothly zooms the lens in and out using 10 different speed levels. Best of all, the adapter can be controlled with Canon's Camera Connect app. The new lens joins Canon's line of Stepper Motor lenses, including the Canon EF-S 35mm f/2.8 Macro IS STM and the 18-55mm f/4-5.6 IS STM kit lens unveiled early in 2017. These lenses, when coupled with a new diaphragm mechanism, provide especially fast and quiet autofocus that's perfect for video capture (where camera noises can be recorded while shooting).

This chapter explains how to select the best lenses for the kinds of photography you want to do.

But Don't Forget the Crop Factor

From time to time you've heard the term *crop factor*, and you've probably also heard the term *lens multiplier factor*. Both are misleading and inaccurate terms used to describe the same phenomenon: the fact that cameras like the T7i (and most other affordable digital SLRs) provide a field of view that's smaller and narrower than that produced by certain other (usually much more expensive) cameras, when fitted with exactly the same lens.

Figure 10.1 quite clearly shows the phenomenon at work. The outer rectangle, marked 1X, shows the field of view you might expect with a 28mm lens mounted on a Canon EOS 5DS, a so-called "full-frame" model. The rectangle marked 1.3X shows the effective field of view from the same vantage point with the exact same lens mounted on the discontinued Canon EOS 1D Mark III camera, while the area marked 1.6X shows the field of view you'd get with that 28mm lens installed on a T7i. It's easy to see from the illustration that the 1X rendition provides a wider, more expansive view, while the other two are, in comparison, *cropped*.

The cropping effect is produced because the sensors of the latter two cameras are smaller than the sensors of the 5D Mark IV. The "full-frame" camera has a sensor that's the size of the standard 35mm film frame, 24mm × 36mm. Your T7i's sensor does *not* measure 24mm × 36mm; instead, it specs out at 22.3mm × 14.9mm, or about 62.5 percent of the area of a full-frame sensor, as shown by the yellow boxes in the figure. You can calculate the relative field of view by dividing the focal

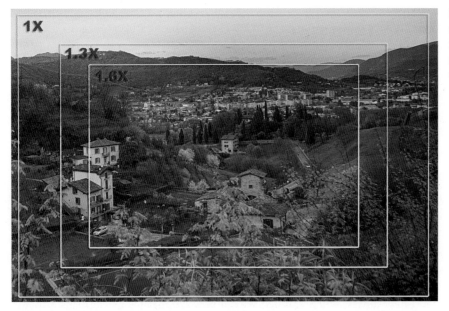

Figure 10.1

Canon offers digital SLRs with full-frame (1X) crops, as well as 1.3X and 1.6X crops.

length of the lens by .625. Thus, a 100mm lens mounted on a T7i has the same field of view as a 160mm lens on the 5DS. We humans tend to perform multiplication operations in our heads more easily than division, so such field of view comparisons are usually calculated using the reciprocal of .625—1.6—so we can multiply instead (100 / .625 = 160; 100 × 1.6 = 160).

This translation is generally useful only if you're accustomed to using full-frame cameras (usually of the film variety) and want to know how a familiar lens will perform on a digital camera. I strongly prefer *crop factor* over *lens multiplier*, because nothing is being multiplied; a 100mm lens doesn't "become" a 160mm lens—the depth-of-field and lens aperture remain the same. (I'll explain more about these later in this chapter.) Only the field of view is cropped. But *crop factor* isn't much better, as it implies that the 24mm × 36mm frame is "full" and anything else is "less." I get e-mails all the time from photographers who point out that they own full-frame cameras with 36mm × 48mm sensors (like the Mamiya 645ZD or Hasselblad H3D-39 medium-format digitals). By their reckoning, the "half-size" sensors found in cameras like the 5D Mark IV are "cropped."

If you're accustomed to using full-frame film cameras, you might find it helpful to use the crop factor "multiplier" to translate a lens's real focal length into the full-frame equivalent, even though, as I said, nothing is being multiplied. Throughout most of this book, I've been using actual focal lengths and not equivalents, except when referring to specific wide-angle or telephoto focal length ranges and their fields of view.

Your First Lens

Back in ancient times (the pre-zoom, pre-autofocus era before the mid-1980s), choosing the first lens for your camera was a no-brainer: you had few or no options. Canon cameras (which used a different lens mount in those days) were sold with a 50mm f/1.4, a 50mm f/1.8, or, if you had deeper pockets, a super-fast 50mm f/1.2 lens. It was also possible to buy a camera as a body alone, which didn't save much money back when a film SLR like the Canon A-1 sold for a street price of $435— *with lens*—in 1978. (Thanks to the era of relatively cheap optics, I still own a total of *eight* 50mm f/1.4 lenses; I picked one up each time I purchased a new or used body.)

Today, your choices are more complicated, and Canon lenses, which now include zoom, autofocus, and, more often than not, built-in image stabilization (IS) features, tend to cost a lot more compared to the price of a camera. (Adjusted for inflation, that $435 A-1 cost $1,587 in today's dollars.)

The Canon EOS T7i is frequently purchased with a lens, even now. I purchased my T7i with the Canon EF-S 18-55mm f/3.5-5.6 IS STM autofocus lens. It added only about $100 to the price tag of the body alone, and was thus an irresistible bargain.

Those looking for a longer zoom range might opt to pay an additional $700 for the older Canon EF-S 18-200mm f/3.5-5.6 IS lens, which provides a very useful 11X zoom range. Some buyers don't need quite that zoom range, and save a few dollars by purchasing the Canon EF 28-135mm f/3.5-5.6 IS USM lens ($480). The latter lens has one advantage. *EF* lenses like the 28-135mm zoom can also be used with any *full-frame* camera you add/migrate to at a later date. You'll learn the difference later in this chapter.

So, depending on which category you fall into, you'll need to decide about what kit lens to buy, or decide what other kind of lenses you need to fill out your existing complement of Canon optics. This section will cover "first lens" concerns, while later in the chapter we'll look at "add-on lens" considerations.

When deciding on a first lens, there are several factors you'll want to consider:

- **Cost.** You might have stretched your budget a bit to purchase your T7i, so you might want to keep the cost of your first lens fairly low. Fortunately, as I've noted, there are excellent lenses available that will add from $100 to $600 to the price of your camera if purchased at the same time.

- **Zoom range.** If you have only one lens, you'll want a fairly long zoom range to provide as much flexibility as possible. Fortunately, the two most popular basic lenses for the T7i have 3X to 5X zoom ranges, extending from moderate wide-angle/normal out to medium telephoto. These are fine for everyday shooting, portraits, and some types of sports.

- **Adequate maximum aperture.** You'll want an f/stop of at least f/3.5 to f/4 for shooting under fairly low-light conditions. The thing to watch for is the maximum aperture when the lens is zoomed to its telephoto end. You may end up with no better than an f/5.6 maximum aperture.

- **Image quality.** Your starter lens should have good image quality, befitting a camera with 24MP of resolution, because that's one of the primary factors that will be used to judge your photos. Even at a low price, the several different lenses sold with the T7i as a kit include extra-low dispersion glass and aspherical elements that minimize distortion and chromatic aberration; they are sharp enough for most applications. If you read the user evaluations in the online photography forums, you know that owners of the kit lenses have been very pleased with their image quality.

- **Size matters.** A good walking-around lens is compact in size and light in weight.

- **Fast/close focusing.** Your first lens should have a speedy autofocus system (which is where the ultrasonic motor/USM and STM system found in many moderately priced Canon lenses is an advantage). Close focusing (to 12 inches or closer) will let you use your basic lens for some types of macro photography.

You can find comparisons of the lenses discussed in the next section, as well as third-party lenses from Sigma, Tokina, Tamron, and other vendors, in online groups and websites. I'll provide my recommendations, but obtaining more information from these additional sources is always helpful when making a lens purchase, because, while camera bodies come and go, lenses may be a lifetime addition to your kit.

Buy Now, Expand Later

The T7i is commonly available with several good, basic lenses that each can serve you well as a "walk-around" lens (one you keep on the camera most of the time, especially when you're out and about without your camera bag). The number of options available to you is actually quite amazing, even if your budget is limited to about $100 to $500 for your first lens. One other vendor, for example, offers only 18mm-70mm and 18mm-55mm kit lenses in that price range, plus a 24mm-85mm zoom. Two popular starter lenses Canon offers are shown in Figures 10.2 and 10.3. Canon's best-bet first lenses are as follows:

■ **Canon EF-S 18-55mm f/3.5-5.6 IS STM autofocus lens.** This lens, shown in Figure 10.2, replaces the old "II" version, and is a bit larger than the older optic. It boasts the new STM stepper motor technology that Canon video fans have found to be so useful. It has image stabilization that can counter camera shake by providing the vibration-stopping capabilities of a shutter speed four stops faster than the one you've dialed in. That is, with image stabilization activated, you can shoot at 1/30th second and eliminate camera shake as if you were using a shutter speed of 1/250th second. (At least, that's what Canon claims; I usually have slightly less impressive results.) Of course, IS doesn't freeze subject motion—that basketball player driving for a layup will still be blurry at 1/30th second, even though the effects of camera shake will be effectively nullified. But this lens is an all-around good choice if your budget is tight.

Figure 10.2
The Canon EF-S 18-55mm f/3.5-5.6 IS STM autofocus lens ships as a basic kit lens for entry-level Canon cameras, including the T7i.

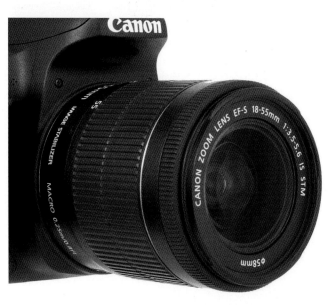

- **Canon EF-S 18-135mm f/3.5-5.6 IS STM autofocus lens.** This lens, priced at about $400, is an upgrade from a similar earlier lens without the stepper motor technology. It's also light, compact (you can see it mounted on the T7i in Figure 10.3), and covers a useful range from true wide-angle to intermediate telephoto. As with Canon's other affordable zoom lenses, image stabilization partially compensates for the slow f/5.6 maximum aperture at the telephoto end by allowing you to use longer shutter speeds to capture an image under poor lighting conditions. I'll explain the advantages of the STM autofocus later in this chapter. However, this economical lens has already been replaced by a newer model, described next.

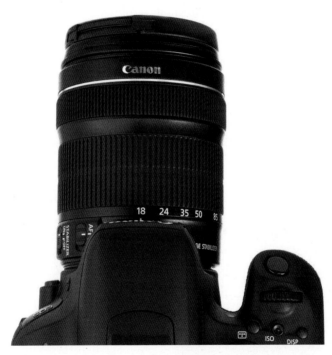

Figure 10.3
The EF-S 18-135mm f/3.5-5.6 IS STM lens is affordable and features near-silent autofocus that's perfect for video shooting.

- **Canon EF-S 18-135mm f/3.5-5.6 IS USM autofocus lens.** Similar in design to the previous model, this one has improved optics and a faster USM motor replacing the STM drive. It's priced at about $600. The extra $250 might be worth it to you to have the latest lens technology.

- **Canon EF-S 18-200mm f/3.5-5.6 IS autofocus lens.** This one, priced at about $700, has been popular as a basic lens for the T7i, because it's light, compact, and covers a full range from true wide-angle to long telephoto. Image stabilization keeps your pictures sharp at the long end of the zoom range, allowing the longer shutter speeds that the f/5.6 maximum aperture demands at 200mm. Automatic panning detection turns the IS feature off when panning in both horizontal and vertical directions. An improved "Super Spectra Coating" minimizes flare and ghosting, while optimizing color rendition.

- **Canon EF-S 17-85mm f/4-5.6 IS USM autofocus lens.** This older lens (introduced in 2004 with the EOS 20D) is a very popular "basic" lens still sold for the T7i. The allure here with this $300 lens is the longer telephoto range, coupled with the built-in image stabilization, which allows you to shoot rock-solid photos at shutter speeds that are at least two or three notches slower than you'd need normally (say, 1/8th second instead of 1/30th or 1/60th second), as long as your subject isn't moving. It also has a quiet, fast, reliable ultrasonic motor (more on that later, too). This is another lens designed for the 1.6X crop factor; all but one of the remaining lenses in this list can also be used on full-frame cameras. (I'll tell you why later in this chapter.)

- **Canon EF 55-200mm f/4.5-5.6 II USM autofocus lightweight compact telephoto zoom lens.** If you bought the 18-55mm kit lens, this one picks up where that one leaves off, going from short telephoto to medium long (88mm-320mm full-frame equivalent). It features a desirable ultrasonic motor. Best of all, it's very affordable at less than $300. If you can afford only two lenses, the 18-55mm and this lens make a good basic set.

- **EF-S 55-250mm f/4-5.6 IS STM telephoto zoom lens.** This is an image-stabilized EF-S lens (which means it can't be used with Canon's 1.3X and 1.0X crop-factor pro cameras), providing the longest focal range in the EF-S range to date, and that 4-stop Image Stabilizer. It's less than $300, and it's worth the cost for the stabilization. (See Figure 10.4.)

Figure 10.4
Some vendors are including the Canon EF-S 55-250mm f/4-5.6 IS STM lens in a bundle with some kits.

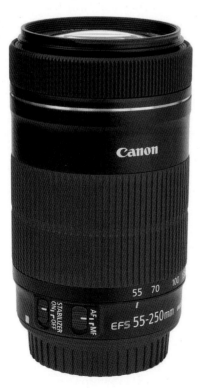

- **Canon EF 24-85mm f/3.5-4.5 USM autofocus wide-angle telephoto zoom lens.** If you can get by with normal focal length to medium telephoto range, Canon offers four affordable lenses, plus one more expensive killer lens that's worth the extra expenditure. All of them can be used on full-frame or cropped-frame digital Canons, which is why they include "wide angle" in their product names. They're really wide-angle lenses only when mounted on a full-frame camera. This lens, priced in the $300 range, offers a useful range of focal lengths, extending from the equivalent of 38mm to 136mm.

- **Canon EF 28-105mm f/3.5-4.5 II USM autofocus wide-angle telephoto zoom lens.** If you want to save about $100 and gain a little reach compared to the 24-85mm zoom, this 45mm-168mm (equivalent lens) might be what you are looking for.

- **Canon EF 28-200mm f/3.5-5.6 USM autofocus wide-angle telephoto zoom lens.** If you want one lens to do everything except wide-angle photography, this 7X zoom lens costs less than $400 and takes you from the equivalent of 45mm out to a long 320mm.

- **Canon EF 24-70mm f/2.8L II USM autofocus zoom wide-angle-telephoto lens.** I couldn't leave this premium lens out of the mix, even though it costs $1900. As part of Canon's L-series (Luxury) lens line, it offers the best sharpness over its focal range than any of the other lenses in this list. Best of all, it's fast (for a zoom), with an f/2.8 maximum aperture that *doesn't change* as you zoom out. Unlike the other lenses, which may offer only an f/5.6 maximum f/stop at their longest zoom setting, this is a *constant aperture* lens, which retains its maximum f/stop. The added sharpness, constant aperture, and ultra-smooth USM motor are what you're paying for with this lens. Another version with an f/4 maximum aperture with image stabilization can be purchased for less than $1,000 if you can find one.

What Lenses Can You Use?

The previous section helped you sort out what lens you need to buy with your T7i (assuming you already didn't own any Canon lenses). Now, you're probably wondering what lenses can be added to your growing collection (trust me, it will grow). You need to know which lenses are suitable and, most importantly, which lenses are fully compatible with your T7i.

With the Canon T7i, the compatibility issue is a simple one: It accepts any lens with the EF or EF-S designation, with full availability of all autofocus, autoaperture, autoexposure, and image-stabilization features (if present). It's comforting to know that any EF (for full-frame or cropped sensors) or EF-S (for cropped sensor cameras only) lens will work as designed with your camera. As I noted at the beginning of the chapter, that's more than 120 million lenses!

But wait, there's more. You can also attach Nikon F mount, Leica R, Olympus OM, and M42 ("Pentax screw mount") lenses with a simple adapter, if you don't mind losing automatic focus and aperture control. If you use one of these lenses, you'll need to focus manually (even if the lens operates in Autofocus mode on the camera it was designed for), and adjust the f/stop to the aperture you want to use to take the picture. That means that lenses that don't have an aperture ring (such as

Nikon G-series lenses) must be used only at their maximum aperture if you use them with a simple adapter. However, Novoflex makes expensive adapter rings (the Nikon-Lens-on-Canon-Camera version is called EOS/NIK NT) with an integral aperture control that allows adjusting the aperture of lenses that do not have an old-style aperture ring. Expect to pay $225 for an adapter of this type. Should you decide to pick up a new Canon EOS-M mirrorless camera, you'll be able to get double-duty with your EF and EF-S lenses, too, with an adapter that will allow you to use the same lenses on your T7i and companion EOS-M cameras.

Because of the limitations imposed on using "foreign" lenses on your T7i, you probably won't want to make extensive use of them, but an adapter can help you when you really, really need to use a particular focal length but don't have a suitable Canon-compatible lens. For example, I occasionally use an older 400mm lens that was originally designed for the Nikon line on my T7i. The lens needs to be mounted on a tripod for steadiness, anyway, so its slower operation isn't a major pain. Another good match is the 105mm Micro-Nikkor I sometimes use with my Canon T7i. Macro photos, too, are most often taken with the camera mounted on a tripod, and manual focus makes a lot of sense for fine-tuning focus and depth-of-field. Because of the contemplative nature of close-up photography, it's not much of an inconvenience to stop down to the taking aperture just before exposure.

The restrictions on use of lenses within Canon's own product line (as well as lenses produced for earlier Canon SLRs by third-party vendors) are fairly clear-cut. The T7i cannot be used with any of Canon's earlier lens mounting schemes for its film cameras, including the immediate predecessor to the EF mount, the FD mount (introduced with the Canon F1 in 1964 and used until the Canon T60 in 1990), FL (1964–1971), or the original Canon R mount (1959–1964). That's really all you need to know. While you'll find FD-to-EF adapters for about $40, you'll lose so many functions that it's rarely worth the bother.

WHY SO MANY LENS MOUNTS?

Four different lens mounts in 40-plus years (five, if you count the EF-M mount for the EOS-M cameras introduced in 2012) might seem like a lot of different mounting systems, especially when compared to the Nikon F mount of 1959, which retained quite a bit of compatibility with that company's film and digital camera bodies during that same span. However, in digital photography terms, the EF mount itself is positively ancient, having remained reasonably stable for more than 25 years. Lenses designed for the EF system work reliably with every EOS film and digital camera ever produced.

However, at the time, yet another lens mount switch, especially a change from the traditional breech system to a more conventional bayonet-type mount, was indeed a daring move by Canon. One of the reasons for staying with a particular lens type is to "lock" current users into a specific camera system. By introducing the EF mount, Canon in effect cut loose every photographer in its existing user base. If they chose to upgrade, they were free to choose another vendor's products and lenses. Only satisfaction with the previous Canon product line and the promise of the new system would keep them in the fold.

In retrospect, the switch to the EF mount seems like a very good idea, as the initial EOS film cameras can now be seen as the beginning of Canon's rise to eventually become the leader in film and (later) digital SLR cameras. By completely revamping its lens mounting system, the company was able to take advantage of the latest advances in technology without compromise.

For example, when the original EF bayonet mount was introduced in 1987, the system incorporated new autofocus technology (EF actually stands for "electro focus") in a more rugged and less complicated form. A tiny motor was built into the lens itself, eliminating the need for mechanical linkages with the camera. Instead, electrical contacts are used to send power and the required focusing information to the motor. That's a much more robust and resilient system that made it easier for Canon to design faster and more accurate autofocus mechanisms just by redesigning the lenses.

EF vs. EF-S

Today, in addition to its EF lenses, Canon offers lenses that use the EF-S (the S stands for "short back focus") mount, with the chief difference being (as you might expect) lens components that extend farther back into the camera body of some of Canon's latest digital cameras (specifically those with smaller than full-frame sensors), such as the T7i. As I'll explain next, this refinement allows designing more compact, less-expensive lenses especially for those cameras, but not for models that include current cameras like the EOS 5D Mark IV.

Canon's EF-S lens mount variation was born in 2003, when the company virtually invented the consumer-oriented digital SLR category by introducing the original EOS 300D/Digital Rebel, a dSLR that cost less than $1,000 *with lens* at a time when all other interchangeable-lens digital cameras (including the T7i's "grandparent," the original EOS 10D) were priced closer to $2,000 with a basic lens. Like the EOS 10D, the EOS T7i features a smaller-than-full-frame sensor with a 1.6X crop factor (Canon calls this format APS-C). But the EOS Digital Rebel accepted lenses that took advantage of the shorter mirror found in APS-C cameras, with elements of shorter focal length lenses (wide angles) that extended *into* the camera, space that was off limits in other models because the mirror passed through that territory as it flipped up to expose the shutter and sensor. (Canon even calls its flip-up reflector a "half mirror.")

In short (so to speak), the EF-S mount made it easier to design less-expensive wide-angle lenses that could be used *only* with 1.6X-crop cameras, and featured a simpler design and reduced coverage area suitable for those non-full-frame models. The new mount made it possible to produce lenses like the ultra-wide EF-S 10-22mm f/3.5-4.5 USM lens, which has the equivalent field of view as a 16mm-35mm zoom on a full-frame camera. (See Figure 10.5.)

Suitable cameras for EF-S lenses include all recent non-full-frame models. The EF-S lenses cannot be used on the APS-C-sensor EOS 10D, the 1D Mark II N/Mark III (which have a 28.7mm × 19.1mm APS-H sensor with a 1.3X crop factor), or any of the full-frame digital or film EOS models, such as the EOS 1D X, EOS 1Ds Mark III, EOS 5D Mark III, or EOS 5DS/5DS R. It's easy

Figure 10.5

The EF-S 10-22mm ultra-wide lens was made possible by the shorter back focus difference offered by the original Digital Rebel and subsequent Canon 1.6X "cropped sensor" models.

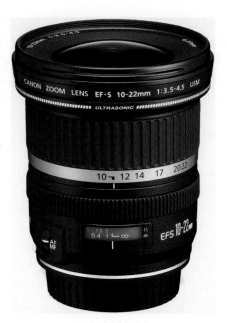

to tell an EF lens from an EF-S lens: The latter incorporate EF-S into their name! Plus, EF lenses have a raised red dot on the barrel that is used to align the lens with a matching dot on the camera when attaching the lens. EF-S lenses and compatible bodies use a white square instead. Some EF-S lenses also have a rubber ring at the attachment end that provides a bit of weather/dust sealing and protects the back components of the lens if a user attempts to mount it on a camera that is not EF-S compatible.

Ingredients of Canon's Alphanumeric Soup

The actual product names of individual Canon lenses are fairly easy to decipher; they'll include either the EF or EF-S designation, the focal length or focal length range of the lens, its maximum aperture, and some other information. Additional data may be engraved or painted on the barrel or ring surrounding the front element of the lens. Here's a decoding of what the individual designations mean:

- **EF/EF-S.** If the lens is marked EF, it can safely be used on any Canon EOS camera, film or digital. If it is an EF-S lens, it should be used only on an EF-S-compatible camera.
- **Focal length.** Given in millimeters or a millimeter range, such as 60mm in the case of a popular Canon macro lens, or 17-55mm, used to describe a medium-wide to short-telephoto zoom.

- **Maximum aperture.** The largest f/stop available with a particular lens is given in a string of numbers that might seem confusing at first glance. For example, you might see 1:1.8 for a fixed focal length (prime) lens, and 1:4.5-5.6 for a zoom. The initial 1: signifies that the f/stop given is actually a ratio or fraction (in regular notation, f/ replaces the 1:), which is why a 1:2 (or f/2) aperture is larger than an 1:4 (or f/4) aperture—just as 1/2 is larger than 1/4. With most zoom lenses, the maximum aperture changes as the lens is zoomed to the telephoto position, so a range is given instead: 1:4.5-5.6. (Some zooms, called *constant aperture* lenses, keep the same maximum aperture throughout their range.)

- **Autofocus type.** Most newer Canon lenses that aren't of the bargain-basement type use Canon's *ultrasonic motor* autofocus system (more on that later) and are given the USM designation. Several of the company's newest optics use the Stepper Motor (STM) technology. If USM or STM does not appear on the lens or its model name, the lens uses the less sophisticated AFD (arc-form drive) autofocus system or the micromotor (MM) drive mechanism.

- **Series.** Canon adds a Roman numeral to many of its products to represent an updated model with the same focal length or focal length range, so some lenses will have a II or III added to their name.

- **Pro quality.** Canon's more expensive lenses with more rugged construction and higher optical quality, intended for professional use, include the letter L (for "luxury") in their product name. You can further differentiate these lenses visually by a red ring around the lens barrel and the off-white color of the metal barrel itself in virtually all telephoto L-series lenses. (Some L-series lenses have shiny or textured black plastic exterior barrels.) Internally, every L lens includes at least one lens element that is built of ultra-low dispersion glass, is constructed of expensive fluorite crystal, or uses an expensive ground (not molded) aspheric (non-spherical) lens component.

- **Filter size.** You'll find the front lens filter thread diameter in millimeters included on the lens, preceded by a Ø symbol, as in Ø67 or Ø72.

- **Special-purpose lenses.** Some Canon lenses are designed for specific types of work, and they include appropriate designations in their names. For example, close-focusing lenses such as the Canon EF-S 60mm f/2.8 Macro USM lens or the new Canon EF-S 35mm f/2.8 Macro IS STM lens incorporate the word *Macro* into their name. Lenses with perspective control features preface the lens name with T-S (for tilt-shift). Lenses with built-in image-stabilization features, such as the nifty EF 28-300mm f/3.5-5.6L IS USM telephoto zoom include *IS* in their product names.

SORTING THE MOTOR DRIVES

Incorporating the autofocus motor inside the lens was an innovative move by Canon, and this allowed the company to produce better and more sophisticated lenses as technology became available to upgrade the focusing system. As a result, you'll find four different types of motors in Canon-designed lenses, each with cost and practical considerations. Most newer lenses use only the latest USM motor, and incorporate that designation in their names.

■ **AFD (Arc-form drive)** and **Micromotor (MM)** drives are built around tiny versions of electro-magnetic motors, which generally use gear trains to produce the motion needed to adjust the focus of the lens. Both are slow, noisy, and not particularly effective with larger lenses. Manual focus adjustments are possible only when the motor drive is disengaged.

■ **Micromotor ultrasonic motor (USM)** drives use high-frequency vibration to produce the motion used to drive the gear train, resulting in a quieter operating system at a cost that's not much more than that of electromagnetic motor drives. With the exception of a couple of lenses that have a slipping clutch mechanism, manual focus with this kind of system is possible only when the motor drive is switched off and the lens is set in manual mode. This is the kind of USM system you'll find in lower-cost lenses.

■ **Ring ultrasonic motor (USM)** drives, available in two different types (*electronic focus ring USM* and *ring USM*), also use high-frequency movement, but generate motion using a pair of vibrating metal rings to adjust focus. Both variations allow a feature called Full Time Manual (FTM) focus, which lets you make manual adjustments to the lens's focus even when the autofocus mechanism is engaged. With electronic focus ring USM, manual focus is possible only when the lens is mounted on the camera and the camera is turned on; the focus ring of lenses with ring USM can be turned at any time.

■ **Stepper motor (STM) drives.** In autofocus mode, the precision motor of STM lenses, along with a new aperture mechanism, allows lenses equipped with this technology to focus quickly, accurately, silently, and with smooth continuous increments. If you think about video capture, you can see how these advantages pay off. Silent operation is a plus, especially when noise from autofocusing can easily be transferred to the camera's built-in microphones through the air or transmitted through the body itself. In addition, because autofocus is often done *during* capture, it's important that the focus increments are continuous. USM motors are not as smooth, but are better at jumping quickly to the exact focus point. You can adjust focus manually, using a focus-by-wire process. As you rotate the focus ring, that action doesn't move the lens elements; instead, your rotation of the ring sends a signal to the motor to change the focus. Figure 10.6 shows the Canon EF-S 40mm f/2.8 STM lens, part of a series that also includes the two kit lenses previously mentioned and a 50mm f/1.8 "nifty fifty" that costs just $125.

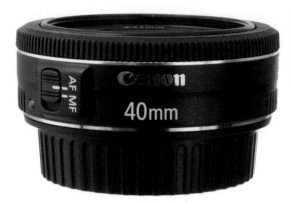

Figure 10.6
Canon's 40mm f/2.8 lens, with an STM motor, is designed for video capture.

Your Second (and Third...) Lens

There are only two advantages to owning just a single lens. One of them is creative. Keeping one set of optics mounted on your T7i all the time forces you to be especially imaginative in your approach to your subjects. I once visited Europe with only a single camera body and a 35mm f/2 lens. The experience was actually quite exciting, because I had to use a variety of techniques to allow that one lens to serve for landscapes, available-light photos, action, close-ups, portraits, and other kinds of images. Canon makes an excellent 35mm f/2 lens (which focuses down to 9.6 inches) that's perfect for that kind of experiment; although, today, my personal choice would be the sublime (and expensive) Canon Wide-Angle EF 35mm f/1.4L USM autofocus lens. I also own the Canon EF 50mm f/1.8 STM lens, which I favor as a very compact and light walkaround/short telephoto/ portrait lens, especially indoors. It makes a great close-up/macro lens, too, and is my choice as a very good second lens. As an EF lens, it works just fine on my Canon full-frame cameras, too.

Of course, it's more likely that your "single" lens is actually a zoom, which is, in truth, many lenses in one, taking you from, say, 17mm to 85mm (or some other range) with a rapid twist of the zoom ring. You'll still find some creative challenges when you stick to a single zoom lens's focal lengths.

The second advantage of the unilens camera is only a marginal technical benefit. If you don't exchange lenses, the chances of dust and dirt getting inside your T7i and settling on the sensor is reduced (but *not* eliminated entirely). Although I've known some photographers who minimized the number of lens changes they made for this very reason, reducing the number of lenses you work with is not a productive or rewarding approach for most of us. The T7i's automatic sensor cleaning feature has made this "advantage" much less significant than it was in the past.

It's more likely that you'll succumb to the malady known as *Lens Lust*, which is defined as an incurable disease marked by a significant yen for newer, better, longer, faster, sharper, anything-er optics for your camera. (And, it must be noted, this disease can *cost* you significant yen—or dollars, or whatever currency you use.) In its worst manifestations, sufferers find themselves with lenses that have overlapping zoom ranges or capabilities, because one or the other offers a slight margin in performance or suitability for specific tasks. When you find yourself already lusting after a new lens before you've really had a chance to put your latest purchase to the test, you'll know the disease has reached the terminal phase.

What Lenses Can Do for You

A saner approach to expanding your lens collection is to consider what each of your options can do for you and then choosing the type of lens that will really boost your creative opportunities. Here's a general guide to the sort of capabilities you can gain by adding a lens to your repertoire.

- **Wider perspective.** Your 18-55mm f/3.5-5.6 or 17-85mm f/4-5.6 or 18-200mm lens has served you well for moderate wide-angle shots. Now you find your back is up against a wall and you *can't* take a step backward to take in more subject matter. Perhaps you're standing on the rim of the Grand Canyon, and you want to take in as much of the breathtaking view as you can. You might find yourself just behind the baseline at a high school basketball game and want an interesting shot with a little perspective distortion tossed in the mix. There's a lens out there that will provide you with what you need, such as the EF-S 10-22mm f/3.5-4.5 USM zoom (about $600). If you want to stay in the sub-$800 price category, you'll need something like the Sigma Super Wide-Angle 10-20mm f/4-5.6 EX DC HSM autofocus lens. The two lenses provide the equivalent of a 16mm to 32/35mm wide-angle view. For a distorted view, there is the Canon Fisheye EF 15mm f/2.8 autofocus, with a similar lens available from Sigma, which offers an extra-wide circular fisheye, and the Sigma Fisheye 8mm f/3.5 EX DG Circular Fisheye. Your extra-wide choices may not be abundant, but they are there. Figure 10.7, left, shows the perspective you get from an ultra-wide-angle, non-fisheye lens.

- **Bring objects closer.** A long lens brings distant subjects closer to you, offers better control over depth-of-field, and avoids the perspective distortion that wide-angle lenses provide. They compress the apparent distance between objects in your frame. In the telephoto realm, Canon is second to none, with a dozen or more offerings in the sub-$650 range, including the Canon EF 100-300mm f/4.5-5.6 USM autofocus and Canon EF 70-300mm f/4-5.6 IS USM autofocus telephoto zoom lenses, and a broad array of zooms and fixed-focal length optics if you're willing to spend up to $1,000 or a bit more. Don't forget that the T7i's crop factor narrows the field of view of all these lenses, so your 70-300mm lens looks more like a 112mm-480mm zoom through the viewfinder. Figure 10.7 center and right were taken from the same position as Figure 10.7, left, but with an 85mm and 500mm lens, respectively.

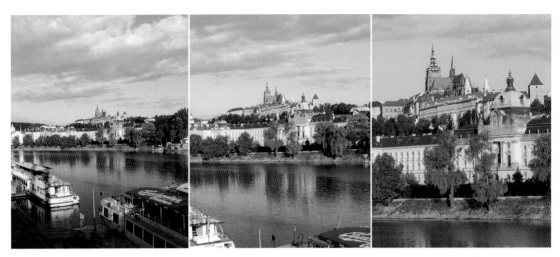

Figure 10.7 An ultra-wide-angle lens provided this view of a castle in Prague, Czech Republic (left). This photo, taken from roughly the same distance, shows the view using a short telephoto lens (center). A longer telephoto lens captured this closer view of the castle from approximately the same shooting position (right).

- **Bring your camera closer.** Macro lenses allow you to focus to within an inch or two of your subject. Canon's best close-up lenses are all fixed focal length optics in the 50mm to 180mm range (including the well-regarded Canon EF-S 60mm f/2.8 compact and Canon EF 100mm f/2.8 USM macro autofocus lenses). But you'll find macro zooms available from Sigma and others. They don't tend to focus quite as close, but they provide a bit of flexibility when you want to vary your subject distance (say, to avoid spooking a skittish creature).

- **Look sharp.** Many lenses, particularly Canon's luxury "L" line, are prized for their sharpness and overall image quality. While your run-of-the-mill lens is likely to be plenty sharp for most applications, the very best optics are even better over their entire field of view (which means no fuzzy corners), are sharper at a wider range of focal lengths (in the case of zooms), and have better correction for various types of distortion.

- **More speed.** Your Canon EF 75-300mm f/4.5-5.6 III telephoto zoom lens (see Figure 10.8) might have the perfect focal length and sharpness for sports photography, but the maximum aperture won't cut it for night baseball or football games, or, even, any sports shooting in daylight if the weather is cloudy or you need to use some unusually fast shutter speed, such as 1/4,000th second. You might be happier with the Canon EF 100mm f/2 medium telephoto for close-range stuff, or even the pricier Canon EF 135mm f/2L. If money is no object, you can spring for Canon's 400mm f/2.8 and 600mm f/4 L-series lenses (both with image stabilization and priced in the four- and five-figure stratosphere). Or, maybe you just need the speed and can benefit from an f/1.8 or f/1.4 lens in the 20mm-85mm range. They're all available in Canon mounts (there's even an 85mm f/1.2 and 50mm f/1.2 for the real speed demons). With any of these lenses you can continue photographing under the dimmest of lighting conditions without the need for a tripod or flash.

Figure 10.8
Canon's EF
75-300mm f/4.5-5.6
III telephoto zoom
doesn't have the
large maximum
aperture needed for
low-light photogra-
phy or for some
sports. In addition,
it gets longer when
you zoom (right).

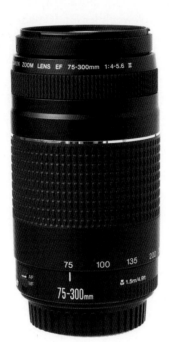
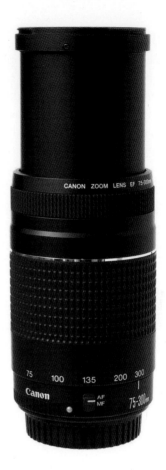

■ **Special features.** Accessory lenses give you special features, such as tilt/shift capabilities to correct for perspective distortion in architectural shots. Canon offers four of these TS-E lenses in 17mm, 24mm, 45mm, and 90mm focal lengths, at more than $1,300 to $2,000 (and up) each. You'll also find macro lenses, including the MP-E 65mm f/2.8 1-5x macro photo lens, a manual-focus lens which shoots *only* in the 1X to 5X life-size range. If you want diffused images, check out the EF 135mm f/2.8 with two soft-focus settings. The fisheye lenses mentioned earlier and all IS (image-stabilized) lenses also count as special-feature optics. The recent Canon EF 8-15mm f/4L Fisheye USM ultra-wide zoom lens is highly unusual in offering a *zoomable* fisheye range. Tokina's 10-17mm fisheye zoom is its chief competitor; I've owned one and it is not in the same league in terms of sharpness and speed as the Canon optic.

Zoom or Prime?

Zoom lenses have changed the way serious photographers take pictures. One of the reasons that I own 12 SLR film bodies is that in ancient times it was common to mount a different fixed focal length prime lens on various cameras and take pictures with two or three cameras around your neck (or tucked in a camera case) so you'd be ready to take a long shot or an intimate close-up or wide-angle view on a moment's notice, without the need to switch lenses. It made sense (at the time) to have a half dozen or so bodies (two to use, one in the shop, one in transit, and a couple backups). Zoom lenses of the time had a limited zoom range, were heavy, and not very sharp (especially when you tried to wield one of those monsters handheld).

That's all changed today. Lenses like the razor-sharp Canon EF 28-300mm f/3.5-5.6L IS USM can boast 10X or longer zoom ranges, in a package that's about 7 inches long, and while not petite at 3.7 pounds, it is quite usable handheld (especially with IS switched on). Although such a lens might seem expensive at close to $2,500, it's actually much less costly than the six or so lenses it replaces.

When selecting between zoom and prime lenses, there are several considerations to ponder. Here's a checklist of the most important factors. I already mentioned image quality and maximum aperture earlier, but those aspects take on additional meaning when comparing zooms and primes.

- **Logistics.** As prime lenses offer just a single focal length, you'll need more of them to encompass the full range offered by a single zoom. More lenses mean additional slots in your camera bag, and extra weight to carry. Just within Canon's line alone you can select from about a dozen general-purpose prime lenses in 28mm, 35mm, 50mm, 85mm, 100mm, 135mm, 200mm, and 300mm focal lengths, all of which are overlapped by the 28-300mm zoom I mentioned earlier. Even so, you might be willing to carry an extra prime lens or two to gain the speed or image quality that lens offers.

- **Image quality.** Prime lenses usually produce better image quality at their focal length than even the most sophisticated zoom lenses at the same magnification. Zoom lenses, with their shifting elements and f/stops that can vary from zoom position to zoom position, are in general more complex to design than fixed focal length lenses. That's not to say that the very best prime lenses can't be complicated as well. However, the exotic designs, aspheric elements, low-dispersion glass, and Canon's diffraction optics (DO) technology (a three-layer diffraction grating to better control how light is captured by a lens) can be applied to improving the quality of the lens, rather than wasting a lot of it on compensating for problems caused by the zoom process itself.

- **Maximum aperture.** Because of the same design constraints, zoom lenses usually have smaller maximum apertures than prime lenses, and the most affordable zooms have a lens opening that grows effectively smaller as you zoom in. The difference in lens speed verges on the ridiculous at some focal lengths. For example, the 18mm-55mm basic zoom gives you a 55mm f/5.6 lens when zoomed all the way out, while prime lenses in that focal length commonly have f/1.8 or faster maximum apertures. Indeed, the fastest f/2, f/1.8, f/1.4, and f/1.2 lenses are all primes, and if you require speed, a fixed focal length lens is what you should rely on. Figure 10.9 shows an image taken with a Canon 85mm f/1.8 Series EF USM telephoto lens.

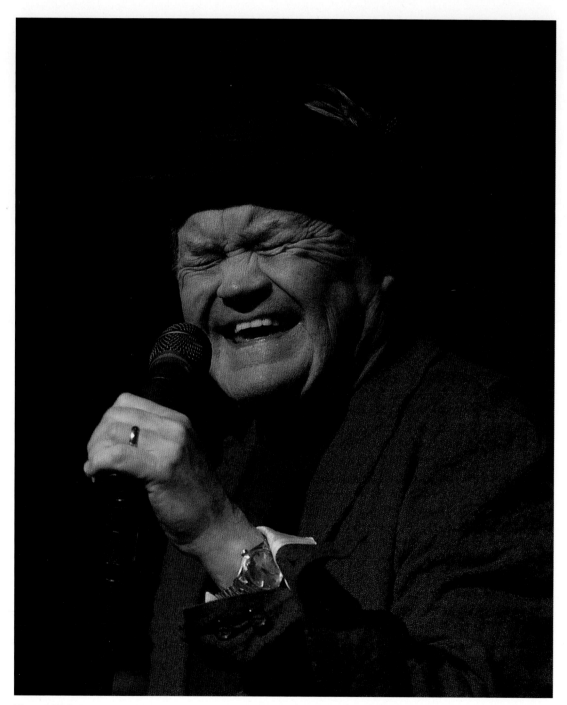

Figure 10.9 An 85mm f/1.8 lens was perfect for this handheld photo of Monkee lead singer Micky Dolenz.

- **Speed.** Using prime lenses takes time and slows you down. It takes a few seconds to remove your current lens and mount a new one, and the more often you need to do that, the more time is wasted. If you choose not to swap lenses, when using a fixed focal length lens, you'll still have to move closer or farther away from your subject to get the field of view you want. A zoom lens allows you to change magnifications and focal lengths with the twist of a ring and generally saves a great deal of time.

- **Special features.** Prime lenses often have special features not found in zoom lenses. For example, the new EF 40mm f/2.8 STM lens boasts that smooth, silent autofocus motor described earlier in this chapter. It functions as a wide-angle lens on a full-frame camera like the 5D Mark III, and as a short telephoto, portrait lens on cameras like the T7i. You'll also find close-focusing capabilities and perspective control features on prime lenses.

Categories of Lenses

Lenses can be categorized by their intended purpose—general photography, macro photography, and so forth—or by their focal length. The range of available focal lengths is usually divided into three main groups: wide-angle, normal, and telephoto. Prime lenses fall neatly into one of these classifications. Zooms can overlap designations, with a significant number falling into the catch-all, wide-to-telephoto zoom range. This section provides more information about focal length ranges, and how they are used.

Any lens with an equivalent focal length of 10mm to 20mm is said to be an *ultra-wide-angle lens*; from about 20mm to 40mm (equivalent) is said to be a *wide-angle lens. Normal lenses* have a focal length roughly equivalent to the diagonal of the film or sensor, in millimeters, and so fall into the range of about 45mm to 60mm (on a full-frame camera). *Telephoto lenses* usually fall into the 75mm and longer focal lengths, while those from about 300mm to 400mm and longer often are referred to as *super-telephotos*.

Using Wide-Angle and Wide-Zoom Lenses

To use wide-angle prime lenses and wide zooms, you need to understand how they affect your photography. Here's a quick summary of the things you need to know.

- **More depth-of-field.** Practically speaking, wide-angle lenses offer more depth-of-field at a particular subject distance and aperture. (But see the sidebar below for an important note.) You'll find that helpful when you want to maximize sharpness of a large zone, but not very useful when you'd rather isolate your subject using selective focus (telephoto lenses are better for that).

- **Stepping back.** Wide-angle lenses have the effect of making it seem that you are standing farther from your subject than you really are. They're helpful when you don't want to back up, or can't because there are impediments in your way.

- **Wider field of view.** While making your subject seem farther away, as implied above, a wide-angle lens also provides a larger field of view, including more of the subject in your photos.

- **More foreground.** As background objects retreat, more of the foreground is brought into view by a wide-angle lens. That gives you extra emphasis on the area that's closest to the camera. Photograph your home with a normal lens/normal zoom setting, and the front yard probably looks fairly conventional in your photo (that's why they're called "normal" lenses). Switch to a wider lens and you'll discover that your lawn now makes up much more of the photo. So, wide-angle lenses are great when you want to emphasize that lake in the foreground, but problematic when your intended subject is located farther in the distance.

- **Super-sized subjects.** The tendency of a wide-angle lens to emphasize objects in the foreground, while de-emphasizing objects in the background can lead to a kind of size distortion that may be more objectionable for some types of subjects than others. Shoot a bed of flowers up close with a wide angle, and you might like the distorted effect of the larger blossoms nearer the lens. Take a photo of a family member with the same lens from the same distance, and you're likely to get some complaints about that gigantic nose in the foreground.

- **Perspective distortion.** When you tilt the camera so the plane of the sensor is no longer perpendicular to the vertical plane of your subject, some parts of the subject are now closer to the sensor than they were before, while other parts are farther away. So, buildings, flagpoles, or NBA players appear to be falling backward, as you can see in Figure 10.10. While this kind of apparent distortion (it's not caused by a defect in the lens) can happen with any lens, it's most apparent when a wide angle is used.

- **Steady cam.** You'll find that you can better handhold a wide-angle lens at slower shutter speeds, without need for image stabilization, than you can with a telephoto lens. The reduced magnification of the wide-lens or wide-zoom setting doesn't emphasize camera shake like a telephoto lens does.

- **Interesting angles.** Many of the factors already listed combine to produce more interesting angles when shooting with wide-angle lenses. Raising or lowering a telephoto lens a few feet probably will have little effect on the appearance of the distant subjects you're shooting. The same change in elevation can produce a dramatic effect for the much-closer subjects typically captured with a wide-angle lens or wide-zoom setting.

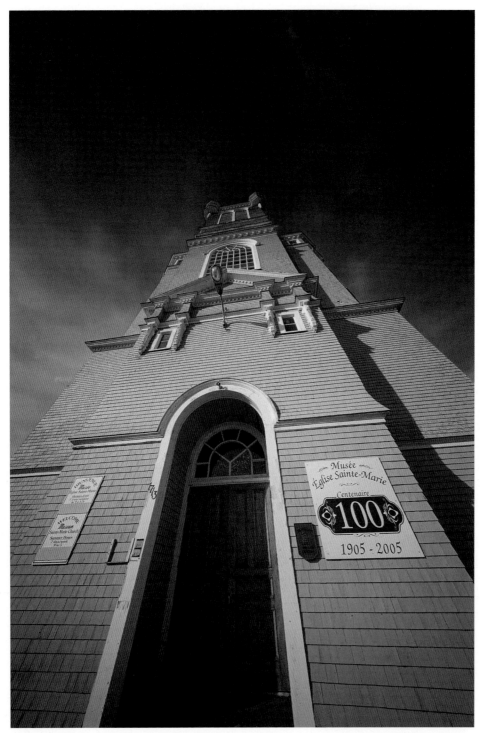

Figure 10.10 Tilting the camera back produces this "falling back" look in architectural photos.

DOF IN DEPTH

The depth-of-field (DOF) advantage of wide-angle lenses is diminished when you enlarge your picture; believe it or not, a wide-angle image enlarged and cropped to provide the same subject size as a telephoto shot would have the *same* depth-of-field. Try it: take a wide-angle photo of a friend from a fair distance, and then zoom in to duplicate the picture in a telephoto image. Then, enlarge the wide shot so your friend is the same size in both. The wide photo will have the same DOF (and will have much less detail, too).

Avoiding Potential Wide-Angle Problems

Wide-angle lenses have a few quirks that you'll want to keep in mind when shooting so you can avoid falling into some common traps. Here's a checklist of tips for avoiding common problems:

- **Symptom: converging lines.** Unless you want to use wildly diverging lines as a creative effect, it's a good idea to keep horizontal and vertical lines in landscapes, architecture, and other subjects carefully aligned with the sides, top, and bottom of the frame. That will help you avoid undesired perspective distortion. Sometimes it helps to shoot from a slightly elevated position so you don't have to tilt the camera up or down.

- **Symptom: color fringes around objects.** Lenses are often plagued with fringes of color around backlit objects, produced by *chromatic aberration*, which comes in two forms: *longitudinal/axial*, in which all the colors of light don't focus in the same plane; and *lateral/transverse*, in which the colors are shifted to one side. Axial chromatic aberration can be reduced by stopping down the lens, but transverse chromatic aberration cannot. Both can be reduced by using lenses with low diffraction index glass (or UD elements, in Canon nomenclature) and by incorporating elements that cancel the chromatic aberration of other glass in the lens. For example, a strong positive lens made of low-dispersion crown glass (made of a soda-lime-silica composite) may be mated with a weaker negative lens made of high-dispersion flint glass, which contains lead.

- **Symptom: lines that bow outward.** Some wide-angle lenses cause straight lines to bow outward, with the strongest effect at the edges. In fisheye (or *curvilinear*) lenses, this defect is a feature, as you can see in Figure 10.11. When distortion is not desired, you'll need to use a lens that has corrected barrel distortion. Manufacturers like Canon do their best to minimize or eliminate it (producing a *rectilinear* lens), often using *aspherical* lens elements (which are not cross-sections of a sphere). You can also minimize less severe barrel distortion simply by framing your photo with some extra space all around, so the edges where the defect is most obvious can be cropped out of the picture.

- **Symptom: dark corners and shadows in flash photos.** The Canon EOS T7i's built-in electronic flash is designed to provide even coverage for lenses as wide as 17mm. If you use a wider lens, you can expect darkening, or *vignetting*, in the corners of the frame. At wider focal lengths, the lens hood of some lenses (my 17mm-85mm lens is a prime offender) can cast a semi-circular shadow in the lower portion of the frame when using the built-in flash. Sometimes removing the lens hood or zooming in a bit can eliminate the shadow. Mounting an external flash unit, such as the mighty Canon Speedlite 600EX-RT II, can solve both problems, as it has zoomable coverage up to 114 degrees with the included adapter, sufficient for a 15mm rectilinear lens. Its higher vantage point eliminates the problem of lens hood shadow, too.

- **Symptom: light and dark areas when using polarizing filter.** If you know that polarizers work best when the camera is pointed 90 degrees away from the sun and have the least effect when the camera is oriented 180 degrees from the sun, you know only half the story. With lenses having a focal length of 10mm to 18mm (the equivalent of 16mm-28mm), the angle of view (107 to 75 degrees diagonally, or 97 to 44 degrees horizontally) is extensive enough to cause problems. Think about it: when a 10mm lens is pointed at the proper 90-degree angle from the sun, objects at the edges of the frame will be oriented at 135 to 41 degrees, with only the center at exactly 90 degrees. Either edge will have much less of a polarized effect. The solution is to avoid using a polarizing filter with lenses having an actual focal length of less than 18mm (or 28mm equivalent).

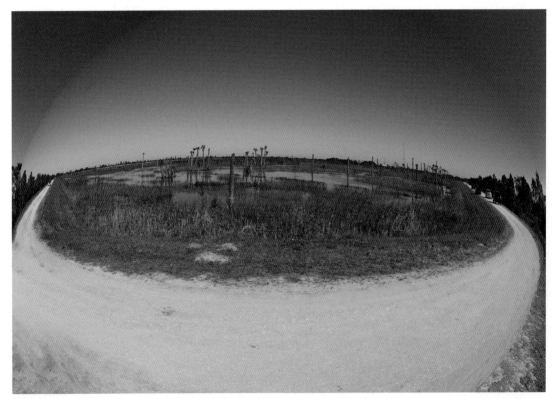

Figure 10.11 Many wide-angle lenses cause lines to bow outward toward the edges of the image; with a fisheye lens, this tendency is especially useful for creating special effects, as in this shot.

Using Telephoto and Tele-Zoom Lenses

Telephoto lenses also can have a dramatic effect on your photography, and Canon is especially strong in the long-lens arena, with lots of choices in many focal lengths and zoom ranges. You should be able to find an affordable telephoto or tele-zoom to enhance your photography in several different ways. Here are the most important things you need to know. In the next section, I'll concentrate on telephoto considerations that can be problematic—and how to avoid those problems.

■ **Selective focus.** Long lenses have reduced depth-of-field within the frame, allowing you to use selective focus to isolate your subject. You can open the lens up wide to create shallow depth-of-field (see Figure 10.12), or close it down a bit to allow more to be in focus. The flip side of the coin is that when you *want* to make a range of objects sharp, you'll need to use a smaller f/stop to get the depth-of-field you need. Like fire, the depth-of-field of a telephoto lens can be friend or foe.

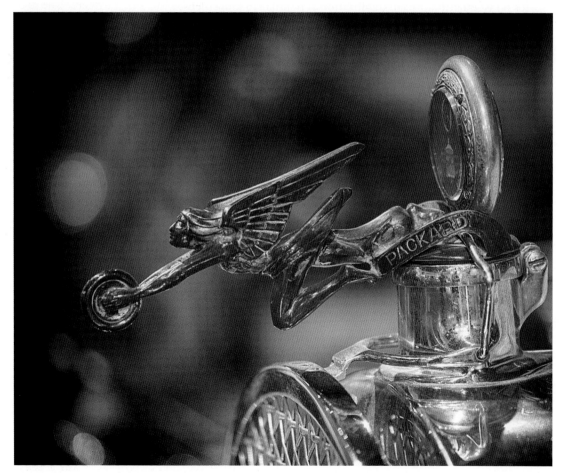

Figure 10.12 A wide f/stop helped isolate this hood ornament, for an interesting effect.

- **Getting closer.** Telephoto lenses bring you closer to wildlife, sports action, and candid subjects. No one wants to get a reputation as a surreptitious or "sneaky" photographer (except for paparazzi), but when applied to candids in an open and honest way, a long lens can help you capture memorable moments while retaining enough distance to stay out of the way of events as they transpire.

- **Reduced foreground/increased compression.** Telephoto lenses have the opposite effect of wide angles: they reduce the importance of things in the foreground by squeezing everything together. This compression even makes distant objects appear to be closer to subjects in the foreground and middle ranges. You can use this effect as a creative tool.

- **Accentuates camera shakiness.** Telephoto focal lengths hit you with a double-whammy in terms of camera/photographer shake. The lenses themselves are bulkier, more difficult to hold steady, and may even produce a barely perceptible see-saw rocking effect when you support them with one hand halfway down the lens barrel. Telephotos also magnify any camera shake. It's no wonder that image stabilization is popular in longer lenses.

- **Interesting angles require creativity.** Telephoto lenses require more imagination in selecting interesting angles, because the "angle" you do get on your subjects is so narrow. Moving from side to side or a bit higher or lower can make a dramatic difference in a wide-angle shot, but raising or lowering a telephoto lens a few feet probably will have little effect on the appearance of the distant subjects you're shooting.

Avoiding Telephoto Lens Problems

Many of the "problems" that telephoto lenses pose are just challenges and not that difficult to overcome. Here is a list of the seven most common picture maladies and suggested solutions.

- **Symptom: flat faces in portraits.** Head-and-shoulders portraits of humans tend to be more flattering when a focal length of 50mm to 85mm is used. Longer focal lengths compress the distance between features like noses and ears, making the face look wider and flat. A wide-angle might make noses look huge and ears tiny when you fill the frame with a face. So, stick with 50mm to 85mm focal lengths, going longer only when you're forced to shoot from a greater distance, and wider only when shooting three-quarters/full-length portraits, or group shots.

- **Symptom: blur due to camera shake.** Use a higher shutter speed (boosting ISO if necessary), consider an image-stabilized lens, or mount your camera on a tripod, monopod, or brace it with some other support. Of those three solutions, only the first will reduce blur caused by *subject* motion; an IS lens or tripod won't help you freeze a race car in mid-lap.

■ **Symptom: color fringes.** Chromatic aberration is the most pernicious optical problem found in telephoto lenses. There are others, including spherical aberration, astigmatism, coma, curvature of field, and similarly scary-sounding phenomena. The best solution for any of these is to use a better lens that offers the proper degree of correction, or stop down the lens to minimize the problem. But that's not always possible. Your second-best choice may be to correct the fringing in your favorite RAW conversion tool or image editor. Photoshop's Lens Correction filter offers sliders that minimize both red/cyan and blue/yellow fringing.

■ **Symptom: lines that curve inward.** Pincushion distortion is found in many telephoto lenses. You might find after a bit of testing that it is worse at certain focal lengths with your particular zoom lens. Like chromatic aberration, it can be partially corrected using tools like Photoshop's Lens Correction filter and Photoshop Elements' Correct Camera Distortion filter.

■ **Symptom: low contrast from haze or fog.** When you're photographing distant objects, a long lens shoots through a lot more atmosphere, which generally is muddied up with extra haze and fog. That dirt or moisture in the atmosphere can reduce contrast and mute colors. Some feel that a skylight or UV filter can help, but this practice is mostly a holdover from the film days. Digital sensors are not sensitive enough to UV light for a UV filter to have much effect. So, you should be prepared to boost contrast and color saturation in your Picture Styles menu or image editor if necessary.

■ **Symptom: low contrast from flare.** Lenses are furnished with lens hoods for a good reason: to reduce flare from bright light sources at the periphery of the picture area, or completely outside it. Because telephoto lenses often create images that are lower in contrast in the first place, you'll want to be especially careful to use a lens hood to prevent further effects on your image (or shade the front of the lens with your hand).

■ **Symptom: dark flash photos.** Edge-to-edge flash coverage isn't a problem with telephoto lenses as it is with wide angles. The shooting distance is. A long lens might make a subject that's 50 feet away look as if it's right next to you, but your camera's flash isn't fooled. You'll need extra power for distant flash shots, and probably more power than your T7i's built-in flash provides. The shoe-mount 600EX-RT II Speedlite, for example, can automatically zoom its coverage down to that of a medium telephoto lens, providing a theoretical full-power shooting aperture of about f/8 at 50 feet and ISO 400. (Try *that* with the built-in flash!)

Telephotos and Bokeh

Bokeh describes the aesthetic qualities of the out-of-focus parts of an image and whether out-of-focus points of light—circles of confusion—are rendered as distracting fuzzy discs or smoothly fade into the background. *Boke* is a Japanese word for "blur," and the h was added to keep English speakers from rendering it monosyllabically to rhyme with *broke*. Although bokeh is visible in blurry portions of any image, it's of particular concern with telephoto lenses, which, thanks to the magic of reduced depth-of-field, produce more obviously out-of-focus areas.

Bokeh can vary from lens to lens, or even within a given lens depending on the f/stop in use. Bokeh becomes objectionable when the circles of confusion are evenly illuminated, making them stand out as distinct discs, or, worse, when these circles are darker in the center, producing an ugly "doughnut" effect. A lens defect called spherical aberration may produce out-of-focus discs that are brighter on the edges and darker in the center, because the lens doesn't focus light passing through the edges of the lens exactly as it does light going through the center. (Mirror or *catadioptric* lenses also produce this effect.)

Other kinds of spherical aberration generate circles of confusion that are brightest in the center and fade out at the edges, producing a smooth blending effect, as you can see at right in Figure 10.13. Ironically, when no spherical aberration is present at all, the discs are a uniform shade, which, while better than the doughnut effect, is not as pleasing as the bright center/dark edge rendition. The shape of the disc also comes into play, with round smooth circles considered the best, and nonagonal or some other polygon (determined by the shape of the lens diaphragm) considered less desirable.

If you plan to use selective focus a lot, you should investigate the bokeh characteristics of a particular lens before you buy. Canon user groups and forums will usually be full of comments and questions about bokeh, so the research is easy.

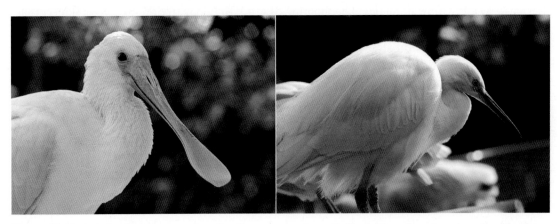

Figure 10.13 Bokeh is less pleasing when the discs are prominent (left), and less obtrusive when they blend into the background (right).

Add-ons and Special Features

Once you've purchased your telephoto lens, you'll want to think about some appropriate accessories for it. There are some handy add-ons available that can be valuable. Here are a couple of them to think about.

Lens Hoods

Lens hoods are an important accessory for all lenses, but they're especially valuable with telephotos. As I mentioned earlier, lens hoods do a good job of preserving image contrast by keeping bright light sources outside the field of view from striking the lens and, potentially, bouncing around inside that long tube to generate flare that, when coupled with atmospheric haze, can rob your image of detail and snap. In addition, lens hoods serve as valuable protection for that large, vulnerable, front lens element. It's easy to forget that you've got that long tube sticking out in front of your camera and accidentally whack the front of your lens into something. It's cheaper to replace a lens hood than it is to have a lens repaired, so you might find that a good hood is valuable protection for your prized optics.

When choosing a lens hood, it's important to have the right hood for the lens, usually the one offered for that lens by Canon or the third-party manufacturer. You want a hood that blocks precisely the right amount of light: neither too much light nor too little. A hood with a front diameter that is too small can show up in your pictures as vignetting. A hood that has a front diameter that's too large isn't stopping all the light it should. Generic lens hoods may not do the job.

When your telephoto is a zoom lens, it's even more important to get the right hood, because you need one that does what it is supposed to at both the wide-angle and telephoto ends of the zoom range. Lens hoods may be cylindrical, rectangular (shaped like the image frame), or petal shaped (that is, cylindrical, but with cut-out areas at the corners which correspond to the actual image area). Lens hoods should be mounted in the correct orientation (a bayonet mount for the hood on the front of the lens usually takes care of this).

Telephoto Extenders

Telephoto extenders (often called teleconverters outside the Canon world), multiply the actual focal length of your lens, giving you a longer telephoto for much less than the price of a lens with that actual focal length. These extenders fit between the lens and your camera and contain optical elements that magnify the image produced by the lens. Available in 1.4X and 2.0X configurations from Canon, an extender transforms, say, a 200mm lens into a 280mm or 400mm optic, respectively. Given the T7i's crop factor, your 200mm lens now has the same field of view as a 448mm or 640mm lens on a full-frame camera. At a little more than $400 each, they're quite a bargain, aren't they?

There are some downsides. While extenders retain the closest focusing distance of your original lens, autofocus is maintained only if the lens's original maximum aperture is f/4 or larger (for the 1.4X extender) or f/2.8 or larger (for the 2X extender). The components reduce the effective aperture of any lens they are used with, by one f/stop with the 1.4X extender, and 2 f/stops with the 2X extender. So, your EF 200mm f/2.8L II USM becomes a 280mm f/4 or 400mm f/5.6 lens. Although Canon extenders are precision optical devices, they do cost you a little sharpness, but that improves when you reduce the aperture by a stop or two. Each of the extenders is compatible only with a set of lenses of 135mm focal length or greater, so you'll want to check Canon's compatibility chart to see if the component can be used with the lens you want to attach to it.

If your lenses are compatible and you're shooting under bright lighting conditions, the Canon Extender EF 1.4x III, and Canon Extender EF 2x III make handy accessories.

Macro Focusing

Some telephotos and telephoto zooms available for the T7i have particularly close-focusing capabilities, making them *macro* lenses. Of course, the object is not necessarily to get close (get too close and you'll find it difficult to light your subject). What you're really looking for in a macro lens is to magnify the apparent size of the subject in the final image. Camera-to-subject distance is most important when you want to back up farther from your subject (say, to avoid spooking skittish insects or small animals). In that case, you'll want a macro lens with a longer focal length to allow that distance while retaining the desired magnification.

Canon makes 50mm, 60mm, 65mm, 100mm, and 180mm lenses with official macro designations. You'll also find macro lenses, macro zooms, and other close-focusing lenses available from Sigma, Tamron, and Tokina. If you want to focus closer with a macro lens, or any other lens, you can add an accessory called an *extension tube*. These add-ons move the lens farther from the focal plane, allowing it to focus more closely. Canon also sells add-on close-up lenses, which look like filters, and allow lenses to focus more closely.

Image Stabilization

Canon has a burgeoning line of more than a dozen lenses with built-in image stabilization (IS) capabilities. This feature uses lens elements that are shifted internally in response to the motion of the lens during handheld photography, countering the shakiness the camera and photographer produce and which telephoto lenses magnify. However, IS is not limited to long lenses; the feature works like a champ at the 17mm zoom position of Canon's EF-S 17-85mm f/4-5.6 IS USM and EF-S 17-55mm f/2.8 IS USM lenses. Other Canon IS lenses provide stabilization with zooms that are as wide as 10-18mm.

Image stabilization provides you with camera steadiness that's the equivalent of at least two or three shutter speed increments. (Canon claims four, which I feel may be optimistic.) This extra margin can be invaluable when you're shooting under dim lighting conditions or handholding a long lens for, say, wildlife photography. Perhaps that shot of a foraging deer calls for a shutter speed of 1/1,000th second at f/5.6 with your EF 100-400mm f/4.5-5.6L IS USM lens. Relax. You can shoot at 1/250th second at f/11 and get virtually the same results, as long as the deer doesn't decide to bound off.

Or, maybe you're shooting a high school play without a tripod or monopod, and you'd really, really like to use 1/15th second at f/4. Assuming the actors aren't flitting around the stage at high speed, your 17-85mm IS lens can grab the shot for you at its wide-angle position. However, keep these facts in mind:

- **IS doesn't stop action.** Unfortunately, no IS lens is a panacea to replace the action-stopping capabilities of a higher shutter speed. Image stabilization applies only to camera shake. You still need a fast shutter speed to freeze action. IS works great in low light, when you're using long lenses, and for macro photography. It's not always the best choice for action photography (unless you're willing to let subject motion become part of your image). In other situations, you may need enough light to allow a sufficiently high shutter speed. But in that case, IS can make your shot even sharper.

- **IS slows you down.** The process of adjusting the lens elements takes time, just as autofocus does, so you might find that IS adds to the lag between when you press the shutter and when the picture is taken. That's another reason why image stabilization might not be a good choice for sports.

- **Use when appropriate.** Some IS lenses produce worse results if you use them while you're panning, although newer Canon IS lenses have a mode that works fine when the camera is deliberately moved from side to side (or up and down) during exposure. Older lenses can confuse the motion with camera shake and overcompensate. You might want to switch off IS when panning or when your camera is mounted on a tripod.

- **Do you need IS at all?** Remember that an inexpensive monopod might be able to provide the same additional steadiness as an IS lens, at a much lower cost. If you're out in the field shooting wild animals or flowers and think a tripod isn't practical, try a monopod first.

11

Working with Light

Unless you're extraordinarily lucky, or supremely observant, great lighting, like most things of artistic value, doesn't happen by accident. It's entirely possible that you'll randomly encounter a scene or subject that's bathed in marvelous lighting, illumination that perfectly sculpts an image in highlights and shadows. But how often can you count on such luck? Ansel Adams is often quoted as saying (although he probably didn't) that "The harder I work, the luckier I get."

The great photographer *was* known for his patience in seeking out the best lighting for a composition, and he *did* say, "A good photograph is knowing where to stand." My own take on excellence in illumination is that you have to possess the ability to *recognize* effective lighting when it is already present, and have the skill to manipulate the light when it is not.

Photography is a form of art. The photographer may have little or no control over the subject (other than posing human subjects) but can often adjust both viewing angle *and* the nature of the light source to create a particular compelling image. The direction and intensity of the light sources create the shapes and textures that we see. The distribution and proportions determine the contrast and tonal values: whether the image is stark or high key, or muted and low in contrast. The colors of the light (because even "white" light has a color balance that the sensor can detect), and how much of those colors the subject reflects or absorbs, paint the hues visible in the image.

As a Rebel T7i photographer, you must learn to be a painter and sculptor of light if you want to move from *taking* a picture to *making* a photograph. This chapter introduces the two main types of illumination: *continuous* lighting (such as daylight, incandescent, or fluorescent sources) and the brief, but brilliant snippets of light we call *electronic flash*.

Continuous Illumination versus Electronic Flash

Continuous lighting is exactly what you might think: uninterrupted illumination that is available all the time during a shooting session. Daylight, moonlight, and the artificial lighting encountered both indoors and outdoors count as continuous light sources (although all of them can be "interrupted" by passing clouds, solar eclipses, a blown fuse, or simply by switching off a lamp). Indoor continuous illumination includes both the lights that are there already (such as incandescent lamps or overhead fluorescent lights indoors) and fixtures you supply yourself, including photoflood lamps or reflectors used to bounce existing light onto your subject.

Electronic flash is notable because it can be much more intense than continuous lighting, lasts only a brief moment, and can be much more portable than supplementary incandescent sources. It's a light source you can carry with you and use anywhere. Indeed, your Rebel T7i has a flip-up electronic flash unit built in.

But you can also use an external flash, either mounted on the T7i's accessory shoe or used off-camera and linked with a cable or triggered wirelessly. Studio flash units are electronic flash, too, and aren't limited to "professional" shooters, as there are economical "monolight" (one-piece flash/power supply) units available in the $200 price range. You can buy a couple to store in a closet and use to set up a home studio, or use as supplementary lighting when traveling away from home.

There are advantages and disadvantages to each type of illumination. Here's a quick checklist of pros and cons:

- **Lighting preview—Pro: continuous lighting.** With continuous lighting, you always know exactly what kind of lighting effect you're going to get and, if multiple light sources are used, how they will interact with each other. Part of the charm of the Romanian doorway shown in Figure 11.1 was the way the lighting from the left side brought out the texture of the hand-carved wood.

- **Lighting preview—Con: electronic flash.** With flash, the general effect you're going to see may be a mystery until you've built some experience, and you may need to review a shot on the LCD monitor, make some adjustments, and then reshoot to get the look you want. (In this sense, a digital camera's review capabilities replace the Polaroid test shots pro photographers relied on in decades past.) An image like the one in Figure 11.1 would have been difficult to achieve with an off-camera battery-powered flash unit, because it would be tricky to preview exactly how the shadows would fall without a true continuous modeling light.

- **Exposure calculation—Pro: continuous lighting.** Your T7i has no problem calculating exposure for continuous lighting, because the illumination remains constant and can be measured through a sensor that interprets the light reaching the viewfinder. The amount of light available just before the exposure will, in almost all cases, be the same amount of light present when the shutter is released. The T7i's Spot metering mode can be used to measure and compare the proportions of light in the highlights and shadows, so you can make an adjustment (such as using more or less fill light) if necessary. You can even use a handheld light meter to measure the light yourself.

- **Exposure calculation—Con: electronic flash.** Electronic flash illumination doesn't exist until the flash fires and so can't be measured by the T7i's exposure sensor when the mirror is flipped up during the exposure. Instead, the light must be measured metering the intensity of a pre-flash triggered an instant before the main flash, as it is reflected back to the camera and through the lens. An alternative is to use a sensor built into an external flash itself and measure reflected light that has not traveled through the lens. If you have a do-it-yourself bent, there are handheld flash meters, too, including models that measure both flash and continuous light.

- **Evenness of illumination—Pro/con: continuous lighting.** Of continuous light sources, day-light, in particular, provides illumination that tends to fill an image completely, lighting up the foreground, background, and your subject almost equally. Shadows do come into play, of course, so you might need to use reflectors or fill-in light sources to even out the illumination further, but barring objects that block large sections of your image from daylight, the light is spread fairly evenly. Indoors, however, continuous lighting is commonly less evenly distributed. The average living room, for example, has hot spots and dark corners. But on the plus side, you can *see* this uneven illumination and compensate with additional lamps.

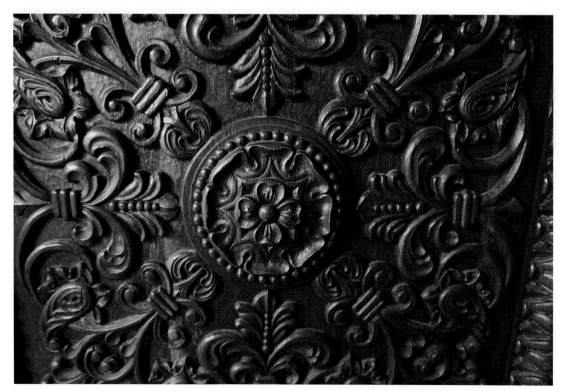

Figure 11.1 You always know how the lighting will look when using continuous illumination.

■ **Evenness of illumination—Con: electronic flash.** Electronic flash units (like continuous light sources such as lamps that don't have the advantage of being located 93 million miles from the subject) suffer from the effects of their proximity. The *inverse square law*, first applied to both gravity and light by Sir Isaac Newton, dictates that as a light source's distance increases from the subject, the amount of light reaching the subject falls off proportionately to the square of the distance. In plain English, that means that a flash or lamp that's 12 feet away from a subject provides only one-quarter as much illumination as a source that's 6 feet away (rather than half as much). (See Figure 11.2.) This translates into relatively shallow "depth-of-light."

■ **Action stopping—Pro: electronic flash.** When it comes to the ability to freeze moving objects in their tracks, the advantage goes to electronic flash. The brief duration of electronic flash serves as a very high "shutter speed" when the flash is the main or only source of illumination for the photo. Your T7i's shutter speed may be set for 1/200th second during a flash exposure, but if the flash illumination predominates, the *effective* exposure time will be the 1/1,000th to 1/50,000th second or less duration of the flash, as you can see in Figure 11.3, because the flash unit reduces the amount of light released by cutting short the duration of the flash. The only fly in the ointment is that, if the ambient light is strong enough, it may produce a secondary, "ghost" exposure, as I'll explain later in this chapter.

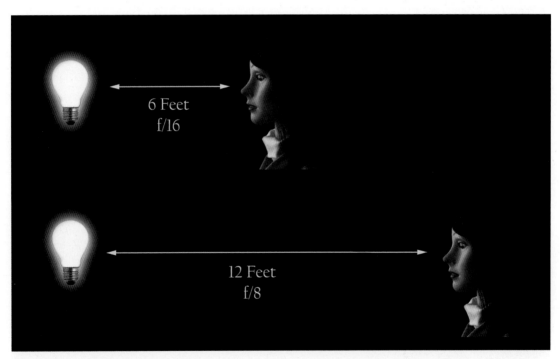

Figure 11.2 A light source that is twice as far away provides only one-quarter as much illumination.

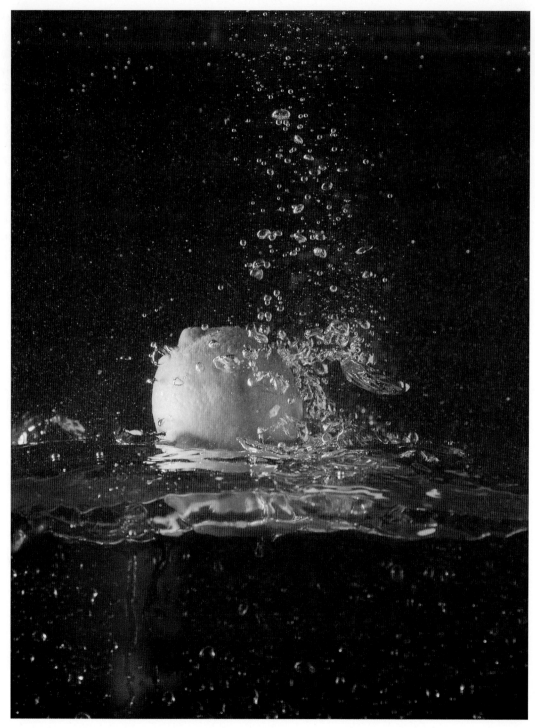

Figure 11.3 Electronic flash can freeze almost any action.

- **Action stopping—Con: continuous lighting.** Action stopping with continuous light sources is completely dependent on the shutter speed you've dialed in on the camera. And the speeds available are dependent on the amount of light available and your ISO sensitivity setting. Outdoors in daylight, there will probably be enough sunlight to let you shoot at 1/2,500th second and f/6.3 with a non-grainy sensitivity setting of ISO 400. That's a fairly useful combination of settings if you're not using a super-telephoto with a small maximum aperture. But inside, the reduced illumination quickly has you pushing your T7i to its limits. For example, if you're shooting indoor sports, there probably won't be enough available light to allow you to use a 1/2,000th second shutter speed (although I routinely shoot indoor basketball at ISO 1600 and 1/500th second at f/4). In many indoor sports situations, you may find yourself limited to 1/500th second or slower.

- **Cost—Pro: continuous lighting.** Incandescent or fluorescent lamps are generally much less expensive than electronic flash units, which can easily cost several hundred dollars. I've used everything from desktop high-intensity lamps to reflector flood lights for continuous illumination at very little cost. There are lamps made especially for photographic purposes, too, priced up to $50 or so. Maintenance is economical, too: many incandescent or fluorescents use bulbs that cost only a few dollars.

- **Cost—Con: electronic flash.** Electronic flash units aren't particularly cheap. The lowest-cost dedicated flash designed specifically for the Canon digital cameras is about $150. Such units are limited in features, however, and intended for those with entry-level cameras. Plan on spending some money to get the features that a sophisticated electronic flash offers.

- **Flexibility—Pro: electronic flash.** Electronic flash's action-freezing power allows you to work without a tripod in the studio (and elsewhere), adding flexibility and speed when choosing angles and positions. Flash units can be easily filtered, and, because the filtration is placed over the light source rather than the lens, you don't need to use high-quality filter material. Roscoe or Lee lighting gels, which may be too flimsy to use in front of the lens, can be mounted or taped in front of your flash with ease.

- **Flexibility—Con: continuous lighting.** Because incandescent and fluorescent lamps are not as bright as electronic flash, the slower shutter speeds required (see Action stopping, above) mean that you may have to use a tripod more often, especially when shooting portraits. The incandescent variety of continuous lighting gets hot enough to have some impact on your photography, especially in the studio, and the side effects range from discomfort (for your human models) to disintegration (if you happen to be shooting perishable foods like ice cream). The heat also makes it more difficult to add filtration to incandescent sources.

Continuous Lighting Basics

While continuous lighting and its effects are generally much easier to visualize and use than electronic flash, there are some factors you need to consider, particularly the color temperature of the light. (Color temperature concerns aren't exclusive to continuous light sources, of course, but the variations tend to be more extreme and less predictable than those of electronic flash.)

Living with Color Temperature

Canon and vendors with equipment compatible with the T7i have been valiant in their efforts to help us tame the color balance monster. One popular color balancing technology lives on in the form of ExpoDisc filter/caps and their ilk (www.expoimaging.com), which allow the camera's built-in custom white balance measuring feature to evaluate the illumination that passes through the disc/cap/filter/Pringle's can lid, or whatever neutral-color substitute you employ. (A white or gray card also works.)

Color temperature, in practical terms, is how "bluish" or how "reddish" the light appears to be to the digital camera's sensor. Indoor illumination is quite warm, comparatively, and appears reddish to the sensor. Daylight, in contrast, seems much bluer to the sensor. Our eyes (our brains, actually) are quite adaptable to these variations, so white objects don't appear to have an orange tinge when viewed indoors, nor do they seem excessively blue outdoors in full daylight. Yet, these color temperature variations are real and the sensor is not fooled. To capture the most accurate colors, we need to take the color temperature into account in setting the color balance (or *white balance*) of the T7i—either automatically using the camera's smarts or manually, using our own knowledge and experience.

Color temperature can be confusing, because of a seeming contradiction in how color temperatures are named: warmer (more reddish) color temperatures (measured in degrees Kelvin) are the *lower* numbers, while cooler (bluer) color temperatures are *higher* numbers. It might not make sense to say that 3,400K is warmer than 6,000K, but that's the way it is. If it helps, think of a glowing red ember contrasted with a white-hot welder's torch, rather than fire and ice.

The confusion comes from physics. Scientists calculate color temperature from the light emitted by a mythical object called a black body radiator, which absorbs all the radiant energy that strikes it, and reflects none at all. Such a black body not only *absorbs* light perfectly, but it *emits* it perfectly when heated (and since nothing in the universe is perfect, that makes it mythical).

At a particular physical temperature, this imaginary object always emits light of the same wavelength or color. That makes it possible to define color temperature in terms of actual temperature in degrees on the Kelvin scale that scientists use. Incandescent light, for example, typically has a color temperature of 3,200K to 3,400K. Daylight might range from 5,500K to 6,000K. Each type of illumination we use for photography has its own color temperature range—with some cautions. The next sections will summarize everything you need to know about the qualities of these light sources.

Daylight

Daylight is produced by the sun, and so is moonlight (which is just reflected sunlight). Daylight is present, of course, even when you can't see the sun. When sunlight is direct, it can be bright and harsh. If daylight is diffused by clouds, softened by bouncing off objects such as walls or your photo reflectors, or filtered by shade, it can be much dimmer and less contrasty.

Daylight's color temperature can vary quite widely. It is highest (most blue) at noon when the sun is directly overhead, because the light is traveling through a minimum amount of the filtering layer we call the atmosphere. The color temperature at high noon may be 6,000K. At other times of day, the sun is lower in the sky and the particles in the air provide a filtering effect that warms the illumination to about 5,500K for most of the day. Starting an hour before dusk and for an hour after sunrise, the warm appearance of the sunlight is even visible to our eyes when the color temperature may dip below 4,500K, as shown in Figure 11.4.

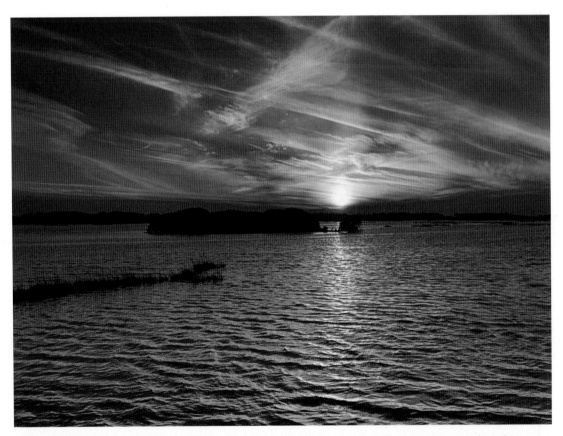

Figure 11.4 At dawn and dusk, the color temperature of daylight may dip below 4,500K, providing this reddish rendition.

Because you'll be taking so many photos in daylight, you'll want to learn how to use or compensate for the brightness and contrast of sunlight, as well as how to deal with its color temperature. I'll provide some hints later in this chapter.

Incandescent/Tungsten Light

The term incandescent or tungsten illumination is usually applied to the direct descendants of Thomas Edison's original electric lamp. Such lights consist of a glass bulb that contains a vacuum, or is filled with a halogen gas, and contains a tungsten filament that is heated by an electrical current, producing photons and heat. Tungsten-halogen lamps are a variation on the basic lightbulb, using a more rugged (and longer-lasting) filament that can be heated to a higher temperature, housed in a thicker glass or quartz envelope, and filled with iodine or bromine ("halogen") gases. The higher temperature allows tungsten-halogen (or quartz-halogen/quartz-iodine, depending on their construction) lamps to burn "hotter" and whiter. Although popular for automobile headlamps today, they are also popular for photographic illumination. Although incandescent illumination isn't a perfect black body radiator, it's close enough that the color temperature of such lamps can be precisely calculated and used for photography without concerns about color variation (at least, until the very end of the lamp's life).

Fluorescent Light/Other Light Sources

Fluorescent light has some advantages in terms of illumination, but some disadvantages from a photographic standpoint, including compact fluorescent lights (CFLs). This type of lamp generates light through an electro-chemical reaction that emits most of its energy as visible light, rather than heat, which is why the bulbs don't get as hot. The type of light produced varies depending on the phosphor coatings and type of gas in the tube. So, the illumination fluorescent bulbs produce can vary widely in its characteristics.

That's not great news for photographers. Different types of lamps have different "color temperatures" that can't be precisely measured in degrees Kelvin, because the light isn't produced by heating. Worse, fluorescent lamps have a discontinuous spectrum of light that can have some colors missing entirely, producing that substandard Color Rendering Index I mentioned. A particular type of tube can lack certain shades of red or other colors (see Figure 11.5), which is why fluorescent lamps and other alternative technologies such as sodium-vapor illumination can produce ghastly looking human skin tones. Their spectra can lack the reddish tones we associate with healthy skin and emphasize the blues and greens popular in horror movies.

Today, LED illumination is rapidly gaining favor over all other types of non-flash artificial illumination, and will continue to do so as prices drop. LED lamps often have more accurate color renditions, are easily dimmable, and can readily be powered by rechargeable batteries instead of AC.

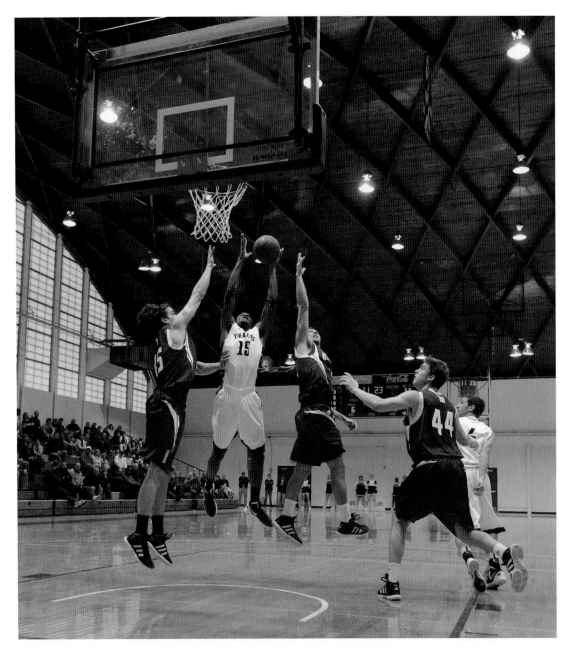

Figure 11.5 The fluorescent lighting in this gym added a distinct greenish cast to the image.

Adjusting White Balance

I showed you how to adjust white balance bracketing in Chapter 8. In most cases, however, the Rebel T7i will do a good job of calculating white balance for you, so Auto can be used as your choice most of the time. Use the preset values or set a custom white balance that matches the current shooting conditions when you need to. The only really problematic light sources are likely to be fluorescents. Vendors, such as GE and Sylvania, may provide a figure known as the *color rendering index* (or CRI), which is a measure of how accurately a particular light source represents standard colors, using a scale of 0 (some sodium-vapor lamps) to 100 (daylight and most incandescent lamps). Daylight fluorescents and deluxe cool white fluorescents might have a CRI of about 79 to 95, which is perfectly acceptable for most photographic applications. Warm white fluorescents might have a CRI of 55. White deluxe mercury vapor lights are less suitable with a CRI of 45, while low-pressure sodium lamps can vary from CRI 0 to 18.

Remember that if you shoot RAW, you can specify the white balance of your image when you import it into Photoshop, Photoshop Elements, or another image editor using your preferred RAW converter. While color-balancing filters that fit on the front of the lens exist, they are primarily useful for film cameras, because film's color balance can't be tweaked as extensively or as easily as that of a sensor.

Electronic Flash Basics

Until you delve into the situation deeply enough, it might appear that serious photographers have a love/hate relationship with electronic flash. You'll often hear that flash photography is less natural looking, and that the built-in flash in most cameras should never be used as the primary source of illumination because it provides a harsh, garish look. Indeed, most "pro" cameras like the Canon EOS 5D Mark IV don't have a built-in flash at all. Available ("continuous") lighting is praised, and built-in flash photography seems to be roundly denounced.

In truth, however, the bias is against *bad* flash photography. Indeed, flash has become the studio light source of choice for pro photographers, because it's more intense (and its intensity can be varied to order by the photographer), freezes action, frees you from using a tripod (unless you want to use one to lock down a composition), and has a snappy, consistent light quality that matches daylight. (While color balance changes as the flash duration shortens, some Canon flash units can communicate to the camera the exact white balance provided for that shot.) And even pros will cede that the built-in flash of the Rebel T7i has some important uses as an adjunct to existing light, particularly to illuminate dark shadows using a technique called *fill flash*.

But electronic flash isn't as inherently easy to use as continuous lighting. As I noted earlier, electronic flash units are more expensive, don't show you exactly what the lighting effect will be (unless you use a second source called a *modeling light* for a preview), and the exposure of electronic flash units is more difficult to calculate accurately.

Fire When Ready!

Once the capacitor is charged, the burst of light that produces the main exposure can be initiated by a signal from the T7i that commands the internal or connected flash units to fire. External strobes can be linked to the camera in several different ways:

- **Camera mounted/hardwired external dedicated flash.** Units offered by Canon or other vendors that are compatible with Canon's lighting system can be clipped onto the accessory "hot" shoe on top of the camera or linked through a wired system such as the Canon Off Shoe Camera Cord OC-E3.

- **Wireless dedicated flash.** A compatible unit can be triggered by signals produced by a pre-flash (before the main flash burst begins), which offers two-way communication between the camera and flash unit. The triggering flash can be the T7i's built-in unit, an external flash unit in Master mode, or a wireless non-flashing accessory, such as the Canon Speedlite Transmitter ST-E2 and new radio-controlled wireless trigger, the Speedlite Transmitter ST-E3-RT, which each do nothing but "talk" to the external flashes. You'll find more on this mode in Chapter 12.

- **Wired, non-intelligent mode.** If you use a third-party adapter for the hot shoe that has a PC/X connector, you can connect non-dedicated flash units, including studio strobes, through a non-intelligent camera/flash link that sends just one piece of information, one way: it tells a connected flash to fire. There is no other exchange of information between the camera and flash. The PC/X adapter connector can be used to link the T7i to studio flash units, manual flash, flash units from other vendors that can use a PC cable, or even Canon-brand Speedlites that you elect to connect to the T7i in "unintelligent" mode.

- **Infrared/radio transmitter/receivers.** Another way to link flash units to the T7i is through third-party wireless infrared or radio *transmitters*, like a Pocket Wizard, Radio Popper, or the Paul C. Buff CyberSync trigger. These are generally mounted on the accessory shoe of the camera, and emit a signal when the T7i sends a command to fire through the hot shoe. The simplest of these function as a wireless PC/X connector, with no other communication between the camera and flash (other than the instruction to fire). However, sophisticated units have their own built-in controls and can send additional commands to the receivers when connected to compatible flash units. I use one to adjust the power output of my Alien Bees studio flash from the camera, without the need to walk over to the flash itself.

■ **Simple slave connection.** In the days before intelligent wireless communication, the most common way to trigger off-camera, non-wired flash units was through a *slave* unit. These can be small external triggers connected to the remote flash (or built into the flash itself), and set off when the slave's optical sensor detects a burst initiated by the camera itself. When it "sees" the main flash (from the T7i's built-in flash, or another flash), the slave flash units are triggered quickly enough to contribute to the same exposure. The main problem with this type of connection—other than the lack of any intelligent communication between the camera and flash—is that the slave may be fooled by any pre-flashes that are emitted by the other strobes, and fire too soon. Modern slave triggers have a special "digital" mode that ignores the pre-flash and fires only from the main flash burst.

How Electronic Flash Works

The bursts of light we call electronic flash are produced by a flash of photons generated by an electrical charge that is accumulated in a component called a *capacitor* and then directed through a glass tube containing xenon gas, which absorbs the energy and emits the brief flash. For the pop-up flash built into the Rebel T7i, the full burst of light lasts about 1/1,000th of a second and provides enough illumination to shoot a subject 10 feet away at f/4 using the ISO 100 setting. In a more typical situation, you'd use ISO 200, f/5.6 to f/8, and photograph something 8 to 10 feet away. As you can see, the built-in flash is somewhat limited in range; you'll see why external flash units are often a good idea later in this chapter.

An electronic flash (whether built in or connected to the Rebel T7i through an adapter's PC terminal or a cable plugged into a hot shoe adapter) is triggered at the instant of exposure, during a period when the sensor is fully exposed by the shutter. As I mentioned earlier in this book, the T7i has a vertically traveling shutter that consists of two curtains. The first curtain opens and moves to the opposite side of the frame, at which point the shutter is completely open. The flash can be triggered at this point (so-called *1st curtain sync*), making the flash exposure. Then, after a delay that can vary from 30 seconds to 1/200th second (with the Rebel T7i; other cameras may sync at a faster or slower speed), a second curtain begins moving across the sensor plane, covering up the sensor again. If the flash is triggered just before the second curtain starts to close, then *2nd curtain sync* is used. In both cases, though, a shutter speed of 1/200th second is the maximum that can be used to take a photo.

Figure 11.6 illustrates how this works. At upper left, you can see a fanciful illustration of a generic shutter (your Rebel T7i's shutter does *not* look like this), with both curtains tightly closed. At upper right, the first curtain begins to move downward, starting to expose a narrow slit that reveals the sensor behind the shutter. At lower left, the first curtain moves downward farther until, as you can see at lower right in the figure, the sensor is fully exposed.

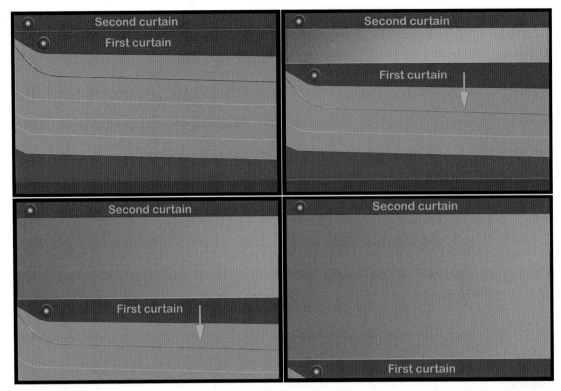

Figure 11.6 A focal plane shutter has two curtains, the upper, or first curtain, and a lower, second curtain.

Ghost Images

The difference between triggering the flash when the shutter just opens, or just when it begins to close might not seem like much. But whether you use 1st curtain sync (the default setting) or 2nd curtain sync (an optional setting) can make a significant difference to your photograph *if the ambient light in your scene also contributes to the image.* You can set either of these sync modes in the Shooting 1 menu, under Flash Control and the Built-in Flash Setting and External Flash Func. Setting options.

At faster shutter speeds, particularly 1/200th second, there isn't much time for the ambient light to register, unless it is very bright. It's likely that the electronic flash will provide almost all the illumination, so 1st curtain sync or 2nd curtain sync isn't very important. However, at slower shutter speeds, or with very bright ambient light levels, there is a significant difference, particularly if your subject is moving, or the camera isn't steady.

In any of those situations, the ambient light will register as a second image accompanying the flash exposure, and if there is movement (camera or subject), that additional image will not be in the same place as the flash exposure. It will show as a ghost image and, if the movement is significant enough, as a blurred ghost image trailing in front of or behind your subject in the direction of the movement.

As I noted, when you're using 1st curtain sync, the flash's main burst goes off the instant the shutter opens fully (a pre-flash used to measure exposure in auto flash modes fires *before* the shutter opens). This produces an image of the subject on the sensor. Then, the shutter remains open for an additional period (30 seconds to 1/200th second, as I said). If your subject is moving, say, toward the right side of the frame, the ghost image produced by the ambient light will produce a blur on the right side of the original subject image, making it look as if your sharp (flash-produced) image is chasing the ghost. For those of us who grew up with lightning-fast superheroes who always left a ghost trail *behind them*, that looks unnatural (see Figure 11.7).

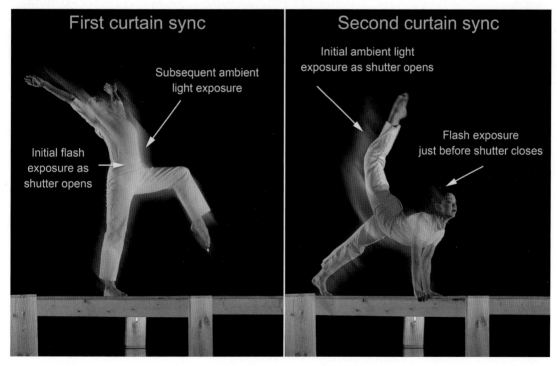

Figure 11.7 First curtain sync produces an image that trails in front of the flash exposure (left), whereas 2nd curtain sync creates a more "natural looking" trail behind the flash image (right).

So, Canon uses 2nd curtain sync to remedy the situation. In that mode, the shutter opens, as before. The shutter remains open for its designated duration, and the ghost image forms. If your subject moves from the left side of the frame to the right side, the ghost will move from left to right, too. *Then*, about 1.5 milliseconds before the second shutter curtain closes, the flash is triggered, producing a nice, sharp flash image *ahead* of the ghost image. I showed you how to switch to 2nd curtain sync in Chapter 8.

Avoiding Sync Speed Problems

Using a shutter speed faster than 1/200th second can cause problems. Triggering the electronic flash only when the shutter is completely open makes a lot of sense if you think about what's going on. To obtain shutter speeds faster than 1/200th second, the T7i exposes only part of the sensor at one time, by starting the second curtain on its journey before the first curtain has completely opened, as shown in Figure 11.8. That effectively provides a briefer exposure as a slit, narrower than the full height of the sensor, passes over the surface of the sensor. If the flash were to fire during the time when the first and second curtains partially obscured the sensor, only the slit that was actually open would be exposed.

You'd end up with only a narrow band, representing the portion of the sensor that was exposed when the picture is taken. For shutter speeds *faster* than 1/200th second, the second curtain begins moving *before* the first curtain reaches the bottom of the frame. As a result, a moving slit, the distance between the first and second curtains, exposes one portion of the sensor at a time as it moves from the top to the bottom. Figure 11.8 shows three views of our typical (but imaginary) focal plane shutter. At left is pictured the closed shutter; in the middle version, you can see the first curtain has moved down about 1/4 of the distance from the top; and in the right-hand version, the second curtain has started to "chase" the first curtain across the frame toward the bottom.

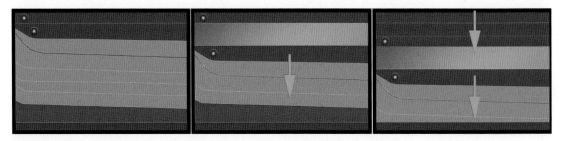

Figure 11.8 A closed shutter (left); partially open shutter as the first curtain begins to move downward (middle); only part of the sensor is exposed as the slit moves (right).

If the flash is triggered while this slit is moving, only the exposed portion of the sensor will receive any illumination. You end up with a photo like the one shown in Figure 11.9. Note that a band across the bottom of the image is black. That's a shadow of the second shutter curtain, which had started to move when the flash was triggered. Sharp-eyed readers will wonder why the black band is at the *bottom* of the frame rather than at the top, where the second curtain begins its journey. The answer is simple: your lens flips the image upside down and forms it on the sensor in a reversed position. You never notice that, because the camera is smart enough to show you the pixels that make up your photo in their proper orientation. But this image flip is why, if your sensor gets dirty and you detect a spot of dust in the upper half of a test photo, if cleaning manually, you need to look for the speck in the *bottom* half of the sensor.

I generally end up with sync speed problems only when shooting in the studio, using studio flash units rather than my T7i's built-in flash or a Canon-dedicated Speedlite. That's because if you're using either type of "smart" flash, the camera knows that a strobe is attached, and remedies any unintentional goof in shutter speed settings. If you happen to set the T7i's shutter to a faster speed in Tv or M mode, the camera will automatically adjust the shutter speed down to 1/200th second. In Av, P, or any of the automatic modes, where the T7i selects the shutter speed, it will never choose a shutter speed higher than 1/200th second when using flash. In P mode, shutter speed is automatically set between 1/60th to 1/200th second when using flash.

Figure 11.9
If a shutter speed faster than 1/200th second is used, you can end up photographing only a portion of the image.

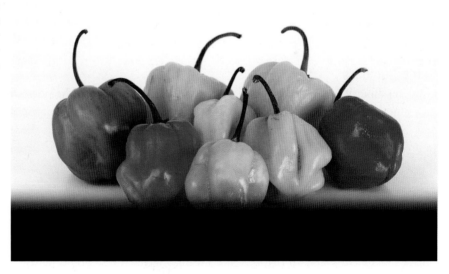

But when using a non-dedicated flash, such as a studio unit plugged into an adapter with a PC/X connector, the camera has no way of knowing that a flash is connected, so shutter speeds faster than 1/200th second can be set inadvertently. Note that the T7i can use a feature called *high-speed sync* that allows shutter speeds faster than 1/200th second with certain external dedicated Canon flash units. When using high-speed sync, the flash fires a continuous serious of bursts at reduced power for the entire duration of the exposure, so that the illumination is able to expose the sensor as the slit moves. High-speed sync is set using the controls on the attached and powered-up compatible external flash.

Determining Exposure

Calculating the proper exposure for an electronic flash photograph is a bit more complicated than determining the settings by continuous light. The right exposure isn't simply a function of how far away your subject is (which the T7i can figure out based on the autofocus distance that's locked in just prior to taking the picture). Various objects reflect more or less light at the same distance so, obviously, the camera needs to measure the amount of light reflected back and through the lens. Yet, as the flash itself isn't available for measuring until it's triggered, the T7i has nothing to measure.

The solution is to fire the flash twice. The initial shot is a pre-flash that can be analyzed, then followed by a main flash that's given exactly the calculated intensity needed to provide a correct exposure. As a result, the primary flash may be longer for distant objects and shorter for closer subjects, depending on the required intensity for exposure. This through-the-lens evaluative flash exposure system, which Canon calls E-TTL II, operates whenever the pop-up internal flash is used, or you have attached a Canon dedicated flash unit to the T7i.

Guide Numbers

Guide numbers, usually abbreviated GN, are a way of specifying the power of an electronic flash in a way that can be used to determine the correct f/stop to use at a particular shooting distance and ISO setting. In fact, before automatic flash units became prevalent, the GN was actually used to do just that. A GN is usually given as a pair of numbers for both feet and meters that represent the range at ISO 100. For example, the Rebel T7i's built-in flash has a GN of 12/39.4 (meters/feet) at ISO 100. To calculate the correct exposure at that ISO setting, you'd divide the guide number by the distance to arrive at the appropriate f/stop.

Using the T7i's built-in flash as an example, at ISO 100 with its GN of 39.4, if you wanted to shoot a subject at a distance of 10 feet, you'd use f/4 (roughly 39.4 divided by 10; rounded to f/4 for simplicity's sake). At 8 feet, an f/stop of f/5.3 (round up to f/5.6) would be used. Some quick mental calculations with the GN will give you any particular electronic flash's range. You can easily see that the built-in flash would begin to peter out at about 15 feet, where you'd need an aperture of roughly f/2.8 at ISO 100. Of course, in the real world you'd probably bump the sensitivity up to a setting of ISO 400 so you could use a more practical f/5.6 at that distance.

Today, guide numbers are most useful for comparing the power of various flash units. You don't need to be a math genius to see that an electronic flash with a GN of, say, 190 would be *a lot* more powerful than your built-in flash (at ISO 100, you could use f/13 instead of f/2.8 at 15 feet).

Getting Started with the Built-in Flash

The Canon Rebel T7i's built-in flash is a handy accessory because it is available as required, without the need to carry an external flash around with you constantly. The next sections explain how to use the built-in flash in the various Basic Zone and Creative Zone modes.

Basic Zone Flash

When the T7i is set to one of the Basic Zone modes (except for Landscape, Sports, Food, Candlelight, HDR Backlight Control, Night Scene, or Flash Off modes), the built-in flash will pop up when needed to provide extra illumination in low-light situations, or when your subject matter is backlit and could benefit from some fill flash. The flash doesn't pop up in Landscape mode because the flash doesn't have enough reach to have much effect for pictures of distant vistas in any case; nor does the flash pop up automatically in Sports mode, because you'll often want to use shutter speeds faster than 1/200th second and/or be shooting subjects that are out of flash range. Pop-up flash is disabled in Flash Off mode for obvious reasons.

If you happen to be shooting a landscape photo and do want to use flash (say, to add some illumination to a subject that's closer to the camera), or you want flash with your sports photos, or you *don't* want the flash popping up all the time when using one of the other Basic Zone modes, switch to an appropriate Creative Zone mode and use that instead.

Creative Zone Flash

When you're using a Creative Zone mode, you'll have to judge for yourself when flash might be useful, and flip it up yourself by pressing the Flash button on the side of the pentamirror housing. The behavior of the internal flash varies, depending on which Creative Zone mode you're using.

- **P.** In this mode, the T7i fully automates the exposure process, giving you subtle fill flash effects in daylight, and fully illuminating your subject under dimmer lighting conditions. The camera selects a shutter speed from 1/60th to 1/200th second and sets an appropriate aperture.

- **Av.** In Aperture-priority mode, you set the aperture as always, and the T7i chooses a shutter speed from 30 seconds to 1/200th second. Use this mode with care, because if the camera detects a dark background, it will use the flash to expose the main subject in the foreground, and then leave the shutter open long enough to allow the background to be exposed correctly, too. If you're not using an image-stabilized lens, you can end up with blurry ghost images even of non-moving subjects at exposures longer than 1/30th second, and if your camera is not mounted on a tripod, you'll see these blurs at exposures longer than about 1/8th second even if you are using IS.

To disable use of a slow shutter speed with flash, access Flash Sync Speed in Av Mode in the Flash Control screen found in the Shooting 2 menu, and change from the default setting Auto to either 1/200-1/60sec. Auto or 1/200sec. (fixed), as described in Chapter 8.

- **Tv.** When using flash in Tv mode, you set the shutter speed from 30 seconds to 1/200th second, and the T7i will choose the correct aperture for the correct flash exposure. If you accidentally set the shutter speed higher than 1/200th second, the camera will reduce it to 1/200th second when you're using the flash.

- **M/B.** In Manual or Bulb exposure modes, you select both shutter speed (30 seconds to 1/200th second) and aperture. The camera will adjust the shutter speed to 1/200th second if you try to use a faster speed with the internal flash. The E-TTL II system will provide the correct amount of exposure for your main subject at the aperture you've chosen (if the subject is within the flash's range, of course). In Bulb mode, the shutter will remain open for as long as the release button on top of the camera is held down, or the release of your remote control is activated.

Flash Range

The illumination of the Rebel T7i's built-in flash varies with distance, focal length, and ISO sensitivity setting.

- **Distance.** The farther away your subject is from the camera, the greater the light fall-off, thanks to the inverse square law discussed earlier. Keep in mind that a subject that's twice as far away receives only one-quarter as much light, which is two f/stops' worth.

- **Focal length.** The built-in flash "covers" only a limited angle of view, which doesn't change. So, when you're using a lens that is wider than the default focal length, the frame may not be covered fully, and you'll experience dark areas, especially in the corners. As you zoom in using longer focal lengths, some of the illumination is outside the area of view and is "wasted." (This phenomenon is why some external flash units, such as the 600EX II-RT II, "zoom" to match the zoom setting of your lens to concentrate the available flash burst onto the actual subject area.)

- **ISO setting.** The higher the ISO sensitivity, the more photons captured by the sensor. So, doubling the sensitivity from ISO 100 to 200 produces the same effect as, say, opening up your lens from f/8 to f/5.6, increasing your effective flash range.

Red-Eye Reduction and Autofocus Assist

When Red-Eye Reduction is turned on in the Shooting 2 menu (as described in Chapter 8), and you are using flash with any shooting mode except for Flash Off, Landscape, Sports, or Movie, the red-eye reduction lamp on the front of the camera will illuminate for about 1.5 seconds when you press down the shutter release halfway, theoretically causing your subjects' irises to contract (if they are looking toward the camera), and thereby reducing the red-eye effect in your photograph. Red-eye effects are most frequent under low light conditions, when the pupils of your subjects' eyes open to admit more light, thus providing a larger "target" for your flash's illumination to bounce back from the retinas to the sensor.

Another phenomenon you'll encounter under low light levels may be difficulty in focusing. Canon's answer to that problem is an autofocus assist beam emitted by the T7i's built-in flash, or by any external dedicated flash unit that you may have attached to the camera (and switched on). In dim lighting conditions, the built-in flash will emit a burst of reduced-intensity flashes when you press the shutter release halfway, providing additional illumination for the autofocus system. Here are some things you need to know about the AF assist beam:

- **Basic Zone activation.** When using a Basic Zone exposure mode other than Flash Off, Landscape, Sports, or Movie, if AF-assist is required, the T7i's built-in flash will pop up automatically.

- **Creative Zone activation.** If you're working with a Creative Zone exposure mode, you must pop up the built-in flash manually using the Flash button to enable AF assist.

- **Focus mode.** The AF-assist beam will fire only if you are using One-Shot AF (single autofocus) or AI Focus AF (automatic autofocus). The beam is disabled if the camera is set to AI Servo AF (continuous autofocus) mode.

- **Distance.** The beam provides autofocus assistance only for subjects closer than roughly 13 feet from the camera. The illumination is too dim at great distances to improve autofocus performance. If you need more of an assist, an external flash such as the 600EX II-RT can provide a focusing aid for subjects as far as 32.8 feet away.

- **Live View.** The AF-assist flash is disabled when using Live View's Live mode and Face Detection focusing modes, for both the built-in flash and external flash. However, if a Canon Speedlite with an LED light is used (such as the 320EX), the beam will illuminate to provide autofocus assistance. The AF-Assist beam functions normally when using Quick mode autofocus in Live View.

- **Enabling/Disabling AF-assist.** You can specify how the AF-assist beam is fired using C.Fn-5, as described below.

AF-Assist with Flash Disabled

You can still use the Autofocus Assist Beam function even when you don't want the flash to contribute to the exposure by disabling flash while enabling autofocus assist, using one of the Flash Control options in the Shooting 2 menu. Just follow these steps:

1. Press the MENU button and navigate to the Shooting 2 menu.

2. Use the directional buttons to select the Flash Control entry.

3. Select Flash Firing, press SET, and choose Disable. That option disables both the built-in flash and any external dedicated flash you may have attached. However, the AF-assist beam will still fire as described earlier.

4. Press the MENU button twice to exit. (Or just tap the shutter release button.)

Enabling/Disabling AF-Assist

Use C.Fn-5 to choose whether the AF-assist beam is emitted by the built-in flash or the external Speedlite. You can disable the feature, activate it for both built-in flash and an external Speedlite, specify only external flash assist, or use only the infrared AF-assist beam included with some Canon flash units, such as the discontinued (but still popular) 580EX II and 600EX II-RT II. That option eliminates the obtrusive visible flashes, but still allows autofocus assistance using IR signals.

Using FE Lock and Flash Exposure Compensation

If you want to lock flash exposure for a subject that is not centered in the frame, you can use the FE Lock button (*) to lock in a specific flash exposure. Just depress and hold the shutter button halfway to lock in focus, then center the viewfinder on the subject you want to correctly expose and press the * button. The FEL (flash exposure lock) message and * icon are displayed in the viewfinder. Then, recompose your photo and press the shutter down the rest of the way to take the photo.

You can also manually add or subtract exposure to the flash exposure calculated by the T7i when using a Creative Zone mode. The easiest way is to use the Quick Control menu. Press the Q button and the screen shown in Figure 11.10 appears. Navigate to the flash exposure compensation box (it's highlighted in gold in the figure), and rotate the Main Dial to set flash compensation.

You can also specify flash compensation using the menus, which can be easy when working with the touch screen, even though there are a few extra steps. Just press the Choose the Flash Control entry in the Shooting 2 menu, then the Built-in Flash Setting, and choose Flash (icon) Exp. Comp. Then use the left/right directional buttons or touch screen to enter flash exposure compensation plus or minus two f/stops. The exposure index scale on the LCD and in the viewfinder will indicate the change you've made, and a flash exposure compensation icon will appear to warn you that an

Figure 11.10
Set flash exposure
compensation in the
Quick Control
screen.

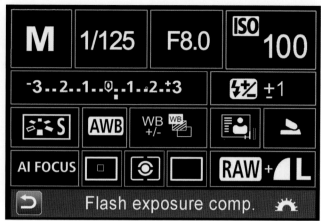

adjustment has been made. As with non-flash exposure compensation, the compensation you make remains in effect for the pictures that follow, and even when you've turned the camera off, remember to cancel the flash exposure compensation adjustment by reversing the steps used to set it when you're done using it.

A third way to access flash exposure compensation is to assign that feature to the SET button, using C.Fn-13, as described in Chapter 9. Thereafter, you can press the SET button when in Shooting mode, and rotate the Main Dial to adjust flash exposure compensation from the screen that pops up on the LCD. Flash exposure compensation can also be adjusted using the controls on your attached and active external flash unit. Those settings (any setting other than 0 dialed in with the external flash) will override any flash exposure compensation you've specified in the camera.

Tip

If you've enabled the Auto Lighting Optimizer in the Shooting 2 menu, as described in Chapter 8, it may cancel out any EV you've subtracted using flash exposure compensation. Disable the Auto Lighting Optimizer if you find your images are still too bright when using flash exposure compensation.

More on Flash Control Settings

I introduced the Shooting 2 menu's Flash Control settings in Chapter 8. This next section offers additional information for using the Flash Control menu. The menu includes six options (see Figure 11.11): Flash Firing, E-TTL II Metering, Flash Sync in AV Mode, Built-in Flash Settings, External Flash Function Settings, and External Flash C.Fn Settings.

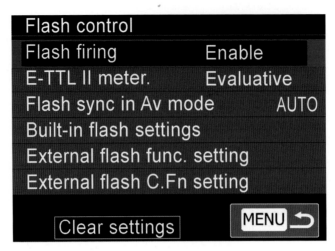

Figure 11.11
Six entries are available from the Flash Control menu.

Flash control

Flash firing	Enable
E-TTL II meter.	Evaluative
Flash sync in Av mode	AUTO
Built-in flash settings	
External flash func. setting	
External flash C.Fn setting	

Clear settings   MENU ↰

Flash Firing

This menu entry has two options: Enable and Disable. It can be used to activate or deactivate the built-in electronic flash and any attached external electronic flash unit. When disabled, the flash cannot fire even if you accidentally elevate it, or have an accessory flash attached and turned on. However, you should keep in mind that the AF-assist beam can still be used. If you want to disable that, too, you'll need to turn it off using C.Fn-5. Disabling the flash here does so for all exposure modes, and so is a better choice than using the Basic Zone Flash Off setting of the Mode Dial.

Here are some applications where I always disable my flash and AF-assist beam, even though my T7i won't pop up the flash and fire without my intervention anyway. Some situations are too important to take chances. (Who knows, maybe I've accidentally set the Mode Dial to Creative Auto?)

■ **Venues where flash is forbidden.** I've discovered that many No Photography signs actually mean "No Flash Photography," either because those who make the decisions feel that flash is distracting or they fear it may potentially damage works of art. Tourists may not understand the difference between flash and available-light photography, or may be unable to set their camera to turn off the flash. One of the first phrases I learn in any foreign language is "Is it permitted to take photos if I do not use flash?" A polite request, while brandishing an advanced camera like the T7i (which may indicate you know what you are doing), can often result in permission to shoot away.

■ **Venues where flash is ineffective anyway.** We've all seen the concert goers who stand up in the last row to shoot flash pictures from 100 yards away. I tend to not tell friends that their pictures are not going to come out, because they usually show me a dismal, grainy shot (actually exposed by the dim available light) that they find satisfactory, just to prove I was wrong.

■ **Venues where flash is annoying.** If I'm taking pictures in a situation where flash is permitted, but mostly supplies little more than visual pollution, I'll disable or avoid using it. Concerts or religious ceremonies may *allow* flash photography, but who needs to add to the blinding bursts when you have a camera that will take perfectly good pictures at ISO 3200? Of course, I invariably see one or two people flashing away at events where flash is not allowed, but that doesn't mean I am eager to join in the festivities.

E-TTL II Metering

The second choice in the Flash Control menu allows you to choose the type of exposure metering the T7i uses for electronic flash. You can select the default Evaluative metering, which selectively interprets the 63 metering zones in the viewfinder to intelligently classify the scene for exposure purposes. Alternatively, you can select Average, which melds the information from all the zones together as an average exposure. You might find the second mode useful for evenly lit scenes, but, in most cases, exposure won't be exactly right and you may need some flash exposure compensation adjustment.

Flash Sync Speed in AV mode

You can select the flash synchronization speed that will be used when working in Aperture-priority mode; choose from Auto (the T7i selects the shutter speed from 30 seconds to 1/200th second) to a range embracing only the speeds from 1/200th to 1/60th second, or fixed at 1/200th second.

Normally, in Aperture-priority mode when using flash, you specify the f/stop to be locked in. The exposure is then adjusted by varying the output of the electronic flash. Because the primary exposure comes from the flash, the main effects of the shutter speed selected is on the secondary exposure from the ambient light on the scene. Your choices include:

■ **Auto.** This is your best choice under most conditions. The T7i will analyze your scene and choose a shutter speed that balances flash exposure and available light. For example, if the camera determines that a flash exposure requires an aperture of f/5.6, and then determines that the background illumination is intense enough to produce an exposure of 1/30th second at f/5.6, it might choose that slow shutter speed to provide a balanced exposure. As you might guess, the chief problem with Auto is that the T7i can choose a shutter speed that is slow enough to cause ghost images, as discussed earlier in this chapter. Don't use Auto if the ambient light is bright and your subject is far from the camera—that combination can lead to large f/stops and slow shutter speeds. (Use a tripod in such situations.) On the other hand, if your subject is fairly close to the camera—10 feet or closer—Auto will rarely get you into trouble. (See Figure 11.12.)

- **1/200-1/60 sec auto.** If you want to ensure that a slow shutter speed won't be used, activate this option to lock out shutter speeds slower than 1/60th second.

- **1/200 sec (fixed).** This setting ensures that the T7i will always select 1/200th second. You'll end up with pitch-black backgrounds much of the time, but you won't have to worry about ghost images.

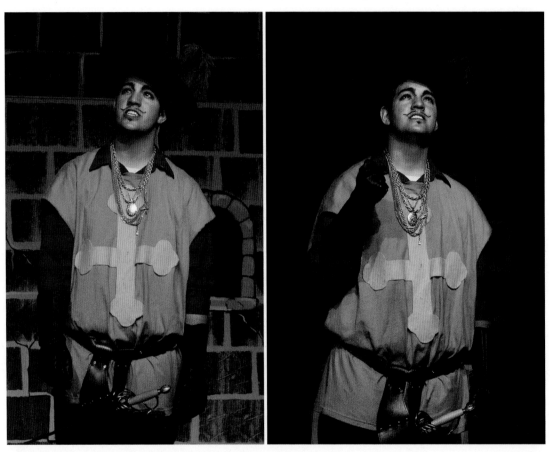

Figure 11.12 At left, a shutter speed of 1/60th second was used, allowing ambient illumination to brighten the background. At right, a 1/200th second shutter speed produced a black background.

Built-in Flash Settings

There are four main choices for this menu choice, which normally appears as shown in Figure 11.13. You cannot select Built-in Flash Settings if an external flash is attached to the accessory shoe. A message will pop up explaining that this menu option has been disabled.

However, that does not mean that you can't use an external flash; your add-on flash unit must be used off-camera and not attached to the T7i's accessory shoe. Indeed, this menu entry has additional settings that apply when using an off-camera wireless external flash, such as Channel and Firing Group (see Figure 11.14), which I'll address in the sections on external flash. Here's a quick summary of the main built-in flash selections, plus additional options that appear when you change the Built-in Flash setting to one of the two wireless flash modes. I'll explain each in more detail in the sections that follow this one, and in Chapter 12.

Figure 11.13
Four entries are available from the Built-in Flash Functions menu.

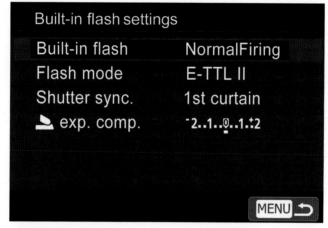

Figure 11.14
Choose Wireless Flash settings and additional options appear.

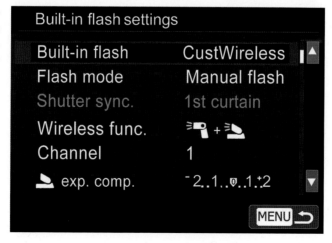

Here are your options:

- **Built-in flash.** Your choices here are Normal Firing, Easy Wireless, and Custom Wireless. The first choice is used when you're working with the built-in flash only. Easy Wireless is a long-needed basic wireless flash shooting mode that allows you to quickly set up your T7i to trigger an external flash that is not physically wired to the camera. Custom Wireless is a more fully featured (and potentially fully confusing) wireless option that requires you to make key settings yourself. I'll explain wireless flash in more detail in Chapter 12.

- **Flash mode.** This entry is available only if you've selected Custom Wireless (above), and allows you to choose automatic exposure calculation (E-TTL II).

- **Shutter sync.** Available only in Normal Firing mode, you can choose 1st curtain sync, which fires the pre-flash used to calculate the exposure before the shutter opens, followed by the main flash as soon as the shutter is completely open. This is the default mode, and you'll generally perceive the pre-flash and main flash as a single burst. Alternatively, you can select 2nd curtain sync, which fires the pre-flash as soon as the shutter opens, and then triggers the main flash in a second burst at the end of the exposure, just before the shutter starts to close. (If the shutter speed is slow enough, you may clearly see both the pre-flash and main flash as separate bursts of light.) This action allows photographing a blurred trail of light of moving objects with sharp flash exposures at the beginning and the end of the exposure. This type of flash exposure is slightly different from what some other cameras produce using 2nd curtain sync.

  If you have an external compatible Speedlite attached, you can also choose High-speed sync, which allows you to use shutter speeds faster than 1/200th second, using the External Flash Function Setting menu.

- **Flash exposure compensation.** You can use the Quick Control screen (press the Q button) and enter flash exposure compensation. If you'd rather adjust flash exposure using a menu, you can do that here. Select this option with the SET button, then dial in the amount of flash EV compensation you want using the directional buttons. The EV that was in place before you started to make your adjustment is shown as a blue indicator, so you can return to that value quickly. Press SET again to confirm your change, then press the MENU button twice to exit.

- **Wireless functions.** These choices appear when you've selected Custom Wireless, and include Mode, Channel, Firing Group, and other options used only when you're working in wireless mode to control an external flash. If you've disabled wireless functions, the other options don't appear on the menu. I'm going to leave the explanation of these options for Chapter 12, which is an entire chapter dedicated to using the Rebel T7i's wireless shooting capabilities.

Using Flash Mode

As I noted, Flash Mode is grayed out and unavailable when the T7i is set to Normal Firing or Easy Wireless. If you select Custom Wireless, you can select Flash Mode and choose one of two options: E-TTL II and Manual Flash.

E-TTL II

You'll leave Flash Mode at this setting most of the time. In this mode, the camera fires a pre-flash prior to the exposure, and measures the amount of light reflected to calculate the proper settings. As noted earlier, when you've selected the E-TTL II Flash mode, you can also choose either Evaluative or Average metering methods. If you select Manual Flash or MULTI Flash (which are only available when using an external flash), that option is removed from the Built-in Flash Setting menu.

Manual Flash

Use this setting when you want to specify exactly how much light is emitted by the flash units, and don't want the T7i's E-TTL II exposure system to calculate the f/stop for you. When you activate this option, the two flash exposure compensation entries are replaced by internal and external flash output scales (the built-in and external flash units are represented by icons). You can select from 1/4th to 1/128th power for the built-in flash, and 1/1 to 1/128th power for the external flash. A blue indicator appears under the previous setting, and a white indicator under your new setting, a reminder that you've chosen reduced power. Click on External flash func. setting, then click ETTL and select M or Multi with the directional buttons.

Here are some situations where you might want to use manual flash settings:

- **Close-ups.** You're shooting macro photos and the E-TTL II exposure is not precisely what you'd like. You can dial in exposure compensation, or set the output manually. Close-up photos are problematic, because the power of the built-in flash may be too much (choose 1/128th power to minimize the output), or the reflected light may not be interpreted accurately by the through-the-lens metering system. Manual flash gives you greater control.

- **Fill flash.** Although E-TTL II can be used in full daylight to provide fill flash to brighten shadows, using manual flash allows you to tweak the amount of light being emitted in precise steps. Perhaps you want just a little more illumination in the shadows to retain a dramatic lighting effect without the dark portions losing all detail. Again, you can try using exposure compensation to make this adjustment, but I prefer to use manual flash settings. (See Figure 11.15.)

- **Action stopping.** The lower the power of the flash, the shorter the effective exposure. Use 1/128th power in a darkened room (so that there is no ambient light to contribute to the exposure and cause a "ghost" image) and you can end up with a "shutter speed" that's the equivalent of 1/50,000th second! Of course, with such a minimal amount of flash power, you need to be very close to your subject and/or increase the ISO sensitivity setting. (See Figure 11.16.)

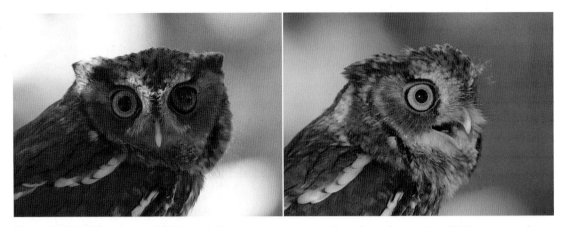

Figure 11.15 When you need fill light (left), you can use your built-in flash, fine-tuning fill illumination by adjusting the output of your camera's built-in flash manually.

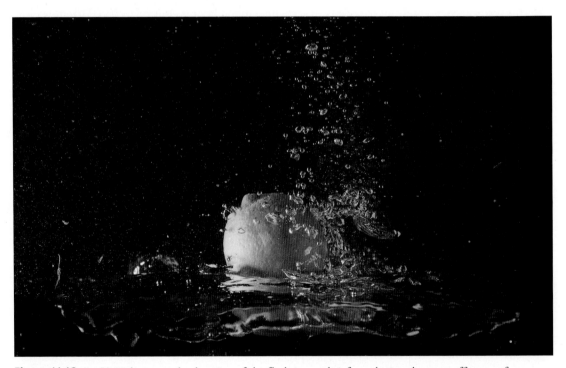

Figure 11.16 At 1/128th power, the duration of the flash is very brief, producing the same effect as a fast shutter speed.

External Flash Function Settings

You can access this menu only when you have a compatible electronic flash attached and switched on. The settings available are shown in Figure 11.17.

- **Flash mode.** This entry allows you to set the flash mode for the external flash, from E-TTL II, Manual flash, and MULTI flash.

- **Wireless functions.** These functions are available when using wireless flash, and will be explained in Chapter 12. This setting allows you to enable or disable wireless functions. You can choose Wireless: Off, Wireless: On (Optical Transmission), or Wireless: On (Radio Transmission). The last choice is shown and available only when using a radio-capable triggering device or flash, such as the 430EX III-RT or 600EX II-RT II.

- **Flash Zoom.** Some flash units can vary their coverage to better match the field of view of your lens at a particular focal length. You can allow the external flash to zoom automatically, based on information provided, or manually, using a zoom button on the flash itself. This setting is disabled when using a flash like the Canon 270EX II, which does not have zooming capability. You can select Auto, in which case the camera will tell the flash unit the focal length of the lens, or choose individual focal lengths including 24mm, 28mm, 35mm, 50mm, 70mm, 80mm, and 105mm. The 600EX II-RT offers an additional setting of 200mm.

- **Shutter synchronization.** As with the T7i's internal flash, you can choose 1st curtain sync, which fires the flash as soon as the shutter is completely open (this is the default mode). Alternatively, you can select 2nd curtain sync, which fires the flash as soon as the shutter opens, and then triggers a second flash at the end of the exposure, just before the shutter starts to close. If a compatible Canon flash, such as the Speedlite 430EX III-RT or 600EX II-RT II is attached and turned on, you can also select High-speed sync. and shoot using shutter speeds faster than 1/200th second. HSS does not work in wireless mode, as I'll explain in Chapter 12.

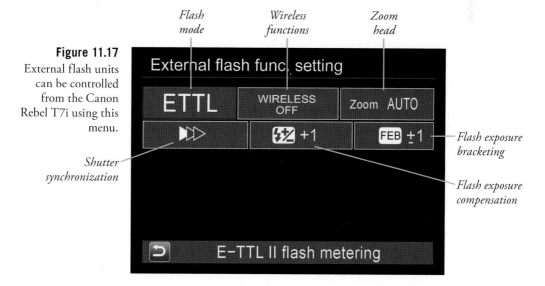

Figure 11.17
External flash units can be controlled from the Canon Rebel T7i using this menu.

Flash mode · *Wireless functions* · *Zoom head* · *Shutter synchronization* · *Flash exposure bracketing* · *Flash exposure compensation*

- **Flash exposure compensation.** You can add/subtract exposure compensation for the external flash unit, in a range of –2 to +2 EV. Dial in the amount of flash EV compensation you want using the directional buttons. The EV that was in place before you started to make your adjustment is shown as a blue indicator, so you can return to that value quickly.

- **Flash exposure bracketing.** Flash Exposure Bracketing (FEB) operates similarly to ordinary exposure bracketing, providing a series of different exposures to improve your chances of getting the exact right exposure, or to provide alternative renditions for creative purposes.

If you enable wireless flash, additional options appear in this menu. I'll cover these in more detail in Chapter 12:

- **Channel.** All flashes used wirelessly can communicate on one of four channels. This setting allows you to choose which channel is used. Channels are especially helpful when you're working around other Canon photographers; each can select a different channel so one photographer's flash units don't trigger those of another photographer.

- **Master flash.** You can enable or disable use of the external flash as the master controller for the other wireless flashes. When set to enable, the attached external flash is used as the master; when disabled, the external flash becomes a slave unit triggered by the T7i's built-in flash.

- **Flash Firing Group.** Multiple flash units can be assigned to a group. This choice allows specifying which groups are triggered, A/B, A/B plus C, or All. The 600EX II-RT offers additional groups when using radio control mode, Groups D and E.

- **A:B fire ratio.** If you select A/B or A/B plus C, this option appears, and allows you to set the proportionate outputs of Groups A and B, in ratios from 8:1 to 1:8 as explained in Chapter 12.

- **Group C exposure compensation.** If you select A/B plus C, this option appears, too, allowing you to set flash exposure compensation separately for Group C flashes.

Learning about MULTI Flash

The MULTI flash setting, available with some flash units, makes it possible to shoot cool stroboscopic effects, with the flash firing several times in quick succession. You can use the capability to produce multiple images of moving objects, to trace movement (say, your golf swing). When you've activated MULTI flash, three parameters appear on the External Flash Function Setting menu, as shown in Figure 11.18. They include:

- **Frequency/Times per second.** This figure specifies the number of bursts per second. With the built-in flash, you can choose (theoretically) 1 to 199 bursts per second. The actual number of flashes produced will be determined by your flash count (which turns off the flash after the specified number of flashes), flash output (higher output levels will deplete the available energy in your flash unit), and your shutter speed.

- **Flash count/Number of shots.** This setting determines the number of flashes in a given burst, and can be set from 1 to 50 flashes.

- **Power level.** Adjust the output of the flash for each burst, from 1/4th to 1/128th power.

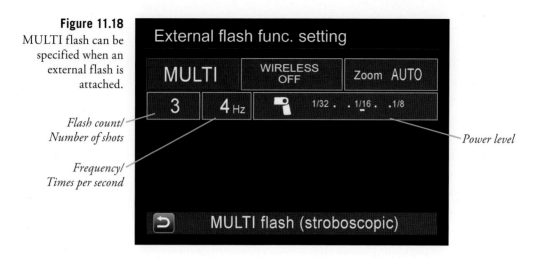

Figure 11.18
MULTI flash can be specified when an external flash is attached.

Flash count/ Number of shots

Power level

Frequency/ Times per second

These factors work together to determine the maximum number of flashes you can string together in a single shot. The exact number will vary, depending on your settings.

High-Speed Sync

High-speed sync is a special mode that allows you to synchronize an *external* flash (but not the built-in flash) at all shutter speeds, rather than just 1/200th second and slower. The entire frame is illuminated by a series of continuous bursts as the shutter opening moves across the sensor plane, so you do *not* end up with a horizontal black band, as shown earlier in Figure 11.9.

HSS is especially useful in three situations, all related to problems associated with high ambient light levels:

■ **Eliminate "ghosts" with moving images.** When shooting with flash, the primary source of illumination may be the flash itself. However, if there is enough available light, a secondary image may be recorded by that light (as described under "Ghost Images" earlier in this chapter). If your main subject is not moving, the secondary image may be acceptable or even desirable. Indeed, the T7i has a provision for slow sync in its Basic Mode Night Portrait setting that allows using a slow shutter speed to record the ambient light and help illuminate dark backgrounds. But if your subject is moving, the secondary image creates a ghost image.

High-speed sync gives you the ability to use a higher shutter speed. If ambient light produces a ghost image at 1/200th second, upping the shutter speed to 1/500th or 1/1,000th second may eliminate it.

Of course, HSS *reduces* the amount of light the flash produces. If your subject is not close to the camera, the waning illumination of the flash may force you to use a larger f/stop to capture the flash exposure. So, while shifting from 1/200th second at f/8 to 1/500th second at f/8 *will* reduce ghost images, if you switch to 1/500th second at f/5.6 (because the flash is effectively less intense), you'll end up with the same ambient light exposure. Still, it's worth a try.

■ **Improved fill flash in daylight.** The T7i can use the built-in flash or an attached unit to fill in inky shadows—both automatically and using manually specified power ratios, as described earlier in this chapter. However, both methods force you to use a 1/200th second (or slower) shutter speed. That limitation can cause three complications.

First, in very bright surroundings, such as beach or snow scenes, it may be difficult to get the correct exposure at 1/200th second. You might have to use f/16 or a smaller f/stop to expose a given image, even at ISO 100. If you want to use a larger f/stop for selective focus, then you encounter the second problem—1/200th second won't allow apertures wider than f/8 or f/5.6 under many daylight conditions at ISO 100. (See the discussion of fill flash with Aperture-priority in the next bullet.)

Finally, if you're shooting action, you'll probably want a shutter speed faster than 1/200th second, if at all possible under the current lighting. That's because, in fill flash situations, the ambient light (often daylight) provides the primary source of illumination. For many sports and fast-moving subjects, 1/500th second, or faster, is desirable. HSS allows you to increase your shutter speed and still avail yourself of fill flash. This assumes that your subject is close enough to your camera that the fill flash has some effect; forget about using fill and HSS with subjects a dozen feet away or farther. The flash won't be powerful enough to have much effect on the shadows.

■ **When using fill flash with Aperture-priority.** The difficulties of using selective focus with fill flash, mentioned earlier, become particularly acute when you switch to Av exposure mode. Selecting f/5.6, f/4, or a wider aperture when using flash is guaranteed to create problems when photographing close-up subjects, particularly at ISO settings higher than ISO 100. If you own an external flash unit, HSS may be the solution you are looking for.

ALL HSS, ALL THE TIME

If you are using a compatible flash unit, it's safe to enable high-speed sync *all the time.* That's because if you set the camera for 1/200th second or slower, the flash will fire normally at its set power output, just as if HSS were not enabled. But once you venture past 1/200th second to a faster shutter speed, the camera/flash combination is smart enough to use HSS. However, it's your responsibility to remember that you've enabled high-speed sync, and realize that as you increase the shutter speed, the effective range of the flash is reduced. At 1/1,000th second, the 600EX II-RT is "good" out to about two feet from the camera. (Remember, HSS does not work in wireless mode, so the flash must be attached to the camera's hot shoe.) At 1/4,000th second, the flash will illuminate subjects no more than about one foot from the flash/camera.

To activate HSS using the 580EX II or 600EX II-RT, just follow these steps:

1. **Attach the flash.** Mount/connect the external flash on the T7i, using the hot shoe or a cable. (HSS cannot be used in wireless mode, nor with a flash linked through an adapter that provides a PC/X terminal.)

2. **Power up.** Turn the flash and camera on.

3. **Select HSS in the camera.** Set the External Flash Function Setting in the camera to HSS as the T7i's sync mode.

   a. Choose Flash Control in the Shooting 2 menu.

   b. Select External Flash Func. Setting.

   c. Navigate to the Shutter Sync. entry, press SET, and choose High-Speed (at the far right of the list). Press SET again to confirm.

4. **Choose HSS on the flash.** Activate HSS (FP flash) on your attached external flash. With the 580EX II, press the High-speed sync button on the back of the flash unit (it's the second from the right under the LCD). (See Figure 11.19.) With the 600EX II-RT, press Function Button 4 (Sync), located at the far right of the row of four buttons just under the LCD.

5. **Confirm HSS is active.** The HSS icon will be displayed on the flash unit's LCD (at the upper-left side with the 580EX II), and at bottom left in the T7i's viewfinder. If you choose a shutter speed of 1/200th second or slower, the indicator will not appear in the viewfinder, as HSS will not be used at slower speeds.

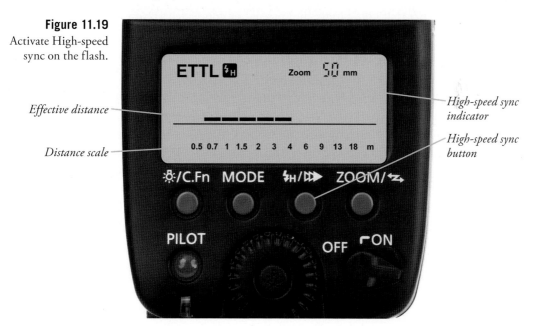

Figure 11.19
Activate High-speed sync on the flash.

Effective distance

Distance scale

High-speed sync indicator

High-speed sync button

6. **View minimum/maximum shooting distance.** Choose a distance based on the maximum shown in the line at the bottom of the flash's LCD display (from 0.5 to 18 meters).

7. **Shoot.** Take the picture. To turn off HSS, press the button on the flash again. Remember that you can't use MULTI flash or Wireless flash when working with High-speed sync.

External Flash Custom Function Settings

Some external Speedlites from Canon include their own list of Custom Functions, which can be used to specify things like flash metering mode and flash bracketing sequences, as well as more sophisticated features, such as modeling light/flash (if available), use of external power sources (if attached), and functions of any slave unit attached to the external flash. This menu entry allows you to set an external flash unit's Custom Functions from your T7i's menu. The settings available in the T7i for the Speedlite 580EX II are shown later in the section that describes that flash.

Clear External Flash Custom Function Setting

This entry allows you to zero-out any changes you've made to your external flash's Custom Functions, and return them to their factory default settings.

Using External Electronic Flash

Once the capacitor is charged, the burst of light that produces the main exposure can be initiated by a signal from the T7i that commands the internal or connected flash units to fire. External strobes can be linked to the camera in several different ways:

- **Camera-mounted/hardwired external dedicated flash.** Units offered by Canon or other vendors that are compatible with Canon's lighting system can be clipped onto the accessory "hot" shoe on top of the camera or linked through a wired system such as the Canon Off Shoe Camera Cord OC-E3.

- **Wireless dedicated flash.** A compatible unit can be triggered by signals produced by a pre-flash (before the main flash burst begins), which offers two-way communication between the camera and flash unit. The triggering flash can be an external flash unit in Master mode, or a wireless non-flashing accessory, such as the Canon Speedlite Transmitter ST-E2 and new radio-controlled wireless trigger, the Speedlite Transmitter ST-E3-RT, which each do nothing but "talk" to the external flashes.

- **Wired, non-intelligent mode.** If you connect a flash to the hot shoe adapter with a PC/X connector, you can use non-dedicated flash units, including studio strobes, through a non-intelligent camera/flash link that sends just one piece of information, one way: it tells a connected flash to fire. There is no other exchange of information between the camera and flash. The PC/X connector can be used to link the T7i to studio flash units, manual flash, flash units from other vendors that can use a PC cable, or even Canon-brand Speedlites that you elect to connect to the T7i in "unintelligent" mode.

- **Infrared/radio transmitter/receivers.** Another way to link flash units to the T7i is through third-party wireless infrared or radio *transmitters*, like a Pocket Wizard, Radio Popper, or the Paul C. Buff CyberSync trigger. These are generally mounted on the accessory shoe of the camera, and emit a signal when the T7i sends a command to fire through the hot shoe. The simplest of these function as a wireless PC/X connector, with no other communication between the camera and flash (other than the instruction to fire). However, sophisticated units have their own built-in controls and can send additional commands to the receivers when connected to compatible flash units. I use one to adjust the power output of my Alien Bees studio flash from the camera, without the need to walk over to the flash itself.

- **Simple slave connection.** In the days before intelligent wireless communication, the most common way to trigger off-camera, non-wired flash units was through a *slave* unit. These can be small external triggers connected to the remote flash (or built into the flash itself), and set off when the slave's optical sensor detects a burst initiated by the camera itself. When it "sees" the main flash (from the T7i's attached external flash, or another flash), the slave flash units are triggered quickly enough to contribute to the same exposure. The main problem with this type of connection—other than the lack of any intelligent communication between the camera and flash—is that the slave may be fooled by any pre-flashes that are emitted by the other strobes, and fire too soon. Modern slave triggers have a special "digital" mode that ignores the pre-flash and fires only from the main flash burst.

Canon offers a broad range of accessory electronic flash units for the T7i. They can be mounted to the flash accessory shoe, or used off-camera with a dedicated cord that plugs into the flash shoe to maintain full communications with the camera for all special features. (Non-dedicated flash units, such as studio flash, can be connected using the camera's PC/X terminal.) They range from the Speedlite 600EX II-RT and Speedlite 580EX II, which can correctly expose subjects up to 24 feet away at f/11 and ISO 200, to the 270EX II, which is good out to 9 feet at f/11 and ISO 200. (You'll get greater ranges at even higher ISO settings, of course.) There are also two electronic flash units specifically for specialized close-up flash photography.

I power my Speedlites with Panasonic Eneloop AA nickel metal hydride batteries. These are a special type of rechargeable battery with a feature that's ideal for electronic flash use. The Eneloop cells, unlike conventional batteries, don't self-discharge over relative short periods of time. Once charged, they can hold onto most of their juice for a year or more. That means you can stuff some of these into your Speedlite, along with a few spares in your camera bag, and not worry about whether the batteries have retained their power between uses. There's nothing worse than firing up your strobe after not using it for a month, and discovering that the batteries are dead.

Speedlite 600EX-RT/600EX II-RT

This flagship of the Canon accessory flash line, and most expensive (in the $500 price range) is the most powerful unit the company offers, with a GN of 197 and a manual/automatic zoom flash head that covers the full frame of lenses from 24mm wide angle to 200mm telephoto. (There's a flip-down, wide-angle diffuser that spreads the flash to cover a 14mm lens's field of view, too.) All angle specifications given by Canon refer to full-frame sensors, but this flash unit automatically converts its field of view coverage to accommodate the crop factor of the T7i and the other 1.6X crop Canon dSLRs. The latest 600EX II-RT version was not available while this book was being written, but Canon states it will have improved continuous flash firing rates (up to 2X faster with an optional CP-E4N battery pack).

The 600EX II-RT shares its basic features with the discontinued (but still widely used) 580EX II, described next, so I won't repeat them here, because the typical veteran Canon owner is more likely to own multiple Speedlites.

The killer feature of this unit is the new wireless two-way radio communication between the camera and this flash (or ST-E3-RT wireless controller and the flash) at distances of up to 98 feet. You can link up to 15 different flash units with radio control, using *five* groups (A, B, C, D, and E), and no line-of-sight connection is needed. (You can hide the flash under a desk or in a potted plant.) With the latest Canon cameras having a revised "intelligent" hot shoe (which includes the T7i), a second 600EX-RT/600EX II-RT can be used to trigger a *camera* that also has a 600EX-RT/600EX II-RT mounted, from a remote location. That means you can set up multiple cameras equipped with multiple flash units to all fire simultaneously! For example, if you were shooting a wedding, you could photograph the bridal couple from two different angles, with the second camera set up on a tripod, say, behind the altar. A pro shooter might find the T7i to be an excellent, affordable second (or third) camera to use in such situations.

600EX (NON-RADIO)

If you see references to a 600EX model (non-RT), you'll find that a version with the radio control crippled is sold only outside the USA in countries where obtaining permission to use the relevant radio spectrum is problematic.

The 600EX II-RT maintains backward compatibility with optical transmission used by earlier cameras. However, it's a bit pricey for the average EOS T7i owner, who is unlikely to be able to take advantage of all its features. If you're looking for a high-end flash unit and don't need radio control, I still recommend the Speedlite 580EX II (described next), which is still widely available and is the most-used high-end flash Canon has ever offered.

Remember that with the 600EX II-RT, you can't use radio control and some other features unless you own at least *two* radio-controlled Speedlites, such as a 600EX II-RT or 430EX III-RT (described later) or one 600EX II-RT plus the ST-E3-RT, which costs about $300. Radio control is possible only between a camera that has a radio-capable flash or ST-E3-RT in the hot shoe, and an additional radio-capable flash or ST-E3-RT.

The Custom Functions of the 600EX II-RT can be set using the T7i's External Flash C.Fn Setting menu. Additional Personal Functions can be specified on the flash itself. The T7i-friendly functions include:

C.Fn-00	Distance indicator display (Meters/Feet)
C.Fn-01	Auto power off (Enabled/Disabled)
C.Fn-02	Modeling flash (Enabled-DOF preview button/Enabled-test firing button/ Enabled-both buttons/Disabled)
C.Fn-03	FEB Flash exposure bracketing auto cancel (Enabled/Disabled)
C.Fn-04	FEB Flash exposure bracketing sequence (Metered > Decreased > Increased Exposure/Decreased > Metered > Increased Exposure)
C.Fn-05	Flash metering mode (E-TTL II/E-TTL/TTL/External metering: Auto/External metering: Manual)
C.Fn-06	Quickflash with continuous shot (Disabled/Enabled)
C.Fn-07	Test firing with autoflash (1/32/Full power)
C.Fn-08	AF-assist beam firing (Enabled/Disabled)
C.Fn-09	Auto zoom adjusted for image/sensor size (Enabled/Disabled)
C.Fn-10	Slave auto power off timer (60 minutes/10 minutes)
C.Fn-11	Cancellation of slave unit auto power off by master unit (within 8 hours/within 1 hour)
C.Fn-12	Flash recycling on external power (Use internal and external power/Use only external power)
C.Fn-13	Flash exposure metering setting button (Speedlite button and dial/Speedlite dial only)
C.Fn-20	Beep (Enable/Disable)
C.Fn-21	Light distribution (Standard, Guide number priority, Even coverage)

C.Fn-22	LCD panel illumination (On for 12 seconds, Disable, Always on)
C.Fn-23	Slave flash battery check (AF-assist beam/Flash lamp, Flash lamp only)

The Personal Functions available include the following. Note that you can set the LCD panel color to differentiate at a glance whether a given flash is functioning in Master or Slave mode.

P.Fn-01	LCD panel display contrast (Five levels of contrast)
P.Fn-02	LCD panel illumination color: Normal (Green, Orange)
P.Fn-03	LCD panel illumination color: Master (Green, Orange)
P.Fn-04	LCD panel illumination color: Slave (Green, Orange)
P.Fn-05	Color filter auto detection (Auto, Disable)
P.Fn-06	Wireless button toggle sequence (Normal > Radio > Optical, Normal < > Radio, Normal < > Optical)
P.Fn-07	Flash firing during linked shooting (Disabled, Enabled)

Speedlite 580EX II

If you were using Canon cameras prior to purchasing your T7i, you might already own this deposed flagship of the Canon accessory flash line. Despite the introduction of the 600EX-RT/600EX II-RT, this unit is still the most widely used Canon Speedlite, popular because of its relatively lower price and wide availability new (from some retailers) or used. The 580EX II is the second-most powerful unit the company offered, with a GN of 190, and a manual/automatic zoom flash head that covers the full frame of lenses from 24mm wide angle to 105mm telephoto, as well as 14mm optics with a flip-down diffuser.

Like the 600EX II-RT, this unit offers full-swivel, 180-degrees in either direction, and has its own built-in AF-assist beam and an exposure system that's compatible with the nine focus points of the T7i. Powered by economical AA-size batteries, the unit recycles in 0.1 to 6 seconds, and can squeeze 100 to 700 flashes from a set of alkaline batteries.

The 580EX II automatically communicates white balance information to your camera, allowing it to adjust WB to match the flash output. You can even simulate a modeling light effect: When you press the depth-of-field preview button on the T7i, the 580EX II emits a one-second burst of light that allows you to judge the flash effect. If you're using multiple flash units with Canon's wireless E-TTL system, this model can serve as a master flash that controls the slave units you've set up (more about this later) or function as a slave itself.

It's easy to access all the features of this unit, because it has a large backlit LCD panel on the back that provides information about all flash settings. There are 14 Custom Functions that can be controlled from the flash, numbered from 00 to 13.

These functions are (the first setting is the default value):

C.Fn-00   Distance indicator display (Meters/Feet)

C.Fn-01   Auto power off (Enabled/Disabled)

C.Fn-02   Modeling flash (Enabled-DOF preview button/Enabled-test firing button/ Enabled-both buttons/Disabled)

C.Fn-03   FEB Flash exposure bracketing auto cancel (Enabled/Disabled)

C.Fn-04   FEB Flash exposure bracketing sequence (Metered > Decreased > Increased Exposure/Decreased > Metered > Increased Exposure)

C.Fn-05   Flash metering mode (E-TTL II-E-TTL/TTL/External metering: Auto/External metering: Manual)

C.Fn-06   Quickflash with continuous shot (Disabled/Enabled)

C.Fn-07   Test firing with autoflash (1/32/Full power)

C.Fn-08   AF-assist beam firing (Enabled/Disabled)

C.Fn-09   Auto zoom adjusted for image/sensor size (Enabled/Disabled)

C.Fn-10   Slave auto power off timer (60 minutes/10 minutes)

C.Fn-11   Cancellation of slave unit auto power off by master unit (within 8 hours/within 1 hour)

C.Fn-12   Flash recycling on external power (Use internal and external power/Use only external power)

C.Fn-13   Flash exposure metering setting button (Speedlite button and dial/Speedlite dial only)

Speedlite 430EX III-RT

This less pricey electronic flash (available for less than $300) is an affordable replacement for the 580EX II for those who don't need the beefy power of the older Speedlite. It also makes radio control wireless triggering available to those who can't afford the 600EX II-RT's price tag. The 430EX III-RT has automatic and manual zoom coverage from 24mm to 105mm, and the same wide-angle pullout panel found on the 600EX II-RT/600EX II-RT that covers the area of a 14mm lens on a full-frame camera, and automatic conversion to the cropped frame area of the T7i and other 1.6X crop Canon dSLRs. The 430EX III-RT also communicates white balance information with the camera, and has its own AF-assist beam. Compatible with Canon's wireless E-TTL system, it makes a good slave unit, but cannot serve as a master flash. It, too, uses AA batteries, and offers recycle times of 0.1 to 3.7 seconds for 200 to 1,400 flashes, depending on subject distance.

This long-overdue replacement for the 430EX II has as its biggest selling point the ability to communicate either optically (as a slave) with any compatible master flash, or by radio transmission (as either master or slave) with other RT flashes, including the 600EX RT. Previously, you needed either two of the expensive 600EX RT/600EX II-RT units or one 600EX RT/600EX II-RT and an ST-E3-RT trigger to use radio communications.

The Canon Speedlite 430EX III-RT offers a sophisticated set of features, including an LCD panel that allows you to navigate the unit's menu and view its status. These features, along with powerful output and automatic zoom means this unit has more in common with Canon's high-end Speedlites than it does with the 320EX or the 270EX II. The Speedlite 430EX III-RT is compatible with E-TTL II and earlier flash technologies. It can serve as a slave unit in an optical wireless configuration. The Speedlite 430EX III-RT has a Guide Number of 43/141 (meters/feet) at ISO 100, at 105mm focal length.

Speedlite 320EX

This $249 flash has a GN of 105. Lightweight and more pocket-sized than the 430EX III-RT and 600EX II-RT, this bounceable (both horizontally and vertically) flash has some interesting features, including a built-in LED video light that can be used for shooting movies with the T7i, or as a modeling light or even AF-assist beam when shooting with live view. Canon says that this efficient LED light can provide up to four hours of illumination with a set of AA batteries. (See Figure 11.20.) It can be used as a wireless slave unit, and has a new flash release function that allows the shutter to be triggered remotely with a two-second delay.

Speedlite 270EX II

The Canon Speedlite 270EX II is designed to work with compatible EOS cameras utilizing E-TTL II and E-TTL automatic flash technologies. This flash unit is entirely controlled from the camera, making it as simple to use as a built-in flash. Its options can be selected and set via the camera's menu system. The 270EX II can also be used as an off-camera slave unit when controlled by a master Speedlite, transmitter unit, or a camera with an integrated Speedlite transmitter. One interesting feature of this unit is that it is also a remote control transmitter, allowing you to wirelessly release the shutter on cameras compatible with certain remote controller units. The Speedlite 270EX II has a Guide Number of 27/89 (meters/feet) at ISO 100, with the flash head pulled forward.

This $170 ultra-compact unit is Canon's entry-level Speedlite, and suitable for T7i owners who want a simple strobe for occasional use, without sacrificing the ability to operate it as a wireless slave unit. With its modest guide number, it provides a little extra pop for fill flash applications. It has vertical bounce capabilities of up to 90 degrees, and can be switched between Tele modes to Normal (28mm full-frame coverage) at a reduced guide number of 72.

Figure 11.20
The Speedlite 320EX has a built-in video lamp.

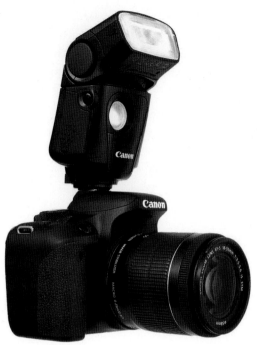

The 270EX II functions as a wireless slave unit triggered by any Canon EOS unit or flash (such as the 430EX III-RT) with a Master function. It also has the new flash release function with a two-second delay that lets you reposition the flash. There's a built-in AF-assist beam, and this 5.5-ounce, 2.6 × 2.6 × 3–inch unit is powered by just two AA-size batteries.

Close-Up Lites

Canon has offered two lites, especially suitable for close-up photography: the Macro Ring Lite MR-14EX II and Macro Twin Lite flash MD-24EX. As you might guess from their names, these lites are especially suitable for close-up, or macro photography, because they provide a relatively shadowless illumination. It's always tricky photographing small subjects up close, because there often isn't room enough between the camera lens and the subject to position lights effectively. Ring lites, like the MR-14EX II, in particular, especially those with their own modeling lamps to help you visualize the illumination you're going to get, mount around the lens at the camera position, and help solve many close-up lighting problems.

But, in recent years, the ring lite has gone far beyond the macro realm and is now probably even more popular as a light source for fashion and glamour photography. The right ring lite, properly used, can provide killer illumination for glamour shots, while eliminating the need to move and reset lights for those shots that lend themselves to ring lite illumination. As you, the photographer, move around your subject, the ring lite moves with you.

One of the key drawbacks to ring lites (whether used for macro or glamour photography) is that they are somewhat bulky and clumsy to use (they must be fastened around the camera lens itself, or the photographer must position the ring lite, and then shoot "through" the opening or ring). That means that you might not be moving around your subject as much as you thought and will, instead, mount the ring lite and camera on a tripod, studio stand, or other support.

Another drawback is the cost. The MR-14EX ring light and MR-24EX twin lite are priced in the $550 and $830 range, respectively. You have to be planning a *lot* of macro or fashion work to pay for one of those. Specialists take note. I tend to favor a third-party substitute for close-up photography, the Alien Bees ABR800 Ringflash. It's priced at about $400, and, besides, it integrates very well with my other Alien Bees studio flash units.

12

Working with Wireless Flash

As I mentioned in the last chapter, one of the chief objections to the use of electronic flash is the stark, flat look of direct/on-camera flash. But as flash wizard Joe McNally, author of *The Hotshoe Diaries*, has proven, small flash units can produce amazingly creative images when used properly.

The key to effective flash photography is to get the flash off the camera, so its illumination can be used to paint your subject in interesting and subtle ways from a variety of angles. But, sometimes, using a cable to liberate your flash from the accessory shoe isn't enough. Nor is the use of just a single electronic flash always the best solution. What we really have needed is a way to trigger one—or more—flash units wirelessly, giving us the freedom to place the electronic flash anywhere in the scene and, if our budgets and time allow, to work in this mode with multiple flashes.

Wireless Evolution

For all Canon cameras prior to the introduction of the Canon EOS 7D, wireless operation was an add-on option. The built-in flash of those earlier cameras was not capable of triggering any off-camera Canon Speedlite with full E-TTL exposure automation. (And, of course, cameras like the EOS 5D Mark III, which do not have any built-in flash at all, were in the same boat.)

Because wireless triggering was not built into the camera itself, to control other flash units it was necessary to use either a Canon Speedlite Transmitter ST-E2 (a $225 accessory that uses hard-to-find and expensive 2CR5 batteries) or mount a "master" flash on the camera. Dedicating a flash meant sinking another $300 or more into a unit like the Speedlite 430EX III-RT, or, more recently, a 600EX II-RT (at a cost north of $500) to your camera just to trigger your wireless strobes. It was especially frustrating when you did not want to use the on-camera flash to contribute to the exposure. Your "triggering" device was invariably an expensive accessory. This, of course, led to the popularity of third-party triggers, like the PocketWizard and RadioPopper product lines.

The situation has changed dramatically now that Canon models like the T7i offer built-in wireless triggering capabilities using the built-in flash. Of course, it's not possible to cover every aspect of wireless flash in one chapter. There are too many permutations involved. For example, you can use the T7i's built-in flash, an external flash, or the ST-E2 optical transmitter (or ST-E3-RT radio transmitter) as the master. You may have one external "slave" flash, or use several. It's possible to control all your wireless flash units as if they were one multi-headed flash, or you can allocate them into "groups" that can be managed individually. You may select one of several "channels" to communicate with your strobes (or any of multiple wireless IDs when using radio-controlled units like the 600EX II-RT). These are all aspects that you'll want to explore as you become used to working with the T7i's amazing wireless capabilities.

What I hope to do in this chapter is provide the introduction to the basics that you won't find in the other guidebooks, so you can learn how to operate the T7i's wireless capabilities quickly, and then embark on your own exploration of the possibilities. Canon has taken a giant step forward by introducing the Easy Wireless feature in the T7i, making this "pro" feature more accessible to owners of a mid-entry-level camera like yours.

This chapter builds on the information in Chapter 11 and shows how to take advantage of the T7i's built-in wireless controller. While it may seem complicated at first, it really isn't. Learning the T7i's controls doesn't take a lot of effort, and once you get the hang of it, you'll be able to make changes quickly.

YOUR STEPS MAY VARY

This chapter is intended to teach you the basics of wireless flash: why to use it, how the T7i or another dedicated flash can be used to trigger and control additional units, and what lighting ratios, channels, and groups are. I'm going to provide instructions on getting set up with wireless flash, but, depending on what flash unit you're working with (and how many you have), your specific steps may vary. The final authority on working with wireless flash has to be the manual furnished with your flash unit.

Elements of Wireless Flash

Here are some of the key concepts to electronic flash and wireless flash that I'll be describing in this chapter. Learn what these are, and you'll have gone a long way toward understanding how to use wireless flash. You need to understand the various combinations of flashes that can be used, how they can be controlled individually and together, and why you might want to use multiple and off-camera flash units. I'm going to address all these points in this section.

Flash Combinations

Your T7i has a built-in flash unit, which can be used alone, or in combination with other, external flash units. Here's a quick summary of the permutations available to you.

■ **Built-in flash used alone.** Your built-in flash can function as the only flash illumination used to take a picture. In that mode, the flash can provide the primary illumination source (the traditional "flash photo") with the ambient light in the scene contributing little to the overall exposure. (See Figure 12.1, left.) Or, the built-in flash can be used in conjunction with the scene's natural illumination to provide a balanced lighting effect. (See Figure 12.1, center.) In this mode, the flash doesn't overpower the ambient light, but, instead, serves to supplement it. Finally, the built-in flash can be used as a "fill" light in scenes that are illuminated predominantly by a natural main light source, such as daylight. In this mode, the flash serves to brighten dark shadows created by the primary illumination, such as the glaring daylight in Figure 12.1, right. I covered the use of the pop-up flash alone in Chapter 11.

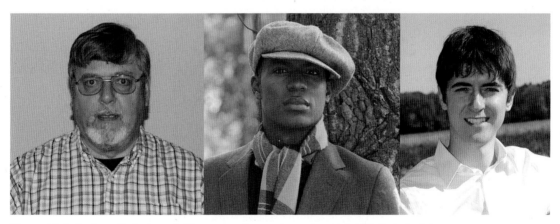

Figure 12.1 Built-in flash alone (left), as a supplement (center), and for fill flash (right).

- **Built-in flash used simultaneously with off-camera flash.** You can use the off-camera flash as a *main light* and supply *fill light* from the built-in flash to produce interesting effects and pleasing portraits.

- **Built-in flash used as a trigger only for off-camera flash.** Use the T7i's built-in wireless flash controller to command single or multiple Speedlites for studio-like lighting effects, without having the pop-up flash contribute to the exposure itself.

Controlling Flash Units

There are multiple ways of controlling flash units, both through direct or wired connections and wirelessly. Here are the primary methods used:

- **Direct connection.** The built-in flash, of course, is directly connected to the T7i, and triggered electronically when a picture is taken. External flash units can also be controlled directly, either by plugging them into the accessory shoe on top of the camera, or by linking them to a camera with a dedicated flash cord that in turn attaches to the accessory hot shoe. When used in these modes, the camera has full communication with the flash, which can receive information about zoom lens position, correct exposure required, and the signals required to fire the flash. There also exist accessory shoe adapters that provide a PC/X connection, allowing non-dedicated strobes, such as studio flash units, to be fired by the camera. These connections are "dumb" and convey no information other than the signal to fire.

- **Dedicated wireless signals.** In this mode, external flash units communicate with the camera through a pre-flash, which is used to measure exposure prior to the "real" flash burst an instant later. The pre-flash can also wirelessly send information from the camera to the flash unit, used to adjust zoom head position (if the flash has that), and required flash duration to produce the desired exposure. In the case of Canon flash units, the pre-flash information is sent and received as pulses of illumination—much like the remote control of your television. (And, also like your TV remote, the optical signal can bounce around the room somewhat, but you more or less need a line-of-sight connection for the communication to work properly.)

- **Dedicated wireless infrared signals.** Some devices, such as the Canon ST-E2 Speedlite Transmitter, can communicate with dedicated flash units through their own infrared signals. The transmitter attaches to the accessory shoe or is connected to the accessory shoe through a dedicated cable. It was an option for wireless flash for Canon cameras prior to the EOS 7D (and later models with a built-in wireless controller), as well as for Canon cameras that have no flash unit at all (such as the EOS 1D, 1Ds, and 5D series). Although the ST-E2 costs about $225, it's still less expensive than using a unit like the 600EX-RT or 600EX II-RT as a master controller, particularly when on-camera flash is not desired.

- **Canon and third-party IR and radio transmitters.** The 600EX II-RT, 430EXIII-RT and ST-E3-RT units from Canon can communicate using radio signals as well as infrared. In addition, some excellent wireless flash controllers that use IR or radio signals to operate external flash units are available from sources like PocketWizard and RadioPopper. One advantage some of these third-party units have is the ability to dial in exposure/output adjustments from the transmitter mounted on the accessory shoe of the camera.

- **Optical slave units.** A relatively low-tech/low-versatility option is to use optical slave units that trigger the off-camera flash units when they detect the firing of the main flash. Slave triggers are inexpensive, but dumb: they don't allow making any adjustments to the external flash units, and are not compatible with the T7i's E-TTL II exposure system. Moreover, you should make sure that the slave trigger responds to the *main* flash burst only, rather than a pre-flash, using a so-called *digital* mode. Otherwise, your slave units will fire before the main flash, and not contribute to the exposure.

Why Use Wireless Flash?

Canon's wireless flash system gives you a number of advantages that include the ability to use directional lighting, which can help bring out detail or emphasize certain aspects of the picture area. It also lets you operate multiple strobes; with models like the old favorite 580EX II that's as many as four flash units in each of three groups, or twelve in all (although most of us won't own 12 Canon Speedlites). With the 600EX-RT and 430EX III-RT, which also have radio control in addition to optical transmission, you can control many more flash units optically, but only 15 radio-controlled Speedlites, in five different groups.

You can set up complicated portrait or location lighting configurations. Since the two top Speedlites pump out a lot of light for a shoe-mount flash, a set of these units can give you near studio-quality lighting. Of course, the cost of these high-end Speedlites approaches or exceeds that of some studio monolights—but the Canon battery-powered units are more portable and don't require an external AC or DC power source.

Key Wireless Concepts

There are three key concepts you must understand before jumping into wireless flash photography: channels, groups, and flash ratios. Here is an explanation of each:

■ **Channel controls.** Canon's wireless flash system offers users the ability to determine on which of four possible channels the flash units can communicate. (The pilots, ham radio operators, or scanner listeners among you can think of the channels as individual communications frequencies.) When using optical transmission, the channels are numbered 1, 2, 3, and 4, and each flash must be assigned to one of them. Moreover, in general, each of the flash units you are working with should be assigned to the *same* channel, because the slave Speedlites will respond *only* to a master flash that is on the same channel.

When using the 600EX II-RT or 430EX III-RT in radio control mode, there are 15 different channels, plus an Auto setting that allows the flash to select a channel. In addition, you can assign a four-digit Wireless Radio ID that further differentiates the communications channel your flashes use.

The channel ability is important when you're working around other photographers who are also using the same system. Photojournalists, including sports photographers, encounter this situation frequently. At any event populated by a sea of "white" lenses you'll often find photographers who are using Canon flash units triggered by Canon's own optical or (now) radio control. Third-party triggers from PocketWizard or RadioPopper are also popular, but Canon's technology remains a mainstay for many shooters.

Each photographer sets flash units to a different channel so as to not accidentally trigger other users' strobes. (At big events with more than four photographers using Canon flash and optical transmission, you may need to negotiate.) I use this capability at workshops I conduct where we have two different setups. Photographers working with one setup use a different channel than those using the other setup, and can work independently even though we're at opposite ends of the same large room.

There is less chance of a channel conflict when working with radio control and all radio-compatible Canon flash units. With 15 channels to select from, and almost 10,000 wireless radio IDs to choose from, any overlap is unlikely. (It's smart not to use a radio ID like 0000, 1111, 2222, etc., to avoid increasing the chances of conflicts. I use the last four digits of my mother-in-law's Social Security Number.) Remember that you must use either all optical or all radio transmission for all your flash units; you can't mix and match.

■ **Groups.** Canon's wireless flash system lets you designate multiple flash units in separate groups. There can be as many as three groups with the T7i's built-in controller and earlier Speedlites like the 580EX II, labeled A, B, and C.

With the 600EX II-RT, 430EX III-RT and ST-E3-RT, up to five groups (A, B, C, D, and E) can be used with as many as 15 different flash units. All the flashes in all the groups use the exact same *channel* and all respond to the same master controller, but you can set the output levels of each group separately. So, Speedlites in Group A might serve as the main light, while Speedlites in Group B might be adjusted to produce less illumination and serve as a fill light. It's convenient to be able to adjust the output of all the units within a given group simultaneously. This lets you create different styles of lighting for portraits and other shots.

> **TIP**
>
> It's often smart to assign flash units that will reside to the left of the camera to the A group, and flashes that will be placed to the right of the camera to the B group. It's easier to adjust the comparative power ratios because you won't have to stop and think where your groups are located. That's because the adjustment controls in the *menus* are always arranged in the same A-B-C left-to-right alignment.
>
> For example, if your A group is used as a main light on the left, and the B group as fill on the right, you intuitively know to specify more power to the A group, and less output to the B group. Reserve the C group (if used) to some other purpose, such as background or hair lights.

■ **Flash ratios.** This ability to control the output of one flash (or set of flashes) compared to another flash or set allows you to produce lighting *ratios*. You can control the power of multiple off-camera Speedlites to adjust each unit's relative contribution to the image, for more dramatic portraits and other effects.

Which Flashes Can Be Operated Wirelessly?

A particular Speedlite can have one of two functions. It can serve as a *master* flash that's capable of triggering other compatible Canon units that are on the same channel. Or, a Speedlite can be triggered wirelessly as a *slave unit* that's activated by a *master*, with full control over exposure through the T7i's eTTL flash system. The second function is easy: all current and many recent Canon shoe-mount flash, including the 600EX-RT, 580EX II, 430EX II, 430EX III, 430EX III-RT, 320EX, and 270EX II can be triggered wirelessly. In addition, some Speedlites and the T7i's built-in flash have the ability to serve as a master flash.

I'm not going to discuss older flash units in this chapter; if you own one, particularly a non-Canon unit, it may or may not function as a slave. For example, the early Speedlite 380EX lacked the wireless capabilities added with later models, such as the 420EX, 430EX, 430EX II, 430EX III, and 430EX III-RT.

Here's a quick run-down of current flash capabilities:

- **Built-in flash.** The flash built into the Canon EOS T7i can serve as a master, triggering any of the other current flash units wirelessly. It shares that capability with the EOS 7D (which introduced wireless in-camera triggering to the Canon line), the T3i, T4i, T5i, and the Canon EOS 60D, 70D, and 80D. At this writing, all other Canon cameras with a built-in flash, introduced *prior* to the T3i, can activate external flash units wirelessly *only* when physically connected to an external flash that has master capabilities, the Canon ST-E2/ST-E3-RT transmitter, or third-party transmitters. The Canon EOS Rebel SL1/100D is a newer camera that cannot function as a master flash. T7i's built-in flash (of course) cannot itself function as a slave unit. (It has no facility for receiving signals from a master flash.)

- **Canon Speedlite 600EX-RT/600EX II-RT.** This top-of-the-line flash can function as a master flash when physically attached to any Canon EOS model, using either optical or radio transmission, and can be triggered wirelessly by another master flash, a compatible camera, another 600EX-RT/600EX II-RT or 580EX II, or the ST-E2/ST-E3-RT transmitters.

- **Canon Speedlite 580EX II.** This flash can function as a master flash when physically attached to any Canon EOS model, and can be triggered wirelessly by an optical (not radio) transmission from another master flash, a camera, another 580EX II, a 600EX-RT/600EX II-RT, 430EX III-RT, the ST-E2 transmitter, or ST-E3-RT transmitter in optical mode.

- **Canon Speedlite 430EX III.** This sibling of the radio-compatible version described next cannot function as a master, but can be used as a slave when working with optical triggering technology.

- **Canon Speedlite 430EX III-RT.** This newer flash can function as a master (in radio mode only) and as a slave when using both optical and radio technology.

- **Canon Speedlite 430EX II.** This discontinued flash cannot function as a master, but can be triggered wirelessly by a master flash (a 7D/60D/70D/T3i/T4i/T5i/T7i camera, a Speedlite 600EX-RT/580EX II, or the ST-E-2 and ST-E3-RT transmitters in optical mode).

- **Canon Speedlite 320EX.** This flash can be triggered wirelessly by a master flash (a 7D/60D/70D/T3i/T4i/T7i camera, a 600EX-RT/580EX II, or the ST-E-2 and ST-E3-RT transmitters in optical mode).

- **Canon Speedlite 270EX II.** This flash can be triggered wirelessly by a master flash (a 7D/60D/70D/T3i/T4i/T7i camera, a 600EX-RT/580EX II, or the ST-E-2 and ST-E3-RT transmitters in optical mode).

You can use any combination of compatible flash units in your wireless setup. The T7i can serve as the master, or you can use an attached 600EX-RT, 580EX II, 430EX III-RT, or ST-E2/ST-E3-RT as a master, with any number of 600EX-RT, 580EX II, 430EX III, 430EX III-RT, 430EX II, 320EX, or 270EX II units (or older compatible Speedlites not discussed in this chapter) as wireless slaves. I'll get you started assigning these flash to groups and channels later on.

Getting Started

The EOS T7i has two wireless flash modes, Easy Wireless Flash Shooting and Custom Wireless Flash Shooting. Since it's necessary to set up both the camera and the strobes for wireless operation, this guide will help you with both, starting with prepping the camera and flash. To configure your equipment for wireless flash, just follow these steps. (I'm going to condense them a bit, because many of these settings have been introduced in previous chapters.)

We're going to begin by assuming that you want to use the T7i's built-in flash as the master controller flash. If that's the case, you need to follow these steps with your external flash units first. I'm going to use the 580EX II as an example, because it's still the most widely used Canon Speedlite. You can adjust the steps for your own flash unit to suit:

1. **Set the wireless off-camera Speedlite to slave mode.** Any of the flash units listed earlier can be used as a slave flash. The first step is to set the off-camera flash to slave mode. The procedure differs for each individual flash model. Check your manual for exact instructions. I'll use the 580EX II as a typical example: Press the ZOOM button for two seconds until the display flashes, then rotate the control dial on the flash until the Slave indicator blinks on the LCD. Press the control dial's center button to confirm your choice.

2. **Assign a channel.** All units must use the same channel. The default channel is 1. If you need to change to a different communications channel, do so using the instructions for your flash unit. With the 580EX II, press the ZOOM button several times until the CH indicator flashes. Then rotate the control dial on the flash until the channel you want appears on the LCD. Press the control dial center button to confirm your choice.

3. **Assign slave to a group.** If you want to use a flash ratio to adjust the output of some slave units separately, you'll want to assign the slave flash to a group, either Group A (the default) or Group B. All units within a group fire at the same proportionate level. If you've set Group B to fire at half power, *all* the Speedlites that have been assigned to Group B will fire at half power.

   And remember that all flash units on a channel are controlled by the same master flash, regardless of the group they belong to. Set the group according to the instructions for your flash. For the 580EX II, press the ZOOM button until the A flashes on the LCD. Then rotate the control dial on the flash to choose B. Press the control dial center button to confirm your choice.

4. **Position the off-camera flash units with the Speedlite's wireless sensor facing the camera/ master flash.** Indoors, you can position the external flash up to 33 feet from the master unit; outdoors, keep the distance to 23 feet or less. Your ability to use a flash wirelessly can depend on whether the Speedlite's sensor can receive communication from the master flash. Factors can include the direction the slave flash is pointed, and whether light can bounce off walls or other surfaces to reach the sensor. When working with the 600EX-RT's radio controls, Canon guarantees "reception" up to 98 feet from the master flash/trigger, but many shooters report no problems at distances of 150 to 200 feet (and no line-of-sight required!).

Easy Wireless Flash Shooting

Wireless flash is a breeze if you're using your camera's built-in flash as the master, and one external flash as the slave. Just follow these steps:

1. **Using the built-in flash as a wireless flash controller.** Start by using a Creative Zone mode and popping up the camera's built-in flash. You can use this flash in conjunction with your remote, off-camera strobes (adding some illumination to your photos), or just to control them (with no illumination from your pop-up flash contributing to the exposure). The built-in flash needs to be in the up position to use the T7i's wireless flash controller either way.

2. **Enable internal flash.** Press the MENU button and navigate to the Shooting 2 menu. Choose the Flash Control entry, as described in Chapter 11, and press the SET button. This brings up the Flash Control menu (which is at the bottom of the menu). Press the SET button to enter the Flash Control menu. Next, select the Flash Firing setting and set the camera to Enable. This activates the built-in flash, which makes wireless flash control with the T7i possible. (See Figure 12.2.)

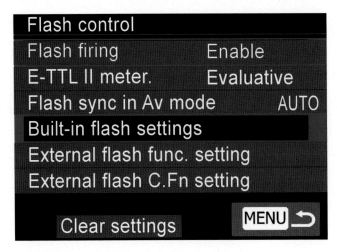

Figure 12.2
Enable the built-in flash.

3. **Confirm/Enable E-TTL II exposure.** Although you can use wireless flash techniques and manual flash exposure, you're better off learning to use wireless features with the EOS T7i set to automatic exposure. So, from the Flash Control menu, choose E-TTL II metering and select Evaluative exposure.

4. **Enable wireless functions.** Next, choose Built-in Flash Settings and select EasyWireless from the Built-in Flash entry. Press MENU to exit.

5. **Choose a channel.** Scroll down to Channel, press SET, and select the channel you want to use (generally that will be Channel 1). Press MENU to exit. The flash will emit a blinking red signal when it is set and waiting for the camera to trigger it.

6. **Take photos.** You're all set! You can now take photos wirelessly.

7. **Exit wireless mode.** When you're finished using wireless flash, navigate to the Built-in Flash setting in the Flash Control menu and select NormalFiring. Wireless flash is deactivated.

If you want to use more than one slave unit, follow these instructions. All additional units using the same communications channel will fire at once, regardless of the slave ID (Group) assignment.

Custom Wireless Flash Shooting

The procedures for using this mode are basically the same as for Easy Wireless Flash shooting, except that you have more options for adjusting things like flash ratios. Just follow these steps:

1. **Using the built-in flash as a wireless flash controller.** Start by using a Creative Zone mode and popping up the camera's built-in flash. You can use this flash in conjunction with your remote, off-camera strobes (adding some illumination to your photos), or just to control them (with no illumination from your pop-up flash contributing to the exposure). The built-in flash needs to be in the up position to use the T7i's wireless flash controller either way.

2. **Enable internal flash.** Press the MENU button and navigate to the Shooting 2 menu. Choose the Flash Control entry, as described in Chapter 11, and press the SET button. This brings up the Flash Control menu (which is at the bottom of the menu). Press the SET button to enter the Flash Control menu. Next, select the Flash Firing setting and set the camera to Enable. This activates the built-in flash, which makes wireless flash control with the T7i possible.

3. **Confirm/Enable E-TTL II exposure.** As with EasyWireless, while you can use wireless flash techniques and manual flash exposure, you're better off learning to use wireless features with the EOS T7i set to automatic exposure. So, from the Flash Control menu, choose E-TTL II metering and select Evaluative exposure.

4. **Enable wireless functions.** Next, choose Built-in Flash Settings and select CustWireless from the Built-in Flash entry. Press SET to confirm and return to the Built-in Flash Settings menu.

5. **Access wireless configuration.** In the Built-in Flash Setting menu, scroll down to Wireless Func. (see Figure 12.3) and press SET.

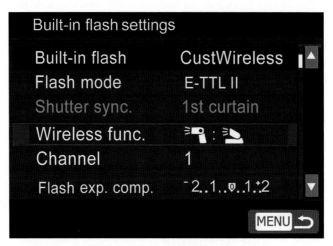

Figure 12.3
Access the wireless configuration screen.

6. **Select wireless configuration.** Choose the External Flash: Built-in Flash icon at the top of the list of choices (see Figure 12.4). Press SET to confirm. The colon between the two flash icons indicates that in this mode you can set a flash *ratio* between the units.

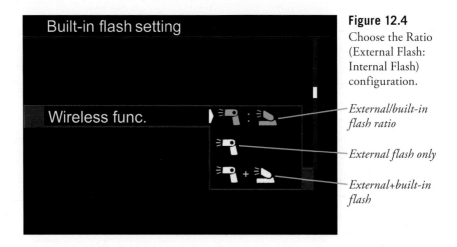

Figure 12.4
Choose the Ratio (External Flash: Internal Flash) configuration.

External/built-in flash ratio

External flash only

External+built-in flash

7. **Choose a channel.** Scroll down to Channel, press SET, and select the channel you want to use (generally that will be Channel 1).

8. **Set flash ratio.** Scroll down to the Ratio Setting entry (it's directly under the Flash Exp. Comp entry) and set a flash ratio between 1:1 (equal output) and 8:1 (external flash 8X the output of the internal flash, or, three stops). Ratios where the internal flash is *more* powerful than the external flash (i.e., 1:2, 1:4, etc.) are not possible.

9. **Take photos.** You're all set! You can now take photos wirelessly.

10. **Exit wireless mode.** When you're finished using wireless flash, navigate to the Built-in Flash Settings in the Flash Control menu and select NormalFiring. Wireless flash is deactivated.

Once you've completed the steps above, your T7i is set up to begin using wireless flash using your camera's built-in flash and one external off-camera flash. Additional options are available for the brave. I'll show you each of these one at a time.

WIRELESS SETTING FOR EXTERNAL FLASH

As noted, you must switch your external flash from normal to wireless modes. The procedure will vary, depending on your flash unit. With the 580EX II, press and hold the ZOOM button for two seconds or longer until the display blinks. Then rotate the flash's control dial until either Master or Slave appears on the flash's LCD. Press the dial's center button to confirm your choice of Master or Slave wireless operation.

REMINDER

Keep in mind that when the Canon Speedlite 580EX II and most other Canon units are ready to fire as a slave, the AF-assist beam will blink at one-second intervals. The unit will *not* go into a sleep mode while it is waiting to be used as a slave, but the camera will shut off at the interval you've specified in the menus.

Setting Up an External Master Flash or Controller

The first step in using an external flash or controller as the master (instead of the built-in flash) is to set up one unit (either a flash or controller) as the external *master*. You can mount a Speedlite 580EX, 580EX II, 430EX III-RT (as a radio control master only), or 600EX-RT/600EX II-RT to your camera, which can serve as the master unit, transmitting E-TTL II optical signals to one or more off-camera Speedlite *slave* units. The master unit can have its flash output set to "off" so that it controls the remote units without contributing any flash output of its own to the exposure. (You will see the pre-flash burst that controls the slave unit, however.) This is useful for images where you don't want noticeable flash illumination coming in from the camera position. The next sections explain your options for setting up a master unit for fully automatic, E-TTL II exposure.

Using a Speedlite or Transmitter as the Master in Optical Mode

Here are the steps to follow to set up and use a compatible Speedlite or transmitter as a camera-mounted master unit in optical triggering mode for automatic exposure.

600EX-RT

1. Press the Wireless button repeatedly until the LCD panel indicates you are in optical wireless master mode.
2. Press MODE to cycle through the ETTL, M, and Multi modes.
3. Use the menu system to control and make changes to RATIO, output, and other options on the master and slave units.

580EX II

1. Press and hold the ZOOM button to bring up the wireless options. Use the Select dial to cycle through the OFF, MASTER on, and SLAVE on options. Select and confirm MASTER on.
2. Press MODE to cycle through the ETTL, M, and Multi modes.
3. Press the ZOOM button repeatedly to cycle through the following options: Flash zoom, RATIO, CH., flash emitter ON/OFF. Use the Select dial and Select/SET button to make any changes to these options.
4. Use the Select/SET button to select and confirm the output power settings when using Manual and Multi modes, or to use FEC or FEB when in ETTL mode.

580EX

1. Slide the OFF/MASTER/SLAVE wireless switch near the base of the unit to MASTER.

2. Press MODE to cycle through the ETTL, M, and Multi modes.

3. Press the ZOOM button repeatedly to cycle through the following options: Flash zoom, RATIO, CH., flash emitter ON/OFF. Use the Select dial and Select/SET button to make any changes to these options.

4. Use the Select/SET button to select and confirm the output power settings when using Manual and Multi modes, or to use FEC or FEB when in ETTL mode.

Using the ST-E2 Transmitter as Master

Canon's Speedlite Transmitter (ST-E2) is mounted on the camera's hot shoe and provides a way to control one or more Speedlites and/or units assigned to Groups A and B. The ST-E2 does not provide any flash output of its own and will not trigger units assigned to Group C. It has the following features and controls:

■ **Transmitter.** Located on the top front of the unit, the transmitter emits E-TTL II pulses through an infrared filter.

■ **AF-assist beam emitter.** Just below the transmitter, the AF-assist beam emitter works similarly to the Speedlite 430EX II and higher models.

■ **Battery compartment.** The ST-E2 uses a 6.0V 2CR5 lithium battery. The battery compartment is accessed from the top of the unit.

■ **Lock slider and mounting foot.** The lock slider is located on the right side of the unit when facing the front. Sliding it to the left lowers the lock pin in the mounting foot (located on the bottom of the unit) to secure it to the camera's hot shoe.

■ **Back panel.** The rear of the unit features several indicators and controls:

• **Ratio indicator.** A series of red LED lights indicating the current A:B ratio setting.

• **Flash ratio control lamp.** A red LED that lights up when flash ratio is in use.

• **Flash ratio setting button.** Next to the flash ratio control lamp. Press this button to activate flash ratio control.

• **Flash ratio adjustment buttons.** Two buttons with raised arrows (same color as buttons) pointing left and right. Use these to change the A:B ratio setting.

• **Channel indicator.** The channel number in use (1–4) glows red.

• **Channel selector button.** Next to the channel indicator. Press this button to select the communication channel.

- **High-speed sync (FP flash) indicator.** A red LED that glows when high-speed sync is in use.
- **High-speed sync button.** Press this button to activate/deactivate high-speed sync.
- **ETTL indicator.** A red LED that glows when E-TTL II is in use.
- **Off/On/HOLD switch.** Slide this switch to turn the unit off, on, or on with adjustments disabled (HOLD). The ST-E2 will power off after approximately 90 seconds of idle time. It will turn back on when the shutter button or test transmission button is pressed.
- **Pilot lamp/Test transmission button.** This lamp works similarly to the Speedlite pilot lamp/test buttons. The lamp glows red when ready to transmit. Press the lamp button to send a test transmission to the slave units.
- **Flash confirmation lamp.** This lamp glows green for about three seconds when the ST-E2 detects a good flash exposure.

Here are the steps to follow to set up and use the ST-E2 transmitter as a camera-mounted master unit:

1. Mount the ST-E2 unit on your T7i.
2. Make sure both the ST-E2 unit and your camera are powered on.
3. Make sure the slave units are set to E-TTL II, assigned to the appropriate group(s), and that all units are operating on the same channel.
4. If you'd like to set a flash ratio between Groups A and B, press the flash ratio setting button and flash ratio adjustment buttons to select the desired ratio. Press the high-speed sync button to use high-speed sync (often helpful with outdoor shooting).

Using the Speedlite 600EX-RT/600EX II-RT as Radio Master

The Speedlite 600EX-RT/600EX II-RT can serve as the master unit when mounted to your camera, transmitting radio signals to one or more off-camera Speedlite 600EX-RT-series slave units. The master unit can have its flash output set to "off" so that it controls the remote units without contributing any flash output of its own to the exposure. This is useful for images where you don't want noticeable flash illumination coming in from the camera position.

Here are the steps to follow to set up and use a Speedlite 600EX-RT-series flash as a camera-mounted master unit for radio wireless E-TTL II operation.

1. Mount the Speedlite 600EX-RT-series flash to your T7i.
2. Make sure the master unit, slave units, and the camera are powered on.
3. Set the camera-mounted flash to radio wireless MASTER mode. Press the Wireless button until the LCD panel indicates you are on radio wireless master mode.

4. Set the slave 600EX-RT/600EX II-RT or 430EX III-RT units to radio wireless SLAVE mode. For each 600EX-RT unit, press the Wireless button until the LCD panel indicates you are on radio wireless slave mode. For each 430EX III-RT slaves, press the left directional key and rotate the Select dial until Slave appears on the LCD. Then press the Select button to confirm.

5. Confirm that all units are set to E-TTL II, assigned to the appropriate group(s), and that all units are operating on the same channel and ID number. The LINK lamps on all units should glow green.

Using the Speedlite 430EX III-RT as Radio Master

The Speedlite 430EX III-RT can serve as a radio master unit to trigger another 430EX III-RT or a 600EX-RT flash. Just follow these steps:

1. Press the left directional key on the Select dial. It's marked with a lightning bolt symbol.

2. Rotate the Select dial until MASTER appears on the LCD.

3. Press the Select button in the center of the Select dial.

4. Set any 600EX-RT-series or 430EX III-RT units that you will be using as slaves to the Slave mode.

   • For the 600EX-RT/600EX II-RT, press the Wireless button until the LCD panel indicates you are in radio wireless slave mode.

   • For any 430EX III-RT slaves, press the left directional key and rotate the Select dial until Slave appears on the LCD. Then press the Select button to confirm.

5. Repeat Step 4 for any additional Slave units.

6. When master and slaves are communicating, the LINK lamps on all units will glow green.

Using the ST-E3-RT as Radio Master

The ST-E3-RT transmitter can be mounted to the camera's hot shoe and used as a master controller to one or more slave Speedlite 600EX-RT units. The ST-E3-RT and the 600EX-RT share essentially the same radio control capabilities except that the ST-E3-RT does not produce flash, provide AF-assist, or otherwise emit light and is therefore incapable of optical wireless transmission.

The layout of the ST-E3-RT's control panel is virtually identical to the 600EX-RT. So is the menu system and operation, except that, as stated earlier, it will only operate as a radio wireless transmitter.

Here are the steps to follow to set up and use the ST-E3-RT transmitter as a camera-mounted master unit for radio wireless E-TTL II operation:

1. Mount the ST-E3-RT unit on your T7i.

2. Make sure both the ST-E3-RT unit and your camera are powered on.

3. Set the slave 600EX-RT/600EX-RT II or 430EX III-RT units to radio wireless SLAVE mode. For each 600EX-RT unit, press the Wireless button until the LCD panel indicates you are on radio wireless slave mode. For each 430EX III-RT slave, press the left directional key and rotate the Select dial until Slave appears on the LCD. Then press the Select button to confirm.

4. Confirm that all units are set to E-TTL II, assigned to the appropriate group(s), and that all units are operating on the same channel and ID number. The LINK lamps on all units should glow green.

The ST-E3-RT controls slave units as described earlier in the section, "Speedlite 600EX-RT as Radio Wireless Master Using E-TTL II."

Setting Up a Slave Flash

The whole point of working wirelessly is to have a master flash/controller trigger and adjust one or more slave flash units. So, once you've defined your master flash, the next step is to switch your remaining Speedlites into slave mode. That's done differently with each particular Canon Speedlite.

- **Speedlite 600EX-RT/600EX II-RT.** Press the Wireless button repeatedly until the LCD panel indicates that the unit is in optical wireless slave mode or radio wireless slave mode. In this mode, the 600EX-RT is assigned a flash mode by the master transmitter, either a flash or ST-E2 or ST-E3-RT.

- **Speedlite 580EX II.** Press and hold the ZOOM button until the wireless setting options appear. Use the Select dial and Select/SET button to select and confirm that wireless is on and in slave mode.

- **Speedlite 430EX III/430EX III-RT.** For each 430EX III-RT slave, press the left directional key and rotate the Select dial until Slave appears on the LCD. Then press the Select button to confirm.

- **Speedlite 430EX II.** Press and hold the ZOOM button for two seconds or more until the wireless setting options appear. Use the Select dial and Select/SET button to select and confirm that wireless is on and in slave mode.

- **Speedlite 320EX.** This flash has an On/Off/Slave switch at the lower left of the back panel. In Slave mode, you can use the flash's C.Fn-10 setting to tell the unit to power down after either 10 or 60 minutes of idle time. That can help preserve the 320EX's batteries. The unit's C.Fn-11 setting can be set to allow the master transmitter to "wake" a sleeping 320EX after your choice of within 1 hour or within 8 hours. Note that the C.Fn settings of the 320EX and 270EX II (described next) can be set only while the Speedlites are connected to the camera with the hot shoe.

- **Speedlite 270EX II.** This flash has an Off/Slave/On switch. If left on and idle, the 270EX II will power itself off after approximately 90 seconds. C.Fn-1 can be used to disable auto power off. As with the 320EX, in Slave mode, you can use the flash's C.Fn-10 setting to tell the unit to power down after either 10 or 60 minutes of idle time. The unit's C.Fn-11 setting can be set to allow the master transmitter to "wake" a sleeping unit after your choice of within 1 hour or within 8 hours.

More Wireless Options and Capabilities

If you're ready to immerse yourself even more deeply in wireless flash photography, the next sections will provide a little more detail on using some of the settings for ratios, channels, and groups.

Internal/External Flash Ratio Setting

Your built-in flash and your wireless flash units have their own individual *oomph*—how much illumination they put out. This option lets you choose the relationship between these units, a *power ratio* between your built-in flash and your wireless flash units—the relative strength of each. That ability can be especially useful if you want to use the built-in flash for just a little fill light (it's not very powerful, anyway), while letting your off-camera units do the heavy work. This setting is the top choice in the Wireless Function menu, designated with icons that show an external flash and a raised camera flash.

Having the ability to vary the power of each flash unit or group of flash units wirelessly gives you greater flexibility and control. Varying the light output of each flash unit makes it possible to create specific types of lighting (such as traditional portrait lighting, which frequently calls for a 3:1 lighting ratio between main light and fill light) or to use illumination to highlight one part of the photo while reducing contrast in another.

Lighting ratios determine the contrast between the main light (sometimes called a "key" light) and fill light. For portraiture, the main light is typically placed at a 45-degree angle to the subject (although there are some variations), with the fill-in light on the opposite side or closer to the camera position. Choosing the right lighting ratio can do a lot to create a particular look or mood. For instance, a 1:1 ratio produces what's known as "flat" lighting. While this is good for copying or documentation, it's not usually as interesting for portraiture. Instead, making the main light more powerful than the fill light creates interesting shadows for more dramatic images. (See Figure 12.5.)

By selecting the power ratio between the flash units, you can change the relative illumination between them. Figure 12.6 shows a series of four images with a single main flash located at a 45-degree angle off to the right and slightly behind the model. The built-in flash at the camera provided illumination to fill in the shadows on the side of the face closest to the camera. The ratio between the external and internal flash were varied using 2:1 (upper-left), 3:1 (upper-right), 4:1 (lower-left), and 5:1 (lower-right) ratios.

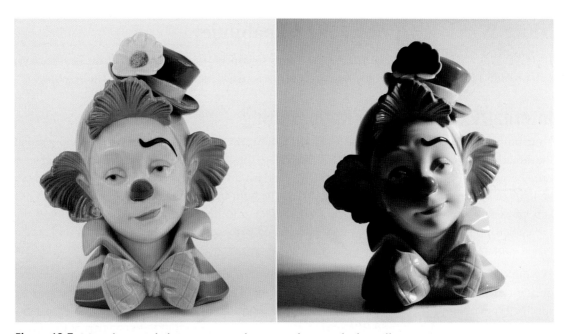

Figure 12.5 More dramatic lighting ratios produce more dramatic-looking illumination.

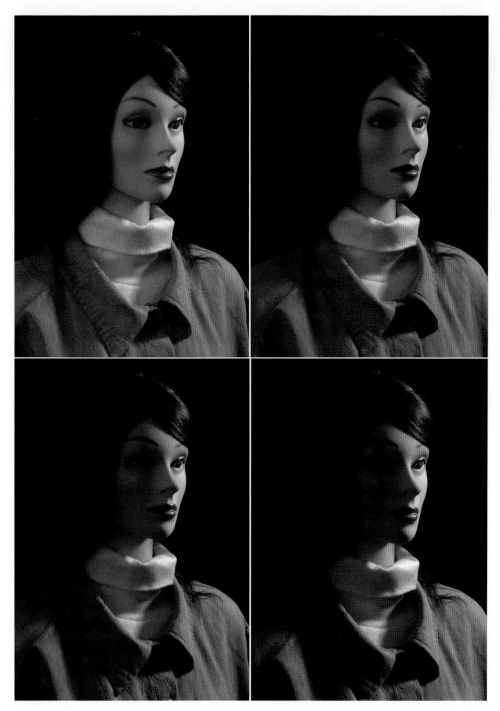

Figure 12.6 The main light (to the right and behind the model) and fill light (at the camera position) were varied using 2:1 and 3:1 (top row, left to right) as well as 4:1 and 5:1 (bottom row, left to right) ratios.

Here's how to set the lighting ratio between the internal flash and one external wireless flash unit:

1. **Enable wireless functions.** Choose Built-in Flash Settings and select CustWireless from the Built-in Flash entry. Press SET.

2. **Choose Ratio Setting in Wireless Func. menu.** In the Built-in Flash Setting menu, highlight Wireless Func., press SET, and choose Ratio Setting (it's the top entry, as shown earlier in Figure 12.4). Press SET again to confirm and return to the previous menu.

3. **Access the Power Ratio entry.** Now you can set the power ratio by scrolling down just below Flash Exp. Comp., represented by a pair of icons corresponding to an external and internal flash unit.

4. **Set the control.** Press the SET button.

5. **Choose the desired ratio.** Then use the directional keys to choose the setting you want. (See Figure 12.7.) Your choices range from 1:1 (the off-camera and built-in flash have equal output) to 8:1 (the off-camera flash supplies 8X output compared to the internal flash). Set the ratio to 4:1, for example, and the external flash will produce four times as much light as the on-camera flash, which is then used as fill illumination. For most subjects, ratios of 2:1 to 5:1 will produce the best results, as shown earlier in Figure 12.6.

6. **Confirm.** Press SET to confirm your ratio.

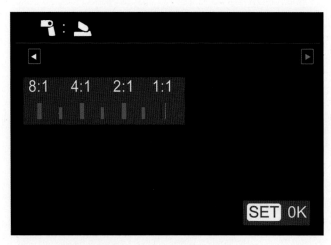

Figure 12.7
Select a ratio from 8:1 to 1:1.

Wireless Flash Only

This setting, represented earlier in Figure 12.4 by an icon of a flash unit alone, allows you to turn off the flash output of your T7i's built-in flash, while allowing it to emit a wireless controller flash that signals the external flash units you're working with. You'll still see a burst from your camera's built-in flash, but that burst will not contribute to the exposure. It will only be used to tell the remote/slave flash units to fire.

This is the setting to choose if you only want to use the flash controller to operate your remote flashes. It's probably the most commonly used choice when you don't want to use the internal flash for fill light, since firing the built-in flash increases the risk of red-eye effects.

Photographers prefer this mode in part because Canon's portable shoe mount flash units are much more powerful than a camera's built-in flash. They want to avoid using a light source that is directly above the lens and close to the lens, since red-eye is caused by light from the flash unit reflecting off the subject's retinas and bouncing back into the lens.

Using off-camera flash lets the photographer precisely control light direction and effect. It also makes it possible for the photographer to move around within the constraints of the flash units' ability to illuminate a scene, without worrying about getting too far from the subject for the flash unit(s) to be effective. Only the camera-to-subject position changes and not the light-to-subject position and ratio. Once you've set up the flash units relative to your subject, you can move around freely.

Being able to control lighting direction is a very useful capability since it can lead to more dramatic images. In Figure 12.8, a single flash unit was used to light the model. A grid (a small light "concentrator") was placed on the flash head to restrict the light from the unit. In this case, the lighting effect is dramatic.

Here are the steps to follow when using wireless flash only (whether you're working with a single external flash, or multiple units).

1. **Choose wireless flash only.** Navigate to the Wireless Func. menu as you did earlier, but choose Wireless Flash Only (the single-flash icon in the middle of the list).

2. **Confirm.** Press the SET button to confirm the Wireless Flash Only setting.

3. **Set the Power Ratio (optional).** If you are using more than one external flash, and have assigned flash units to different groups, you can then set the power ratios between groups. (I'll explain groups later in this chapter.) If you are using only one flash, or all the flash units are assigned to the same group, you don't need to do this; setting a power ratio won't make any difference. The Firing Group entry will read "All" and the fire ratio entry will not be visible. You can only select a power ratio if you've chosen A:B in the Firing Group entry. (Remember to change the power ratio back to normal when you are finished with a session; Canon's Speedlites retain the settings you make, even after a quick battery change.)

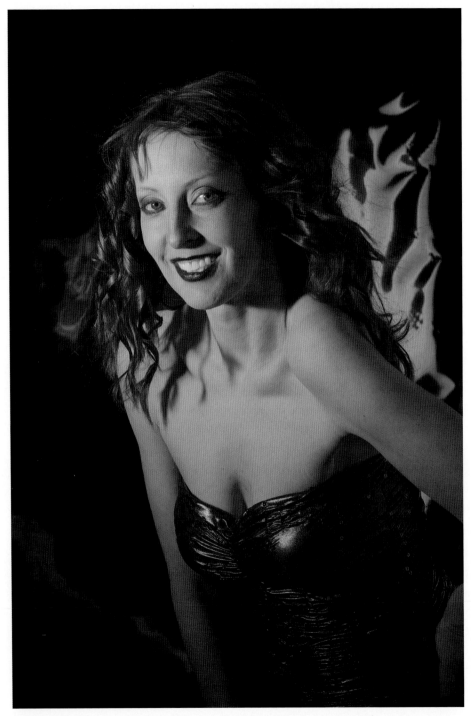

Figure 12.8 The subject was lit by a Canon 600EX-RT flash unit. The flash unit was placed on a light stand positioned to the left of the model and angled slightly downward.

Using Wireless and Built-in Flash

This option in the Wireless Func. screen, represented by an icon of an external unit *plus* an icon of a raised camera flash, adds the built-in flash to whatever wireless groups you're using. You can then use the built-in flash in conjunction with whatever firing groups you've set up. In this case you're still using the external flash units as the main sources of light, but the built-in flash can either serve to provide some extra fill (such as to illuminate the face under the brim of a hat) or to provide a second light when you only have one off-camera flash available.

It is also possible to set up a two-light portrait using an off-camera flash as a main light (about 45 degrees to the model) and the built-in flash as the fill light, as discussed earlier. Use the External/Internal Flash Ratio Setting to adjust their relative contribution to the image.

Some photographers do like to position their fill light directly above the camera and straight toward the model. The lighting ratio for such a setup would have the built-in and external strobes set to 1:1 or 2:1. Keep in mind that if using such a configuration, the light from the built-in flash is striking the subject head on and needs to be added to your calculations for the main light. In other words, setting your lighting ratio to 1:1 would actually provide a 2:1 effective lighting ratio since you would have 1 part light from the main light and 1 part light from the built-in flash illuminating one side of the subject and just 1 part light from the built-in flash illuminating the other side. Setting your lighting ratio to 2:1 would effectively provide a 3:1 lighting ratio this way. If you have set the camera to E-TTL II exposure as recommended, the lighting you choose will be automatically accounted for in the exposure selected by the camera, so no calculations are necessary by the photographer.

Working with Groups

With what you've already learned, you can shoot wirelessly using your camera's built-in flash and one or more external flash units. All these strobes will work together with the T7i for automatic exposure using E-TTL II exposure mode. You can vary the power ratio between your built-in flash and the external units. As you become more comfortable with wireless flash photography, you can even switch the individual external flash units into manual mode, and adjust their lighting ratios manually.

But there's a lot more you can do if you've splurged and own two or more compatible external flash units (some photographers I know own five or six Speedlite 580EX II or 600EX-RT units). Canon wireless photography lets you collect individual strobes into *groups*, and control all the Speedlites within a given group together. You can operate as few as two strobes in two groups or three strobes in three groups, while controlling more units if desired. You can also have them fire at equal output settings (A+B+C mode) versus using them at different power ratios (A:B or A:B C modes). Setting each group's strobes to different power ratios gives you more control over lighting for portraiture and other uses. Canon's radio-compatible devices can communicate with up to five groups in radio mode, although you would rarely need that capability (or, more likely, not own enough flashes to distribute among five groups). This is one of the more powerful options of the EOS wireless flash system. I prefer to keep my Speedlites set to different groups normally. I can always set the power ratio to 1:1 if I want to operate the flash units all at the same power. If I change my mind and need to make adjustments, I can just change the wireless flash controller and then manipulate the different groups' output as desired.

The ST-E2 is a hot shoe mount device that offers wireless flash control for a wide variety of Canon wireless flash capable strobes and can even control flash units wirelessly for High-speed sync (HSS) photography. (HSS is described in Chapter 11.) The ST-E2 can only control three flash groups though and also can support flash exposure bracketing. Its range isn't as great as the T7i's though.

Canon flash units that can be operated wirelessly include: 580EX II, 580EX, 550EX, 430EX III-RT, 430EX, 420EX, 320EX, 270EX II, MR-14EX, and MT-24EX. The 270EX, 220EX, 380EX, and earlier Canon flash units cannot be operated wirelessly via Canon's wireless flash system. There are third-party flash units that can (such as the Sigma I use), but you must use one designed to work with Canon's wireless flash system only.

Here's how you set up groups:

1. **Determine lighting setup.** Decide whether you're using the built-in flash as part of your lighting scheme or just using the external flash units. If you do want the internal flash to contribute to the exposure, then you can scroll down in the Built-in Flash Setting entry to the External Flash/Built-in Flash Lighting Ratio Control (if you're using lighting ratios) and set that control (from 8:1 to 2:1, as noted earlier).

2. **Access lighting groups.** If you're not using the built-in flash (Wireless Func. is set to the external flash only icon), scroll down to the Firing Group entry that appears and press SET.

3. **Select the group configuration you want.** From top to bottom, the choices are as follows:

   • **All external.** Multiple external flash units functioning as one big flash.

   • **A:B.** Multiple external units in two groups.

   I'll explain exactly what these two configurations do next.

4. **Allocate flash units into groups.** You must do this at the flash unit itself. You'll need to tell each flash which group it "belongs" to, so it will respond, along with any other strobes (if any) in its group, to wireless commands directed at that group. The procedure for setting each flash unit's slave ID/group varies depending on what flash you are using, so consult your Speedlite's manual.

Ratio Control

By default, all the flashes in each group will fire at full power. However, for more advanced lighting setups, you can select lighting ratios.

Here's how to set the lighting ratio between the internal flash and one external wireless flash unit:

1. **Navigate to the T7i's Flash Group selection option.** With wireless flash already activated, visit the External Speedlite Control entry in the Shooting 2 menu, navigate to the Flash Function Settings choice, Flash Functions. Navigate to the Flash Group choice at the lower left of the screen and choose SET.

2. **Choose Group Configuration.** You can select ALL, A:B, or A:B C. If you're using the 600EX-RT in radio transmission mode, you can also select Groups D and E. Press SET to confirm.

3. **Select Ratio.** If you've chosen A:B C, navigate to the A:B Ratio Control option, and select a ratio from 8:1 to 1:8. At 8:1, Group A supplies 8X output of Group B. At 1:8, the ratio is reversed.

4. **Confirm.** Press SET to confirm your ratio.

Here's how the various basic Group Configurations work:

- **ALL.** All groups will fire at the power level set at the flash unit itself. That may be full power, or you may have set individual flashes to fire at some other power level. It's usually simpler to set your flashes at full power and allow the master to control their output.

- **A:B.** In this configuration, you can specify the ratio of the power levels of Groups A and B, as described in Step 3 above.

- **A:B C.** In this Group configuration, you can specify the power ratio between Groups A and B, but *not* the output of Group C flashes. Those can be controlled only using Flash Exposure Compensation.

Choosing a Channel

Canon's wireless flash system can work on any of four channels in optical mode, so if more than one photographer is using the Canon system, each can set his gear to a different channel so they don't accidentally trigger each other's strobes. You need to be sure all of your gear is set to the same channel. Selecting a channel is done differently with each flash model.

The ability to operate flash units on one of four channels in optical mode isn't really important unless you're shooting in an environment where other photographers are also using the Canon wireless flash system. If the system only offered one channel, then each photographer's wireless flash controller would be firing every Canon flash set for wireless operation. By having four channels available, the photographers can coordinate their use to avoid that problem. Such situations are common at sporting events and other activities that draw a lot of shooters.

It's always a good idea to double-check your flash units before you set them up to make sure they're all set to the same channel, and this should also be one of your first troubleshooting questions if a flash doesn't fire the first time you try to use it wirelessly.

You do this as follows:

1. **Set flash units to the channel you want to use for all your groups.** Each flash unit may use its own procedure for setting that strobe's channel. Consult your Speedlite's manual for instructions. With the 580EX II, press the ZOOM button repeatedly until the CH. Indicator blinks, then rotate the control dial to select Channel 1, 2, 3, or 4. Press the control dial center button to confirm.

2. **Navigate to the T7i's channel selection option.** In the Built-in Flash Func. Settings screen, use the directional buttons to scroll down to the Channel Setting and push the SET button.

3. **Select the channel your flashes are set to.** You can then use the up/down directional buttons to advance the channel number from 1 to 4 or back down again (you have to reverse the directional buttons direction to get back to one; you can't just keep advancing it to get there—it doesn't "wrap around").

4. **Double-check to make sure your flash units are set to the appropriate channel.** Your wireless flash units must be set to the same channel as the T7i's wireless flash controller; otherwise, the Speedlites won't fire.

Flash Release Function

The Canon Speedlite 430EX III, 320EX and Speedlite 270EX II have a nifty feature called the Remote Release Function, which, as I write this, is completely novel in the Canon accessory flash lineup. The feature allows you to detach the Speedlite from certain EOS cameras (right now the 5DS/5DS R, 5D Mark II, Mark III, Mark IV, 6D, 7D, 7D II, 60D, 70D, 80D, 77D, T7i, T6s, T6i, T5i, T4i, T3i, T2i, T1i, Xsi, Xti, XT, and 2003-era original Digital Rebel), and then use a button on the flash unit as a remote control to trigger the camera from up to 16 feet away. That's right, your 320EX and 270EX II can function as a wireless remote control, just like the Canon RC-6, RC-5, and RC-1 infrared controls!

As you can see from the list of cameras, it works with any EOS camera that can be triggered by an IR remote. There's a (mandatory) two-second delay after you press the flash's remote release, and the flash itself does not have to fire and contribute to the exposure. An invisible infrared signal emitted by the flash triggers the camera.

To use the feature with the T7i, use the Drive function, described earlier, and select the self-timer/ infrared remote option. If you don't want the T7i's flash to fire, make sure it's set to P or a Creative Zone mode where the flash doesn't pop up automatically. With the 320EX or 270EX II turned on and detached from the camera, position the flash so it "sees" the remote-control sensor on the front of the camera. Press the remote release button on the side of the flash, and the camera will fire two seconds later. If you're taking a picture of yourself, this delay allows you to stash the flash out of sight and grin. The flash will not fire.

If you prefer to have the flash fire and contribute to the exposure, move the On/Off switch on the back to the middle "slave" position. In this mode, the camera itself must serve as the master, or you must have another master unit physically attached to the camera. To use the camera in master mode, use the Built-in Flash Control menu entry to activate the T7i's master mode, as described previously. Or, you can connect a 580EX II, set to master mode, either by putting it in the accessory shoe or linked with a cable, such as the Off Camera Cord OC-E3. Alternatively, you can connect the Speedlite Transmitter ST-E2.

When you're ready, point the 320EX or 270EX II at the front of the camera/master flash within 16 feet of the camera, and press the remote control button on the side of the flash. During the two-second delay, you can then point the 320EX or 270EX II in a different direction (as is likely, because you're probably using this feature to illuminate the scene, not the camera). That's the real reason for the two-second delay, by the way: giving you the ability to reposition the "remote" release flash.

The 600EX-RT has its own remote release function, which allows you to use a slave unit to trigger your camera by remote control when using radio transmission mode. EOS cameras released since 2012 (including the T7i) can be triggered in this way through the intelligent hot shoe, using a 600EX-RT mounted on the camera as a receiver, and the slave 600EX-RT off camera as the remote trigger. Older cameras can still be used in this mode, but you'll need to connect the on-camera 600EX-RT to the camera's N3 remote control terminal using an optional Release Cable SR-N3. (If your camera uses a different type of remote release, you're out of luck.)

Troubleshooting and Prevention

One of the nice things about modern electronic cameras like the Canon EOS T7i is that they have fewer mechanical moving parts to fail, so they are less likely to "wear out." No film transport mechanism, no wind lever or motor drive, and no complicated mechanical linkages from camera to lens to physically stop down the lens aperture. Instead, tiny, reliable motors are built into each lens (and you lose the use of only that lens should something fail), and one of the few major moving parts in the camera itself is a lightweight mirror (its small size one of the results of the T7i's 1.6X crop factor) that flips up and down with each shot.

Of course, the camera also has a moving shutter that can fail, but the shutter is built rugged enough that you can probably expect it to last 100,000 shutter cycles or more. Unless you're shooting sports in continuous mode day in and day out, the shutter on your T7i is likely to last as long as you expect to use the camera.

The only other things on the camera that move are switches, dials, buttons, the flip-up electronic flash, and the door that slides open to allow you to remove and insert the memory card. Unless you're extraordinarily clumsy or unlucky or give your built-in flash a good whack while it is in use, there's not a lot that can go wrong mechanically with your EOS T7i.

On the other hand, one of the chief drawbacks of modern electronic cameras is that they are modern *electronic* cameras. Your T7i is fully dependent on two different batteries. Without them, the camera can't be used. There are numerous other electrical and electronic connections in the camera (many connected to those mechanical switches and dials), and components like the color LCD that can potentially fail or suffer damage. The camera also relies on its "operating system," or *firmware*, which can be plagued by bugs that cause unexpected behavior. Luckily, electronic components are generally more reliable and trouble-free, especially when compared to their mechanical counterparts from the pre-electronic film camera days. (Film cameras of the last 10 to 20 years have had almost as many electronic features as digital cameras, but, believe it or not, there were whole generations of film cameras that had *no* electronics or batteries.)

Digital cameras have problems unique to their breed, too; the most troublesome being the need to clean the sensor of dust and grime periodically. This chapter will show you how to diagnose problems, fix some common ills, and, importantly, learn how to avoid some of them in the future.

Updating Your Firmware

As I said, the firmware in your EOS T7i is the camera's operating system, which handles everything from menu display (including fonts, colors, and the actual entries themselves), what languages are available, and even support for specific devices and features. Upgrading the firmware to a new version makes it possible to add new features while fixing some of the bugs that sneak in.

Official Firmware

Official firmware for your T7i is given a version number that you can view by turning the power on, pressing the MENU button, and navigating to Firmware Ver. x.x.x in the Set-up 4 menu. As I write this chapter, the current version is still 1.0.1. The first number in the string represents the major release number, while the second and third represent less significant upgrades and minor tweaks, respectively. I haven't actually had to do a firmware update with either camera, but I've done it many times with my other Canon cameras so I am familiar with the procedure.

Firmware upgrades are used for both cameras and certain lenses, most frequently to fix bugs in the software, and much less frequently to add or enhance features. For example, previous firmware upgrades for Canon cameras have mended things like incorrect color temperature reporting when using specific Canon Speedlites, or problems communicating with memory cards under certain conditions. The exact changes made to the firmware are generally spelled out in the firmware release announcement. You can examine the remedies provided and decide if a given firmware patch is important to you. If not, you can usually safely wait a while before going through the bother of upgrading your firmware—at least long enough for the early adopters to report whether the bug fixes have introduced new bugs of their own. Each new firmware release incorporates the changes from previous releases, so if you skip a minor upgrade you should have no problems.

Upgrading Your Firmware

If you're computer savvy, you might wonder how your EOS T7i is able to overwrite its own operating system—that is, how can the existing firmware be used to load the new version on top of itself? It's a little like lifting yourself by reaching down and pulling up on your bootstraps. Not ironically, that's almost exactly what happens: At your command (when you start the upgrade process), the T7i shifts into a special mode in which it is no longer operating from its firmware but, rather, from a small piece of software called a *bootstrap loader*, a separate, protected software program that functions only at startup or when upgrading firmware. The loader's function is to look for firmware to launch or, when directed, to copy new firmware from a memory card or your computer to the internal memory space where the old firmware is located. Once the new firmware has replaced the old, you can turn your camera off and then on again, and the updated operating system will be loaded.

Because the loader software is small in size and limited in function, there are some restrictions on what it can do. For example, the loader software isn't set up to go hunting through your memory card for the firmware file. It looks only in the top or root directory of your card, so that's where you must copy the firmware you download. Once you've determined that a new firmware update is available for your camera and that you want to install it, just follow these steps. (If you chicken out, any Canon service center can install the firmware upgrade for you.)

WARNING

Use a fully charged battery or Canon's optional AC adapter kit to ensure that you'll have enough power to operate the camera for the entire upgrade. Moreover, you should not turn off the camera while your old firmware is being overwritten. Don't open the memory card door or do anything else that might disrupt operation of the T7i while the firmware is being installed.

---

1. Download the firmware from Canon (you'll find it in the Downloads section of the Support portion of Canon's website) and place it on your computer's hard drive. The firmware is contained in a self-extracting file for either Windows or Mac OS. It will have a name such as T7I000102.fir.

2. In your camera, format a memory card. Choose Format from the Set-up menu, and initialize the card (make sure you don't have images you want to keep before you do this!).

3. You can copy the upgrade software to the card either using a memory card reader or by connecting the camera to your computer with a USB cable and using the EOS Utility application furnished with your camera (and described in the next section). The Firmware Version entry in the Set-up 4 menu will remind you that a memory card containing the firmware is required before you can proceed.

4. Insert the memory card in the camera and then turn the camera on. With the T7i set to any mode other than Creative Auto or Full Auto, press MENU and scroll to Firmware Ver. x.x.x in the Set-up 4 menu (see Figure 13.1) and press SET.

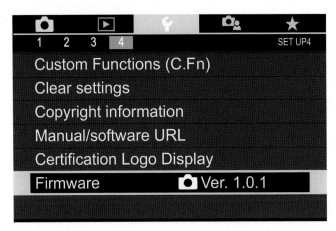

Figure 13.1
Determine the current version number.

5. You'll see the current firmware version, and an option to update, as shown in Figure 13.2. (This is a "fictional" update, as no new firmware has been released for the T7i as I write this, so the screens you see may be slightly different from the ones shown. Choose OK and press the SET button to begin loading the update program.

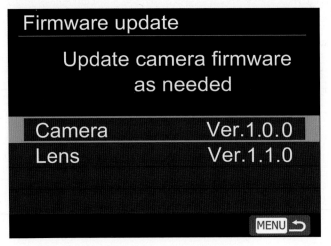

Figure 13.2

6. A confirmation screen will appear (see Figure 13.3). Select OK and press SET to continue. As the Firmware Update Program loads, you'll see the screen shown in Figure 13.4.

7. Next, you'll get the opportunity to confirm that the version you're upgrading to is the one you want, as you can see in Figure 13.5. You can press the MENU button to cancel. (Yes, I know there are a lot of confirmation screens; Canon wants to make sure you don't upgrade your firmware by accident, or, possibly, intentionally.)

8. Finally, the very last confirmation screen is shown in Figure 13.6. Select OK, and press SET, and, I promise, the actual firmware update will really begin.

9. While the firmware updates, you'll be warned not to turn off the power switch or touch any of the T7i's buttons. (See Figure 13.7.)

10. When the update complete screen appears (Figure 13.8), you can turn off the EOS T7i, remove the AC adapter, if used, and replace or recharge the battery. Then turn the camera on to boot up your camera with the new firmware update.

11. Be sure to reformat the card before returning it to regular use to remove the firmware software.

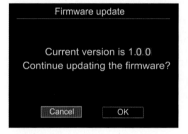

Figure 13.3

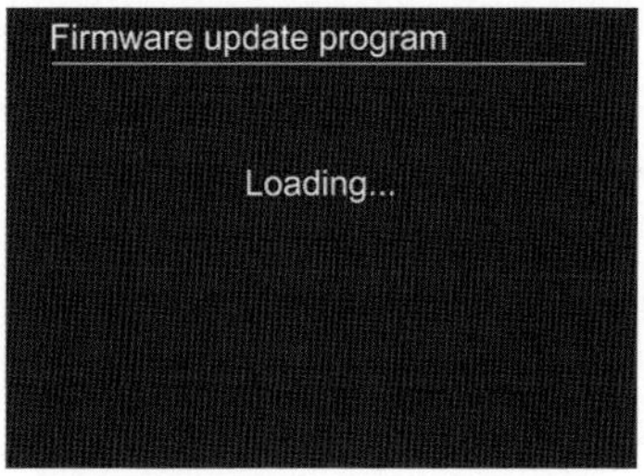

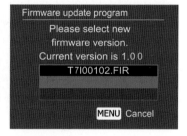

Figure 13.4

Figure 13.5

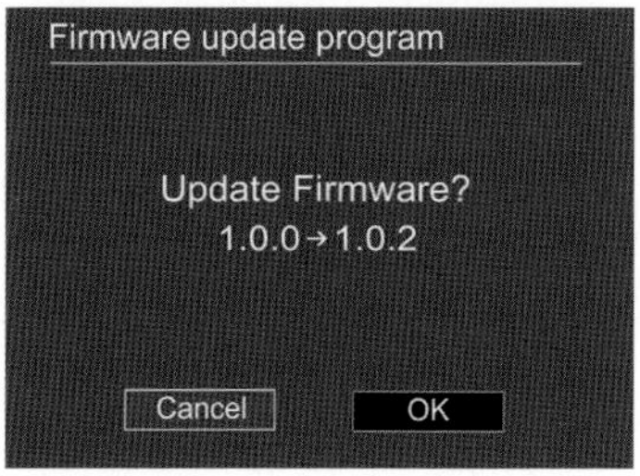

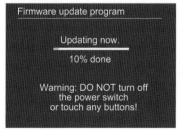

Figure 13.6

Figure 13.7

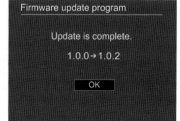

Figure 13.8

Using Direct Camera USB Link to Copy the Software

The procedure is slightly different (and a little more automated) if you choose to transfer the firmware software to the camera through a USB linkup. Follow these instructions to get started:

1. Connect the camera (with a freshly charged battery or attached to the AC Adapter) to the computer using the USB cable and turn it on.

2. Load the EOS Utility.

3. Click the Camera/Settings/Remote Shooting button.

4. Select the Firmware Update option. When the Update Firmware window appears at the bottom of the EOS Utility, choose OK.

5. Click Yes in the confirmation screen.

6. Follow the instructions in the dialog boxes that pop up next by pressing the SET button on the camera.

Protecting Your LCD

The color LCD on the back of your EOS T7i almost seems like a target for banging, scratching, and other abuse. Fortunately, it's quite rugged, and a few errant knocks are unlikely to shatter the protective cover over the LCD, and scratches won't easily mar its surface.

Of course, you can always flip it around so the LCD is facing the back of the camera. That's almost sure-fire protection, but it means you'll have to reverse the screen every time you want to use the camera—at least if you're in the mood to review the images you've taken on the screen, or liable to visit a few menus.

However, if you want to be on the safe side, there are a number of other protective products you can purchase to keep your LCD safe—and, in some cases, make it a little easier to view. I've found that the capacitive touch screen does continue to be responsive to touches and gestures with the protectors I've tried, and with the thinnest you should still be able to reverse your screen. But I haven't tried them all.

Plastic/glass overlays are the simplest solution. These adhere either by static electricity or through a light adhesive coating that's even less clingy than stick-it notes. You can cut down overlays made for PDAs (although these can be pricey at up to $19.95 for a set of several sheets), or purchase overlays sold specifically for digital cameras. I like the GGS brand available on eBay and Amazon. These products will do a good job of shielding your T7i's LCD screen from scratches and minor impacts, but will not offer much protection from a good whack. These are your best choice if you plan to reverse the LCD so it faces the camera; thicker shields may not allow the LCD panel to close completely in the reversed position.

Troubleshooting Memory Cards

Sometimes good memory cards go bad. Sometimes good photographers can treat their memory cards badly. It's possible that a memory card that works fine in one camera won't be recognized when inserted into another. In the worst case, you can have a card full of important photos and find that the card seems to be corrupted and you can't access any of them. Don't panic! If these scenarios sound horrific to you, there are lots of things you can do to prevent them from happening, and a variety of remedies available if they do occur. You'll want to take some time—before disaster strikes—to consider your options.

All Your Eggs in One Basket?

The debate about whether it's better to use one large memory card or several smaller ones has been going on since even before there were memory cards. I can remember when computer users wondered whether it was smarter to install a pair of 200MB (not *gigabyte*) hard drives in their computer, or if they should go for one of those new-fangled 500MB models. By the same token, a few years ago the user groups were full of proponents who insisted that you ought to use 128MB memory cards rather than the huge 512MB versions. Today, most of the arguments involve 16GB cards versus 32GB or 64GB cards, and I expect that as prices for 128GB memory cards continue to drop, they'll find their way into the debate as well. Size is especially important when you're using a camera like the T7i that captures 20-megapixel images.

Why all the fuss? Are 16GB memory cards more likely to fail than 8GB cards? Are you risking all your photos if you trust your images to a larger card? Isn't it better to use several smaller cards, so that if one fails you lose only half as many photos? Or, isn't it wiser to put all your photos onto one larger card, because the more cards you use, the better your odds of misplacing or damaging one and losing at least some pictures?

In the end, the "eggs in one basket" argument boils down to statistics, and how you happen to use your T7i. The rationales can go both ways. If you have multiple smaller cards, you do increase your chances of something happening to one of them, so, arguably, you might be boosting the odds of losing some pictures. If all your images are important, the fact that you've lost 100 rather than 200 pictures isn't very comforting.

Also consider that the eggs/basket scenario assumes that the cards that are lost or damaged are always full. It's actually likely that your 16GB card might suffer a mishap when it's less than half-full (indeed, it's more likely that a large card won't be completely filled before it's offloaded to a computer), so you really might not lose any more shots with a single 16GB card than with multiple 8GB cards.

If you shoot photojournalist-type pictures, you probably change memory cards when they're less than completely full in order to avoid the need to do so at a crucial moment. (When I shoot sports, my cards rarely reach 80 to 90 percent of capacity before I change them.) Using multiple smaller cards means you have to change them that more often, which can be a real pain when you're taking a lot of photos. In my book, I prefer keeping all my eggs in one basket, and then making very sure that nothing happens to that basket.

There are only two good reasons to justify limiting yourself to smaller memory cards when larger ones can be purchased at the same cost per-gigabyte. One of them is when every single picture is precious to you and the loss of any of them would be a disaster. If you're a wedding photographer, for example, and unlikely to be able to restage the nuptials if a memory card goes bad, you'll probably want to shoot no more pictures than you can afford to lose on a single card, and have an assistant ready to copy each card removed from the camera onto a backup hard drive or DVD onsite.

To be even safer, you'd want to alternate cameras or have a second photographer at least partially duplicating your coverage so your shots are distributed over several memory cards simultaneously. (Strictly speaking, the safest route of all is to beam the images to a computer as you shoot them using a Wi-Fi connection—if you have the time.)

If none of these options are available to you, consider *interleaving* your shots. Say you don't shoot weddings, but you do go on vacation from time to time. Take 50 or so pictures on one card, or whatever number of images might fill about 25 percent of its capacity. Then, replace it with a different card and shoot about 25 percent of that card's available space. Repeat these steps with diligence (you'd have to be determined to go through this inconvenience), and, if you use four or more memory cards, you'll find your pictures from each location scattered among the different memory cards. If you lose or damage one, you'll still have *some* pictures from all the various stops on your trip on the other cards. That's more work than I like to do (I usually tote around a portable hard disk and copy the files to the drive as I go), but it's an option.

What Can Go Wrong?

There are lots of things that can go wrong with your memory card, but the ones that aren't caused by human stupidity are statistically very rare. Yes, a memory card's internal bit bin or controller can suddenly fail due to a manufacturing error or some inexplicable event caused by old age. However, if your memory card works for the first week or two that you own it, it should work forever. There's not a lot that can wear out.

The typical memory card is rated for a Mean Time Between Failures of 1,000,000 hours of use. That's constant use 24/7 for more than 100 years! According to the manufacturers, they are good for 10,000 insertions in your camera, and should be able to retain their data (and that's without an external power source) for something on the order of 11 years. Of course, with the millions of memory cards in use, there are bound to be a few lemons here or there.

Given the reliability of solid-state memory, compared to magnetic memory, though, it's more likely that your memory problems will stem from something that you do. Memory cards are small and easy to misplace if you're not careful. For that reason, it's a good idea to keep them in their original cases. Always placing your memory card in a case can provide protection from the second-most common mishap that befalls memory cards: the common household laundry. If you slip a memory card in a pocket, rather than a case or your camera bag, often enough, sooner or later it's going to end up in the washing machine and probably the clothes dryer, too. There are plenty of reports of relieved digital camera owners who've laundered their memory cards and found they still worked fine, but it's not uncommon for such mistreatment to do some damage.

Memory cards can also be stomped on, accidentally bent, dropped into the ocean, chewed by pets, and otherwise rendered unusable in myriad ways. It's also possible to force a card into your T7i's memory card slot incorrectly if you're diligent enough, doing little damage to the card itself, but damaging the contacts in the camera, eliminating its ability to read or write to any memory card. Or, if the card is formatted in your computer with a memory card reader, your T7i may fail to recognize it. Occasionally, I've found that a memory card used in one camera would fail if used in a different camera (until I reformatted it in Windows, and then again in the camera). Every once in awhile, a card goes completely bad and—seemingly—can't be salvaged.

Another way to lose images is to do commonplace things with your memory card at an inopportune time. If you remove the card from the T7i while the camera is writing images to the card, you'll lose any photos in the buffer and may damage the file structure of the card, making it difficult or impossible to retrieve the other pictures you've taken. The same thing can happen if you remove the memory card from your computer's card reader while the computer is writing to the card (say, to erase files you've already moved to your computer). You can avoid this by *not* using your computer to erase files on a memory card but, instead, always reformatting the card in your T7i before you use it again.

What Can You Do?

Pay attention: If you're having problems, the *first* thing you should do is *stop* using that memory card. Don't take any more pictures. Don't do anything with the card until you've figured out what's wrong. Your second line of defense (your first line is to be sufficiently careful with your cards that you avoid problems in the first place) is to *do no harm* that hasn't already been done. Read the rest of this section and then, if necessary, decide on a course of action (such as using a data recovery service or software described later) before you risk damaging the data on your card further.

Now that you've calmed down, the first thing to check is whether you've inserted a card in the camera. If you've set the camera in the Shooting menu so that Shoot w/o Card has been turned on, it's entirely possible (although not particularly plausible) that you've been snapping away with no memory card to store the pictures to, which can lead to massive disappointment later. Of course, the No Memory Card message appears on the LCD when the camera is powered up, and it is super-imposed on the review image after every shot, but maybe you're inattentive, or aren't using picture review. You can avoid all this by turning the Release Shutter w/o Card feature off in the Shooting 1 menu and leaving it off.

Things get more exciting when the card itself is put in jeopardy. If you lose a card, there's not a lot you can do other than take a picture of a similar card and print up some Have You Seen This Lost Flash Memory? flyers to post on utility poles all around town.

If all you care about is reusing the card, and have resigned yourself to losing the pictures, try refor-matting the card in your camera. You may find that reformatting removes the corrupted data and restores your card to health. Sometimes I've had success reformatting a card in my computer using a memory card reader (this is normally a no-no because your operating system doesn't understand the needs of your T7i), and *then* reformatting again in the camera.

If your memory card is not behaving properly, and you *do* want to recover your images, things get a little more complicated. If your pictures are very valuable, either to you or to others (for example, a wedding), you can always turn to professional data recovery firms. Be prepared to pay hundreds of dollars to get your pictures back, but these pros often do an amazing job. You wouldn't want them working on your memory card on behalf of the police if you'd tried to erase some incriminat-ing pictures. There are many firms of this type, and I've never used them myself, so I can't offer a recommendation. Use a Google search to turn up a ton of them. I use a software program called RescuePro, which came free with one of my SanDisk memory cards.

A more reasonable approach is to try special data recovery software you can install on your com-puter and use it to attempt to resurrect your "lost" images yourself. They may not actually be gone completely. Perhaps your memory card's "table of contents" is jumbled, or only a few pictures are damaged in such a way that your camera and computer can't read some or any of the pictures on the card. Some of the available software was written specifically to reconstruct lost pictures, while other utilities are more general-purpose applications that can be used with any media, including floppy disks and hard disk drives. They have names like OnTrack, Photo Rescue 2, Digital Image Recovery, MediaRecover, Image Recall, and the aptly named Recover My Photos. A quick Google search will locate some of your options.

DIMINISHING RETURNS

Usually, once you've recovered any images on a memory card, reformatted it, and returned it to ser-vice, it will function reliably for the rest of its useful life. However, if you find a card going bad more than once, you'll almost certainly want to stop using it forever. See if you can get it replaced by the manufacturer, if you can, but, in the case of memory card failures, the third time is never the charm.

Cleaning Your Sensor

There's no avoiding dust. No matter how careful you are, some of it is going to settle on your camera and on the mounts of your lenses, eventually making its way inside your camera to settle in the mirror chamber. As you take photos, the mirror flipping up and down causes the dust to become airborne and eventually make its way past the shutter curtain to come to rest on the anti-aliasing filter atop your sensor. There, dust and particles can show up in every single picture you take at a small enough aperture to bring the foreign matter into sharp focus. No matter how careful you are and how cleanly you work, eventually you will get some of this dust on your camera's sensor. Some say that CMOS sensors, like the one found in the EOS T7i, "attract" less dust than CCD sensors found in cameras from other vendors. But even the cleanest-working photographers using Canon cameras are far from immune.

Fortunately, one of the EOS T7i's most useful features is the automatic sensor cleaning system that reduces or eliminates the need to clean your camera's sensor manually. Canon has applied anti-static coatings to the sensor and other portions of the camera body interior to counter charge build-ups that attract dust. A separate filter over the sensor vibrates ultrasonically each time the T7i is powered on or off, shaking loose any dust.

Although the automatic sensor cleaning feature operates when you power the camera up or turn it off, you can activate it at any time. Choose Sensor Cleaning from the Set-up 3 menu, and select Clean Now. If you'd rather turn the feature on or off, choose Auto Cleaning instead, and then choose either Enable or Disable with the directional buttons. Press SET, then press the MENU button to return to the Set-up 3 menu (see Figure 13.9).

If some dust does collect on your sensor, you can often map it out of your images (making it invisible) using software techniques with the Dust Delete Data feature in the Shooting 4 menu. Operation of this feature is described in Chapter 8. Of course, even with the EOS T7i's automatic sensor cleaning/dust resistance features, you may still be required to manually clean your sensor from time

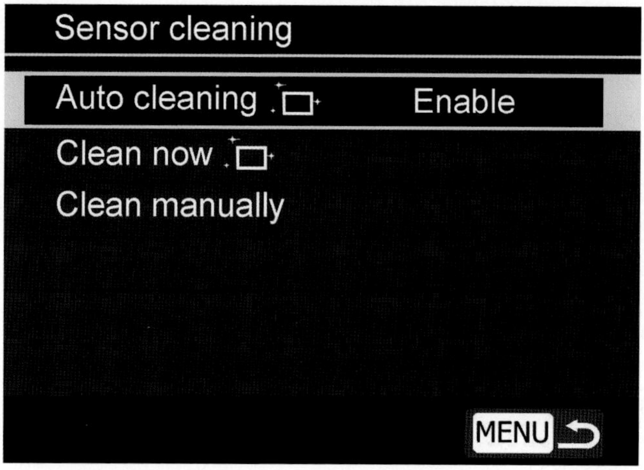

Figure 13.9
You can activate automatic sensor cleaning immediately or enable/disable the feature.

to time. This section explains the phenomenon and provides some tips on minimizing dust and eliminating it when it begins to affect your shots. I also cover this subject in my book, *Digital SLR Pro Secrets*, with complete instructions for constructing your own sensor cleaning tools. However, I'll provide a condensed version here of some of the information in that book, because sensor dust and sensor cleaning are two of the most contentious subjects Canon EOS T7i owners have to deal with.

Dust the FAQs, Ma'am

Here are some of the most frequently asked questions about sensor dust issues.

Q. I see tiny specks in my viewfinder. Do I have dust on my sensor?

A. If you see sharp, well-defined specks, they are clinging to the underside of your focus screen and not on your sensor. They have absolutely no effect on your photographs, and are merely annoying or distracting.

Q. I can see dust on my mirror. How can I remove it?

A. Like focus screen dust, any artifacts that have settled on your mirror won't affect your photos. You can often remove dust on the mirror or focus screen with a bulb air blower, which will loosen it and whisk it away. Stubborn dust on the focus screen can sometimes be gently flicked away with a soft brush designed for cleaning lenses. I don't recommend brushing the mirror or touching it in any way. The mirror is a special front-surface-silvered optical device (unlike conventional mirrors, which are silvered on the back side of a piece of glass or plastic) and can be easily scratched. If you can't blow mirror dust off, it's best to just forget about it. You can't see it in the viewfinder, anyway.

Q. I see a bright spot in the same place in all my photos. Is that sensor dust?

A. You've probably got either a "hot" pixel or one that is permanently "stuck" due to a defect in the sensor. A hot pixel is one that shows up as a bright spot only during long exposures as the sensor warms. A pixel stuck in the "on" position always appears in the image. Both show up as bright red, green, or blue pixels, usually surrounded by a small cluster of other improperly illuminated pixels, caused by the camera's interpolating the hot or stuck pixel into its surroundings, as shown in Figure 13.10. A stuck pixel can also be permanently dark. Either kind is likely to show up when they contrast with plain, evenly colored areas of your image.

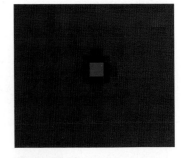

Figure 13.10 A stuck pixel is surrounded by improperly interpolated pixels created by the T7i's demosaicing algorithm.

Finding one or two hot or stuck pixels in your sensor is unfortunately common. They can be "removed" by telling the T7i to ignore them through a simple process called *pixel mapping*. If the bad pixels become bothersome, Canon can remap your sensor's pixels with a quick trip to a service center.

Bad pixels can also show up on your camera's color LCD panel, but, unless they are abundant, the wisest course is to just ignore them.

Q. I see an irregular out-of-focus blob in the same place in my photos. Is that sensor dust?

A. Yes. Sensor contaminants can take the form of tiny spots, larger blobs, or even curvy lines if they are caused by minuscule fibers that have settled on the sensor. They'll appear out of focus because they aren't on the sensor surface but, rather, a fraction of a millimeter above it on the filter that covers the sensor. The smaller the f/stop used, the more in-focus the dust becomes. At large apertures, it may not be visible at all.

Q. I never see any dust on my sensor. What's all the fuss about?

A. Those who never have dust problems with their EOS T7i fall into one of four categories: those for whom the camera's automatic dust removal features are working well; those who seldom change their lenses and have clean working habits that minimize the amount of dust that invades their cameras in the first place; those who simply don't notice the dust (often because they don't shoot many macro photos or other pictures using the small f/stops that makes dust evident in their images); and those who are very, very lucky.

Identifying and Dealing with Dust

Sensor dust is less of a problem than it might be because it shows up only under certain circumstances. Indeed, you might have dust on your sensor right now and not be aware if it. The dust doesn't settle on the sensor itself, but, rather, on a protective filter a very tiny distance above the sensor, subjecting it to the phenomenon of *depth-of-focus*. Depth-of-focus is the distance the focal plane can be moved and still render an object in sharp focus. At f/2.8 to f/5.6 or even smaller, sensor dust, particularly if small, is likely to be outside the range of depth-of-focus and blur into an unnoticeable dot.

However, if you're shooting at f/16 to f/22 or smaller, those dust motes suddenly pop into focus. Forget about trying to spot them by peering directly at your sensor with the shutter open and the lens removed. The period at the end of this sentence, about .33mm in diameter, could block a group of pixels measuring 40 × 40 pixels (160 pixels in all!). Dust spots that are even smaller than that can easily show up in your images if you're shooting large, empty areas that are light colored. Dust motes are most likely to show up in the sky, as in Figure 13.11, or in white backgrounds of your seamless product shots and are less likely to be a problem in images that contain lots of dark areas and detail.

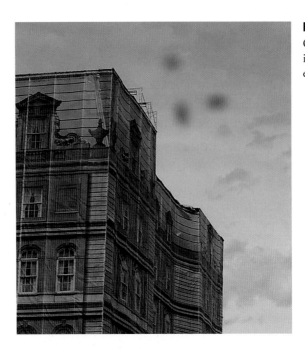

Figure 13.11
Only the dust spots in the sky are apparent in this shot.

To see if you have dust on your sensor, take a few test shots of a plain, blank surface (such as a piece of paper or a cloudless sky) at small f/stops, such as f/22, and a few wide open. Open Photoshop, copy several shots into a single document in separate layers, then flip back and forth between layers to see if any spots you see are present in all layers. You may have to boost contrast and sharpness to make the dust easier to spot.

Avoiding Dust

Of course, the easiest way to protect your sensor from dust is to prevent it from settling on the sensor in the first place. Some Canon lenses come with rubberized seals around the lens mounts that help keep dust from infiltrating, but you'll find that dust will still find a way to get inside. Here are my tips for eliminating the problem before it begins.

- **Clean environment.** Avoid working in dusty areas if you can do so. Hah! Serious photographers will take this one with a grain of salt, because it usually makes sense to go where the pictures are. Only a few of us are so paranoid about sensor dust (considering that it is so easily removed) that we'll avoid moderately grimy locations just to protect something that is, when you get down to it, just a tool. If you find a great picture opportunity at a raging fire, during a sandstorm, or while surrounded by dust clouds, you might hesitate to take the picture, but, with a little caution (don't remove your lens in these situations, and clean the camera afterward!) you can still shoot. However, it still makes sense to store your camera in a clean environment. One place cameras and lenses pick up a lot of dust is inside a camera bag. Clean your bag from time to time, and you can avoid problems.

- **Clean lenses.** There are a few paranoid types that avoid swapping lenses in order to minimize the chance of dust getting inside their cameras. It makes more sense just to use a blower or brush to dust off the rear lens mount of the replacement lens first, so you won't be introducing dust into your camera simply by attaching a new, dusty lens. Do this before you remove the lens from your camera, and then avoid stirring up dust before making the exchange.

- **Work fast.** Minimize the time your camera is lens-less and exposed to dust. That means having your replacement lens ready and dusted off, and a place to set down the old lens as soon as it is removed, so you can quickly attach the new lens.

- **Let gravity help you.** Face the camera downward when the lens is detached so any dust in the mirror box will tend to fall away from the sensor. Turn your back to any breezes, indoor forced air vents, fans, or other sources of dust to minimize infiltration.

- **Protect the lens you just removed.** Once you've attached the new lens, quickly put the end cap on the one you just removed to reduce the dust that might fall on it.

- **Clean out the vestibule.** From time to time, remove the lens while in a relatively dust-free environment and use a blower bulb like the one shown in Figure 13.12 (*not* compressed air or a vacuum hose, please!) to clean out the mirror box area. A blower bulb is generally safer than a can of compressed air, or a strong positive/negative airflow, which can tend to drive dust further into nooks and crannies.

- **Be prepared.** If you're embarking on an important shooting session, it's a good idea to clean your sensor *now*, rather than come home with hundreds or thousands of images with dust spots caused by flecks that were sitting on your sensor before you even started.

- **Clone out existing spots in your image editor.** Photoshop and other editors have a clone tool or healing brush you can use to copy pixels from surrounding areas over the dust spot or dead pixel. This process can be tedious, especially if you have lots of dust spots and/or lots of images to be corrected. The advantage is that this sort of manual fix-it probably will do the least damage to the rest of your photo. Only the cloned pixels will be affected.

- **Use filtration in your image editor.** A semi-smart filter like Photoshop's Dust & Scratches filter can remove dust and other artifacts by selectively blurring areas that the plug-in decides represent dust spots. This method can work well if you have many dust spots, because you won't need to patch them manually. However, any automated method like this has the possibility of blurring areas of your image that you didn't intend to soften.

Figure 13.12
Use a robust air bulb for cleaning your sensor.

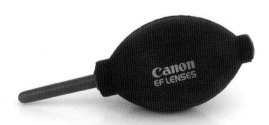

Sensor Cleaning

Those new to the concept of sensor dust hesitate before deciding to clean their camera themselves. Isn't it a better idea to pack up your T7i and send it to a Canon service center so their crack technical staff can do the job for you? Or, at the very least, shouldn't you delegate the task to the friendly folks at your local camera store (if you're lucky, you have one nearby)?

Of course, if you choose to let someone else clean your sensor, they will be using methods that are more or less identical to the techniques you would use yourself. None of these techniques are difficult, and the only difference between their cleaning and your cleaning is that they might have done it dozens or hundreds of times. If you're careful, you can do just as good a job.

Of course, vendors like Canon won't tell you this. It's not that difficult for a real goofball to mess up his camera by hurrying or taking a shortcut. Perhaps the person uses the "Bulb" method of holding the shutter open and a finger slips, allowing the shutter curtain to close on top of a sensor cleaning brush. Or, someone tries to clean the sensor using masking tape, and ends up with goo all over its surface. If Canon recommended *any* method that's mildly risky, someone would do it wrong, and then the company would face lawsuits from those who'd contend they did it exactly in the way the vendor suggested, so the ruined camera is not their fault. If you visit Canon's website, you'll find this recommendation: "If the image sensor needs cleaning, we recommend having it cleaned at a Canon service center, as it is a very delicate component."

You can see that vendors like Canon tend to be conservative in their recommendations, and, in doing so, make it seem as if sensor cleaning is more daunting and dangerous than it really is. Some vendors recommend only dust-off cleaning, through the use of reasonably gentle blasts of air, while condemning more serious scrubbing with swabs and cleaning fluids. However, these cleaning kits for the exact types of cleaning they recommended against are for sale in Japan only, where, apparently, your average photographer is more dexterous than those of us in the rest of the world. These kits are similar to those used by official repair staff to clean your sensor if you decide to send your camera in for a dust-up.

As I noted, sensors can be affected by dust particles that are much smaller than you might be able to spot visually on the surface of your lens. The filters that cover sensors tend to be fairly hard compared to optical glass. Cleaning the 22.3mm × 14.9mm sensor in your Canon T7i within the tight confines of the mirror box can call for a steady hand and careful touch. If your sensor's filter becomes scratched through inept cleaning, you can't simply remove it yourself and replace it with a new one.

There are three basic kinds of cleaning processes that can be used to remove dusty and sticky stuff that settles on your dSLR's sensor. All of these must be performed with the shutter locked open. I'll describe these methods and provide instructions for locking the shutter later in this section.

- **Air cleaning.** This process involves squirting blasts of air inside your camera with the shutter locked open. This works well for dust that's not clinging stubbornly to your sensor.

- **Brushing.** A soft, very fine brush is passed across the surface of the sensor's filter, dislodging mildly persistent dust particles and sweeping them off the imager.

- **Liquid cleaning.** A soft swab dipped in a cleaning solution such as ethanol is used to wipe the sensor filter, removing more obstinate particles.

Placing the Shutter in the Locked and Fully Upright Position for Cleaning

Make sure you're using a fully charged battery or an optional AC adapter.

1. Remove the lens from the camera and then turn the camera on.

2. Set the EOS T7i to any one of the non–fully automatic modes.

3. You'll find the Clean Manually menu choice in the Set-up 3 menu under Sensor Cleaning (see Figure 13.9, shown earlier). Press the SET button.

4. Select OK and press SET again. The mirror will flip up and the shutter will open.

5. Use one of the methods described below to remove dust and grime from your sensor. Be careful not to accidentally switch the power off or open the memory card or battery compartment doors as you work. If that happens, the shutter may be damaged if it closes onto your cleaning tool.

6. When you're finished, turn the power off, replace your lens, and switch your camera back on.

Air Cleaning

Your first attempts at cleaning your sensor should always involve gentle blasts of air. Many times, you'll be able to dislodge dust spots, which will fall off the sensor and, with luck, out of the mirror box. Attempt one of the other methods only when you've already tried air cleaning and it didn't remove all the dust.

Here are some tips for doing air cleaning:

- **Use a clean, powerful air bulb.** Your best bet is bulb cleaners designed for the job, like the Giottos Rocket. Smaller bulbs, like those air bulbs with a brush attached sometimes sold for lens cleaning or weak nasal aspirators, may not provide sufficient air or a strong enough blast to do much good.

- **Hold the EOS T7i upside down.** Then look up into the mirror box as you squirt your air blasts, increasing the odds that gravity will help pull the expelled dust downward, away from the sensor. You may have to use some imagination in positioning yourself. (See Figure 13.13.)

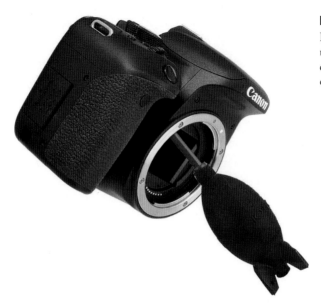

Figure 13.13
Hold the camera upside down when cleaning to allow dust to fall out.

- **Never use air canisters.** The propellant inside these cans can permanently coat your sensor if you tilt the can while spraying. It's not worth taking a chance.

- **Avoid air compressors.** Super-strong blasts of air are likely to force dust under the sensor filter.

Brush Cleaning

If your dust is a little more stubborn and can't be dislodged by air alone, you may want to try a brush, charged with static electricity, which can pick off dust spots by electrical attraction. One good, but expensive, option is the Arctic Butterfly sold at www.visibledust.com. A motor built into the brush is used to "flutter" the tip for a few seconds prior to cleaning (see Figure 13.14, left), charging the brush's anti-static properties. Then, the motor is turned off (Figure 13.14, right) and the brush tip is passed above the surface of the sensor. (It's not necessary to touch the sensor.) The dust is attracted to the brush and removed by another quick flutter once you've removed the brush from the mirror chamber. A cheaper, inanimate, sensor cleaning brush can be purchased from a variety of sources. You need a 16mm version. It can be stroked across the short dimension of your T7i's sensor.

Ordinary artist's brushes are much too coarse and stiff and have fibers that are tangled or can come loose and settle on your sensor. A good sensor brush's fibers are resilient and described as "thinner than a human hair." Brush cleaning is done with a dry brush by gently swiping across the surface of the sensor filter with the tip. The dust particles are attracted to the brush particles and cling to them. You should clean the brush with compressed air before and after each use, and store it in an appropriate air-tight container between applications to keep it clean and dust-free. Although these special brushes are expensive, one should last you a long time.

Figure 13.14
A proper brush like this Arctic Butterfly is required for dusting off your sensor.

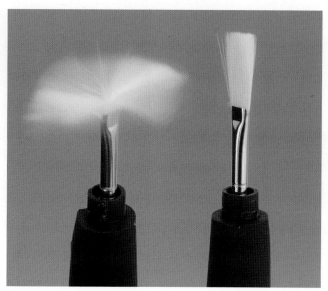

Liquid Cleaning

Unfortunately, you'll often encounter stubborn dust spots that can't be removed with a blast of air or flick of a brush. These spots may be combined with some grease or a liquid that causes them to stick to the sensor filter's surface. In such cases, liquid cleaning with a swab may be necessary. During my first clumsy attempts to clean my own sensor, I accidentally got my blower bulb tip too close to the sensor, and some sort of deposit from the tip of the bulb ended up on the sensor. I panicked until I discovered that liquid cleaning did a good job of removing whatever it was that took up residence on my sensor.

You can make your own swabs out of pieces of plastic (some use fast-food restaurant knives, with the tip cut at an angle to the proper size) covered with a soft cloth or Pec-Pad, as shown in Figures 13.15 and 13.16. However, if you've got the bucks to spend, you can't go wrong with good-quality commercial sensor cleaning swabs, such as those sold by Photographic Solutions, Inc. at their web site (www.photosol.com) or from other retailers, such as Amazon.

You want a sturdy swab that won't bend or break so you can apply gentle pressure to the swab as you wipe the sensor surface. Use the swab with methanol (as pure as you can get it, particularly medical grade; other ingredients can leave a residue), or the Eclipse solution also sold by Photographic Solutions. Eclipse is quite a bit purer than even medical-grade methanol. A couple drops of solution should be enough, unless you have a spot that's extremely difficult to remove. In that case, you may need to use extra solution on the swab to help "soak" the dirt off.

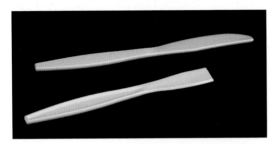

Figure 13.15 You can make your own sensor swab from a plastic knife that's been truncated.

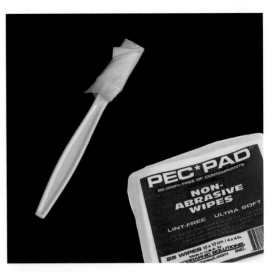

Figure 13.16 Carefully wrap a Pec-Pad around the swab.

Once you overcome your nervousness at touching your T7i's sensor, the process is easy. You'll wipe continuously with the swab in one direction, then flip it over and wipe in the other direction. You need to completely wipe the entire surface; otherwise, you may end up depositing the dust you collect at the far end of your stroke. Wipe; don't rub.

If you want a close-up look at your sensor to make sure the dust has been removed, you can pay $50–$100 for a special sensor "microscope" with an illuminator. Or, you can do like I do and work with a plain old Carson MiniBrite PO-55 illuminated 5X magnifier, as seen in Figure 13.17. It has a built-in LED and, held a few inches from the lens mount with the lens removed from your T7i, provides a sharp, close-up view of the sensor, with enough contrast to reveal any dust that remains. You can read more about this great device at http://dslrguides.com/carson.

Figure 13.17
An illuminated magnifier like this Carson MiniBrite PO-55 can be used as a 'scope to view your sensor.

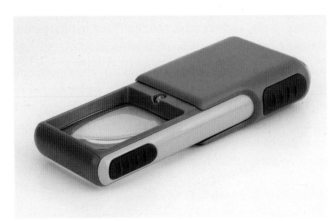

Index

A

A setting. *See* **Scene Intelligent Auto setting**
AC Adapter Kit ACK-E18, 6, 9
access lamp, 52–53
access menus, 16
action, stopping, 188, 191, 340–342
activating features, 53
Adobe RGB color space, 235–237
AE lock
  button, 51
  displaying in live view, 140–141
  live view in Movie mode, 151
AEB (automatic exposure bracketing). *See also* **bracketing**
  default value, 297
  explained, 93–95
  menu, 226–227
  range readout, 61–62, 64
AF (autofocus) mode. *See also* **focus modes; Live 1-Point AF; One-Shot AF**
  assist beam, 290
  with color tracking, 131–132
  contrast detection, 116–117
  cross-type focus point, 121–124
  Dual Pixel CMOS AF, 120–121
  versus manual focusing, 116
  options, 127–129

parameters, 132
phase detection, 117–120
sensor array, 118
sensors, 124
setting buttons, 216
AF Area Selection modes
  built-in flash, 32–33
  button, 56–57
  choosing, 30–31, 129–131, 291
  default value, 297
  displaying, 64
  parameters, 132
  self-timer, 32
  white balance and ISO, 31
AF method
  default value, 299
  displaying in live view, 140
  live view, 151
  using with live view, 138, 141, 144–147
AF mode button, 52, 54
AF operation
  default value, 297, 299
  displaying in live view, 140–141
AF point, 61
  displaying in live view, 140, 142
  live view, 151
AF Point Display During Focus, 132, 291–292
AF Point Display menu, 270, 298

AF point readouts, 61–62
AF point Selection
  Magnify button, 52
  shooting tips, 38, 40, 42
AF points and lens groups, 123–124
AF with shutter button during movie recording, default value, 300
AF-Assist, enabling and disabling, 358
AF-Assist Beam Firing, 132
AFD (Arc-form drive), 317
AF/MF switch, moving, 29
AF-point selection, shooting tips, 38
AI Focus mode, 30
AI Servo mode, 30, 128. *See also* **Servo AF**
air bulb, using on dust, 425
air cleaning sensors, 427–428
albums, adding video snapshots, 164
all purpose, shooting tips, 38–39
Ambience settings, 111–113
angle finder c right-angle viewer, 6. *See also* **rubber eyecup Ef**
Anti-Flicker Shooting. *See also* **flicker detection**
  default value, 297
  menu, 254
  tips, 38, 40, 43

aperture
    displaying in live view,
        140–141
    in exposure triangle, 71
    and f/stop, 73
    lenses, 308
    live view in Movie mode, 151
    readout, 61–62
Aperture Priority setting, 24
Area AF frame, 60–61
Art Bold Effect, 264
Art effects, using with HDR,
    97
Aspect Ratio
    default value, 297
    frames, 60
    menu, 255
attenuator, live view in Movie
    mode, 151
audio and video, 182–184. *See*
    also Sound recording;
    video/sound
Auto AF Point Selection, 291
auto cleaning, default value,
    298
Auto Lighting Optimizer
    default value, 297
    displaying, 64
    displaying in live view, 140,
        142
    live view in Movie mode, 151
    menu, 232–234
    shooting tips, 38, 40, 43
Auto Picture Style, 240
Auto power off
    default value, 298
    shooting tips, 38, 41, 43
Auto Power Off option, 279
Auto Rotate
    default value, 298
    option, 277
Autoexposure lock/Auto
    Exposure Bracketing
    in-progress, 61–62
autofocus lenses, 307

Autofocus modes
    displaying, 64
    shooting tips, 38, 40, 42
autofocus points, 60–61
Autofocus/Manual focus
    switch, 58–59
automatic focus, switching to
    manual, 29
Av (Aperture-priority) mode
    close-up photography, 85
    Creative Zone modes, 27–28
    equivalent exposure, 75
    Exposure compensation
        button, 52–53
    exposure meters, 91
    landscape photography,
        83–84
    macro photography, 85
    portrait photography, 84
    tabs, 214
Average metering, 228
axial chromatic aberration,
    224, 327

B

B & W effect, using with
    movies, 166
back focus, 132
back panel, 49–55
back-button focus, 132–134.
    See also focus modes
Background Blur setting, 111
backlighting, 69
Basic Zone shooting modes,
    24–26, 82, 108–114
batteries
    chargers, 8–9
    charging, 7, 10
    dangers of mishandling, 7
    decoding, 7–8
    keeping extras, 5, 8
    Movie mode, 150
    power options, 8–9
    third-party sellers, 7–8

battery charger LC-E17/E17E,
    3
battery cover door, 57
battery grips, 9
Battery Info. option, 285
battery level
    displaying, 64
    displaying in live view, 140,
        142
    live view, 151
battery pack LP-E17, 3
Beep
    default value, 298
    option, 285
    shooting tips, 38, 41–43
BG-E18 battery grip, 9
"blinkies," 106
blue channel, 107
Bluetooth function
    default value, 299
    displaying, 64
    displaying in live view,
        140–141
    live view in Movie mode, 151
    using, 199–206
blur, reducing and adding,
    85–86
blurring subjects, 197
body cap RF-3, 3
bokeh, 332
Bold effect, 27
bootstrap loader, 413
bottom of camera, 57
bracketing. *See also* AEB
    (automatic exposure
    bracketing)
    exposures, 92–95
    and Merge to HDR, 98–101
    WB (white balance), 64
Brightness Histogram,
    101–102
brightness options, 280
brush cleaning sensors,
    428–429
buffer and bursts, 186–187

built-in electronic flash. *See also* **electronic flash; flash; Speedlites; wireless flash**
  AF (autofocus) Assist, 357–358
  Basic Zone modes, 355
  capabilities, 388
  clearing settings, 230
  Creative Zone modes, 355–356
  FE Lock, 358–359
  flash exposure compensation, 358–359
  flash range, 356
  power rating, 32
  recharging readout, 61–62
  Red-Eye Reduction and AF-Assist, 357–358
  settings, 64, 229–230, 363–364
  as Speedlite trigger, 5
  using, 32–33
  and wireless flash, 405
bulb exposures, 61–62, 149, 193. *See also* **exposure**
bursts
  availability, 61, 63
  maximum in live view, 140, 142
  size, 186
Busy readout, 61–62
buttons. *See* **controls; directional buttons**

C

cable. *See* **interface cable; USB cables**
calibration systems, 237
camera
  manuals, 301
  turning on, 24
camera bottom, 57

camera settings. *See also* **Display Level Settings**
  changing, 46, 65
  choosing, 56
  date and time, 20, 22–23
  default values, 296–300
  navigating, 28
  verifying, 215
camera shake
  vanquishing, 191
  video, 174
Candlelight setting, 26, 109, 113
Canon Camera Connect app, 201–212
Canon EF lenses, 311
Canon EF-S lenses, 309–311
Canon EOS Rebel T7i/800D. *See* **camera**
Canon Image Gateway, 200, 211–212
Canon lenses, 307. *See also* **lenses**
Canon Speedlites. *See* **Speedlites**
capacitor, use with electronic flash, 349
Card error readout, 61–62
Card full warning, 61–62
card slot cover, 46
Center-weighted metering, 29, 81
Certification Logo Display option, 301
C.Fn (custom functions)
  AF (autofocus) assist beam, 290
  AF Area selection, 291
  AF parameters, 132
  AF Point Display During Focus, 291–292
  all purpose, 39
  Auto AF Point Selection, 291
  back-button focus, 133
  Color Tracking, 291
  defaults, 39, 297
  e-mail, 44

    Exposure Compensation Auto Cancel, 289
    exposure level increments, 288
    external flash, 372
    HDR, 41–42
    Highlight Tone Priority, 289–290
    ISO expansion, 288–289
    landscape, 44
    LCD Display When Power On, 296
    long exposures, 41–42
    macro, 44
    mirror lockup feature, 292–293
    option, 286–296
    portraits, 41–42
    Retract Lens on Power Off, 296
    SET button, 295
    settings, 287–288
    Shutter button/AE Lock button, 294
    Speedlite 580EX II, 377
    Speedlite 600EX-RT/600EX II-RT, 375
    sports, 39
    stage performances, 41–42
    studio flash, 44
    travel, 44
    VF Display Illumination, 292
    Viewfinder Warnings, 293–294
channels and histograms, 107
charging batteries, 7, 10
chromatic aberration, 222, 224, 298, 327
CIPA (Camera & Imaging Products Association), 7
circles of confusion, 125–126
cleaning sensor, 421–430
Clear Settings option, 296–300
close-up lites, 379–380
close-up photography, 85

Close-Up setting, 24, 26, 109, 113

close-ups, video, 178–179

CMOS sensors, susceptibility to noise, 90–91

color channels, correcting, 107–108

color filters, applying, 244. *See also* Creative Filters; filters versus toning

color fringes, reducing, 222

color management, 237

Color Space. *See also* RGB histogram
information display, 66–67
menu, 235–237
shooting tips, 38, 40, 43

color temperature, 343, 345

color tone adjustment, 240

Color Tracking, 291

color tracking and AF, 131–132

Colormunki website, 237

communications, enabling, 203

composition, video, 176–179

computers, shooting from, 136

concerts, 86

Connect app, 201–212

Connect Station storage, 199, 210

contacts, 47–48

continuous autofocus, 148. *See also* AI Servo mode

continuous lighting
action stopping, 342
color temperature, 343
cost, 342
daylight, 344–345
versus electronic flash, 337–342, 347
evenness of illumination, 339
exposure calculation, 338–339
flexibility, 342

fluorescent/other light sources, 345–346

incandescent/tungsten, 345

lighting preview, 338

white balance, 346

Continuous shooting, 185–187

contrast, changing, 105–106

Contrast control, 240

contrast detection, 116–117

Control over HDMI, default value, 299

controls, using, 16. *See also* directional buttons

Copyright Information

Creative Auto setting, 24–25, 109–111, 214

Creative Filters. *See also* color filters; filters versus toning
default value, 297, 299–300
displaying in live view, 140
live view, 142–143
live view in Movie mode, 151
menu, 261–264
movies, 165–167
settings, 24, 26, 114
tabs, 214
types, 27

Creative Zone modes, 24, 27–28, 30, 63. *See also* exposure modes

crop factor, 306–307

Cropping menu, 264–265

cross-type focus point, 121–124

Ctrl over HDMI menu, 271

curtain sync, 349–351

custom functions (C.Fn)
AF (autofocus) assist beam, 290
AF Area selection, 291
AF parameters, 132
AF Point Display During Focus, 291–292
all purpose, 39

Auto AF Point Selection, 291

back-button focus, 133

Color Tracking, 291

defaults, 39, 297

e-mail, 44

Exposure Compensation Auto Cancel, 289

exposure level increments, 288

external flash, 372

HDR, 41–42

Highlight Tone Priority, 289–290

ISO expansion, 288–289

landscape, 44

LCD Display When Power On, 296

long exposures, 41–42

macro, 44

mirror lockup feature, 292–293

option, 286–296

portraits, 41–42

Retract Lens on Power Off, 296

SET button, 295

settings, 287–288

Shutter button/AE Lock button, 294

Speedlite 580EX II, 377

Speedlite 600EX-RT/600EX II-RT, 375

sports, 39

stage performances, 41–42

studio flash, 44

travel, 44

VF Display Illumination, 292

Viewfinder Warnings, 293–294

Custom White Balance
default value, 298
menu, 247–248

Custom Wireless Flash Shooting, 389

D

D+ symbol, appearance of, 90

"dark frame," 251

dark frame subtraction, 91

darkness, showing, 197–198

date and time, setting, 22–23

Date/Time/Zone option

 default value, 298

 options, 281–282

daylight, color temperature, 344–345

DC cord hole, 46–47

defaults

 settings, 296–300

 shooting tips, 38–39

degrees Kelvin, 345

delayed exposures, 198–200. *See also* exposure

deleting images, 34, 259

details, optimizing, 240

dials, number of, 45

diffraction

 correction, 222, 224–226

 default value for correction, 298

 explained, 70

DIGIC7 image processing, 219

digital terminal, 49

Digital Zoom

 default value, 299

 live view in Movie mode, 151

diopter correction, 11–12, 50

DIP (digital image processing) chip, 219

direct printing, 200

directional buttons, 16, 53–54, 215. *See also* controls

DISP. Button

 locating, 56

 turning off screen, 65

Display Level Settings. *See also* camera settings

 accessing, 19–20, 301

 default values, 297

displaying images, 34–35

displays, making visible, 28

distance scale, 59

distortion correction, 222, 224

 default value, 298

DOF (depth-of-field)

 circles of confusion, 125

 and f/stops, 70

 lenses, 319

 preview button, 48

 video, 172

 wide-angle and wide-zoom lenses, 324–327

Dolenz, Micky, 323

DPOF (Digital Print Order Format), 259–261

dragging to select, 17–18

Dramatic B & W effect, using with movies, 166

Drive mode

 button, 52, 54

 default value, 297

 displaying, 64

 displaying in live view, 140–141

 options, 33

 setting buttons, 216

 shooting tips, 38, 40, 42

 specifying, 186

Drive/Flash Modes, 111

Dual Pixel CMOS AF, 120–121

Dust Delete Data

 default value, 298

 menu, 253

dust on sensor

 avoiding, 424–425

 FAQs, 422–423

 identifying and dealing with, 423–424

dynamic range, 71. *See also* HDR (High Dynamic Range); Merge to HDR and bracketing

E

Easy Connection wizard, 205–206

Easy Wireless Flash Shooting, 389–390

Edgerton, Harold, 189

editing movies, 170–171

EF and EF-S lenses, 309–312, 314–315

EF lens mount index, 47, 58

EF lenses, 308

EF-S mounting index, 47, 58

EF-S/EF mounting index, 59

electrical contacts, 58–59

electronic flash. *See also* built-in electronic flash; flash; Speedlites; wireless flash

 action stopping, 340–341

 capacitor, 349

 versus continuous lighting, 347

 cost, 342

 curtain sync, 349–351

 evenness of illumination, 340

 exposure, 354–355

 exposure calculation, 339

 flexibility, 342

 freezing action, 188

 functioning, 349–354

 ghost images, 350–352

 lighting preview, 338

 and shutter speed, 189

 shutter speed, 353

 sync speed, 352–354

electronic level, 61–62, 65, 140

Electronic Manual Focus, 226. *See also* focus modes

electronic release cable, 6

e-mail, shooting tips, 42–44

Embossed effect, 27

enlarging and reducing images, 18

EOS Digital Solution Disc CD, 5

EOS Utility
music files, 268
Picture Style, 246–247
remote control, 210
equivalent exposures, 73–75
erasing images, 34, 259
Error code readout, 61–62
establishing shot, video, 178
E-TTL II Metering, 228, 297,
361, 365
EV (exposure value)
changes, 91–92
ISO settings, 89
Evaluative metering, 29, 79,
228
EW-400D wide strap, 3
ExpoDisc filter/caps, 343
exposure. *See also* **bulb**
exposures; delayed
exposures; long
exposures; short
exposures
adjusting with ISO settings,
89–91
bracketing, 92
calculating, 75–77
displaying in live view, 140,
142
electronic flash, 354–355
equivalent, 73–74
fixing with histograms,
101–108
highlights and shadows,
71–72
impact, 70–71
and light, 70–73
locking in, 56
merging, 101
setting, 73
simulation, 142
triangle, 70–71
exposure bracketing range,
displaying in live view,
140–141

exposure compensation
amount, 61–62
Auto Cancel, 289
button, 52–53
displaying, 64
displaying in live view,
140–141
live view in Movie mode, 151
menu, 226–227
and non-bracketing, 94
readout, 61, 63
Exposure Compensation/AEB,
default value, 297
exposure level increments, 288
exposure level indicator
described, 63
displaying, 64
displaying in live view,
140–141
live view in Movie mode, 151
viewfinder, 61
exposure modes. *See also*
Creative Zone modes
Av (Aperture-priority), 82–85
Basic Zone, 82
displaying, 64
getting information about, 14
M (Manual), 87–89
P (Program), 86–87
shooting tips, 38, 40, 42
Tv (Shutter-priority), 85–86
exposure simulation, displaying
in live view, 140, 142
external electronic flash
close-up lites, 379–380
Custom Function, 372
linking to camera, 372–373
radio transmitters, 373
slave connection, 373
Speedlite 270EX II, 378–379
Speedlite 320EX, 378
Speedlite 430EX III-RT,
377–378
Speedlite 580EX II, 376–377
Speedlite 600EX-RT/600EX
II-RT, 374–376
wireless setting, 393

External Flash Function
settings, 230
external master flash/
controller, setting up,
394–399
external strobes, linking to
camera, 348–349
eyecup, 3
Eye-Fi Settings option, 279
Eye-Fi transmission
default value, 299
displaying in live view,
140–141
transmission status, 64, 151

F

Face Detection+Tracking
Mode, 144–145
Faithful Picture Style, 241
FE lock
built-in electronic flash,
358–359
button, 51
readout, 61–62
Feature Guide, changing, 20
FEB (flash exposure
bracketing), displaying
in live view, 140, 142
File Numbering
default value, 298
option, 276–277
files, transferring to
computers, 23
fill flash, 365–366
Filter Effects, 240, 244
filter thread, 57–58
filters versus toning, 244. *See*
also **color filters;**
Creative Filters
Fine Detail Picture Style, 240
firmware, updating, 301,
412–416
Fish-Eye effect, 27, 114, 262
fisheye lenses, 327

flash. *See also* built-in flash; electronic flash; Speedlites
> button, 48–49
> capabilities, 388
> ISO settings, 90
> and M (Manual) exposure, 88

Flash Control settings
> action stopping, 365
> Built-in Flash Settings, 229–230, 363–364
> curtain sync, 367
> E-TTL II Metering, 228, 361, 365
> External Flash Function, 367–372
> fill flash, 365–366
> Flash firing, 228, 360–361
> Flash mode, 365–366
> Flash Sync Speed in Av mode, 229, 361–362
> HSS (high-speed sync), 369–372
> manual flash, 365
> MULTI Flash, 368–369
> wireless flash options, 368

flash exposure compensation
> built-in electronic flash, 358–359
> default value, 297
> displaying, 64
> FE lock/Flash exposure bracketing in-progress, 61–62
> live view, 141
> using, 230

Flash Firing, 228, 297, 360–361

Flash mode, 365–366

Flash Off
> displaying in live view, 140, 142
> settings, 24–25, 109
> tabs, 214

flash ratio setting, 399–402

flash ready, displaying in live view, 140, 142

Flash Release function, wireless flash, 408–409

Flash status indicator/High-speed sync, 61–62

flash sync contacts, 56

Flash Sync Speed in Av mode, 229, 297, 361–362

flash-ready indicator, 61–62

flat lighting, 181

flicker detection, 61–62. *See also* Anti-Flicker Shooting

fluorescent/other light sources, 345–346

focal plane mark, 56

focus, locking in, 56

focus distance, 58

focus indicator, 61, 63

focus modes. *See also* AF (autofocus) mode; back-button focus; Electronic Manual Focus; manual focus
> adjustment screen, 143
> choosing, 29–30
> circles of confusion, 125–126

focus priority, 148

focus ring, 58–59

focusing, live view, 144–148

folders, selecting, 274–276

Food setting, 26, 109, 113

Format Card option, 278

formatting memory cards, 23–24

frame rate
> live view in Movie mode, 151
> resolution, 152–154

freezing action, 188, 191, 340–342

front view, 46–49

front-curtain sync, 351

f/stops, 70, 73–74

Full auto setting, 25

G

"ghosts," eliminating, 369

"ghoul lighting," 181

GN (guide numbers), 354–355

GPS connection
> displaying in live view, 140
> live view in Movie mode, 151

GPS data, displaying, 64, 66, 68

GPS Device Settings option, 283–284

Grainy B/W effect, 27, 114, 262

gray cards, 75, 77–78

grayscale images, 103

green channel, 107

Grid display
> default value, 299–300
> live view, 138
> viewfinder, 60–61

grip, 46–47

Group Photo setting, 26, 113

groups, wireless flash, 405–406

guided menus, 15

Guided shooting mode
> information screen, 25
> interface, 14

H

Halsman, Philippe, 189

Handheld Night Scene setting, 26, 110, 113

HD movies. *See* movies

HDMI port, 49

HDR (High Dynamic Range). *See also* dynamic range; Merge to HDR
> Backlight Control, 95–97
> shooting tips, 40–42
> special effects, 97

HDR Art effects, 27, 114

HDR Backlight Control, 26, 110, 113

HDR movies, shooting, 165
HDTV (high-definition television), viewing images, 284
High ISO noise reduction. *See also* noise reduction
  default value, 298
  menu, 252
  shooting tips, 38, 40, 43
Highlight Tone Priority
  displaying in live view, 140, 143
  explained, 63–64, 289–290
  live view in Movie mode, 151
  viewfinder, 61
highlighting, moving, 16
High-Speed Sync
  live view, 140
  viewfinder, 61–62
histograms
  channels, 107
  and contrast, 104–105
  default value, 298
  displaying, 66–68, 140, 143, 271
  features, 101–102
  overexposure, 106–107
  tonal range, 102–104
  underexposure, 106
  using, 105–108
horizontal lines, aligning, 138–139
hot shoe, 56–57
HSS (high-speed sync), 369–372

illumination. *See* lighting
Image Jump with Main Dial
  default value, 298
  menu, 269–270
  options, 55

Image Quality
  default value, 297
  displaying, 64
  lenses, 308
  menu, 217–220
  shooting tips, 38, 40, 42
Image Review
  default value, 298
  menu, 221
  shooting tips, 38, 40, 42
image-recording
  quality, 140–141
  settings, 297–298
images. *See also* photos; pictures
  capacity on memory card, 261
  displaying, 34–35
  erasing, 34, 259
  jumping forward and back, 35
  previewing on TV, 136
  protecting, 256–258
  rating, 266
  reducing and enlarging, 18
  resizing, 265
  reviewing, 34–35
  rotating, 258
  saving to Connect Station, 210
  scrolling, 18, 35
  searching, 268–269
  transferring between cameras, 207–208
incandescent/tungsten lighting, 345
Index button, 51
index display, zooming out and viewing, 35
index views, navigating, 36
INFO button
  live view, 140
  locating, 34, 50
  using, 35
information screens, 65–66
instruction manual, 4

interface cable, 5. *See also* USB cables
IR (infrared)
  focus adjustment, 58–59
  sensors, 6
IS (image stabilization)
  explained, 334–335
  Movie mode, 152
  switch, 58–59
ISO, exposure triangle, 71
ISO Auto
  default value, 297
  menu, 232
  shooting tips, 38, 40, 43
ISO expansion, 288–289
ISO noise, 90–91
ISO settings
  adjusting exposure, 89–91
  D+ symbol, 90
  displaying, 64
  locating, 216
ISO speed
  button, 56
  default value, 297
  displaying in live view, 140–141
  live view in Movie mode, 151
  menu, 231–232
  readout, 61, 63

J
JPEG compression, 217–220
Jump method, 54, 269–270

K
Kids setting, 26, 109, 113
knobs, number of, 45

L

landscape
  Picture Style, 240
  setting, 24, 26, 109, 113
  shooting tips, 42–44, 83–84, 86
Language option, 282, 298
lapel microphones, 184
Large Zone AF, 61–62, 129–130
latches
  locating, 57
  number of, 45
lateral/transverse chromatic aberration, 224, 327
LCD brightness
  default value, 298
  option, 280
  shooting tips, 38, 41, 43
LCD Display When Power On, 296
LCD monitor, 50–51. *See also* Touch screen
  protecting, 19, 416
  screens, 63–65
  turning on and off, 56
LCD Off/On Button
  default value, 298
  option, 280–281
LC-E17/E17E battery charger, 3
LED illumination, 345
Lens aberration correction
  data, 66, 68
  menu, 221–226
  shooting tips, 38, 40, 43
lens aperture
  displaying in live view, 64, 140–141
  in exposure triangle, 71
  and f/stop, 73
  lenses, 308
  live view in Movie mode, 151
  readout, 61–62

lens components, 57–59
lens electronic manual focus, default value, 298
lens groups and AF points, 123–124
lens hood, 57–58, 333
lens hood bayonet, 57–58
Lens Lust, 318
lens mount bayonet, 58
lens mounts, 47, 59, 313
lens multiplier factor, 306–307
lens release button/locking pin, 47–48
lens switches, 48
lenses. *See also* Canon lenses
  adapter rings, 313
  aperture, 308
  aperture maximum, 316
  aspherical, 327
  autofocus, 307
  autofocus type, 316
  buying, 309–312
  capabilities, 319–321
  categories, 324
  collecting, 318–324
  compatibility, 312–315
  components, 57–59
  curvilinear, 327
  DOF (depth-of-field), 319
  EF, 308
  filter size, 316
  first time, 307–309
  fisheye, 327
  focal length, 315
  focusing, 308
  image quality, 308
  IS (image stabilization), 334–335
  kit in box, 3
  macro, 316
  mounting, 10–11
  movies, 172–173
  pro quality, 316
  rectilinear, 327
  series, 316

  special-purpose, 316
  telephoto and tele-zoom, 329–332
  telephoto zoom, 320–321
  ultra-wide-angle, 320
  USM and STM system, 308
  wide-angle and wide-zoom, 324–327
  zoom versus prime, 322–324
Lexar cards, 5
light
  and exposure, 70–72, 75
  high shutter speeds, 188
light fall-off, fixing, 222
light meters, 78, 88
light trails, producing, 196
lighting
  external strobes, 348–349
  LED illumination, 345
  video, 179–181
liquid cleaning sensors, 429–430
lithium-ion battery pack. *See* batteries
Live 1-Point AF, 146. *See also* AF (autofocus)
live view
  activating, 139–143
  AF method, 144–147
  autofocus, 116
  button, 50
  default value, 299
  enabling, 137–139
  features, 136–137
  focus operation, 148
  focusing, 144–148
  information display, 140
  movie shooting, 151
  power usage, 137
  Q (Quick Control), 143
  Servo AF, 148
  Shooting option, 256
  Still mode, 150
  tabs, 214
  Touch Shutter, 149

**Long Exposure Noise
    Reduction**
    default value, 298
    menu, 250–251
    shooting tips, 38, 40, 43
**long exposures, 40–42, 192–
    198.** *See also* **exposure**
**longitudinal/axial chromatic
    aberration, 224, 327**
LP-E17 battery pack, 3

M

M (Manual) mode
    Creative Zone, 27–28
    flash functions, 33
    tabs, 214
    using, 87–89
**macro photography, 42–44,
    85, 316, 334**
**Macro Ring Lite MR-14EX II,
    377–378**
**Macro Twin Lite flash
    MD-24EX, 377–378**
Macs, transferring images, 37
Magnified View, 140, 143, 147
magnifier MG-Ef, 6
Magnify button, 52
**Magnify/Digital Zoom, live
    view in Movie mode, 151**
Main Dial
    described, 56
    image jump, 269–270
    locating, 46
    using, 16
manual focus. *See also* **focus
    modes**
    activating, 125, 129–131
    switching to automatic, 29
manual for camera, 4, 301
Manual setting, 24
**Manual/Software URL option,
    301**

master
    controller flash, 389–390
    Speedlite or transmitter,
    394–399
    ST-E2 transmitter, 395–396
Matrix metering, 29, 79, 228
McNally, Joe, 377–378
medium shot, video, 178–179
memory cards. *See also* **Release
    Shutter without Card**
    capacity, 261
    formatting, 23–24, 278
    inserting, 12
    Movie mode, 150
    No card warning, 61–62
    transferring images, 37
    troubleshooting, 417–420
**Memory effect, using with
    movies, 166**
MENU button, 16, 50
Menu Display, changing, 20
menus
    guided mode, 15
    modes and tabs, 214
    navigating, 16, 215
    tabs, 216
    viewing, 15
**Merge to HDR and bracketing,
    98–101.** *See also* **dynamic
    range; HDR (High
    Dynamic Range)**
Metering modes
    choosing, 28–29, 78–79
    default value, 297
    displaying, 64, 140–141
    versus M (Manual) exposure,
    89
    menus, 234
    shooting tips, 38, 40, 43
metering timer
    default value, 299
    live view, 138
microphones, 47–48
    input, 49
    video, 182–183
    wind noise reduction, 184

**Miniature effect, 27, 114, 166–
    167, 263–264**
mirror, 47–48
**mirror lockup feature, 199,
    292–293**
MM (Micromotor) drive, 317
Mode Dial, 55–56
modeling light, 347
moiré effects, correcting, 222
**Monochrome Picture Style,
    241**
**motion blur, reducing and
    adding, 85–86**
motor drives, 317
mounting lenses, 10–11
Movie button, 50
**movie clips, versus Video
    Snapshots, 164**
**Movie digital image
    stabilization, default
    value, 300**
**Movie ISO Auto, default value,
    299**
**Movie ISO Speed, default
    value, 299**
Movie modes
    batteries, 150
    file size, 153–154
    Final Image Simulation, 152
    frame rates, 152–154
    HDR Movies, 165
    image stabilizer, 152
    live view, 151
    memory cards, 150
    recording time, 153–154
    resolution, 150, 152–154
    shooting in, 150
    silent running, 152
    tabs, 214
    Time-Lapse, 167–169
    Video Snapshots, 161–164
**Movie recording size, default
    value, 299**
**Movie Servo AF, default value,
    299**

Movie Shooting menus
AF method, 159
AF w/shutter button during
movie recording, 159
Auto Lighting Optimizer, 156
default values, 299–300
Digital Zoom, 154–156
exposure compensation, 156
Grid display, 159
Lens aberration correction,
155
Lens electronic manual focus,
155
Metering timer, 159
Movie Digital Image
Stabilization, 159–160
Movie ISO Auto, 156
Movie ISO Speed, 156
Movie rec. size, 154
Movie Servo AF, 158–159
Picture Style, 157
Remote control, 159–160
Sound recording, 155
Time-lapse movie, 159–160
Video snapshot, 159–160
White Balance, 157
Movie switch, 56
movies. *See also* **video**
audio, 182–184
camera shake, 174
close-ups, 178–179
composition, 176–179
Creative Filters, 165–167
DOF (depth-of-field), 172
establishing shot, 178
information display, 161
lenses, 172–173
lighting, 179–181
medium shot, 178–179
over-the-shoulder shots,
178–179
playback and editing,
170–171
shooting scripts, 174–175
storyboards, 175

storytelling, 176
two shots, 178–179
video/sound, 160–161
zooming, 173
MULTI Flash, 368–369
**Multi-Shot Noise Reduction,
64, 140, 142.** *See also*
noise reduction
**music, adding to slide shows,
268**
My Menu, 299–304

N

navigating settings, 28, 215
neck strap, 3
Neutral Picture Style, 241
**NFC (Near Field
Communications), 57,
199–206**
nickname, changing, 204–205
**Night Portrait setting, 26, 109,
113.** *See also* **Portrait
setting**
**No card warning readout,
61–62**
Noise Ninja website, 91
noise reduction, 64. *See also*
**High ISO speed noise
reduction; Multi-shot
noise reduction; visual
noise**
activating, 91
information display, 66–67
numbering files, 276–277

O

**Old Movies effect, using with
movies, 166**
One-Shot AF, 30, 128, 148. *See
also* **AF (autofocus) mode**
On/Off/Movie switch, 56
**Optical mode, Speedlite or
transmitter, 394–399**
orientation, rotating, 277

outdoor lighting, 181
overexposure, 76–77, 106–107
**over-the-shoulder shot, video,
178–179**

P

P (Program) mode
Creative Zone, 27–28
flash functions, 33
tabs, 214
using, 86–87
pairing with smart device, 203
Partial metering, 29, 80
passive phase detection, 117
PC, transferring images, 37
**Peripheral Illumination
Correction, 222–223**
default value, 297
**Personal Functions, Speedlite
600EX-RT/600EX II-RT,
375**
phase detection, 117–120
Photobook Set-up menu, 261
**photos, transferring to
computers, 36–37.** *See
also* **images; pictures**
PictBridge, 200
**Picture Control, displaying,
64–67**
Picture Style
button, 52, 54
changing settings, 246–247
creating and loading, 245
default value, 297
defining, 242–243
displaying in live view, 140,
142
Editor, 243
EOS Utility, 246–247
Filter Effects, 244
live view in Movie mode, 151
menu, 238–247
selecting, 241–242
setting buttons, 216

sharpness parameter, 239
shooting tips, 38, 40, 43
Toning Effects, 244
uploading, 246
pictures, taking, 34. *See also*
images
pinching LCD screen, 18
playback
button, 52–53
displays, 65–68
information, 59
movies, 170–171
options, 34–35
Playback menus
AF Point Display, 270
Creative Filters, 261–264
Cropping, 264–265
Ctrl over HDMI, 271
Erase Images, 259
Histogram Display, 271
Image Jump with Main Dial,
269–270
Photobook Set-up, 261
Print Order, 259–261
Protect Images, 256–257
Rating, 266
Resize, 265
Rotate Images, 258
Set Image Search Conditions,
268–269
Slide Show, 266–268
playback mode, Reduce/Index/
AE lock/FE lock button,
52
pop-up electronic flash. *See*
built-in electronic flash,
49
portrait photography, 84
Portrait settings, 24, 26,
40–42, 109, 113, 204.
See also **Night Portrait**
setting
power options, 24, 279
prime versus zoom lenses,
322–324

Print Order menu, 259–261
printing, 200, 211
Program Auto setting, 24
Protect Images menu, 256–257

Q

Q (Quick Control)
button, 16, 52–53, 65
changing metering modes, 28
Creative Auto setting, 111
display, 64
displaying in live view, 140,
142
live view in Movie mode, 151
screen, 64
QR code, displaying, 301
Quick Start suggestions, 15

R

radio master
Speedlite 430EX III-RT, 397
Speedlite 600EX-RT/600EX
II-RT, 396–397
ST-E3-RT, 397–398
radio transmitters, external
electronic flash, 373
Rating menu, 266
ratio control, wireless flash,
407
RAW files, 218–220
rear-curtain sync, 351
reciprocity failure, 188
recording level, live view in
Movie mode, 151
red channel, 107
Red-eye reduction
default value, 297
lamp on, 61–62
menu, 231
self-timer lamp, 47
Reduce/Index/AE lock/FE lock
button, 51
reducing and enlarging images,
18

registration card, 4–5
release cable, 6
Release Shutter without Card.
See also **memory cards**
default value, 298
menu, 221
remote control
default value, 300
EOS Utility, 210
terminal, 49
using, 47, 200
remote controller RC-6, 6
Remote Release Function,
wireless flash, 408–409
remote switch RS-60E3, 6
Resize menu, 265
resolution
and frame rates, 152–154
image quality, 217
Retract Lens on Power Off,
296
reviewing images, 34–35
RF-3 body cap, 3
RGB histogram, 66–67, 101–
102. *See also* **Color Space**
right-angle viewer, 6
ring (USM) ultrasonic motor
drive, 317
Rotate Images menu, 258
rotating orientation, 277
rubber eyecup Ef, 3. *See also*
Angle Finder C right-
angle viewer

S

Saturation parameter, 240
saving images to Connect
Station, 210
scales, adjusting, 17–18
Scene Intelligent Auto setting,
24–25, 108, 110, 214
Scene modes, 113, 214
SCN Mode, 26, 109, 297
screen off mode, 65
scrolling images, 18, 35

**SD (Secure Digital) card,
  inserting, 12**
searching images, 268–269
Select Folder option, 274–276
selecting items, 17–18
self-timer, 32, 47, 198–199
**Sensor Cleaning option, 20,
  22, 285–286, 421–430**
Sepia filter, 244
Servo AF, 148. *See also* AI
  Servo mode
SET button, 52, 295
**Set Image Search Conditions
  menu, 268–269**
SET/OK button, 16, 53
settings. *See also* Display Level
  Settings
  changing, 46, 65
  choosing, 56
  date and time, 20, 22–23
  default values, 296–300
  navigating, 28
  verifying, 215
Set-up menu options
  Auto Power Off, 279
  Auto Rotate, 277
  Battery Info., 285
  Beep, 285
  Certification Logo Display,
    301
  Clear Settings, 296–300
  Copyright Information,
    300–301
  Custom Functions, 286–296
  Date/Time/Zone, 281–282
  Eye-Fi Settings, 279
  File Numbering, 276–277
  Firmware Version, 301
  Format Card, 278
  GPS Device Settings,
    283–284
  Language, 282
  LCD Brightness, 280

  LCD Off/On Button,
    280–281
  Manual/Software URL, 301
  Select Folder, 274–276
  Sensor Cleaning, 285–286
  Touch Control, 284
  Video System, 284
  Viewfinder Display, 282
  Wireless Communication
    Settings, 278
sharpness
  achieving, 84
  Picture Style setting, 239
**shooting function settings,
  63–64**
**shooting information display,
  59, 65–66**
Shooting menus
  AEB (automatic exposure
    bracketing), 226–227
  Anti-Flicker Shooting, 254
  Aspect Ratio, 255
  Auto Lighting Optimizer,
    232–234
  Color Space, 235–237
  Custom White Balance,
    247–248
  Dust Delete Data, 253
  Electronic Manual Focus,
    226
  Exposure Compensation, 226
  Flash Control, 228–230
  High ISO Speed Noise
    Reduction, 252
  Image Quality, 217–220
  Image Review, 221
  ISO Auto, 232
  ISO Speed, 231–232
  Lens Aberration Correction,
    221–226
  Live View Shooting, 256
  Long Exposure Noise
    Reduction, 250–251
  Metering Mode, 234
  Picture Style, 238–247

  Red-Eye Reduction, 231
  Release Shutter without Card,
    221
  White Balance, 247
  White Balance Shift and
    Bracketing, 248–249
**Shooting Mode Guide,
  changing, 20**
shooting modes
  displaying in live view,
    140–141
  getting information about, 14
  Reduce/Index/AE lock/FE
    lock button, 51
  selecting, 24–28
Shooting Screen
  changing, 20
  Guided and Standard
    settings, 21
**shooting scripts, using for
  video, 174–175**
**shooting settings, default
  values, 297**
shooting tips
  all purpose, 38–39
  defaults, 38–39
  e-mail, 42–44
  HDR, 40–42
  landscape, 42–44
  long exposures, 40–42
  macro, 42–44
  portraits, 40–42
  sports, 38–39
  stage performances, 40–42
  studio flash, 42–44
  travel, 42–44
short exposures, 189–192. *See
  also* exposure
shotgun microphones, 184
**shots possible, displaying in
  live view, 140, 142**
**shots remaining, displaying,
  64**
**shutter, releasing without card,
  221**

Shutter button, 46, 56, 294
shutter speed
    displaying, 64
    displaying in live view,
        140–141
    and electronic flash, 189
    in exposure triangle, 71
    freezing action, 188
    and f/stops, 74
    live view in Movie mode, 151
    specifying ranges, 82
    viewfinder, 61–62
shutter sync, 229–230
Shutter-priority (Tv) mode
    concerts, 86
    Creative Zone, 27–28
    explained, 85–86
    exposure meters, 91
    flash functions, 33
    landscape photography, 86
    selecting, 24
    stage performances, 86
    tabs, 214
single autofocus, 30, 128, 148.
        See also AF (autofocus)
        mode
Single-point AF, 129–130
slave connection, 373
slave flash, setting up,
        398–399
slice of time, shooting,
        188–192
Slide Show menu, 266–268
smart device
    communication, 208–210
    pairing, 203
smartphones, connecting to,
        199
Smooth Zone, 145–146
Soft Focus effect, 27, 114, 262
software. *See* firmware
Sound recording, default value,
        299. *See also* audio and
        video; video/sound

speaker, 48
Special Scene settings, 24–26
Speedlites. *See also* built-in
        electronic flash;
        electronic flash; flash;
        wireless flash
    270EX II, 378–379, 388, 399
    320EX, 378–379, 399
    430EX II, 388, 398
    430EX III/III-RT, 388, 398
    430EX III-RT, 377–378, 397
    580EX, 394
    580EX II, 376–377, 388, 394,
        398
    600EX-RT, 394, 409
    600EX-RT/600EX II-RT,
        374–376, 388,
        396–398
    master and slave unit, 387
    triggering remotely, 5
sports
    freezing action, 188
    RAW files, 220
    shooting tips, 38–39
Sports setting, 24, 26, 109, 113
Spot metering, 29, 60–61, 80
Spyder 5 Pro color correction
        system, 237
sRGB color space, 235–237
stage performances, 40–42, 86
Standard Picture Style, 240
standby mode, 20, 22
status information, Guided
        shooting mode, 14
ST-E2
    hot shoe mount, 406
    transmitter, master, 395–396
ST-E3-RT, radio master,
        397–398
Still mode, using in live view,
        150
STM (stepper motor) drives,
        317–318
storyboards, using for video,
        175

storytelling in video, 176
strap mount, 48
streaks, creating, 195
strobes, linking to camera,
        348–349
stroboscope, 188
studio, working in, 88
studio flash, shooting tips,
        42–44
swiping to select, 17–18
switches, number of, 45
sync speed, avoiding problems,
        352–354

T

T7i. *See* camera
tablets, connecting to, 199
tabs
    arrangement, 216
    moving between, 15
tapping to select, 17
telephoto and tele-zoom lenses,
        329–332. *See also*
        zooming
telephoto
    extenders, 333–334
    zoom lens, 320–321
terminal covers, 48
three-point lighting, 181
thumbnails
    displaying, 36, 52
    viewing, 34
    zooming in and out, 18
time exposures, 193
time zone, setting, 281–282
timed exposures, 193
Time-lapse movies, default
        value, 300
time-lapse movies, 167–169
tonal range, 102–104
toning, versus filters, 244
Toning Effects, 240, 244
top of camera, 55–57

Touch Control
default value, 299
option, 284
touch features, enabling and disabling, 19
Touch screen, 17, 50–51. *See also* **LCD monitor**
Touch Shutter
default value, 299
displaying in live view, 140–141, 149
using with live view, 138
Toy Camera effect, 27, 114, 264
transferring images, 36–37, 207–208
transverse chromatic aberration, 224, 327
Trash button, 52–53
travel, shooting tips, 42–44
tripod socket, 57
tripods
and HDR (High Dynamic Range), 96
long exposures, 196
shooting from, 137
tungsten/incandescent lighting, 345
turning on camera, 24
Tv (Shutter-priority) mode
concerts, 86
Creative Zone, 27–28
explained, 85–86
exposure meters, 91
flash functions, 33
landscape photography, 86
selecting, 24
stage performances, 86
tabs, 214
TV (television), viewing images, 136, 284
Tv (Time Value) mode
displaying, 14
equivalent exposure, 75
two shots, video, 178–179

U

ultra-wide-angle lens, 320
underexposure, 76–77, 106
UPstrap website, 3–4
USB cables, using to transfer images, 5, 37. *See also* **interface cable**
USM (Ultrasonic motor)
drives, 317
STM system, 308

V

vertical lines, aligning, 138–139
vertical orientation, rotating, 277
VF Display Illumination, 292
video, microphones, 182–184. *See also* **movies**
Video Snapshot
default value, 300
live view in Movie mode, 151
versus movie clips, 161–164
Video System
default value, 299
option, 284
video/sound, capturing, 160–161. *See also* **audio and video; Sound recording**
Viewfinder display
contrast detection, 116–117
default value, 297
illumination, 132
option, 282
phase detection, 117–120
readouts, 60–63
viewfinder eyepiece, 50
Viewfinder Warnings, 293–294
vignetting, 222–223, 327–328
visible light, 72
visual noise, 90–91. *See also* **noise reduction**
Vivid effect, 27

W

warning icon, 61–63
warranty card, 4
water, blurring, 197
Water Painting effect, 27, 114, 264
WB-BKT, default value, 298
Web service, uploading to, 211–212
Web upload, 200
white balance
bracketing, 64
button, 52, 54
correction default value, 298
customizing, 247
default value, 298
displaying, 64, 140, 142
library, 248
live view in Movie mode, 151
menu, 247
setting buttons, 216
Shift and Bracketing menu, 248–249
wide-angle and wide-zoom lenses, 324–328
wide-angle shots, 319
Wi-Fi
button, 52–53
communications, 199–206
default value, 299
manual, 206
signal strength, 64
Wi-Fi function
displaying, 64
displaying in live view, 140–141
live view in Movie mode, 151
Wi-Fi lamp, 56–57
Wi-Fi printer, 211
Wi-Fi signal strength
displaying in live view, 140–141
live view in Movie mode, 151

wind filter, live view in Movie
    mode, 151
wind noise reduction, 184
Wireless Communication
    Settings, 202, 278
wireless features, 199–200, 230
wireless flash. *See also* built-in
    electronic flash;
    electronic flash
  advantages, 385
  and built-in flash, 405
  channel controls, 386
  channels in optical mode,
    407–408
  combinations, 383–384
  custom shooting, 391–393
  direct connection, 384

flash ratios, 387
Flash Release function,
    408–409
groups, 387, 405–406
IR and radio transmitters,
    385
modes, 389
optical slave units, 385
ratio control, 407
triggering, 377–378
wireless infrared signals, 384
wireless signals, 384
wireless mode, switching to,
    393
wireless options, flash ratio
    setting, 399–402

Z
Zone AF, 129–130
zoom ring, 58–59
zoom scale, 58–59
zoom versus prime lenses,
    322–324
zooming. *See also* telephoto
    and tele-zoom lenses
  in and out, 18, 34–35
  video, 173